Living Lines

Five Contemporary Artists on Edvard Munch's Drawings

Marlene Dumas
Terje Nicolaisen
Nalini Malani
Georg Baselitz
Tracey Emin

There exist in Nature
two fixed given lines
– two Major lines –
the horizontal – Reclining line
and vertical – Gravitative line
– Around these move
the living Lines – the
bursting Lines [–] Life

Edvard Munch
Undated sketchbook, 1910s

Foreword

Stein Olav Henrichsen
Director

It is with great pleasure that MUNCH is publishing a book that will shed light on Edvard Munch's drawings – a lesser-known side of his artistic production than the paintings and prints.

What prompted the publication of this book is the digitalisation of the approximately 7700 drawings that Munch left behind, which have been catalogued and are now available to the public on the museum's website. Behind the digitalisation work is a three-year research project, which has been made possible by the patronage of the Bergesen Foundation. We would like to thank the Bergesen Foundation for its generous support of the work behind making this important material available to everyone interested in Munch's oeuvre. Including the previously digitalised catalogues raisonnés of Munch's graphic works, paintings and writings, we are proud to announce that his entire artistic production has now been published.

Edvard Munch's art has a unique way of captivating people from all over the world. Artists in particular have been inspired by his work. To celebrate the new digital catalogue of drawings, in this book we have invited five artists to compile their own personal selections of Munch's drawings: Marlene Dumas, Terje Nicolaisen, Nalini Malani, Georg Baselitz, and Tracey Emin. Each of the selections forms its own exhibition of sorts, and together they offer unexpected and multiple glimpses into this abundant and comprehensive material. I would like to take this opportunity to thank the artists who have delved into Munch's drawings and opened them up to so many refreshing and thought-provoking perspectives.

I would also like to thank all of our professional staff members, who have contributed to carrying out the research project and this publication.

Index

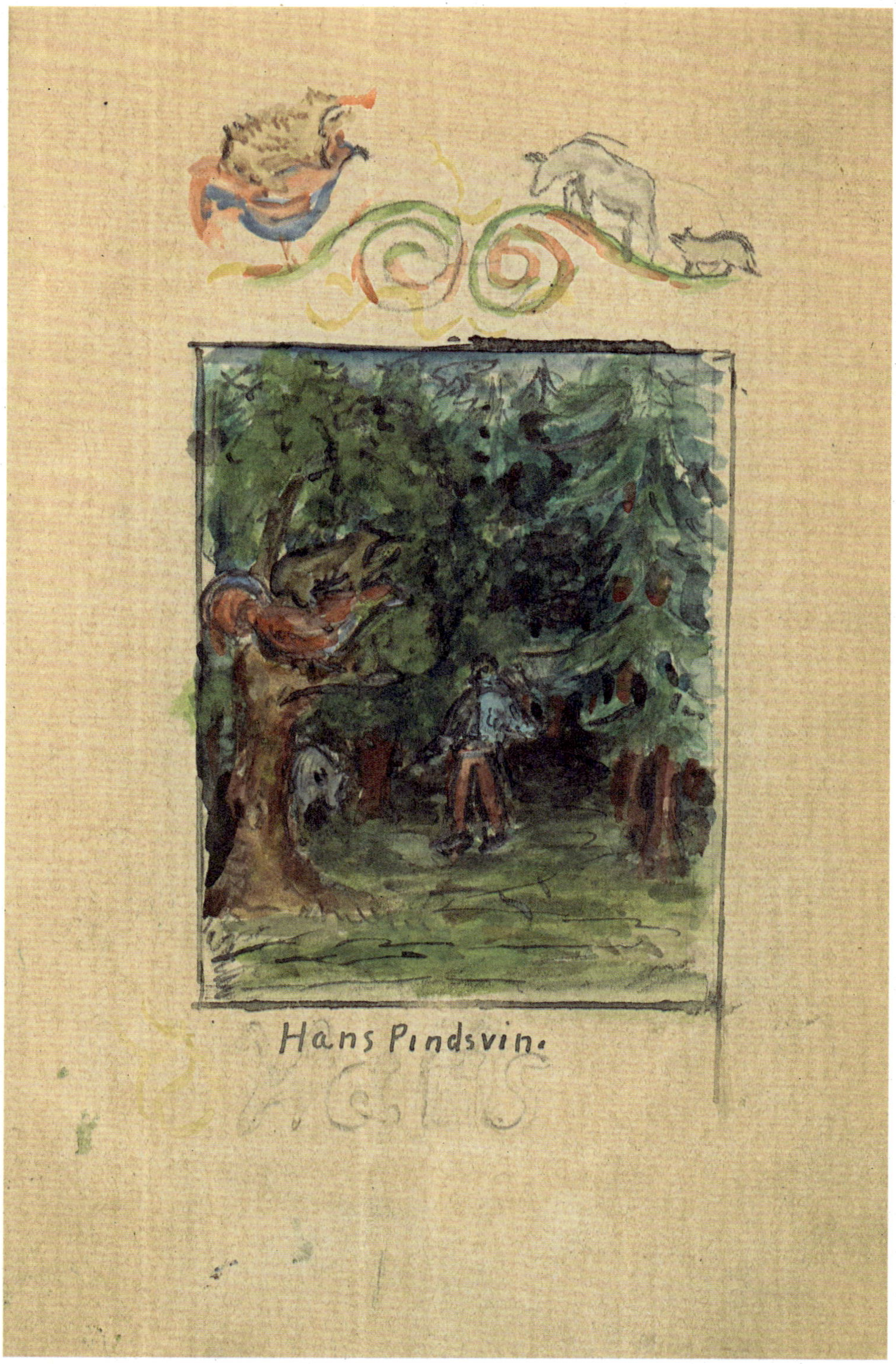

Hans Hedgehog
1873–76
Watercolour and pencil
135 × 97 mm

Introduction
Edvard Munch's Drawings in Perspective

Jon-Ove Steihaug

For Edvard Munch (1863–1944) drawing served as an artistic laboratory, tightly interwoven with his work as a painter and printmaker. He drew throughout his entire life, and some of the earliest drawings we know of are small watercolours in a book of fairy tales by the brothers Grimm, which he made when he was ten–twelve years old. Throughout his more than sixty-year-long career as an artist, hardly a day passed without him picking up a pencil, charcoal stick, chalk or pen, and he preserved almost everything.

The majority of Edvard Munch's preserved drawings are in Munchmuseet's collection and form part of the large gift he bequeathed to the City of Oslo. Altogether there are nearly 7700 drawings from his hand, on loose sheets of paper or in one of the many sketchbooks he always had at the ready. During the period 2015–18 Munchmuseet implemented a major endeavour to register all of Munch's drawings. The work was headed by former Senior Curator Magne Bruteig, who describes the project in his article "The Work Behind the Catalogue Raisonné of Munch's Drawings" (p. 227). This voluminous material has been published digitally and thus made available to a broader public on the museum's website. This book represents the missing piece in the museum's years long enterprise of cataloguing Munch's entire artistic oeuvre.

From playing with drawing and watercolours during his childhood, in the digital catalogue you can follow how Munch gradually makes more elaborate studies through his adolescent years, as his visual proficiency improves. The motifs in these drawings are often taken from his close surroundings; drawing tools on the desk in front of him, the interior of his childhood home, the working class neighbourhood they lived in on the east side of Oslo (called Kristiania then), and the landscapes he studied during excursions to the tracts of forest surrounding the city. We also find humorous scenes, caricatures, rebuses, boyish motifs of "cowboys and Indians", and occasionally schoolwork. When in the autumn of 1880, not quite 17, he began his more formal art education at the Royal School of Design in Kristiania, it did not cause any noticeable break in his drawings as far as we can see – apart from an increasing number filled with distinctive character types and everyday scenes from city life. But eventually we see that nude studies and portraits of his closest family and acquaintances begin to appear. During these years he also makes a series of studies of a characteristic medieval church surrounded by a cluster of houses, which he was able to observe from the family's apartment. Old Aker Church would also become a motif for some of his first oil paintings.

Throughout the 1880s Munch typically fills his sketchbooks with rapidly jotted down sketches and the beginnings of motifs. Quick sketches of this type would become an essential aspect of his drawings as a whole, freely executed and totally without any desire to excel. There are of course a number of more elaborate drawings from his hand. Among others, the nude drawings from the period when Munch studied under Léon Bonnat in Paris around 1889–90 demonstrate that he was a skilled draughtsman when he so desired. Drawing nudes, traditionally one of the foundations of instruction at the art academies, was something he fully mastered early on. In a number of studies of a reclining male figure, for instance, he solves the challenging foreshortening of the body quite effortlessly (p. 218). Munch was obviously adept at it, and this may be one of the reasons why he was not interested in showing off his skills.

Beginning in the early 1890s we find sketches for what are considered among his iconic works today, such as *The Scream*, *Kiss*, *Vampire* and *Melancholy*. His drawings for the painting *The Voice*, for example, are remarkably evocative variations on this motif. This way of developing and modifying motifs we find throughout his entire oeuvre. It applied for instance to the monumental paintings he later executed for the University of Oslo's festivity hall, the Aula, and other commissions. During the years following 1909 – when he settled permanently in Norway after twenty nomadic years – one can see among other things that he returns to the nude motif with renewed interest, in the form of swiftly executed croquis drawings. And in a number of watercolours from around 1920, he elevates this artistic practice to new heights. One might also mention the many drawings inspired by Henrik Ibsen's plays, in particular from the last half of his artistic career. On the whole, Munch's drawings cover an exceptionally broad gamut, yet with important exceptions it is the consistently quick observation or recording of an idea that dominates.

The idea behind this book is to look at Munch's drawings through the gaze of artists living today. We have invited five artists to compile their own individual selection of his drawings – Marlene Dumas, Terje Nicolaisen, Nalini Malani, Georg Baselitz, and Tracey Emin. What they primarily have in common in this context is an interest in Munch's art and the fact that drawing is a central aspect of their own artistic practice. Their respective selections offer a number of different ingresses into the magnitude of material represented by the drawings in the museum's holdings, which have now been compiled in a catalogue; many of the selected works have hardly been exhibited before. With their different perspectives they bring to light the range as well as the depth of Munch's draughtsmanship. In the interviews with the artists, this is elaborated further; here they discuss their respective selections, their relationship to Munch, and their own art.

Café Scene
1881
Pencil
74 × 139 mm

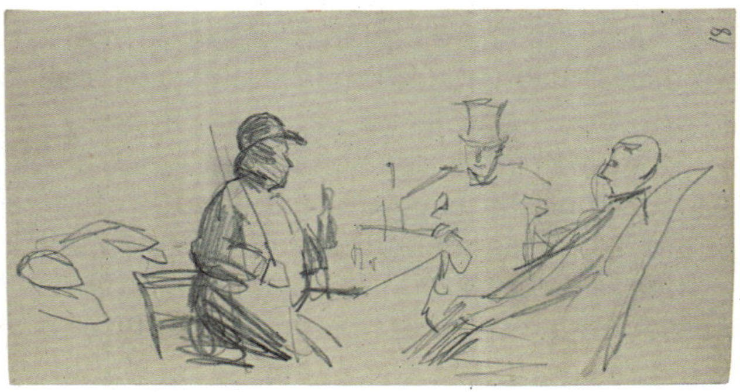

↓ *Landscape. Hakloa in Nordmarka*
1881
Pencil
170 × 237 mm

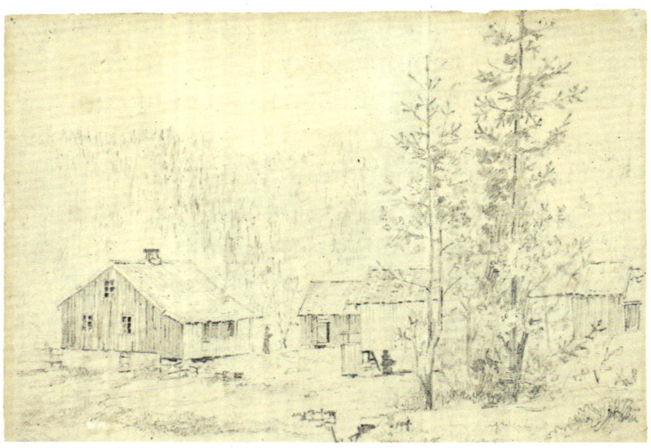

Rag Collector
1880–82
Pen
150 × 220 mm

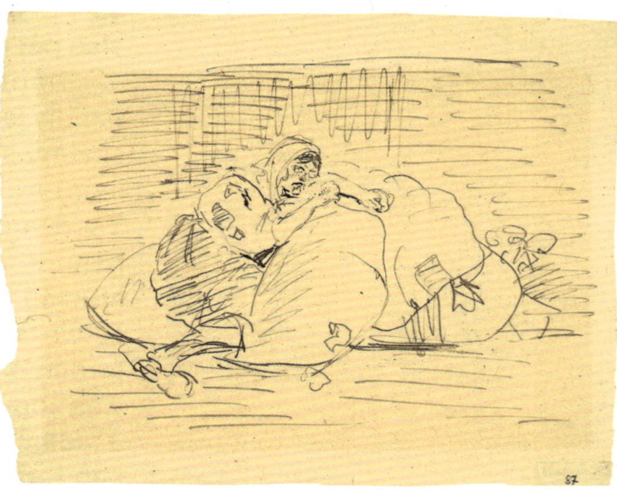

The Voice
1893
Charcoal
499 × 647 mm

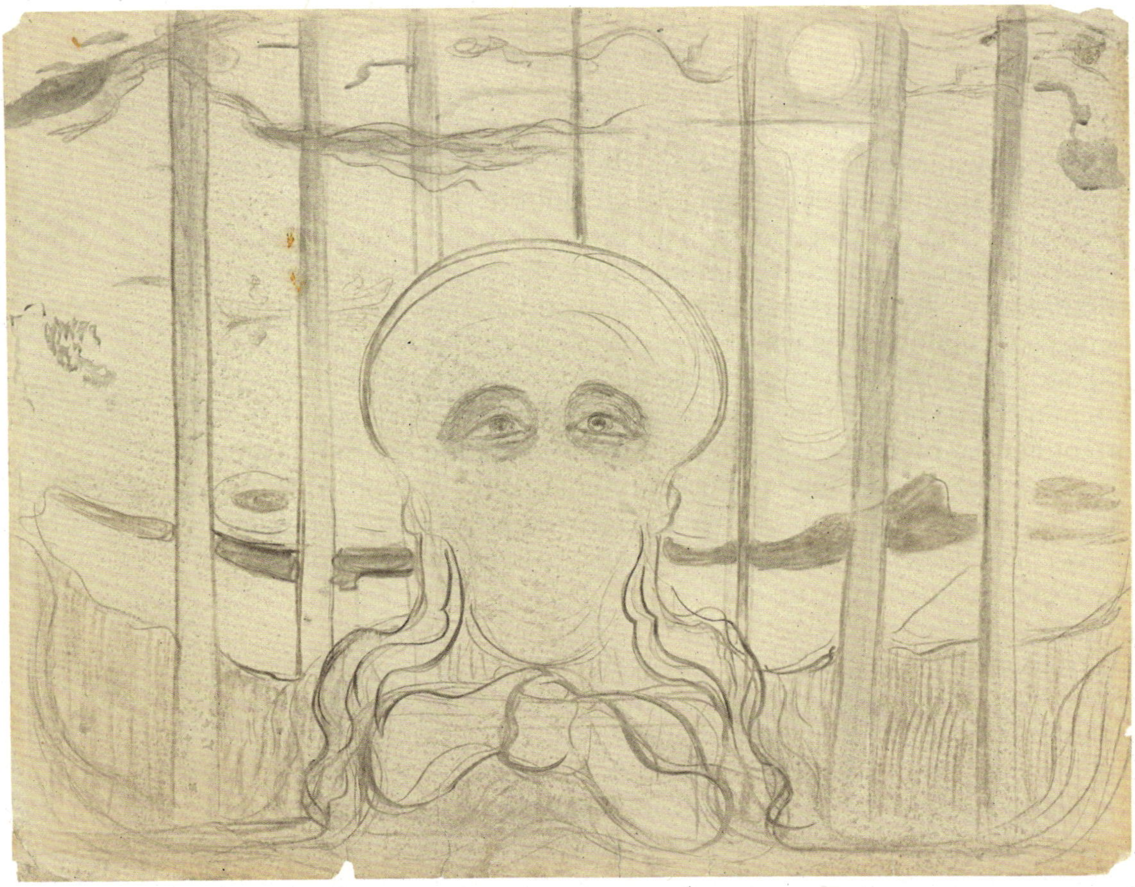

The selection Marlene Dumas (b. 1953) has made reveals the more satirical and burlesque side of Munch. One can view it as a continuation of the exploration of his works that she made for the exhibition *Moonrise. Marlene Dumas & Edvard Munch* at the museum in 2018–19. Her own point of departure as an artist is precisely drawing. As in Munch, the nude and the human figure are a central motif in her pictures. They have a raw intensity whether they speak of sexuality, love, abuse or death. Another overall feature is that they are always based on photographs, cut out of magazines and newspapers or snapshots of friends and family. The relationship between drawing and painting is fluid, which we can see in her many ink washes in a large format and in other works on paper. Dumas has written somewhere: "I would like to make one-stroke ink brush paintings like the ancient Chinese aspired to. They call it painting and we call it drawing."

As an artist born and living in Norway, Terje Nicolaisen (b. 1964) was raised on Munch's art so to speak. In his native country Munch is seen as a kind of national saint; this naturally affects Nicolaisen's relationship with him, and in many different ways. In Nicolaisen's art there is a consistent humoristic and unpretentious sideways glance at life and the art world, one that accepts imperfection and failure. Drawing is a central part of his oeuvre, which is also evidenced by numerous artists' books, multiples, and ideas for unrealised projects. He is a member of the artist group Tegneklubben (the Drawing Club), comprised of five artists who since 2004 have come together for collective drawing séances where they cultivate the spontaneity and fallibility inherent in the medium. About his relationship with Munch, Nicolaisen has the following to say: "I'd say that where Munch and I meet eye to eye is where he stumbles, although the two of us stumble in different ways. In his case, it's a deliberate tactic to outwit his inherent skilfulness, and it often works." In keeping with this, Nicolaisen's selection encompasses drawings by Munch where he does not appear as the familiar master. It's almost as though we are on the inside of the mask and can sense Munch's human and naked ordinariness.

Nalini Malani (b. 1946) became acquainted with Munch's art when she was an art student in Bombay (Mumbai) in the late 60s, and her exposure to Munch was deepened when she came to Paris on a grant from the French government a few years later. Malani's selection of Munch drawings touches on various themes expressed by catchwords such as absurd, hieroglyphs, proletariat, puberty, fear, machismo. They point to subjects in her own art, which is founded upon a strong political consciousness. From primarily having worked with painting and drawing, since the 90s Malani has expanded her work to include large room installations where she combines light projection, painting and video. Together they create a form of shadow play, in which the motifs that are painted and drawn on cylinders of transparent film are projected onto the walls in the room. The compound motifs circle around and overlap each other in a continuous movement. Malani also explores drawing as a medium in the form of large charcoal depictions drawn directly on the wall, which are erased in a ritual-like manner as the exhibition comes to an end.

Georg Baselitz (b. 1938) has in his selection focused on Munch's drawn self-portraits. He too has often used himself as a model in his pictures, frequently together with his wife Elke. Baselitz has throughout his long artistic career worked simultaneously with drawing, painting and printmaking. The first drawings from the early 60s are characterised by existential uneasiness and discomfort. As a young man he sought out art that represented a counterweight to abstract art, which dominated the international art scene in the post-war era. This included Expressionism, Surrealism and outsider artists. Edvard Munch was an artist Baselitz became aware of early on. He has referred to Munch in many of his works and also mentioned him in interviews. A constant feature of Baselitz's drawings is that the gesture itself, the expressive action that is embodied in the line or brushstroke, is just as important as what the motif represents. When he began to consistently paint his motifs upside down in the late 60s, it was in order to reset the contrast between abstraction and figuration.

Drawing permeates Tracey Emin's (b. 1963) entire oeuvre. Aside from drawings in a more traditional sense, it also includes her paintings, applications and textual works, whether they are composed in neon or written/drawn by hand. The expressive drawn line in her works may be fragile and sensitive, organically flowing or angular and more aggressive, respectively. Emin has on many occasions spoken about the significance Munch's art has had for her from very early on and throughout her career. She explores this affinity in the exhibition *Tracey Emin / Edvard Munch: The Loneliness of the Soul* (2020–21), made in collaboration with MUNCH and also shown at the Royal Academy of Arts in London. In addition, she has made the monumental bronze sculpture *The Mother*, as a landmark and a tribute to Munch on a pier outside the new museum. The drawings Emin has chosen for this book point among other things to her interest in the way Munch combines poetic texts with drawing. She has also chosen a number of unusual female motifs, an important theme in her own art as well. More generally Emin has unearthed drawings that reveal Munch at his most evocative and emotional.

Altogether the selections made by the five artists offer a multidimensional and varied picture of Munch's drawings while simultaneously saying something about his continued relevance today. The drawings provide a unique glimpse into Munch's creative process, and we hope that this book will also inspire you, the reader, to continue exploring this voluminous material.

Ambiguity is Munch's Middle Name

Marlene Dumas
interviewed by Mieke Bal

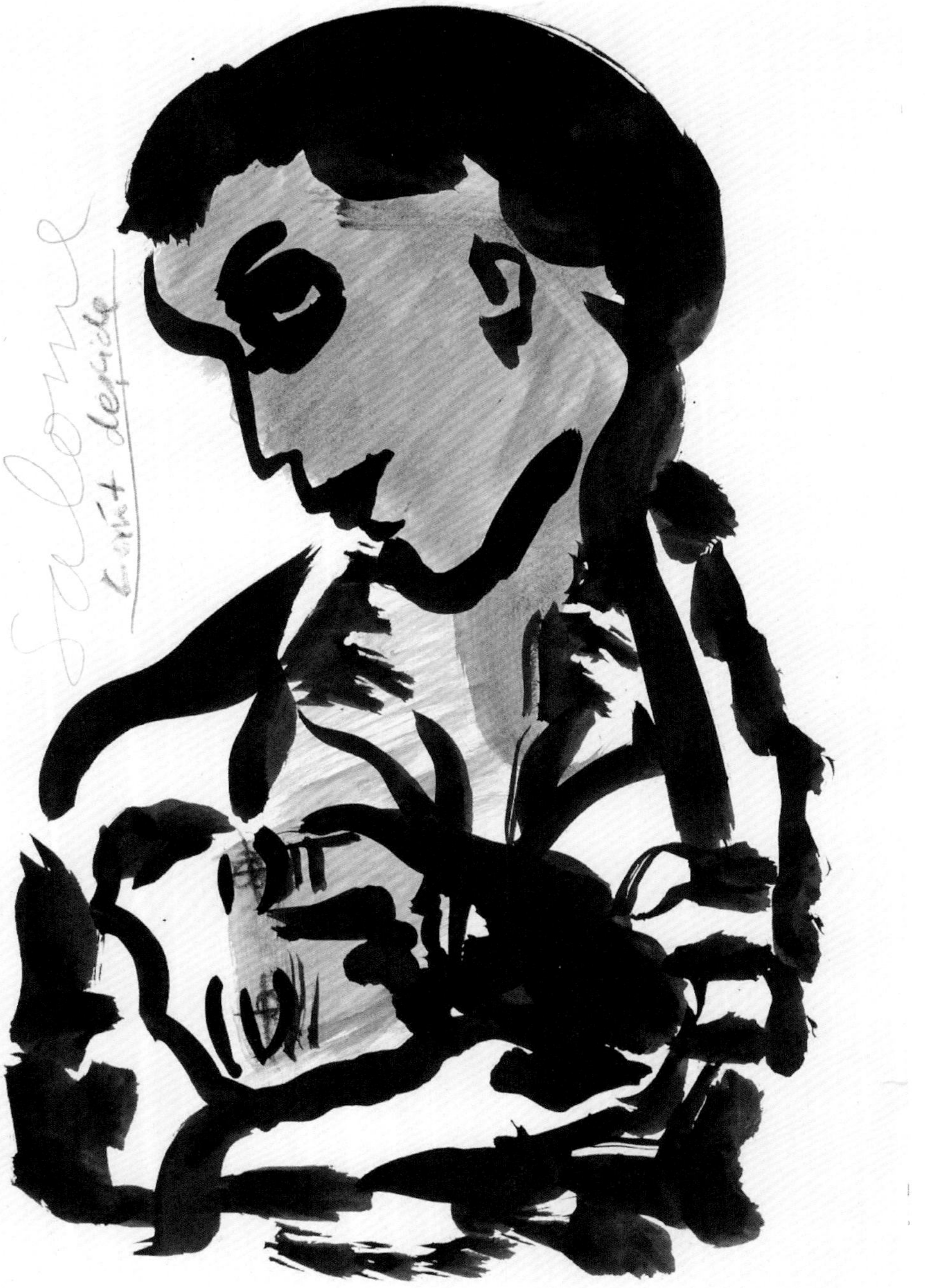

Marlene Dumas
Salomé Can't Decide, c. 1987
Ink and watercolour in paper
29.5 × 21 cm

Marlene Dumas has a great artistic imagination. Never painting or drawing from "nature", always from earlier images such as press photographs or famous iconographies, her interest is in visual culture. She sees painting as a means to overcome traditional oppositions: paint as material versus optic; the tension between form and colour; and the tension between abstraction and figuration. And in opening up possibilities, she involves the political – the antagonisms that constitute human societies. In these aspects of her work, her interest in poetry, and her sensitivity to the integration of images and words, I recognise what also fascinates me in Edvard Munch's work. Her selection of drawings and what she says about them in this interview demonstrate interests that are central to her art.

Bal — What is the starting point for your selection?

Dumas — I discovered Munch's "The City of Free Love" in the catalogue for an exhibition at Munchmuseet in the 1980s.[1] It has always intrigued me, fascinated me. This is really a book of sorts, with sketches combined with an amazing narrative-dramatic text. It deals with a reversal of the usual power relations between men and women, and with the fragility of the artist. The words are written in different styles, with different relations to the images. So, the word-image combinations were my number one interest. Secondly, Munch was also great at making sketches. Artists don't necessarily do that anymore. These two aspects seem to go together. I also combine texts and drawings in my work; just like Munch I do this especially in smaller formats rather than in large paintings. A few years ago, the writer Hafid Bouazza asked me to "illustrate" his translation of Shakespeare's *Venus and Adonis*, which I did with ink drawings.[2]

B — Yes, that is a fabulous book. The drawings have that watery effect that makes them almost seem to flow into the text (p.17).

D — They do; that is because Bouazza's request compelled me to rethink the idea of illustration. It put me in the mood again for more integrated and non-hierarchical combinations of words and images than the notion of illustration normally allows. Traditionally, that word suggests that the visual images are subordinate to the text, which they must clarify. I wanted to avoid that hierarchy. Recently Bouazza asked me to do a second collaboration, this time for Baudelaire's *Paris Spleen*. By chance he saw a painting of mine that made him think of the fifth prose poem in the collection, "The Double Room".

B — Munch also made sketches to accompany Baudelaire's *Les fleurs du mal*, though he never finished them (p.28). What is your relationship to Baudelaire?

D — I do find Baudelaire a great poet, even though I have strived to be a modernist rather than a symbolist, like everyone else in my generation. I am especially interested in the fact that things – images, line drawings, text fragments – mean so many different things in his poems. I find that inspiring. Nothing is straightforward. For example, there are many allegories of time.

B — Can you give an example?

D — Oh yes. The figure of Woman signifies time. Or, an ode to absinth or other narcotic substances may take the shape of a woman. Baudelaire constantly played with reality and fiction. Everything can be turned around in one unexpected blow. And his poems are full of dark humour and social satire. I like Daumier for the same reason. I have never really studied literature, but forms such as Baudelaire's prose-poems have given me insight into a lot of things I didn't know before. And the mixtures and mergings of forms in Munch fascinate me.

I am not surprised by that interest in Munch's literary activities. Your own titles B
and short texts are amazing, really poetry. Your book *Sweet Nothings* is in fact a book of poetry.[3] [Marlene Dumas shrugs this off.] And your own ink drawings have that appealing sketchiness, too. Perhaps sketchiness is another form of nudity, like poetry, as you see it. On a card in one of your exhibitions you wrote: "I would like my paintings to be like poems. Poems are like sentences that have taken their clothes off. The meaning of a poem is what its beat and rhythm do. How the words move on the page. Poetry is writing that breathes and makes jumps and leaves spaces open, so we can read between the lines." To me this is a visualisation of poetry; a figural prose-poem. It gives nakedness such a rich and specific meaning!

I am not really a writer, but I love the feel of words. And certainly, Munch must D
have felt like that as well. Sometimes I come up with a title and realise it can apply to many different things. But people tend to reduce it to a single one of the many meanings it harbours. I find that impoverishing, a great loss of cultural richness. It is a misunderstanding of how images, language, and meaning work.

Baudelaire was very keen on merging the different senses. His poems had a special B
synaesthetic quality, where sound, vision, smell, and touch interacted. His most famous poem in this respect is the 1857 sonnet "Correspondances" which begins thus:

Nature is a temple where living pillars
Let escape sometimes confused words;
Man traverses it through forests of symbols
That observe him with familiar glances.

I think this nicely sums up what you were saying about symbols, allegory, and ambiguity. "Confused words" is a positive term here. And the familiarity mentioned is what you phrased earlier as recognition. That poem is a programmatic one, like your text on the card which I just cited.

Reading is important. I think visual artists should also read. They shouldn't be con- D
tent with picking up ideas that float around. Instead, they should really read what other people have to say, not to endorse it uncritically, but to consider what they read as a "second person" whom their work addresses; its "you". The text is an interlocutor, to use one of your terms, Mieke. Then they can see, or even feel captured by the resulting spiderweb of experience. No one can do without others and the ideas they generate. That is culture. My ethics professor at Cape Town University said: "We think, therefore I am".

Oh yes, I love that. Individual existence depends on collectivity. We can endlessly B
take off from Descartes, even though he is constantly belittled as "obsolete". That's why I made the film about him.[4] But tell me more about the process of selecting Munch's drawings!

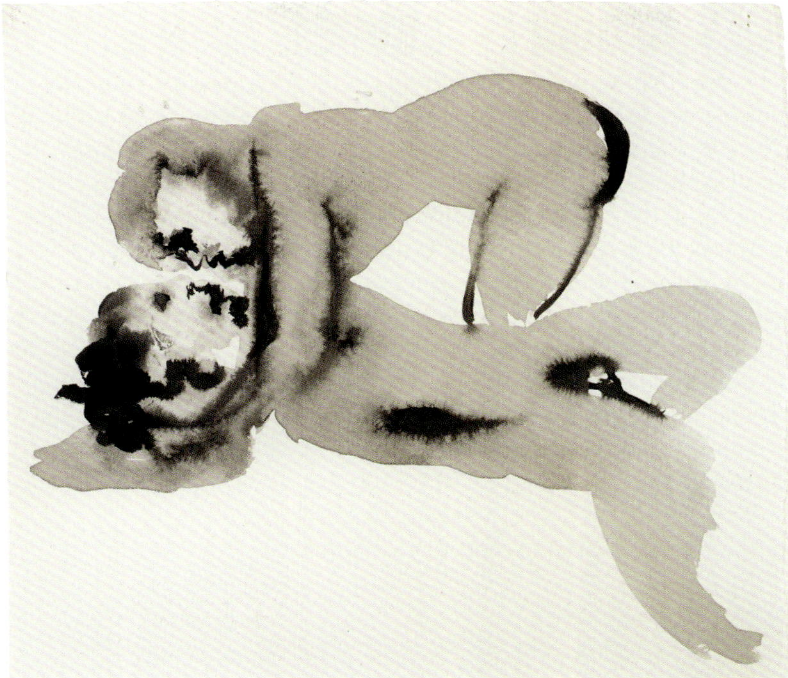

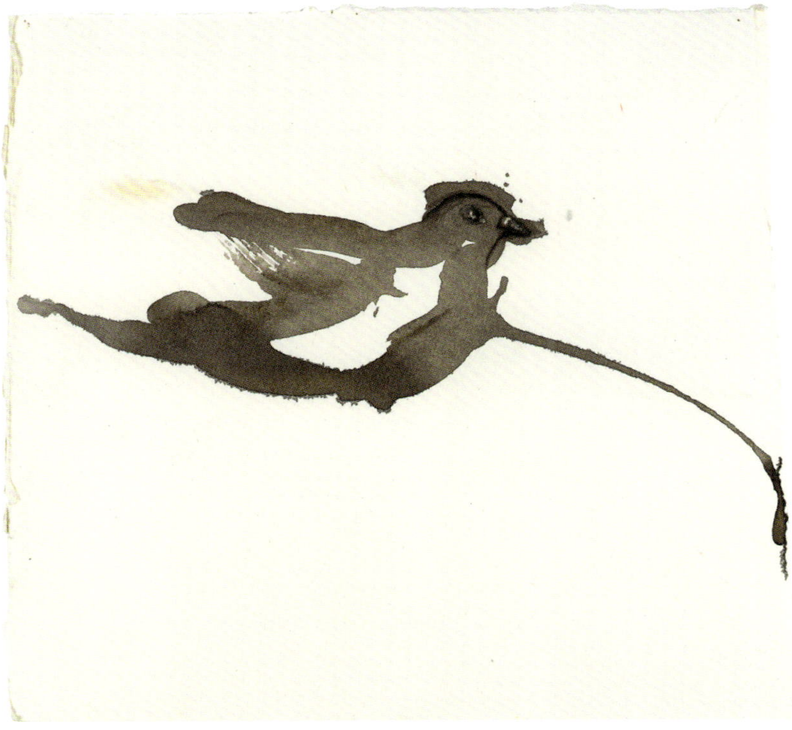

Marlene Dumas
Venus with Body of Adonis, 2015–16
Ink wash and metallic acrylic on paper
25.5 × 28.5 cm

Marlene Dumas
The Dove, 2015–2016
Ink wash and metallic acrylic on paper
27 × 30.5 cm

I didn't want to return to "Alpha & Omega", however beautiful it is. I already used that series as the basis for my exhibition at Munchmuseet in 2018–19, where I showed the entire series.[5] What made it difficult to compose the selection for this book was that I really want to talk about Munch's sketchbooks. After the word-image interaction and the sketchiness, this is the third thing that has been on my mind when working on this selection: the materiality of the object. And there are so many of those sketchbooks, and they are in such different formats that it's impossible for anyone to find their way linearly or chronologically in that material. There are so many versions of *The Scream*, for example, in different formats and media. And also, they are accompanied by many text fragments, sometimes almost the same, but not quite, and made in different years. Figures with the head of John the Baptist, of Tulla Larsen ... dancing women, a head on a plate – where does it fit in? Anitra in Grieg's and Ibsen's *Peer Gynt*, just as much as Salomé. Look at these! How to find a context for this in those thousands and thousands of sketches? Never mind, since ambiguity is Munch's middle name. D

Your selection is complex and perhaps complicated to reproduce, I suppose. B

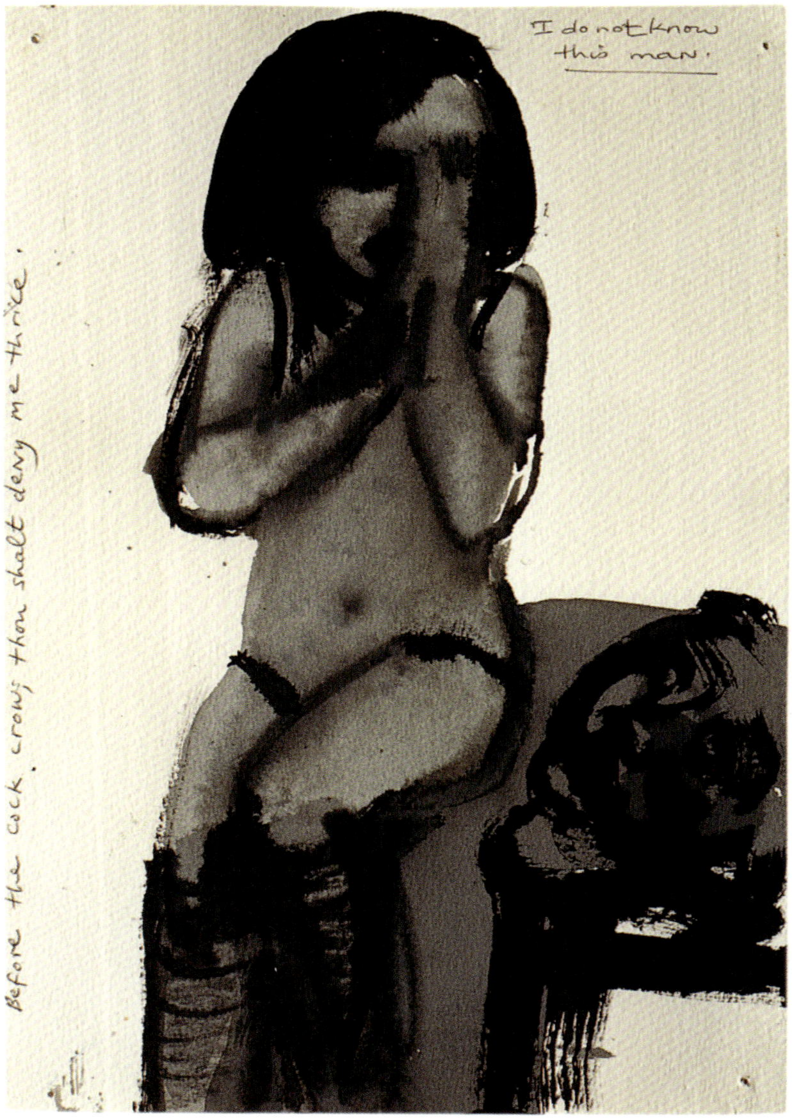

Marlene Dumas
I Do Not Know / This Man from the series "Give Me the Head of John the Baptist", 1992
Ink, crayon and pencil on paper
35.2 × 26.7 cm

D

Yes, it will probably be a bit of a challenge. For, in connection with my interest in Munch's sketchbooks, there is another special wish I have. I would like to see the sketches printed in their actual formats, whenever possible. The reproductions should give the reader/viewer a sense of the physical quality of the sketches, just as in the museum where one sees the scale and all the textures and colour nuances of the paintings exhibited. Take this sketch in green-blue lines of *Stooped Man Looking at Himself in the Mirror*. That double image, where the two figures are not identical. The one with a weird shadow looking at his mirror image, and the other at the viewer (p.26).

B

That gives a sense of material reality. So, let's first look at some of the sheets from "The City of Free Love". Are there special bits you are interested in, in connection with your own work?

D

Well, yes, in 1992 I made a series of drawings titled "Give me the Head of John the Baptist", with a young girl as the murderer and seducer (p.18, 20 and 24). When I saw the dancing women and a woman with a humanoid "golden" pig on her lap (p.33) the John the Baptist theme came up, inevitably. But it goes off on all kinds of tracks. I do that also in my series "Give me the Head". Some motifs re-occur in different years and in different contexts too. Munch's texts are staggering: funny and, in a sense, tragic. And political. "The City of Free Love" is full of satirical allusions to capitalism and other forms of exploitation. On the front page, the main character, the minstrel, stands in front of a closed city gate. On top of it, a variety of heads pop up. The man in front of the door stoops down a bit while looking up, as if humbly begging for entry (p.29). Once inside, he discovers that the freedom is not as free as it seems. Kissing must be done in large quantities. In the end he is brought to justice for not having kissed enough. His weak defence is that he is unable to do so because he was ill.

B

This is a mix of literary forms, and the narrative merges with theatre.

D

Yes, it begins with narrative. The introductory paragraph describes that he is exhausted and has suffered, and now he longs for love. He thinks he will be happy in that city. In the end he is more or less executed, pushed into a ditch in the ground. This happens after he has been sentenced by a judge not coincidentally called Moses. The figure who seems to reign over the city, significantly called The Dollar Princess, is a kind of rich patron of the arts. She is given the singer's head on a plate in a pen sketch from 1905 (p.35).

B

The Dollar Princess looks like a caricature of a "grande dame". She wears the ornate hat known from some of Munch's paintings. Two humanoid pigs sit on a kind of throne at the back. On the left, an elongated dog. Such figures recur in Munch's drawings. You recognise them, don't you?

D

Yes, indeed. We can also recognise figures from other sketches, such as *Frame with Caricatured Figures* (p.32). The man with the potato nose on the left and the female bust-without-body on the right, with a wavery line hinting at the same ornate hat: we see them all over Munch's work, and especially in the drawings. The frame locks more like a theatre stage or door – depending on which perspective one chooses.

B

Munch's ambiguity-oriented mindset is at work again here.

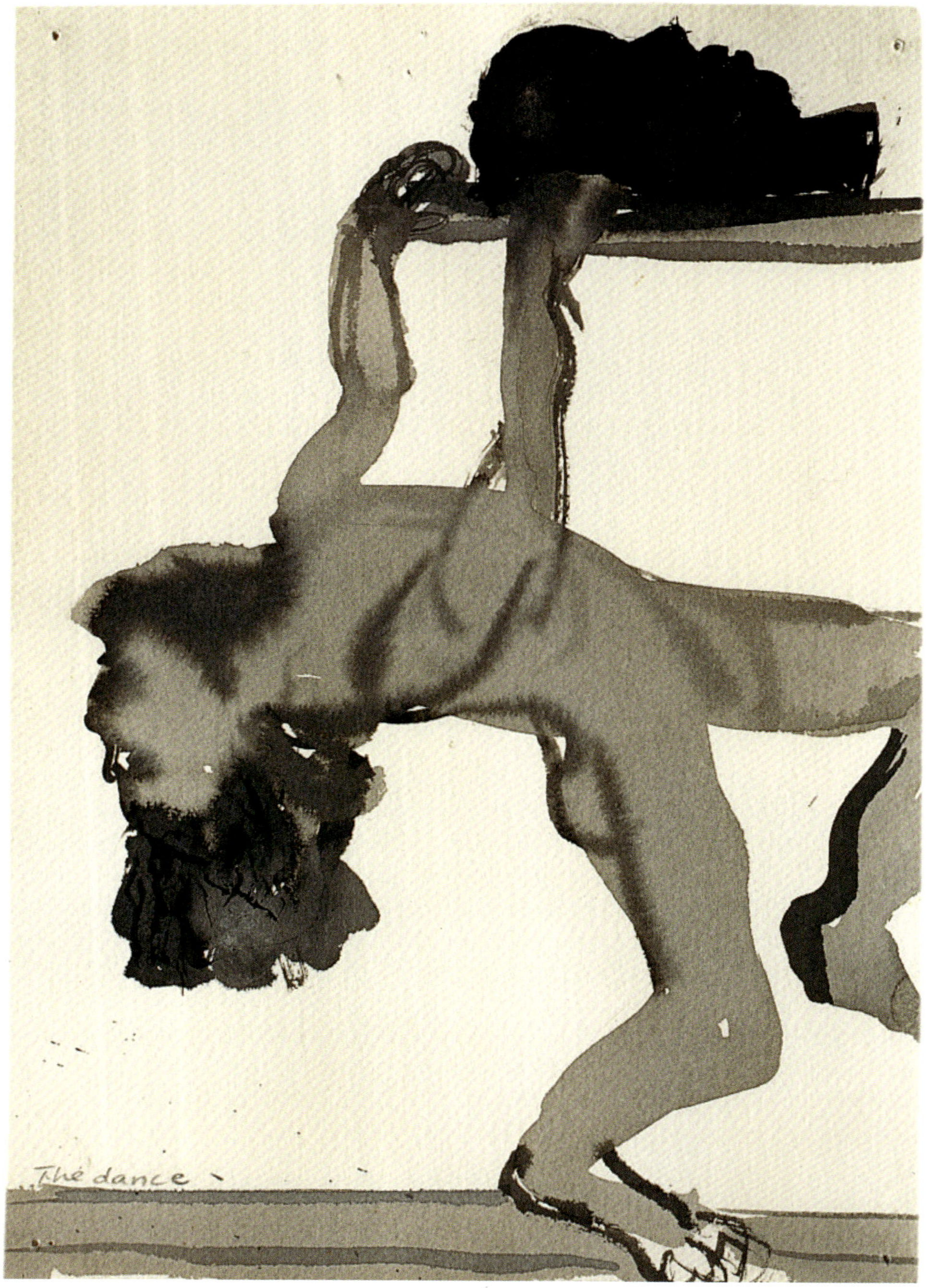

Marlene Dumas
The Dance from the series "Give Me the Head of John the Baptist", 1992
Ink, crayon and pencil on paper
35.2 × 26.7 cm

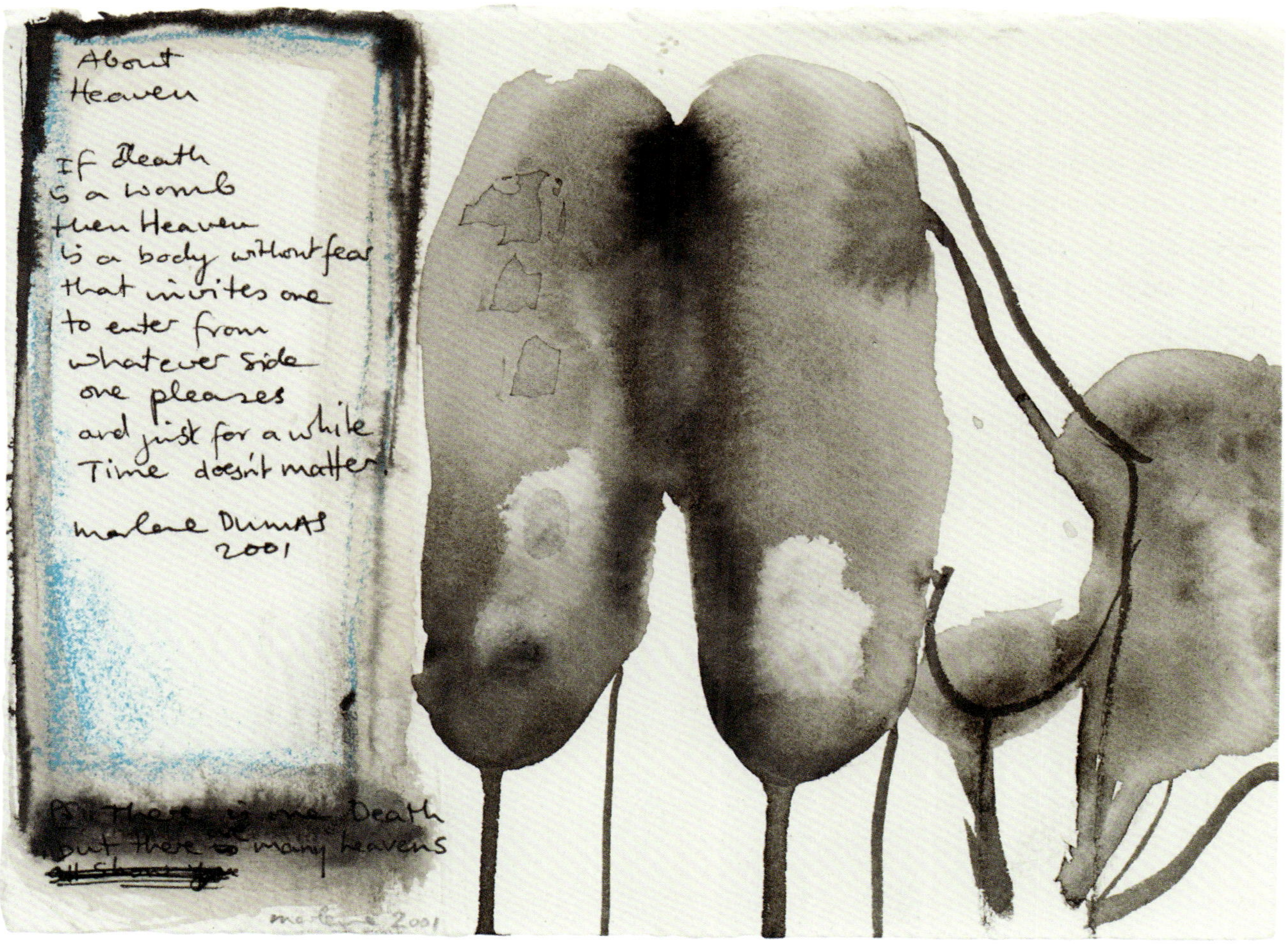

21

Marlene Dumas
About Heaven, 2001
Ink and crayon on paper
16 × 22 cm

The fragmented bits of text in "The City of Free Love" are as sketchy as the drawings they are combined with. But they are in fact very well written, and the story is quite gripping. A tone of caricature and reversals make it a very politically resonating text. The mob-like background of the sketch where the minstrel is kicked into the grave (p. 39) assembles all the characters, with the victim in the foreground. The figures of these women are not very erotic, but rather off-putting. The same may be said of the men in this city. The pen drawing *Caricature of a Couple* (p. 31) suggests lust in the grin on the female figure's mouth. And the man in full dress leans a bit backwards. D

I am very intrigued by your choice of that sketch for, or variation of, the painting called *Vision*, which I had in my exhibition at Munchmuseet in 2017.[6] This comes with an incredible poem (p. 27). It is narrative, but with a predominance of description. It reads like this: B

I lived down in the depths
amid slime and creatures –
I forced my way up to the
water's surface out of longing
for the bright colours
A blinding white
swan glided by over there on
the gleaming surface its
clean lines mirrored in
the water – which also reflected
the sky's light clouds
I reached out to it
with my hands – entreated it to come
But it could not
simply could not reach past the
ring of scum and slime that
surrounded me – it dirtied
its head and breast and glided away[7]

"Down in the depths" and cut off from others who would shun dirtying themselves with "scum and slime" around him: don't you think this is the most poignant expression of loneliness and rejection imaginable? Even animals abandon him. And the painting shows that loneliness.

But this sketch does not work quite in the same way. It is not an illustration of the poem. Change something, and everything changes. Munch is an expert at expressing alienation. I chose this page as an example of how the handwriting and the drawing interact and become one. It's all a puzzle, and it's all done with lines on paper. D

Munch also drew very sensual, erotic scenes when the chosen story allowed it, for example his illustrations for Ibsen's play *Peer Gynt*. In a scene from Peer's journey to Africa, you see how the woman teases him and uses her body. This is not a lady from "The City of Free Love". Munch can make lines dance on paper. This is a medium he loved and understood. Therefore, I am moved and delighted. Never mind meaning; how about pleasure?

B With these interpretations, the question of Munch's life remains. How do you see the relationship between Munch's life and his work?

D That is very important to me, but not in the simple one-to-one equation that is so often applied on Munch. He refers to, or alludes to, events and people in his life, but not all the time, and never literally, in my view. He had a deep interest in the cinema, which was introduced during his lifetime. Images, figures, movements that he saw on his frequent visits to movie theatres also ended up, in different configurations, in his sketches. In that sense, the sketch books were notebooks. That's why some are so small. He carried them in his pocket. And there, the fragmentation is also very strong. Sometimes he only filled a few pages or made a partial drawing of something. It is clear that Munch was very intelligent. And his intelligence refused to distinguish visual from literary expression as a matter of principle. He was clearly a thinker. If you imagine, for example, the task of "imaging" jealousy. Look at what he did! It is fantastic, isn't it? We all have such emotions. How to make that into something of that calibre ... It requires life experience, the biographical critics say, and turn the artist into a nasty jealous man.

B That is so limiting. It makes it harder, not easier, to see the works. Another way of doing justice to the many facets and meanings of artworks is to talk about them with others. But for that to happen, museums must provide seating.

D Yes, absolutely. And maybe a bed or two for those who, like me, can see better when lying down, and may imagine holding one of Munch's sketchbooks in their hand.

1 *Edvard Munch: Alpha & Omega,* Munchmuseet, 25 March–31 August 1981.
2 William Shakespeare, *Venus and Adonis*. Translated into Dutch with a commentary and an epilogue by Hafid Bouazza and illustrations by Marlene Dumas (Amsterdam: Athenaeum-Polak & Van Gennep, 2016).
3 Dumas' short texts, notes, and titles are collected in the volume *Sweet Nothings: Notes and Texts by Marlene Dumas*, ed. Mariska van den Berg (Amsterdam: Uitgeverij De Balie / Galerie Paul Andriesse, 1998). Second revised edition, *Sweet Nothings: Notes and Texts by Marlene Dumas, 1982–2014* (Cologne: Walther König, 2014).
4 Mieke Bal, *Reasonable Doubt: Scenes from Two Lives*, 2016.
5 See the book *Omega's Eyes: Marlene Dumas on Edvard Munch. Guest star: René Daniëls* (Oslo: Munchmuseet / Brussels: Mercatorfonds, 2018).
6 *Vision*, 1892–93 (MM T 2908), in *eMunch.no: Text and Image,* ed. Mai Britt Guleng (Oslo: Munchmuseet 2011), p. 274–75; The line breaks are as in the original.

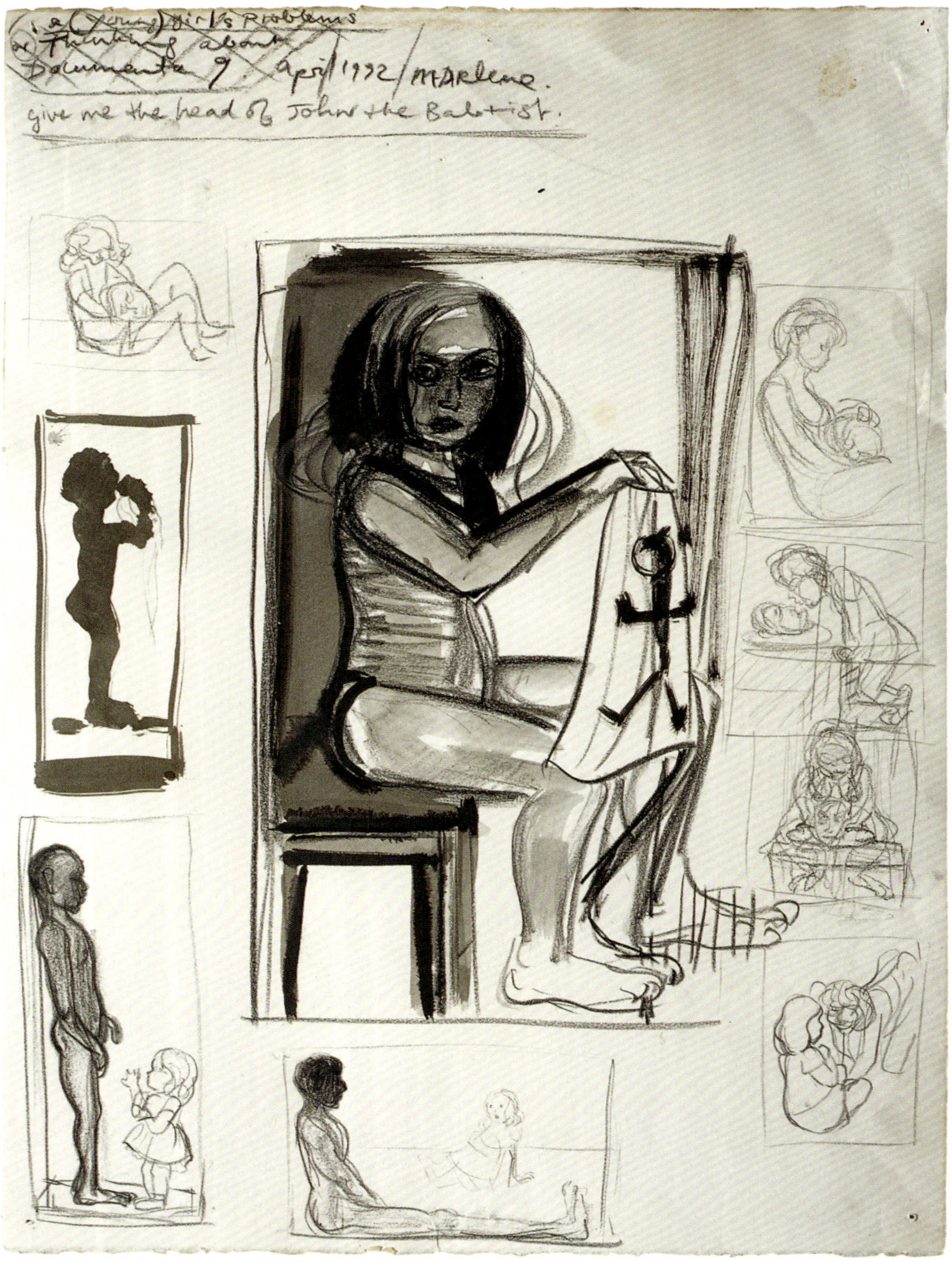

Marlene Dumas
A (Young) Girl's Problems / Or Thinking about / Give Me the Head of John the Baptist
from the series "Give Me the Head of John the Baptist", 1992
Ink, crayon and pencil on paper
74.2 × 58.2 cm

Dumas chooses Munch

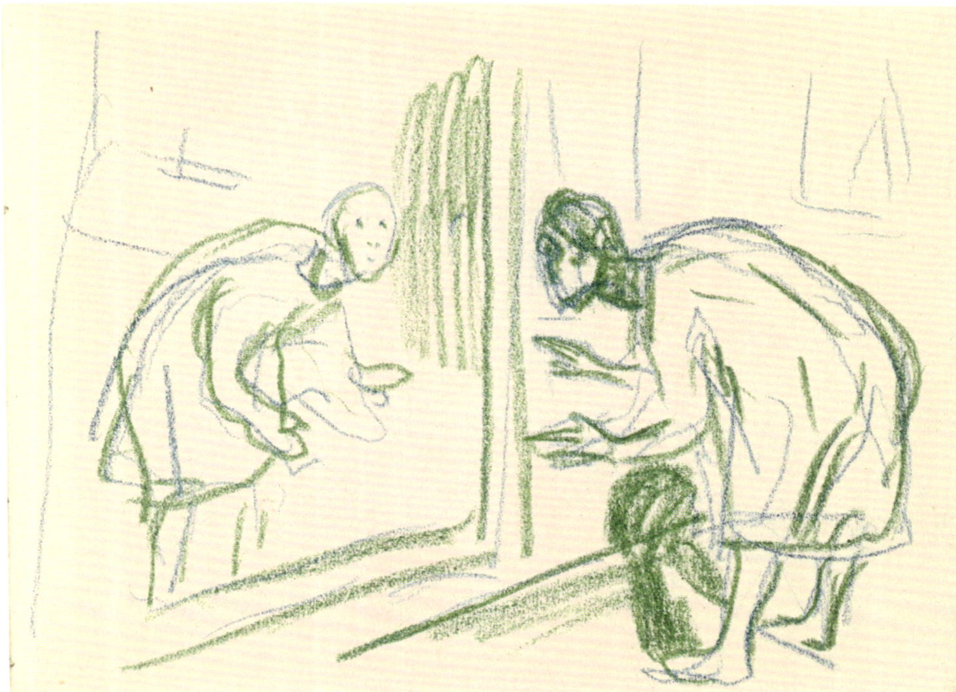

Stooped Man Looking at Himself in the Mirror
1919
Crayon
128 × 178 mm

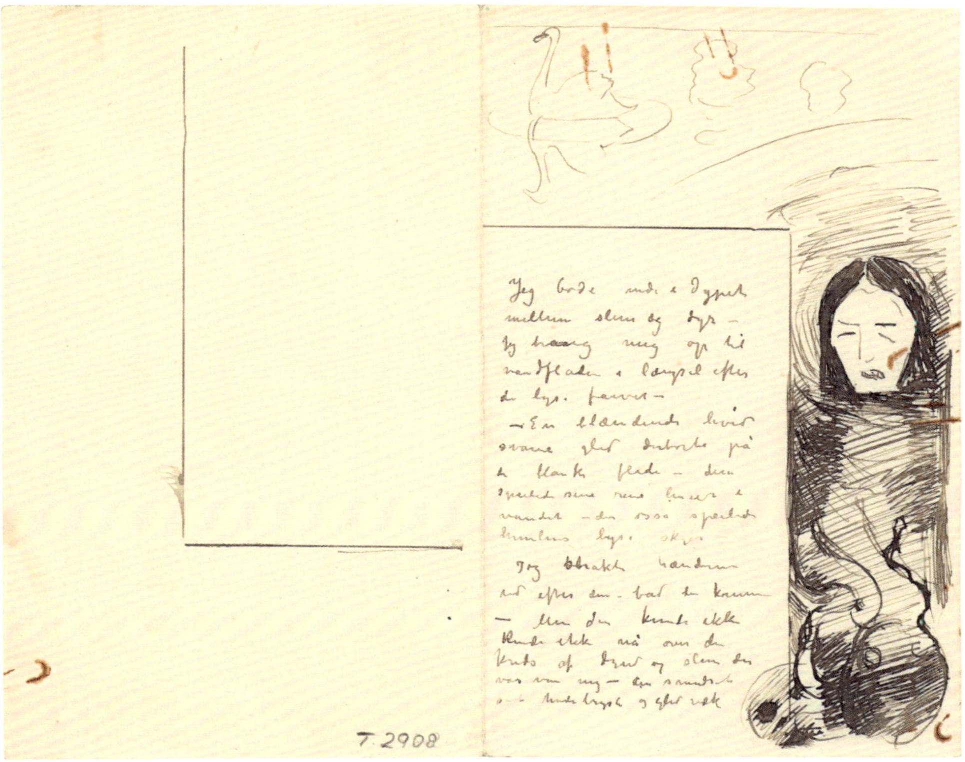

27

Sketch of *Vision* with text
1892–93
Pen
181 × 230 mm

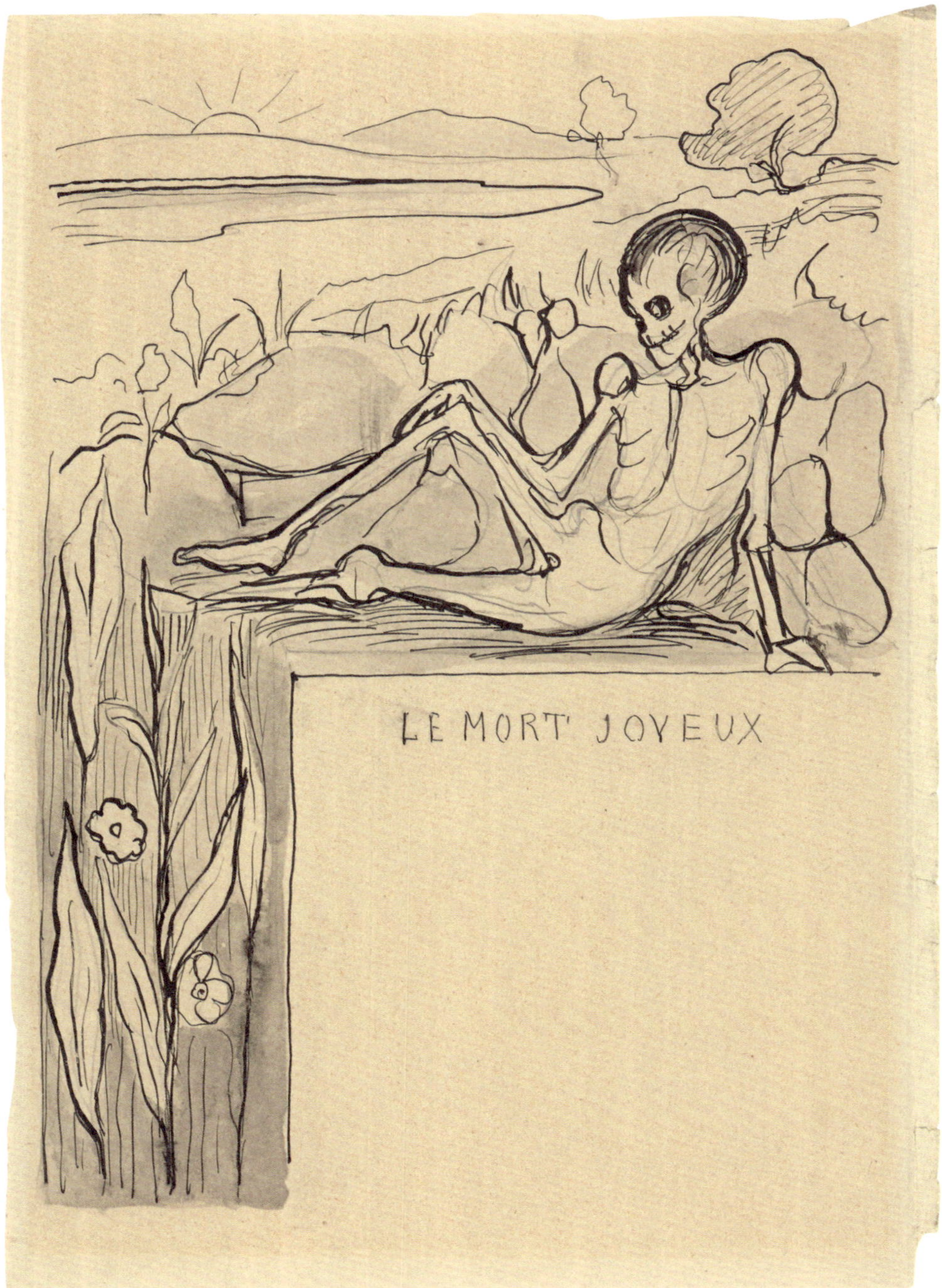

Le Mort Joyeux. Illustration for Charles Baudelaire's
Les fleurs du mal
1896
Pen, wash and pencil
280 × 205 mm

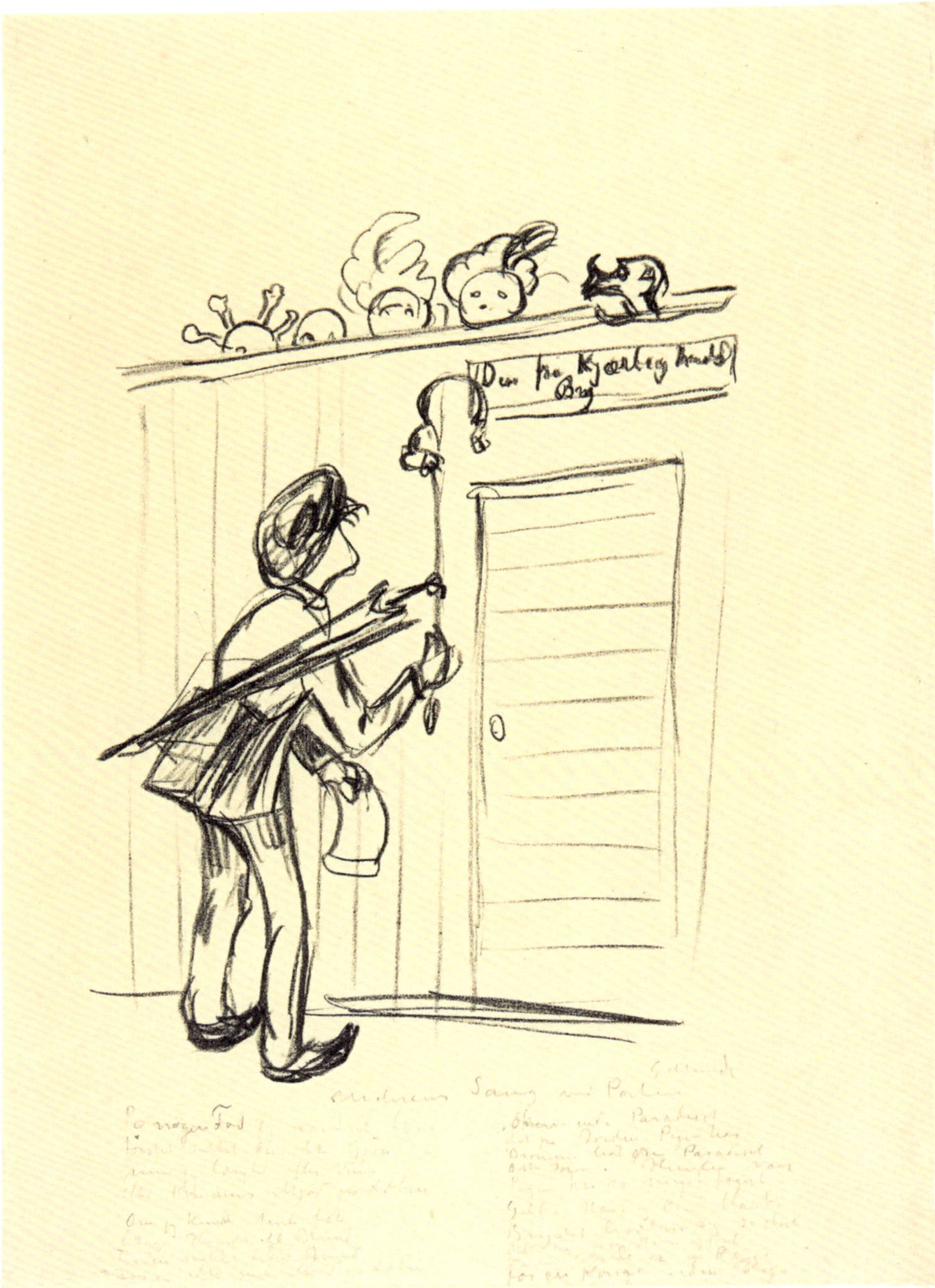

The City of Free Love
1908–09
Lithograph
310 × 230 mm

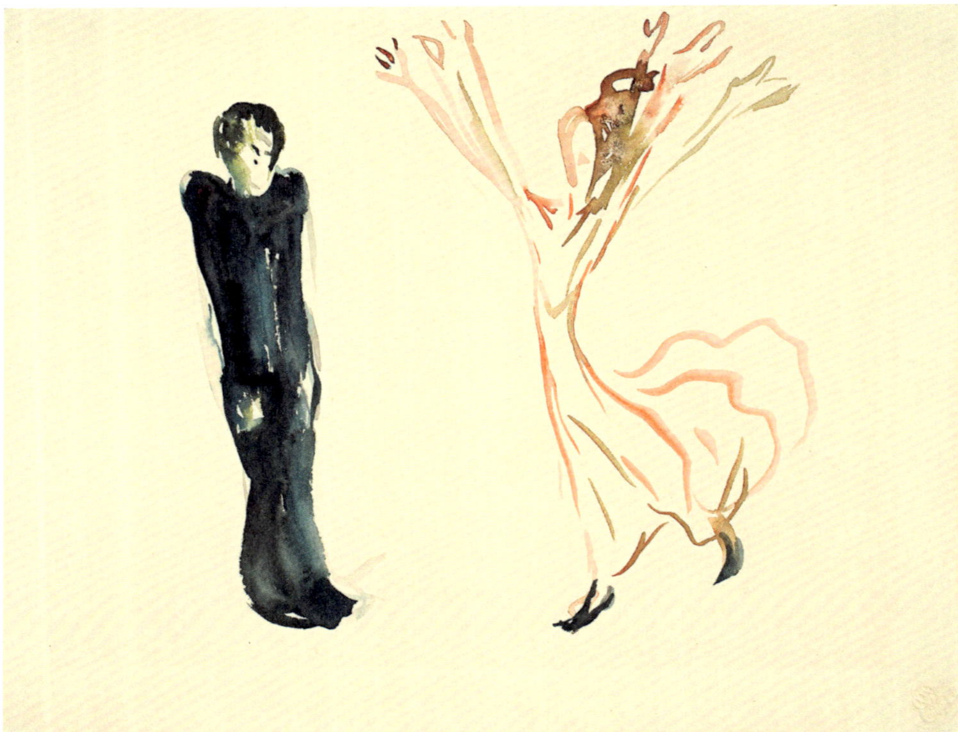

Standing Man and Dancing Woman
1908–09
Watercolour
240 × 314 mm

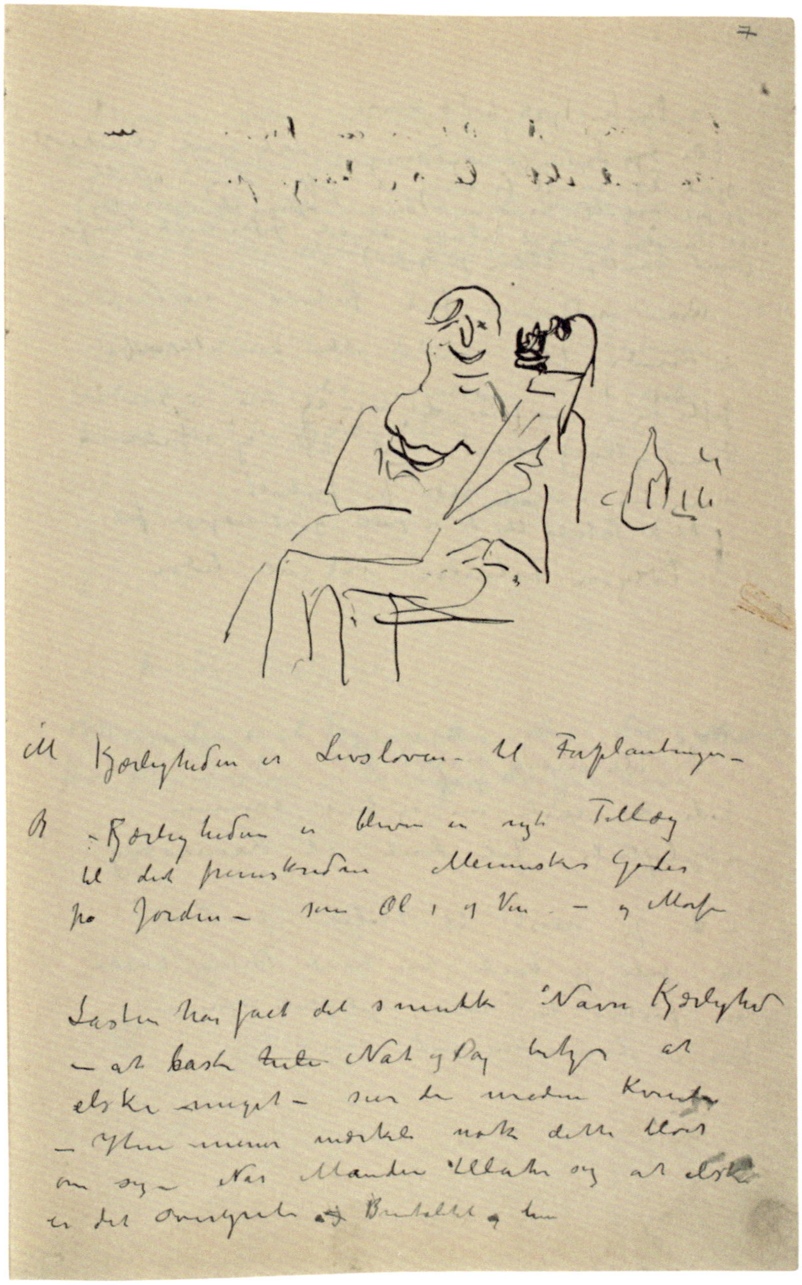

Caricature of a Couple
1909–11
Pen
339 × 223 mm

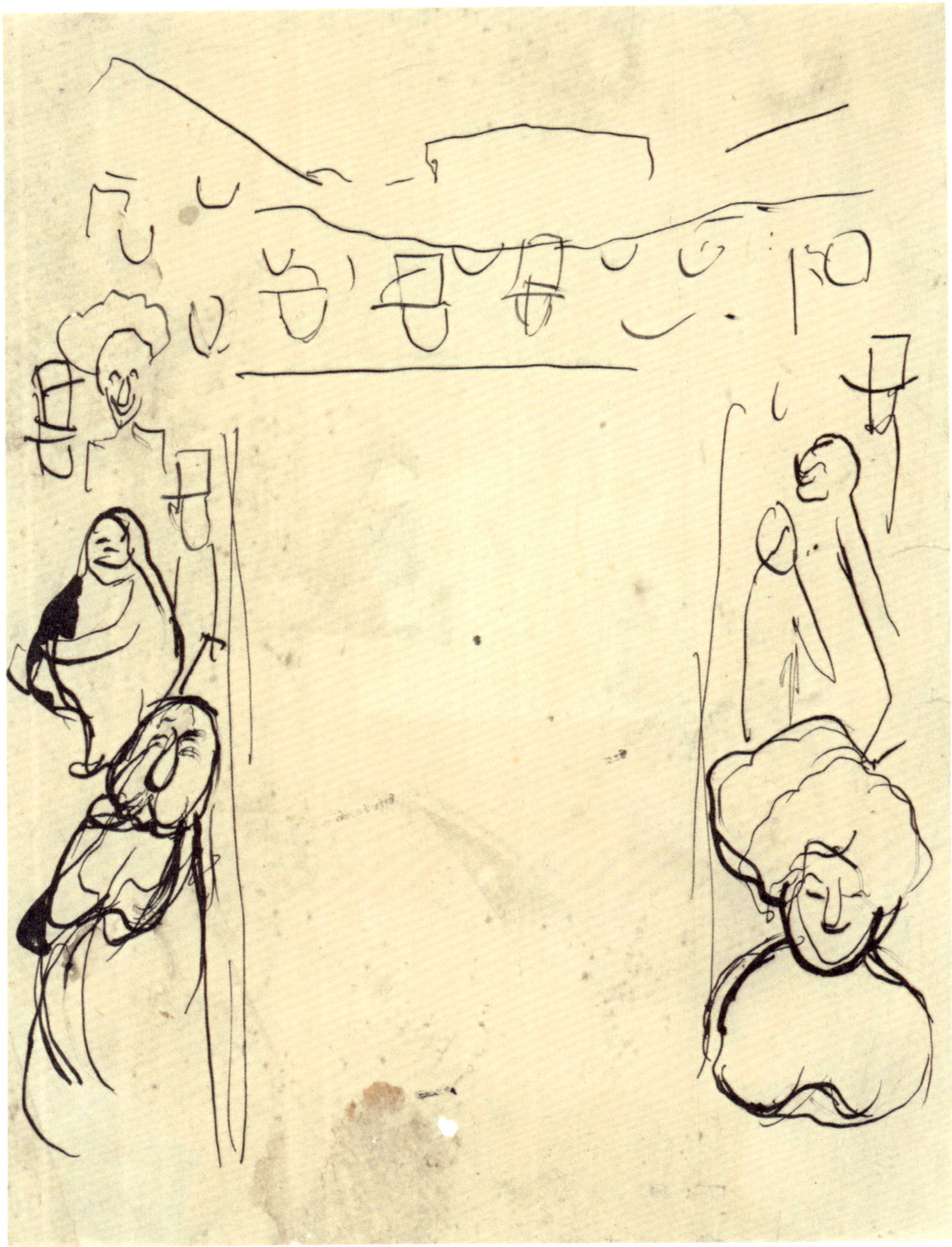

Frame with Caricatured Figures
1905–06
Pen
280 × 215 mm

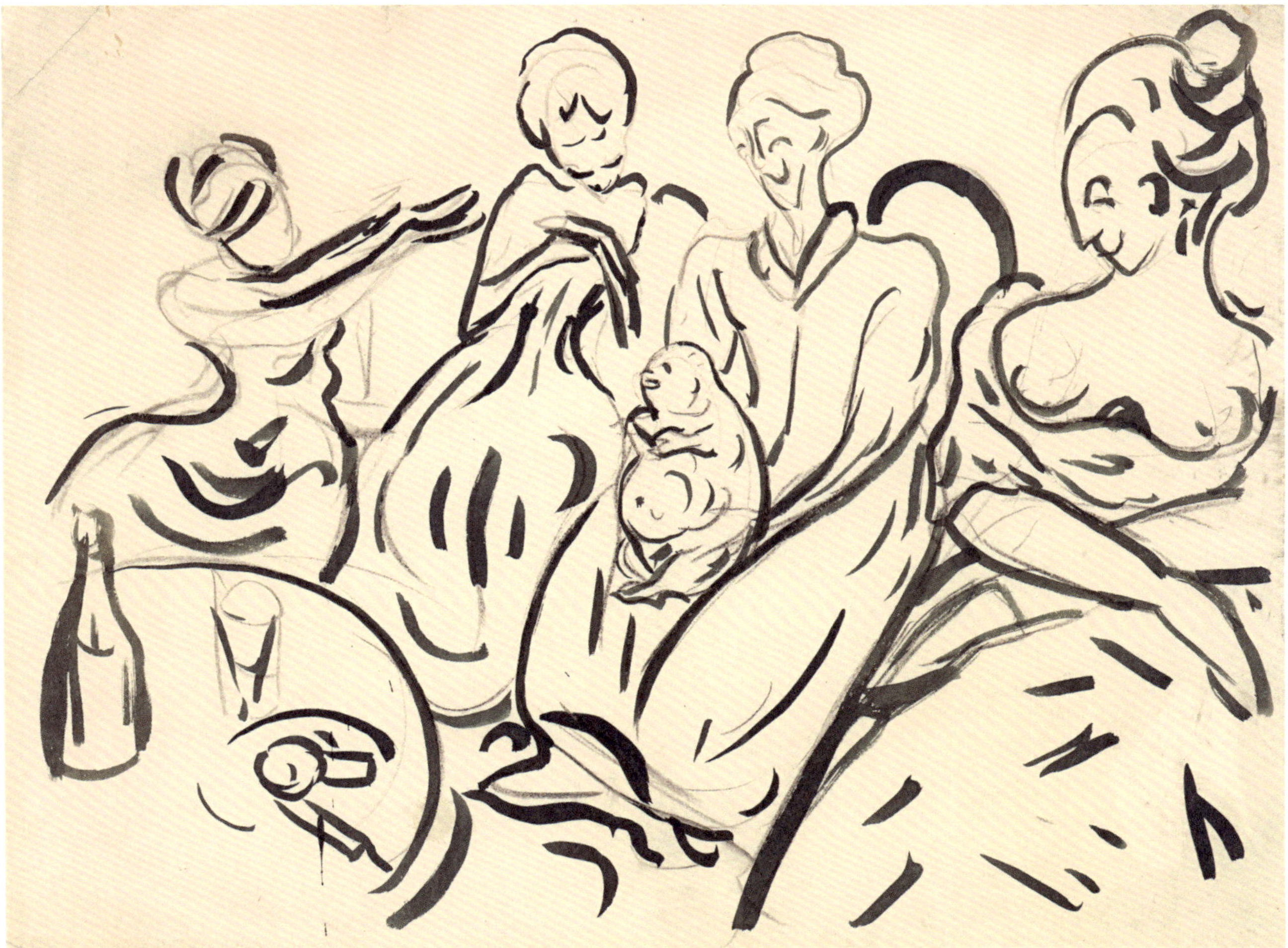

The City of Free Love: The Lap Piggy
1908–10
Brush and crayon
480 × 650 mm

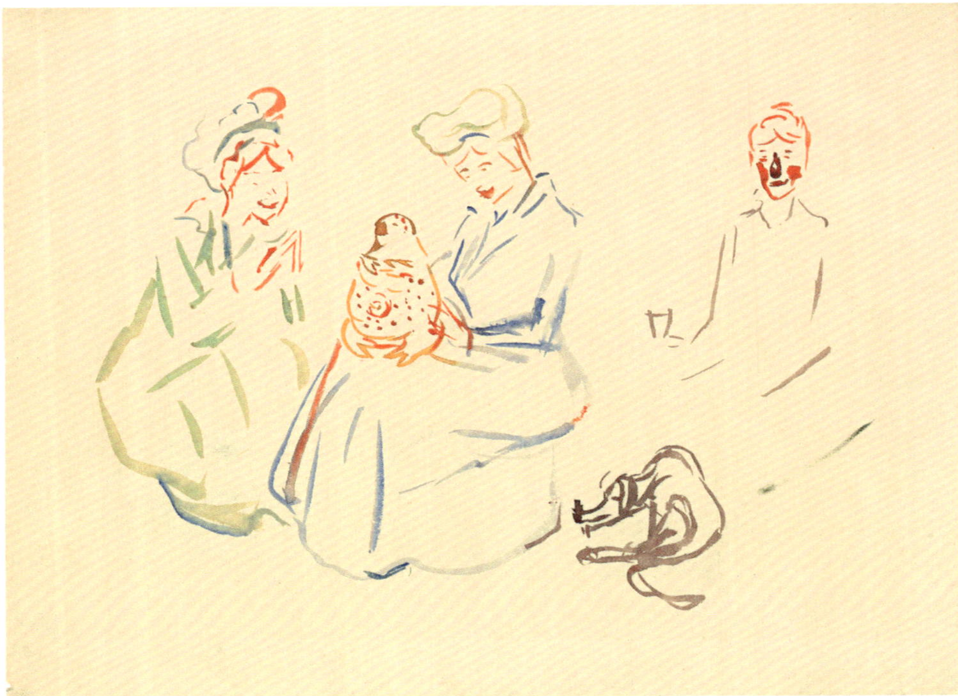

Caricature: Women, Toad-Piglet and Dog
1908–09
Watercolour
260 × 361 mm

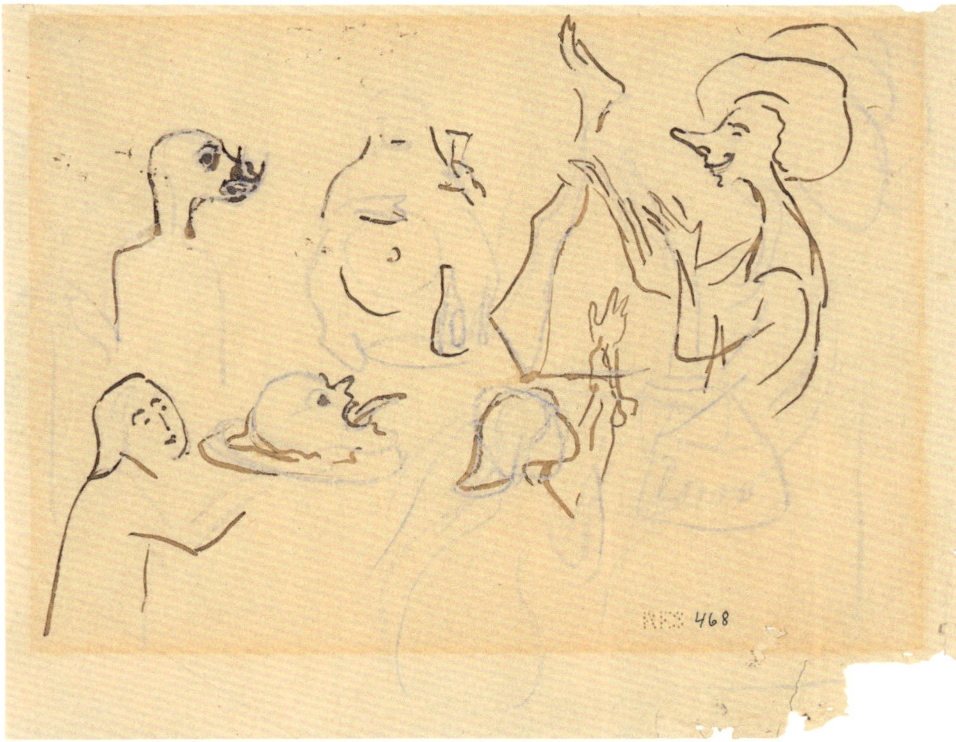

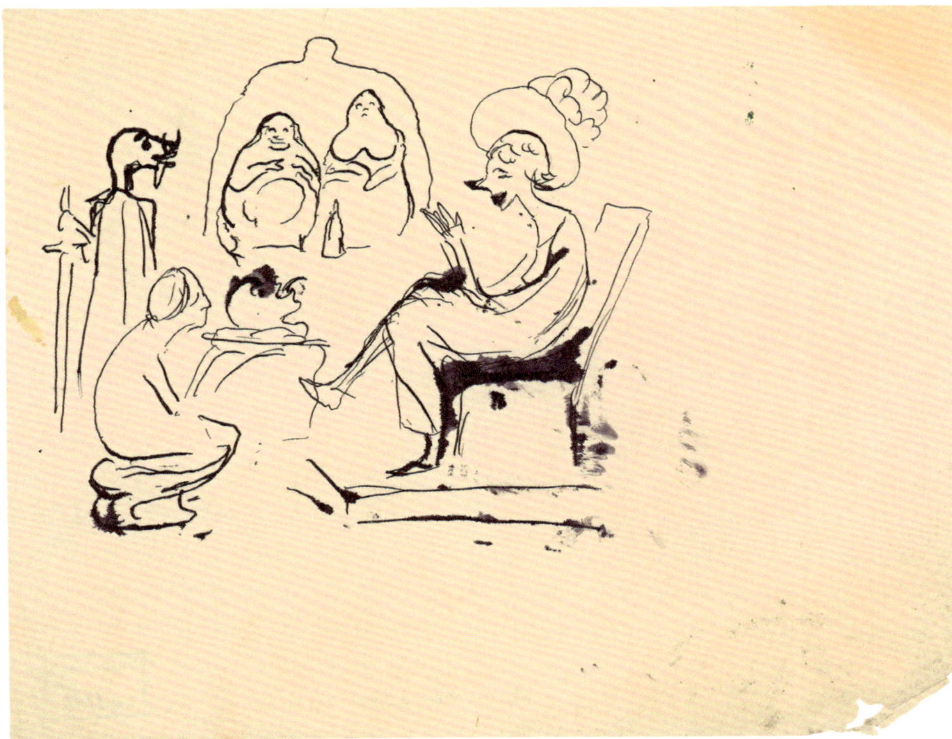

Caricature. John the Baptist's Head on a Platter.
Variation of the engraving *Ghosts*
1905
Pen and crayon(?)
214 × 280 mm

The City of Free Love: The Dollar Princess with the Singer's Head on a Plate
1905–06
Pen
215 × 280 mm

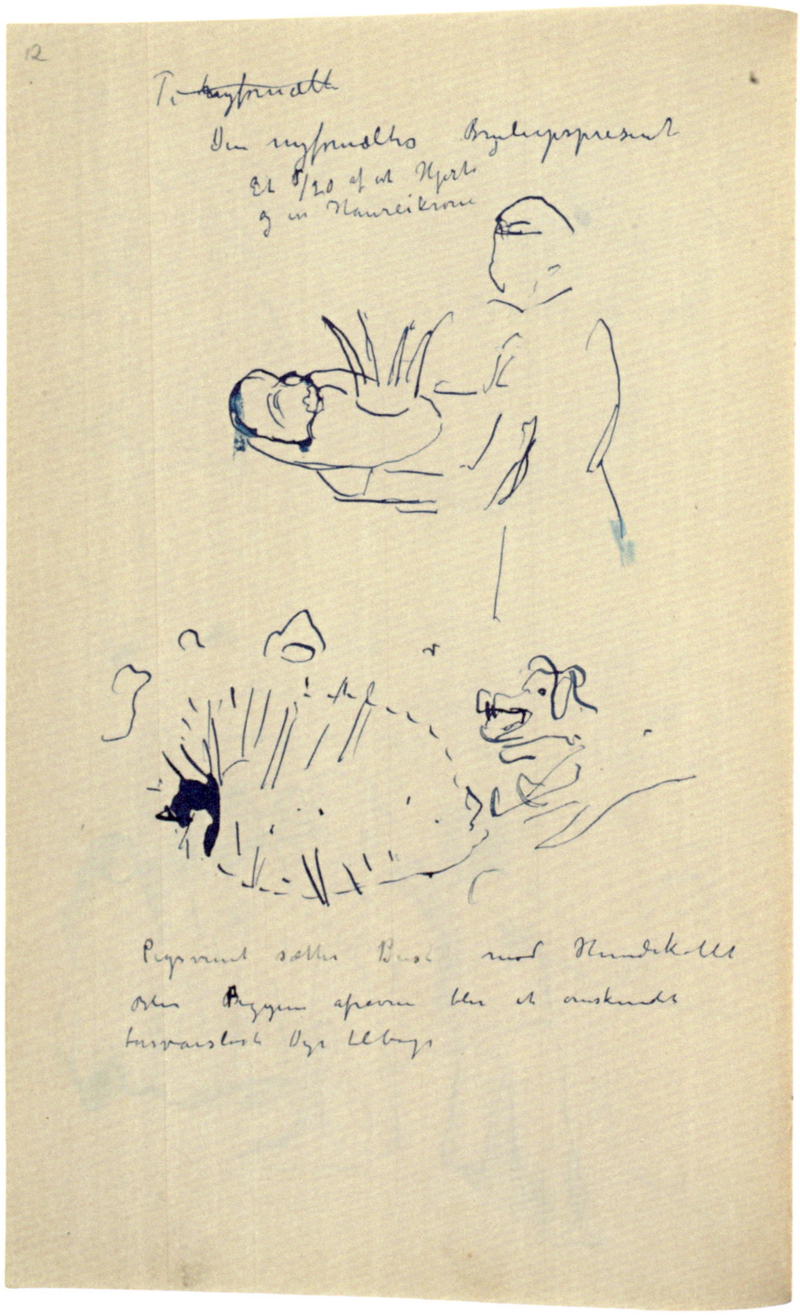

The Wedding Present
1909–11
Pen
339 × 223 mm

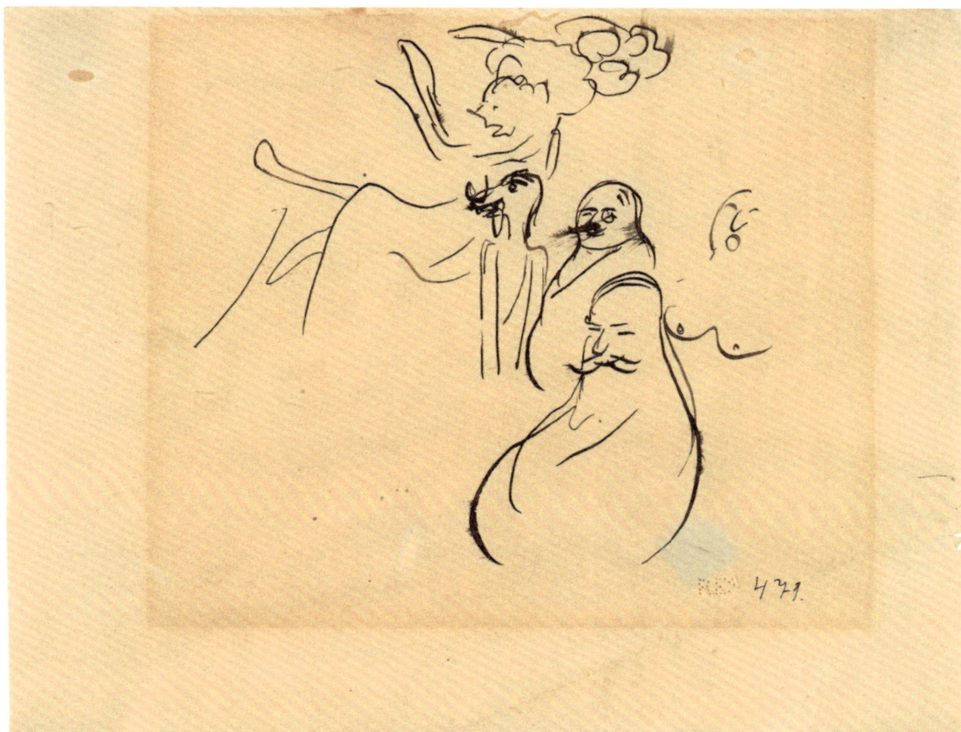

Caricature. Tulla Larsen, Sigurd Bødtker, Gunnar Heiberg and Christian Krohg
1905–06
Pen
214 × 280 mm

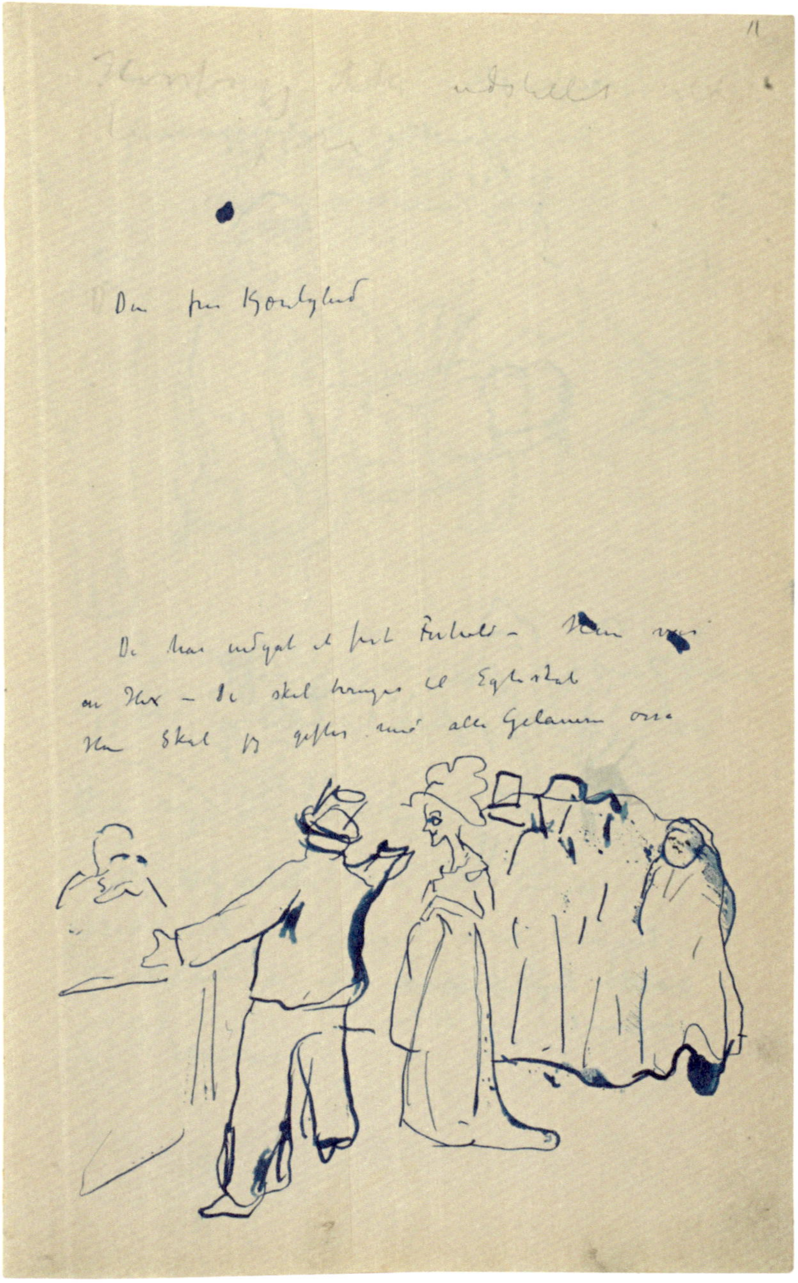

The City of Free Love
1909–11
Pen
339 × 223 mm

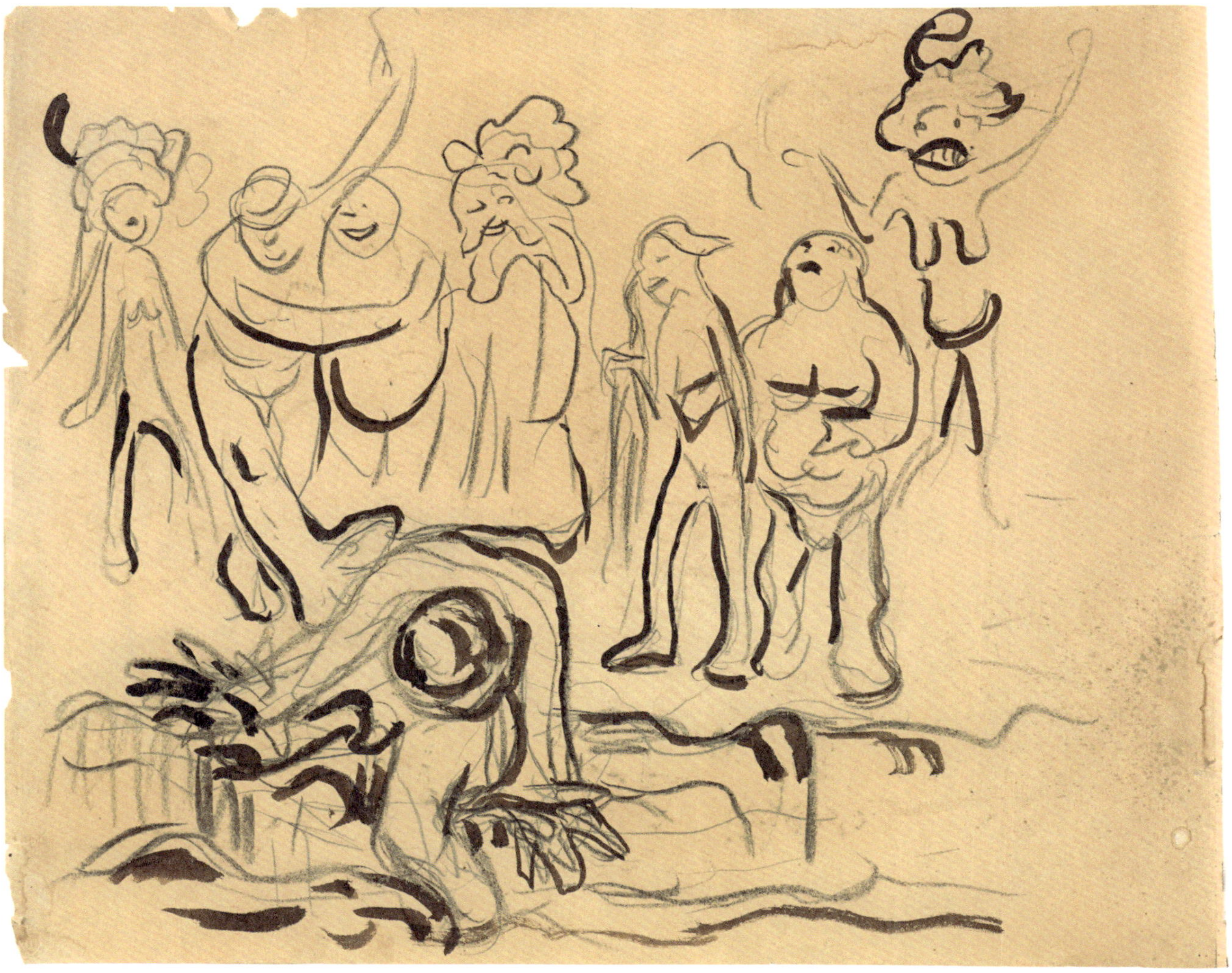

The Dancer Kicked into the Grave
1909–10
Pencil, crayon and brush
504 × 632 mm

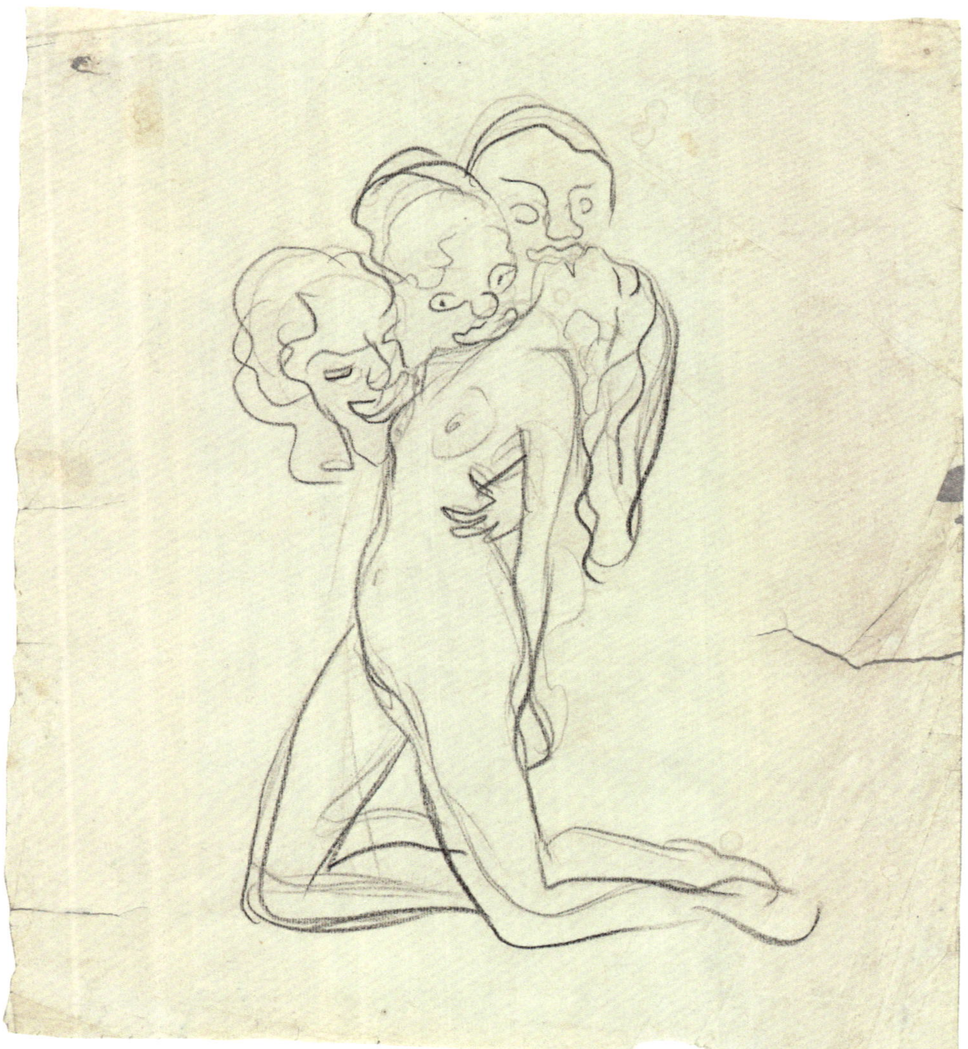

Desire
1898
Crayon
395 × 355 mm

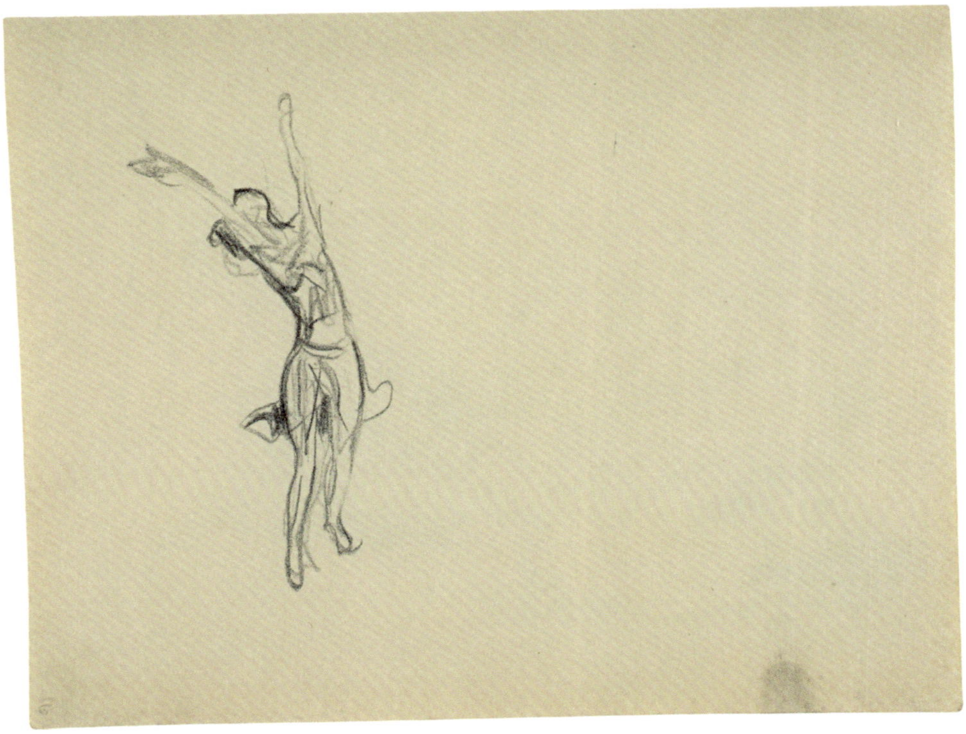

Peer Gynt: Anitra's Dance
1916–20
Crayon
208 × 265 mm

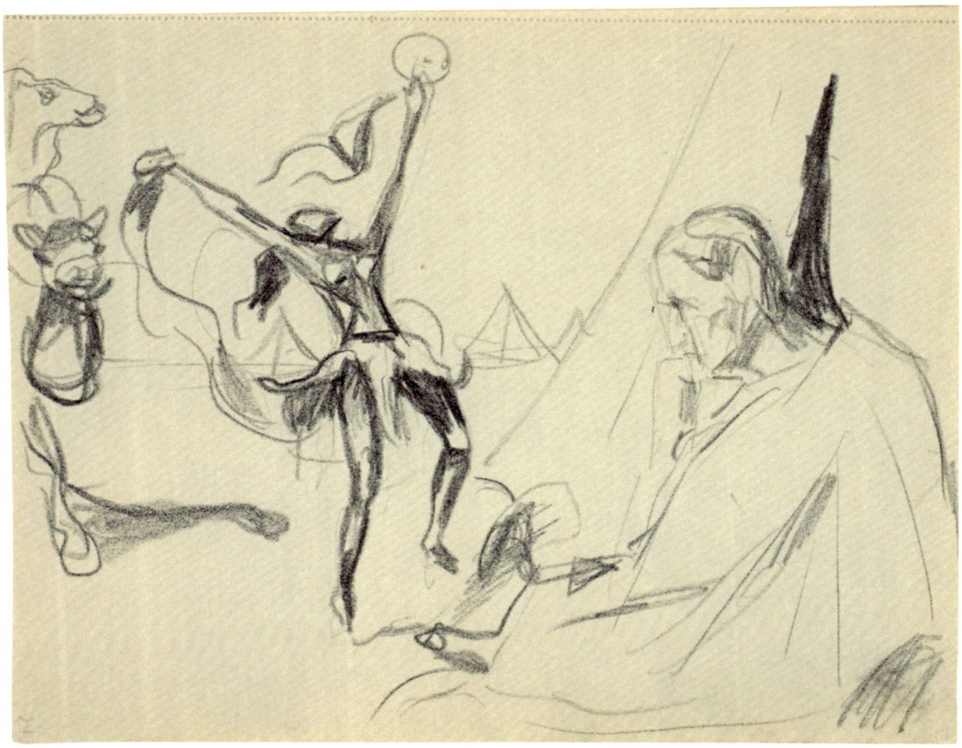

Peer Gynt: Anitra's Dance
1916–20
Crayon
208 × 265 mm

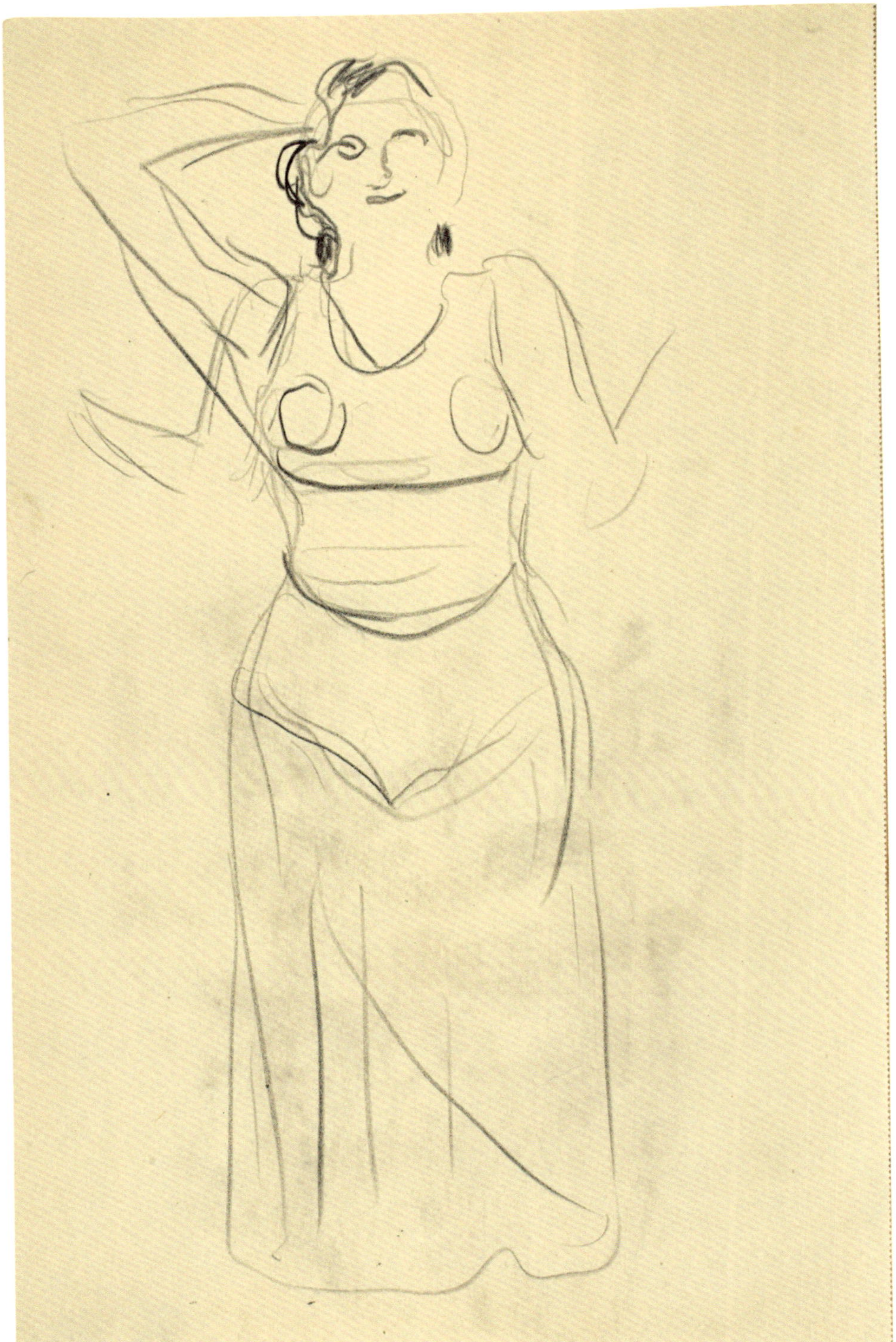

Peer Gynt: Anitra
1916
Crayon
411 × 268 mm

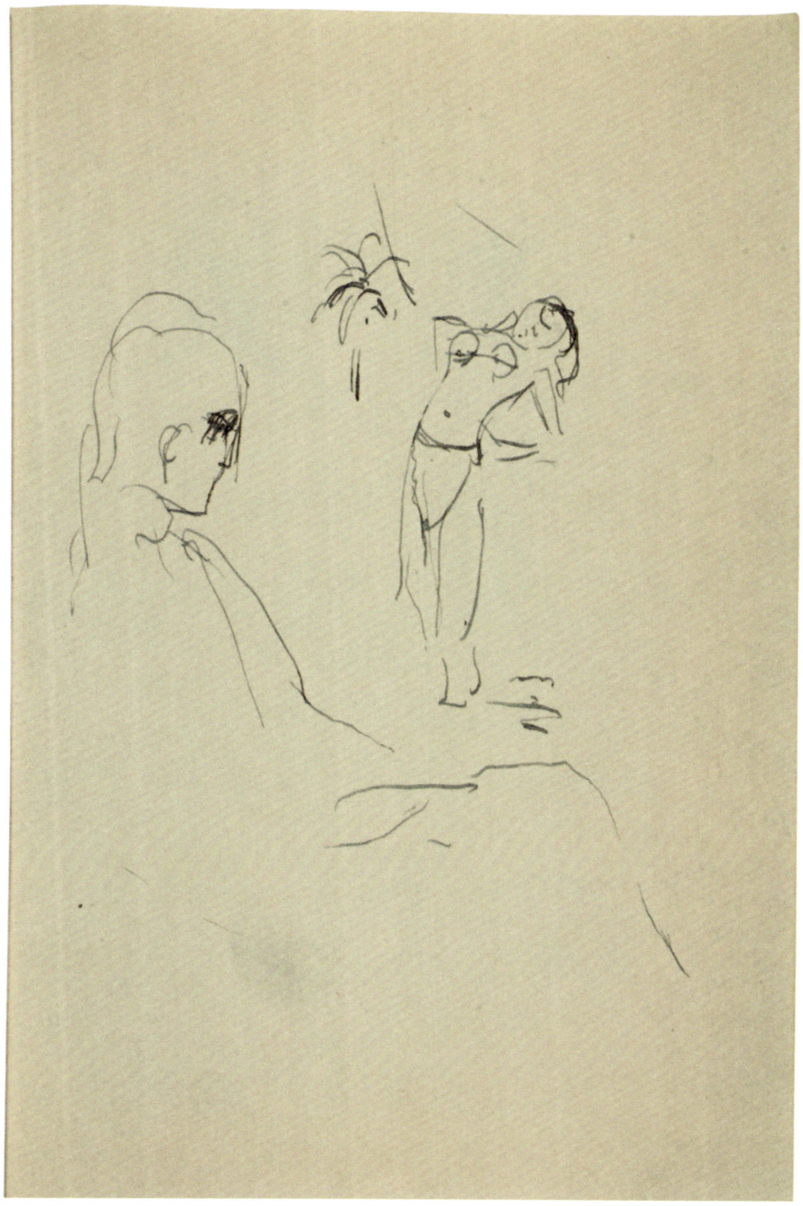

Peer Gynt: Anitra's Dance
1920
Pen
206 × 128 mm

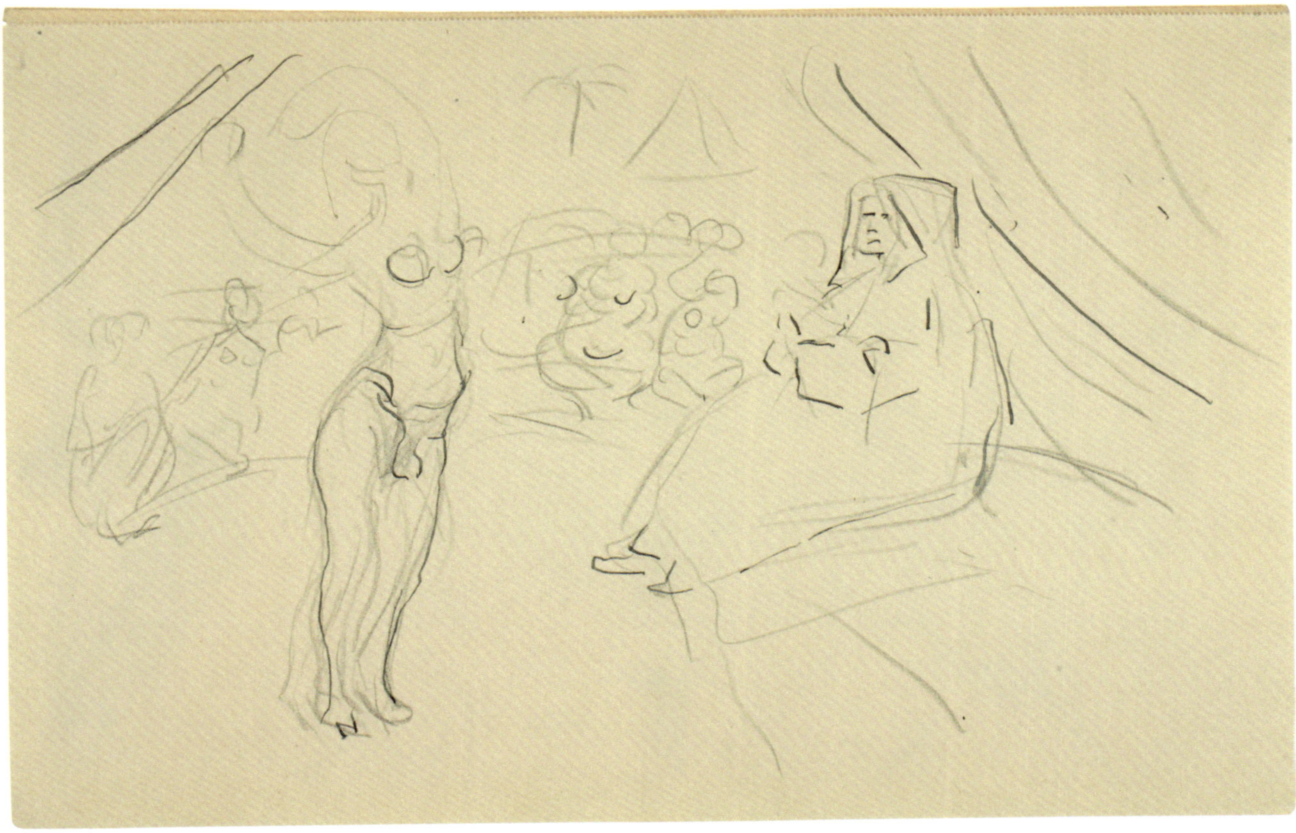

Peer Gynt: Anitra's Dance
1913
Crayon and pen
258 × 410 mm

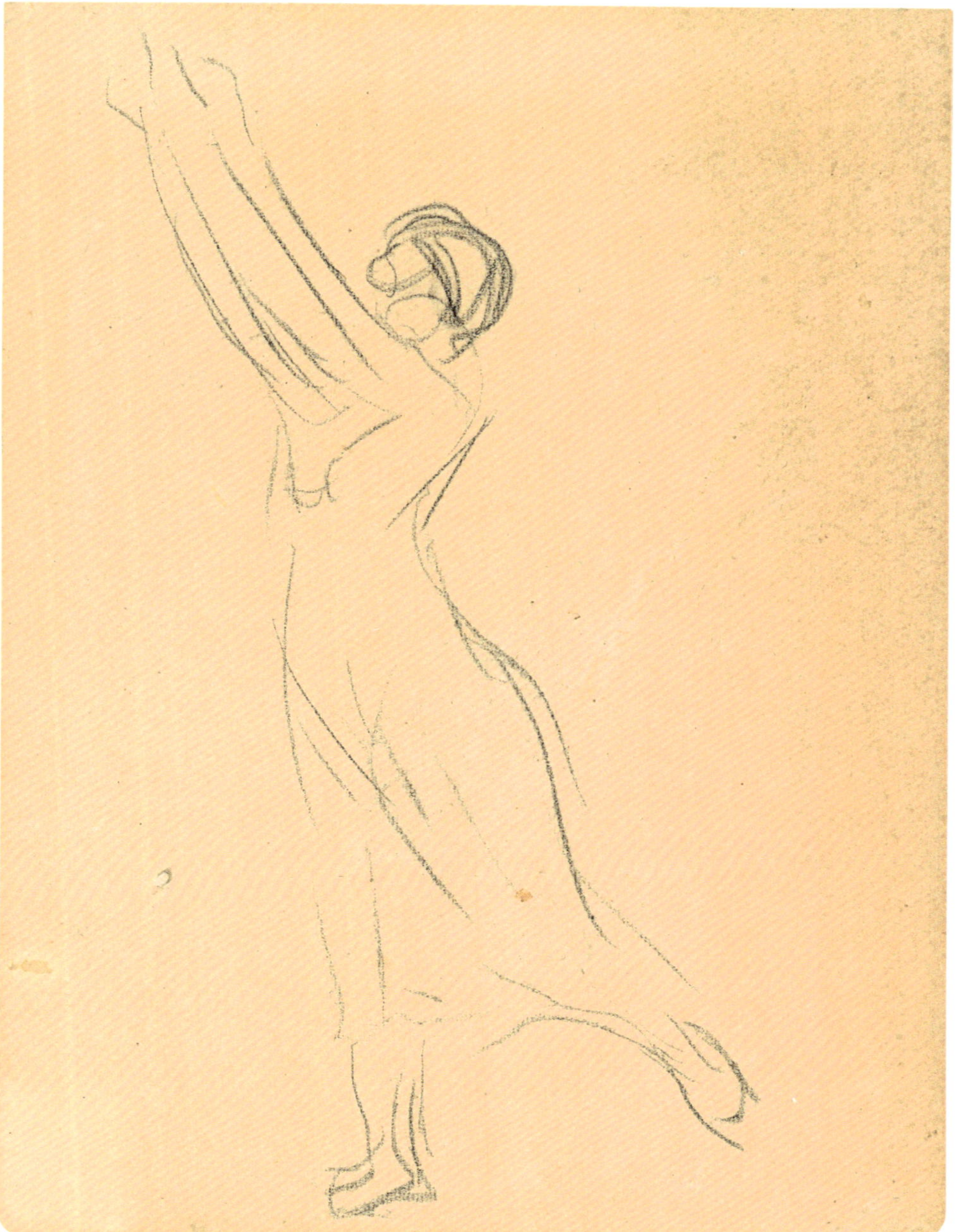

Peer Gynt: Anitra's Dance
1916
Crayon
329 × 253 mm

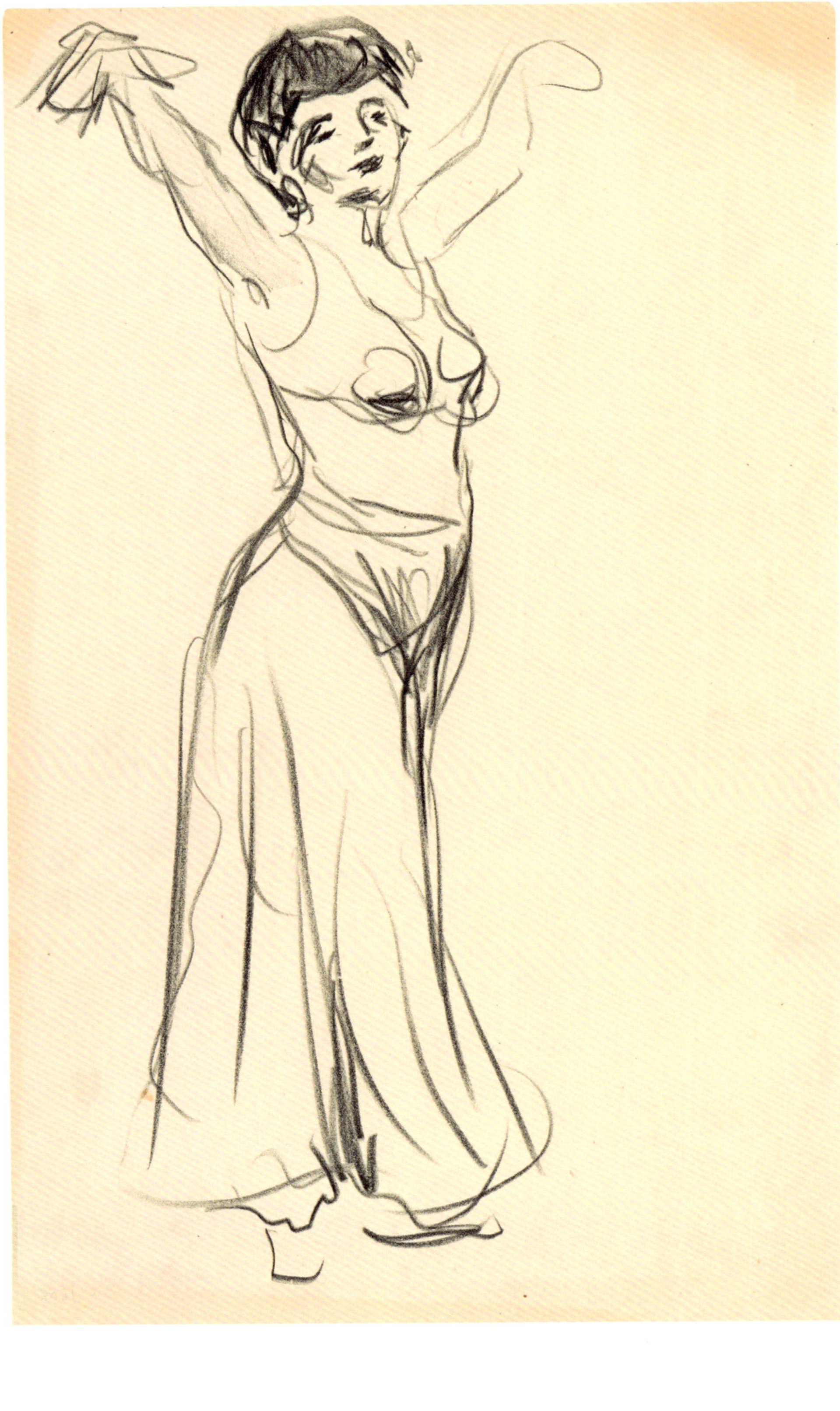

Peer Gynt: Anitra's Dance
1913
Crayon
411 × 258 mm

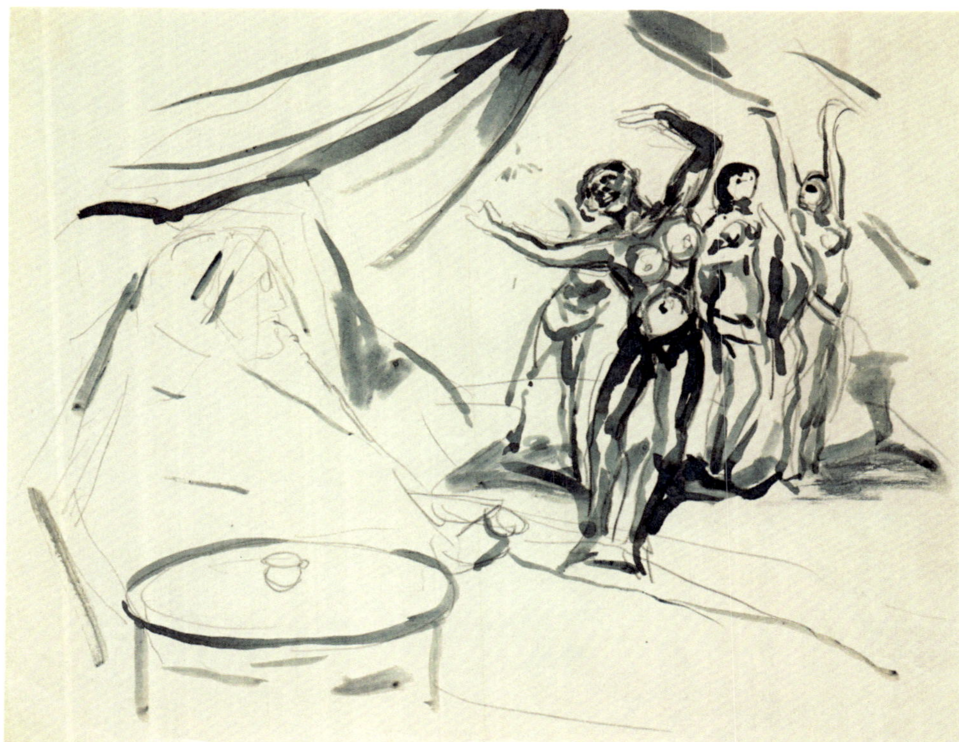

Peer Gynt: Anitra's Dance
1932–34
Brush and pencil
225 × 290 mm

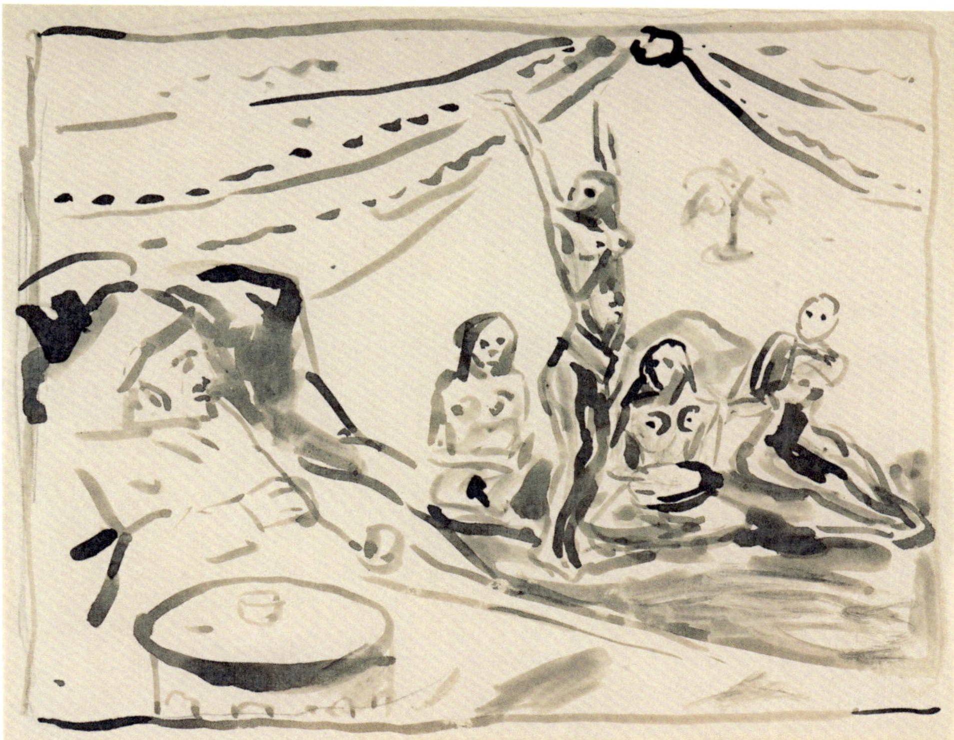

Peer Gynt: Anitra's Dance
1932–34
Brush
225 × 290 mm

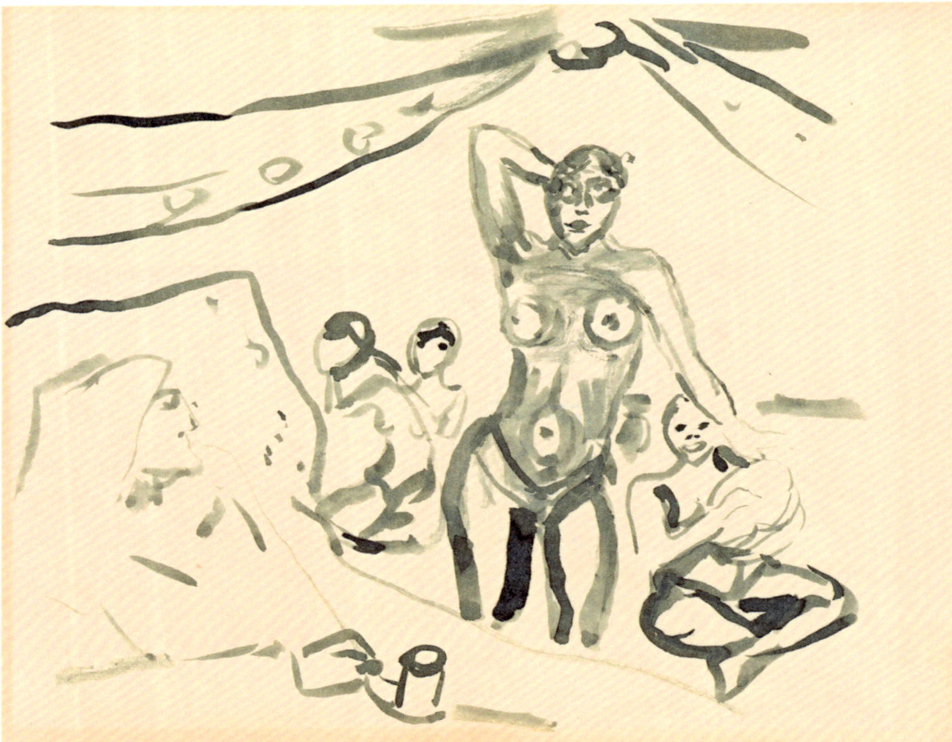

Peer Gynt: Anitra's Dance
1932–34
Brush
225 × 290 mm

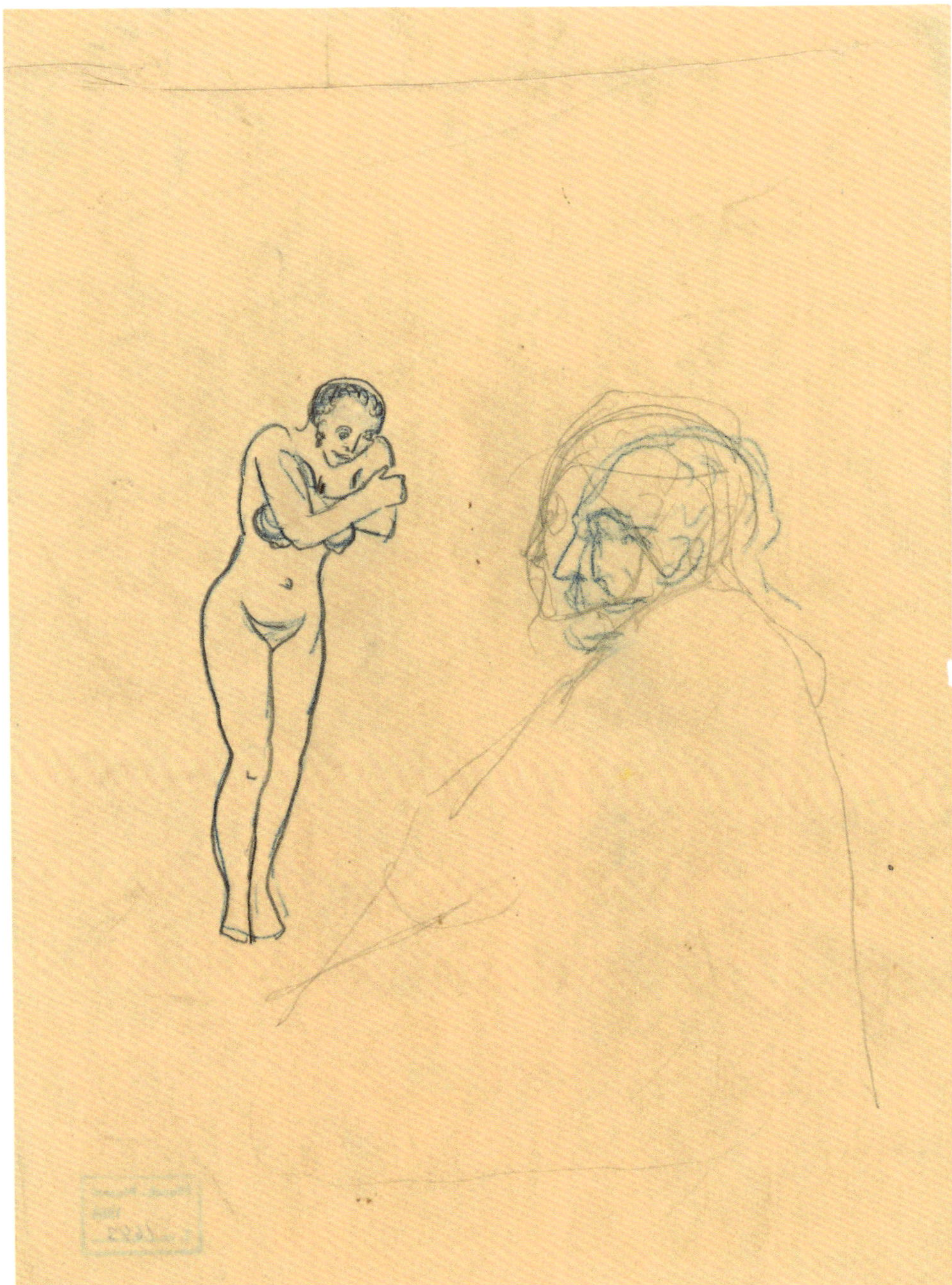

Peer Gynt: Peer and Anitra
1930–33
Pencil and carbon paper(?)
313 × 233 mm

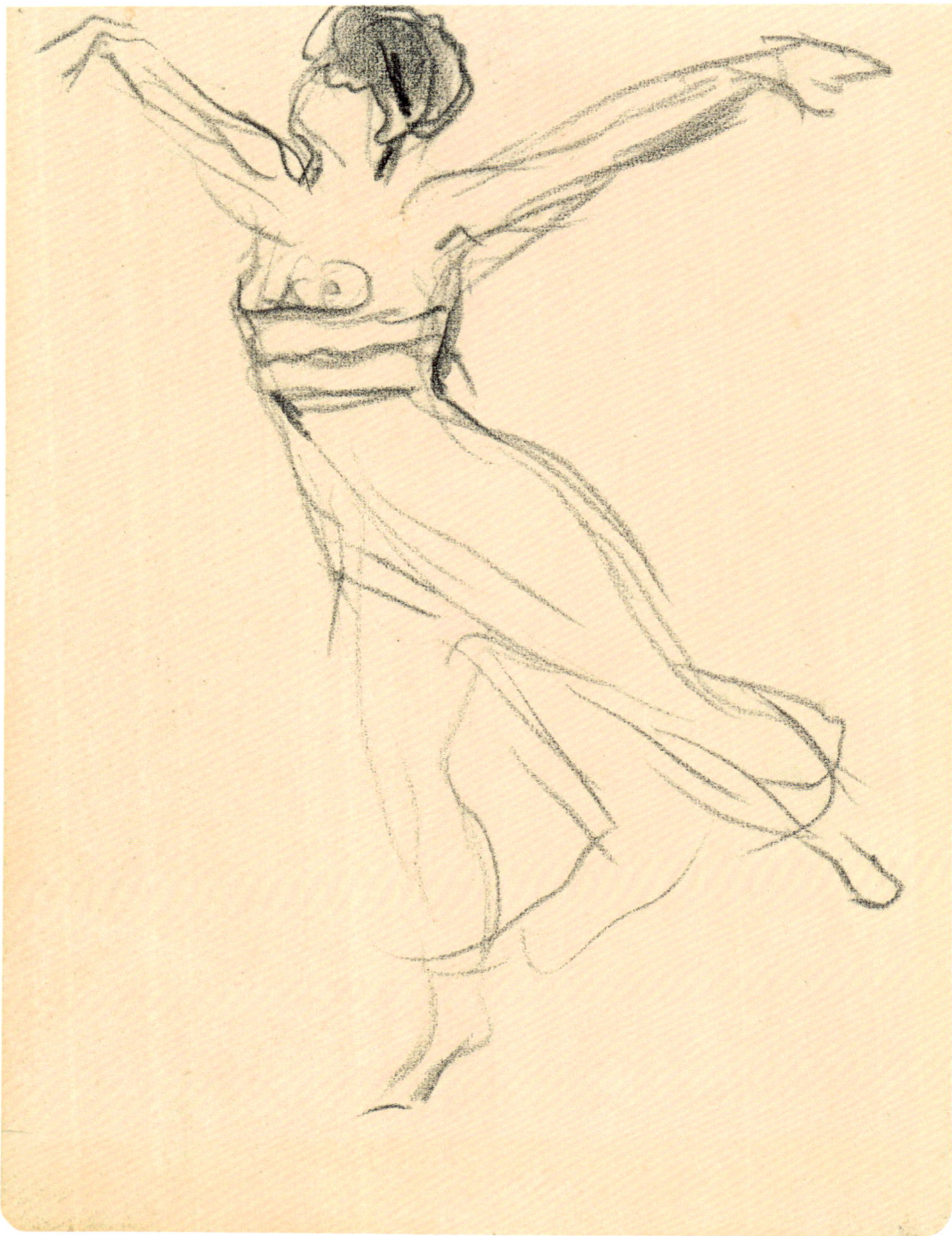

Peer Gynt: Anitra's Dance
1916
Crayon
325 × 253 mm

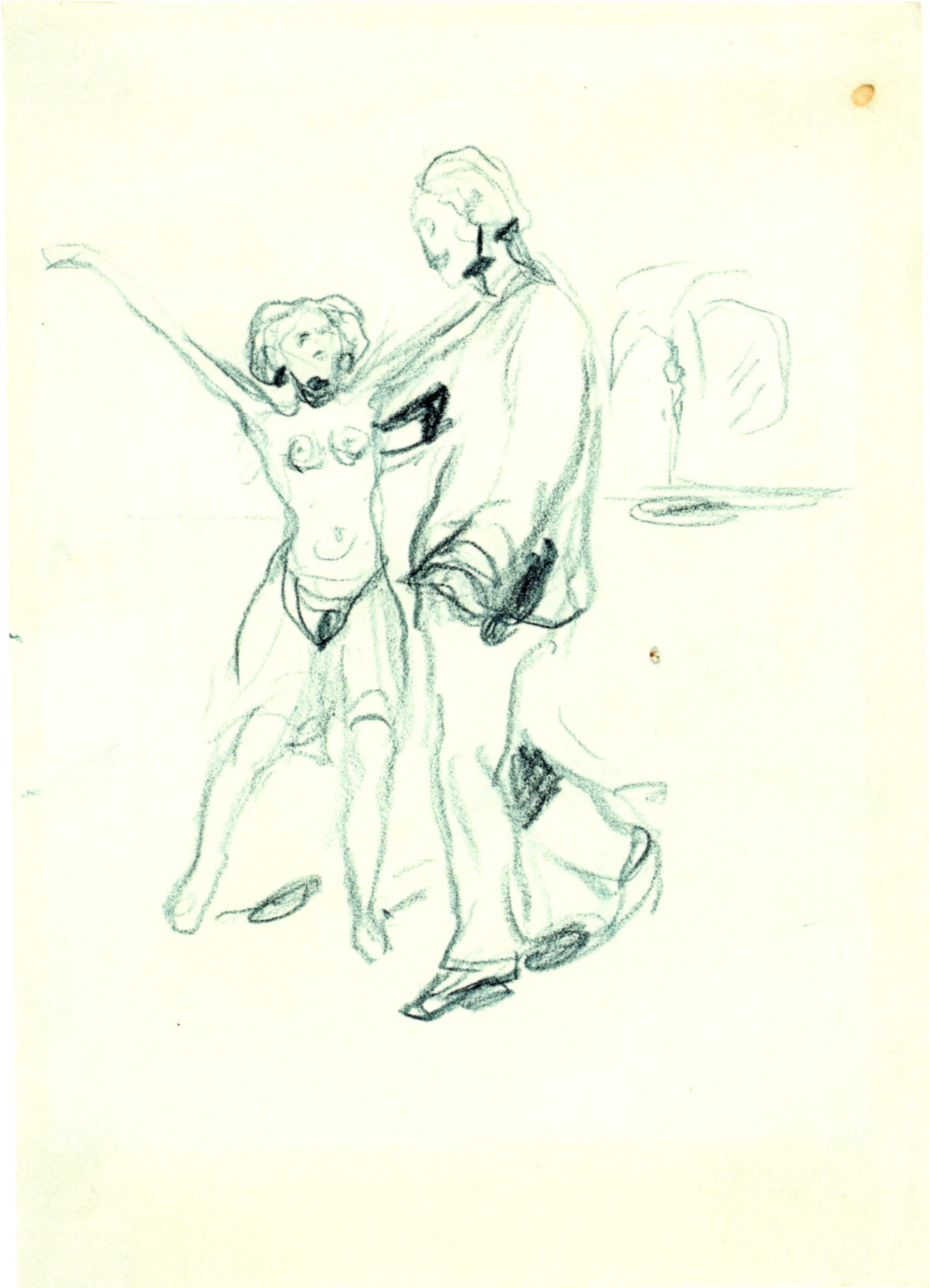

Peer Gynt: Peer and Anitra
1913
Crayon
355 × 253 mm

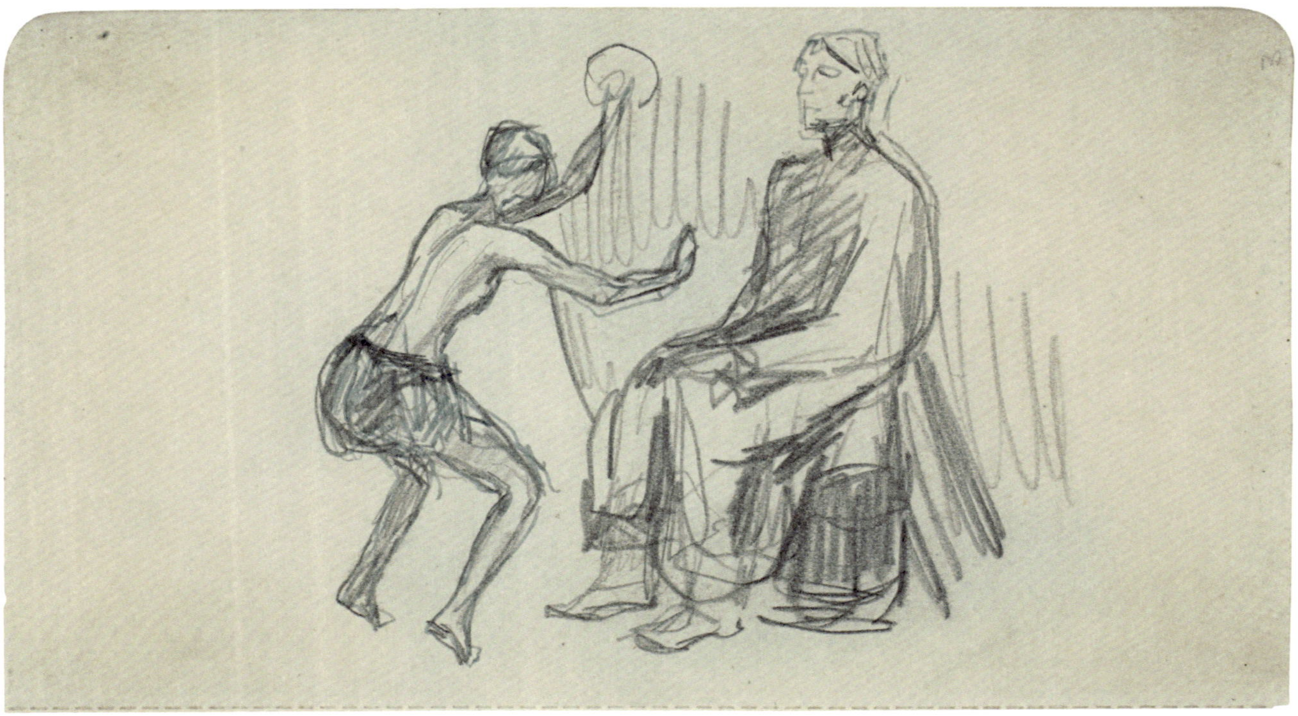

Peer Gynt: Anitra's Dance
1916–17
Pencil
112 × 183 mm

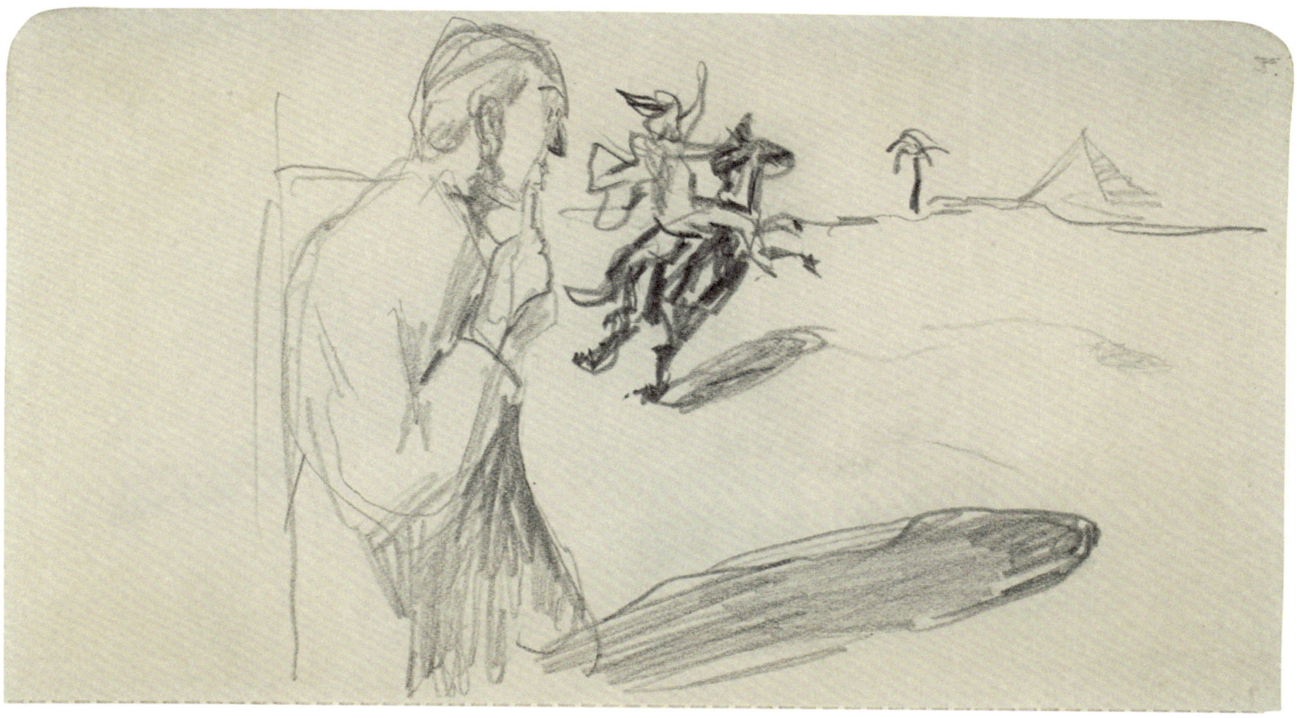

Peer Gynt: Anitra's Escape
1916–17
Pencil
112 × 183 mm

The Same Free, Interesting Zone

Terje Nicolaisen interviewed by Halvor Haugen

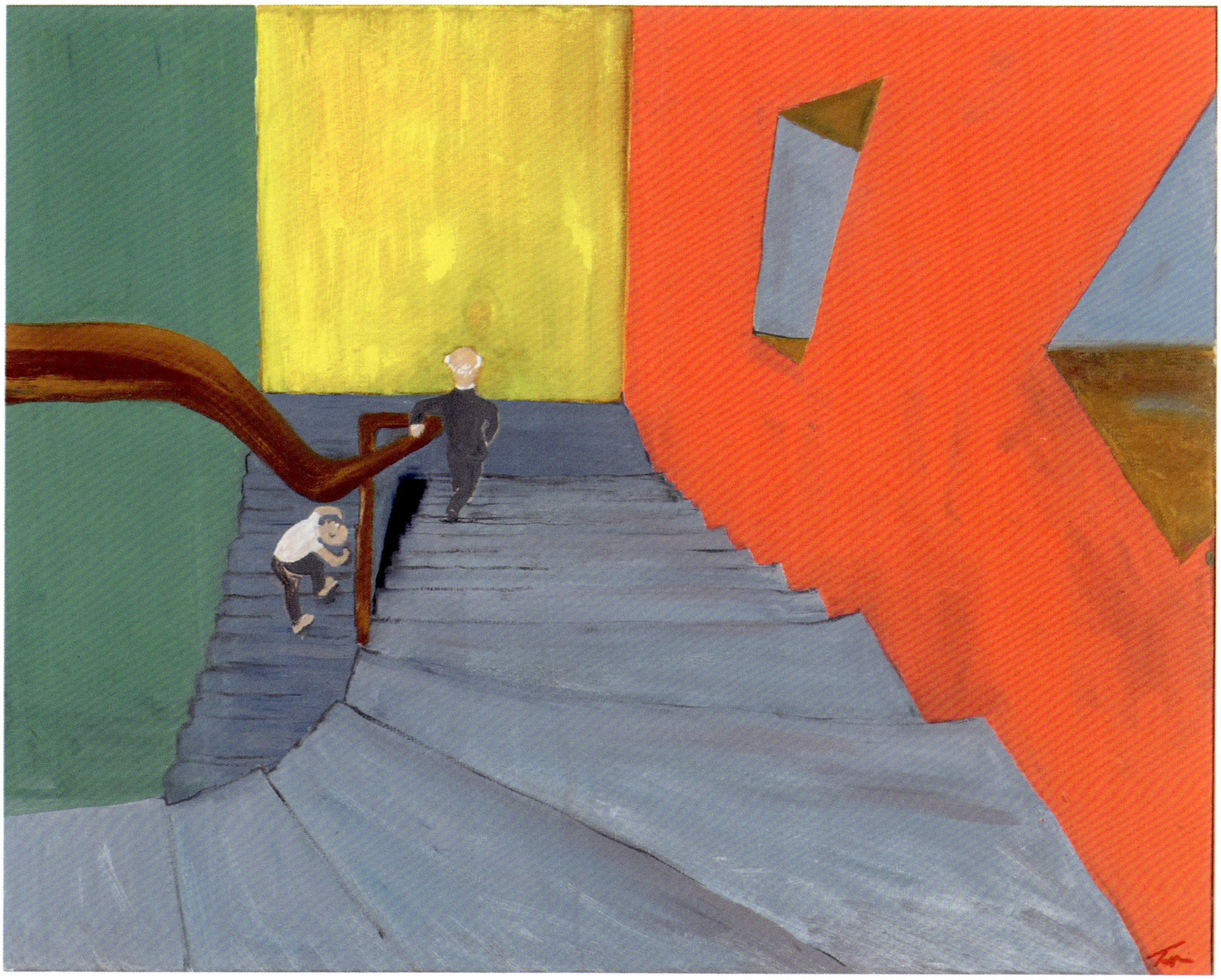

Terje Nicolaisen
Encounter on the Landing, 2020
Oil on canvas
80 × 100 cm

In Terje Nicolaisen's art, drawing serves as an effective antidote to pretension, both one's own and that of others. His drawings capture a mix of spontaneous ideas, unintended errors, and strokes of serendipity. In making his selection of Edvard Munch's drawings for this book, he has focused on modest points of similarity between himself and Norway's most canonical artist by far – it's all about the moments when one stumbles and takes oneself by surprise.

Haugen

I imagine Munch makes many artists feel a bit nervous, perhaps especially here in Norway. Is that true for you?

Nicolaisen

No, in fact I'd say there's nothing difficult about my relationship with Munch. I see him as a friend, or at least an inspiration. My studio is close to the museum at Tøyen and I often stop by to see the exhibitions there. For me, Munch always has surprises in store; I'm constantly discovering things I hadn't noticed before. And then there's his brushwork, which can sometimes be pretty reckless or sloppy, and that I find reassuring.

But I should add that Munch and I start out from very different places. He was an incredibly good draughtsman right from childhood, and he came from a family steeped in culture. I for my part trained as a bricklayer before entering the art academy. Art wasn't really part of my background, and I found myself thrust onto a stage where I didn't know the rules. I'd say that where Munch and I meet eye to eye is where he stumbles, although the two of us stumble in different ways. In his case, it's a deliberate tactic to outwit his inherent skilfulness, and it often works. I don't have his level of skill; when I stumble, it's because I'm seriously trying to create something good, or perhaps to be clever. But I don't have a chance. So where he comes stumbling down the stairs, I'm struggling to make my way up. And that's where we meet, on the landing half-way.

H

What have you been looking for in selecting from Munch's drawings?

N

First and foremost, I've looked for things outside the standard canon. I've avoided works that are finished, or that have a clear purpose, and I have excluded his illustrations, caricatures, and studies for better known works. That means I have ruled out a vast number of the pictures I love. Instead, I've looked for things that give me a sense of being on a level with Munch. Don't get me wrong; in suggesting we're on the same level, it's those stumbles on the stairs I'm talking about. My approach has been: Is something too precise? Is it too good? Or too entertaining?

H

Let's take a closer look at some of the drawings you have picked out.

N

This one's beautiful (p. 71). Although there's something here that suggests a human figure, with two dashes of sky beyond, it isn't the purpose of the drawing that matters. Viewers can decide for themselves what they see. I would say the major challenge for any artist is to figure out how to give an artwork a sense of openness. With Munch, there's usually a lot of intention; there's a story he wants to tell, and very often the visual storytelling is so good that we're simply captivated. But in some cases he's looser, and the work becomes more open, allowing us to enter it in different ways without following his narrative. Before you read the title *Ragnarok: Two Escapees on the Beach* (p. 85), the elements in the picture are open to a variety of readings.

H — Does your selection include different kinds of openness?

N — In some of his drawings he is simply exploring something, like the map of the Oslo Fjord (p.73). You could call it an unintentional drawing. It represents a conceptual space. Here, Munch has been thinking about the geographical relationship between Oslo and Åsgårdstrand, and the upshot is a figure that can be interpreted in very different ways. This one here, *Male Head in Front of a Window* (p.94), is more deliberately exploratory. I feel he's trying to work out how to place the person within the space, something he's very good at. One eye is very intense and is at the forefront of the pictorial space. Then he has asked himself: What if the background is allowed to bleed through? To me it's as if he were trying to make things move back and forth. We glimpse the background through the face, which makes the figure recede into the room. And that's exciting!

H — In this portrait of a woman (p.95), could it be that the suggestion of openness has to do with the use of watercolour?

N — Yes, when working with materials things happen that you can't foresee, although you learn to control it to some extent through routine. On one side of her face, the red follows the contour of her eye, while on the other it has just settled in the corner, so perhaps that part wasn't wet enough. The hair is just a few quick strokes. Here I feel it doesn't matter who is portrayed – the picture speaks for itself.

H — There are many bending male bodies in your selection.

N — It's as if the drawing of the man in front of the mirror (p.26), was done during a thinking phase, before the idea had become clear. Munch is exploring the relationship between the figure and the mirror, but without any clear symbolism or prepared narrative. I immediately identified with the two workers (p.74–75); to me they're probably bricklayers, and this is the dance they perform day in, day out. A bricklayer does around 1500 such bends in an average working day. No wonder I have back pain.

H — You have also selected a drawing with the title *Handicraft* (p.99).

N — Yes, here it would seem he hasn't quite captured the man at his work, and the picture doesn't give us any clear impression of the man's emotional state. One could just as easily imagine that he's a bit ham-fisted, that he's stressed or anxious, or one could even see him as an expression of small-town romanticism. That really appeals to me.

H — The drawings of Foldal, a character in Ibsen's play *John Gabriel Borkman*, are studies of a body that is bent over for other reasons (p.76–78).

N — Munch's interest in this theme is interesting in itself, I find. Foldal is a minor character in the play, a slightly pitiful poet of no great importance. In the final act, his daughter heads off in a sleigh together with Borkman's son. As they pass by, they nearly run Foldal over, who ends up in a ditch. But these drawings don't really need Ibsen or the play. One has to find one's pictures somewhere, and what interested Munch here was, I feel, the body and the posture; there's this element of things merging with each other, like one sees in many of his pictures, such as *Two Nudes, Man and Woman, Half Figure* (p.98). This is more of a rough sketch than a real study, and here again it's the openness that attracts me. He doesn't really let us see their faces. She stands with her head bent forward, as if a little shy or maybe coquettish, but the relationship between the two is barely hinted at. They could belong to one of so many short stories.

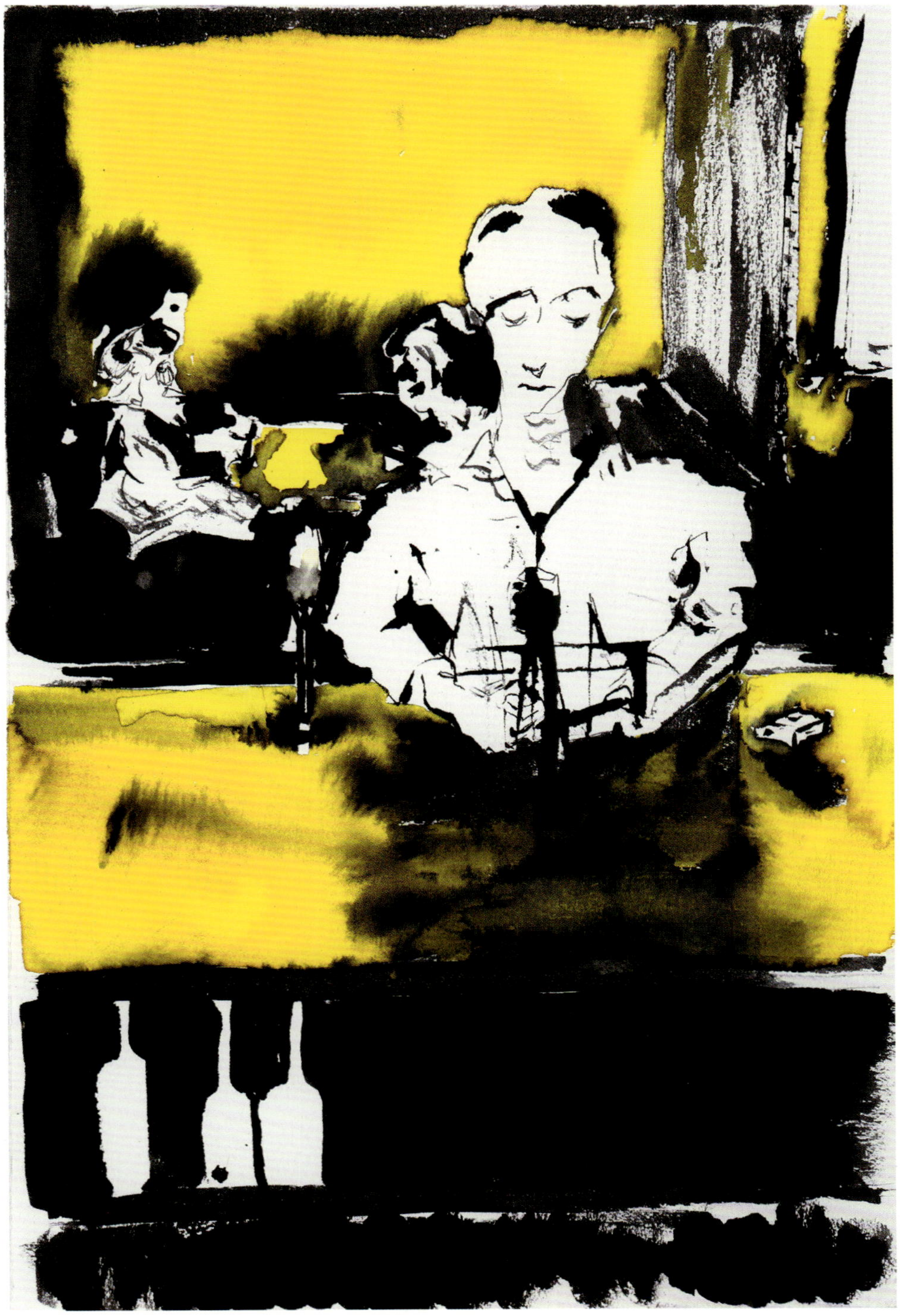

Terje Nicolaisen
At the Bar, 2013
Ink and watercolour on paper
390 × 267 mm

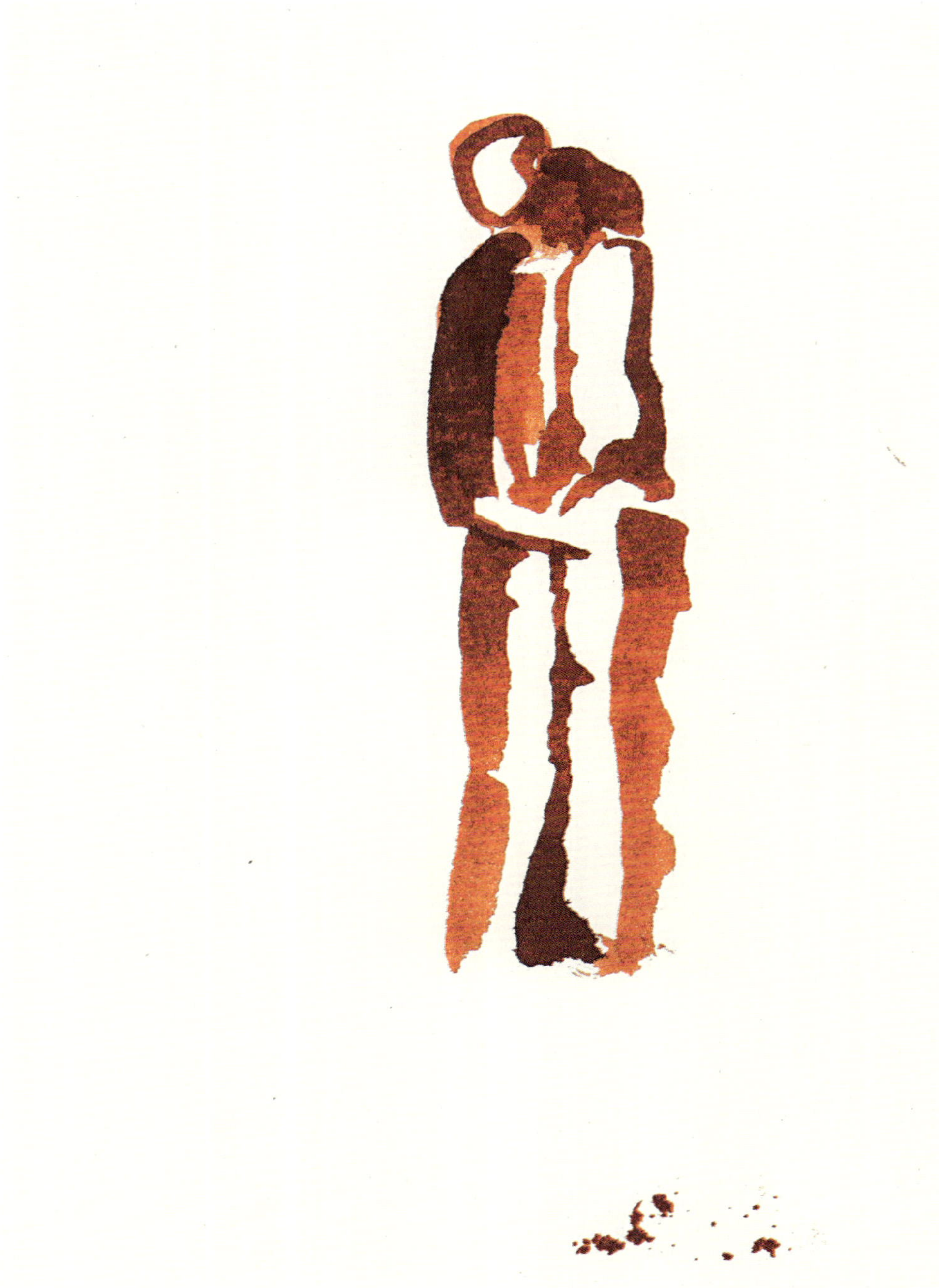

Terje Nicolaisen
Two Lovers, 2015
Ink on paper
280 × 210 mm

H Does this kind of merging also occur in his landscape drawings?

N There's one incredibly cheeky but elegant depiction of a group of trees (p.86–87). He simply puts a rope round it. After studying all these drawings by Munch, this is how I now see the trees around me, especially in winter when they're without their leaves and the many branches form a kind of drawing. He sketches whole groups of trees, deciding to make them into just one entity, a single form in the landscape rather than ten thousand lines. A brilliant simplification.

H Munch's drawings of people he fell out with can be a bit mean. It's one thing to harbour a dislike of someone with very different opinions, but to bear a grudge against a neighbour's dog even years after it died, as Munch did (p.88–89), doesn't exactly seem gracious.

N Munch is an expert at showing us emotions. Some of his drawings might be rather mean or self-righteous, but you can't hold that against him. He's also hard on himself, as in the self-portrait where he bears a striking similarity to his neighbour's dog at Ekely. Someone who's mean is effectively showing his hand, not least to himself. It might sound a bit strange to call it generosity, but that's what I'd say it is, in the sense that Munch is prepared to share and own up to his feelings, even when they're nothing to be proud of.

There's also something generous about the fact that Munch never threw any of his drawings away. It's remarkable that someone as proud as he was should hang on to all this stuff. He also worked very fast, which I find a fantastic quality in an artist. I'm not saying that those who work slowly necessarily make bad art, but it's the quick, performative, experimental approach that appeals to me personally. Munch was extremely productive. On the other hand, although 7700 drawings might sound like a lot, I've also thought that it isn't actually such a vast amount – not if you add in all the sketchbooks and scribbles in his letters.

H How many drawings do you think you yourself have?

N I've never counted, but four or five thousand for sure. And so far I've produced only sketches, just tentative suggestions of certain works. If I'm lucky, I can go on making art for another twenty to thirty years.

H There's a good deal of humour in the Munch drawings you have selected, even though you said you didn't want to include the caricatures.

N No, I simply don't find the true caricatures all that funny. There's something laboured about them, something almost affected. Such things only become amusing when they're involuntary.

H Does it have to do with the openness we were talking about?

N Yes, it's another aspect of that same free, interesting zone that I find so fascinating. It's not a place you can just choose to go to, because then it would be intentional, right? But Munch gropes around, and shares it with us. He freely admits it, and that's what makes it somehow amusing, but with a warmth. I too tend to use a lot of humour. And it's complex and difficult. It's like when someone says: Tell us a joke, then! It's horrible to receive a challenge like that. You can't be funny when it's demanded of you. Fundamentally, I don't really want to be funny. The funniest of my works were made with the utmost seriousness.

H

But what about your own work and the proposals you make for projects and monuments? You present yourself as an artist who ponders remote problems and thinks up ways to gain access to the art world. There was your suggestion to use Munch's famous pillars of moonlight on information signs; isn't that a deliberate attempt to be funny?

N

That's one intention, in a way. Clearly many of these ideas can't be put into practice. But it's not as if I sit there thinking, now I'm going to make a book about an artist trying to get into the art world in order to realise all these projects. It might be a dumb thing to admit, but I really am someone who's trying hard to be professional and to find a place in the art world, and I've made many proposals which I've now collected in a book. So if that's amusing, it's probably because I happen to be such a person. As far as the work with the info sign is concerned, there's an element of humour about it. But it's also about flagging up the fact that when it comes to culture, I'm not especially knowledgeable; I confess that this somewhat tacky idea came to me while looking at Munch.

H

One question that has cropped up on various levels in the process of selecting from Munch's drawings is how one can escape oneself in this kind of work. But at the same time, isn't it a task where you need your analytical, reflective faculties?

N

It's a difficult question. Where Munch hits his mark, as he does in some of the pictures I've selected, he succeeds in getting away from himself. Then he's little more than a factotum with something in his hand – a charcoal stick – who stumbles and achieves something he didn't intend. And perhaps it's the same with me. But one of my main concerns has been to be free and utterly honest about the fact that I myself could never have drawn a realistic portrait of, say, Dag Solstad or Allen Ginsberg (p. 66–67). No matter how hard I tried, the result would look like something completely different. I always do the best I can, and I also try to admit the fact.

H

But I would say that both these drawings are examples of portraits that capture a likeness. The comical aspect in the drawing of Solstad might well be at his expense, but I dare say that wasn't the original intention.

N

Certainly, for Solstad it isn't a flattering portrait, but it definitely wasn't meant as an insult. Quite the contrary, I'm a great fan of his books. I feel the humour is also at my own expense, precisely because my portraits are in some way so unsatisfactory. The drawing has something of the same devil-may-care attitude that I feel is present in many of the Munch drawings I have selected – a kind of stunt; one throws oneself into it.

H

Do you curate your own things in the same way that you have gone about selecting the drawings by Munch?

N

Choosing my own stuff is something I always struggle with. It's very hard to sort the wheat from the chaff. When curators visit me in my studio, I'm generally surprised by what they choose; often it's things I myself feel ashamed of. There's always been a gulf between what I consider good and what others find interesting. It's almost as if I feel unable to choose from my own works. Maybe it's because my pictures are not the product of analysis. The action of applying colour to a sheet of paper gives me a kick that can't be shared. One consequence of trying to get this kick is that it results in a work. And then I have to evaluate it. Is it any good? Could I submit it to the National Annual Autumn Exhibition? No, but then maybe nothing is genuinely good. Consequently, I've decided for myself that it isn't my task to decide. It's too complicated, at least if I'm supposed to make pictures at the same time. I feel that artists who have learnt to evaluate while expressing themselves end up creating designs that merely resemble art.

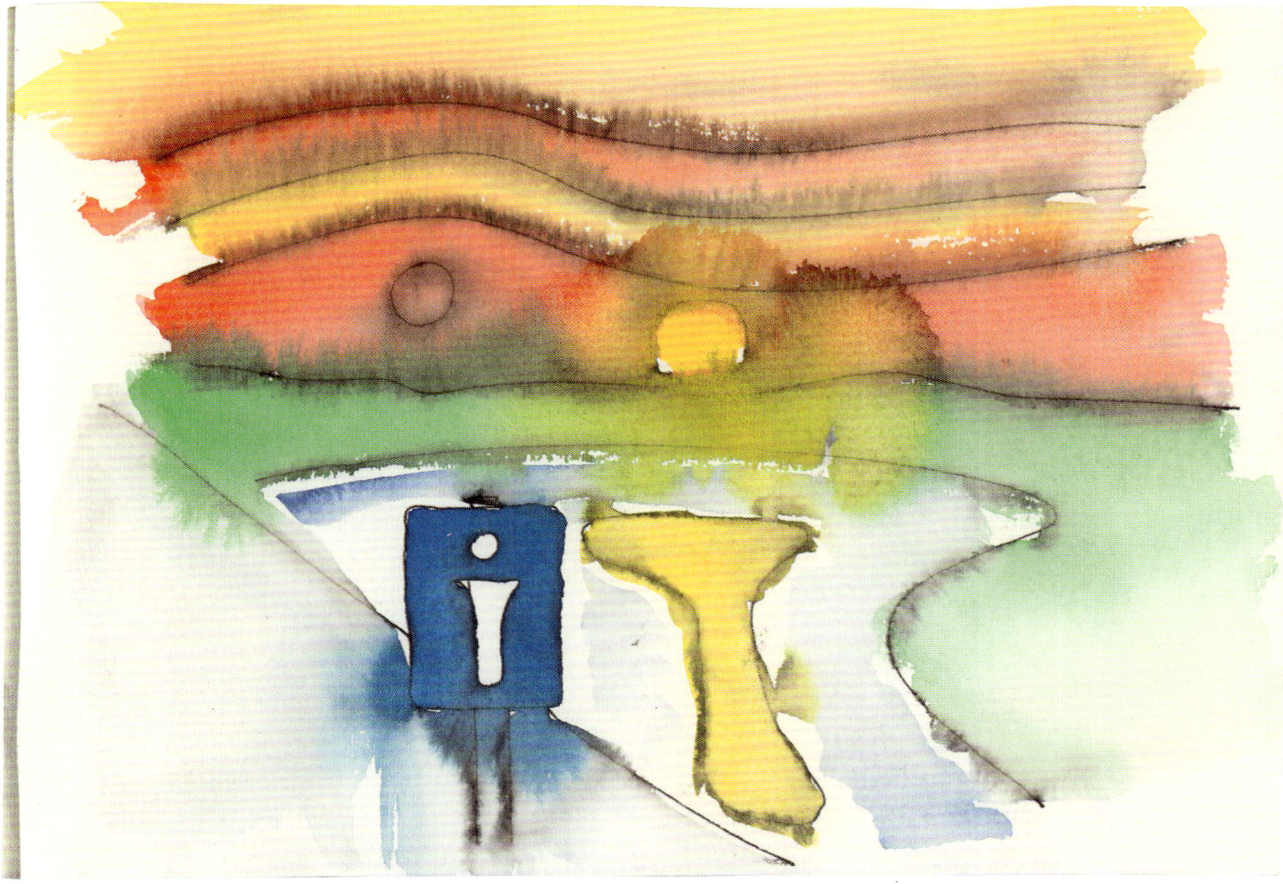

Terje Nicolaisen
From the Artist Book *Proposals*, 2001
Ink and watercolour on paper
173 × 255 mm

So is there a message in your selection? H

At the least there's a desire to show Munch as a probing, hesitant artist. But another point might be that, in order to create art, you have to be straight with yourself. N

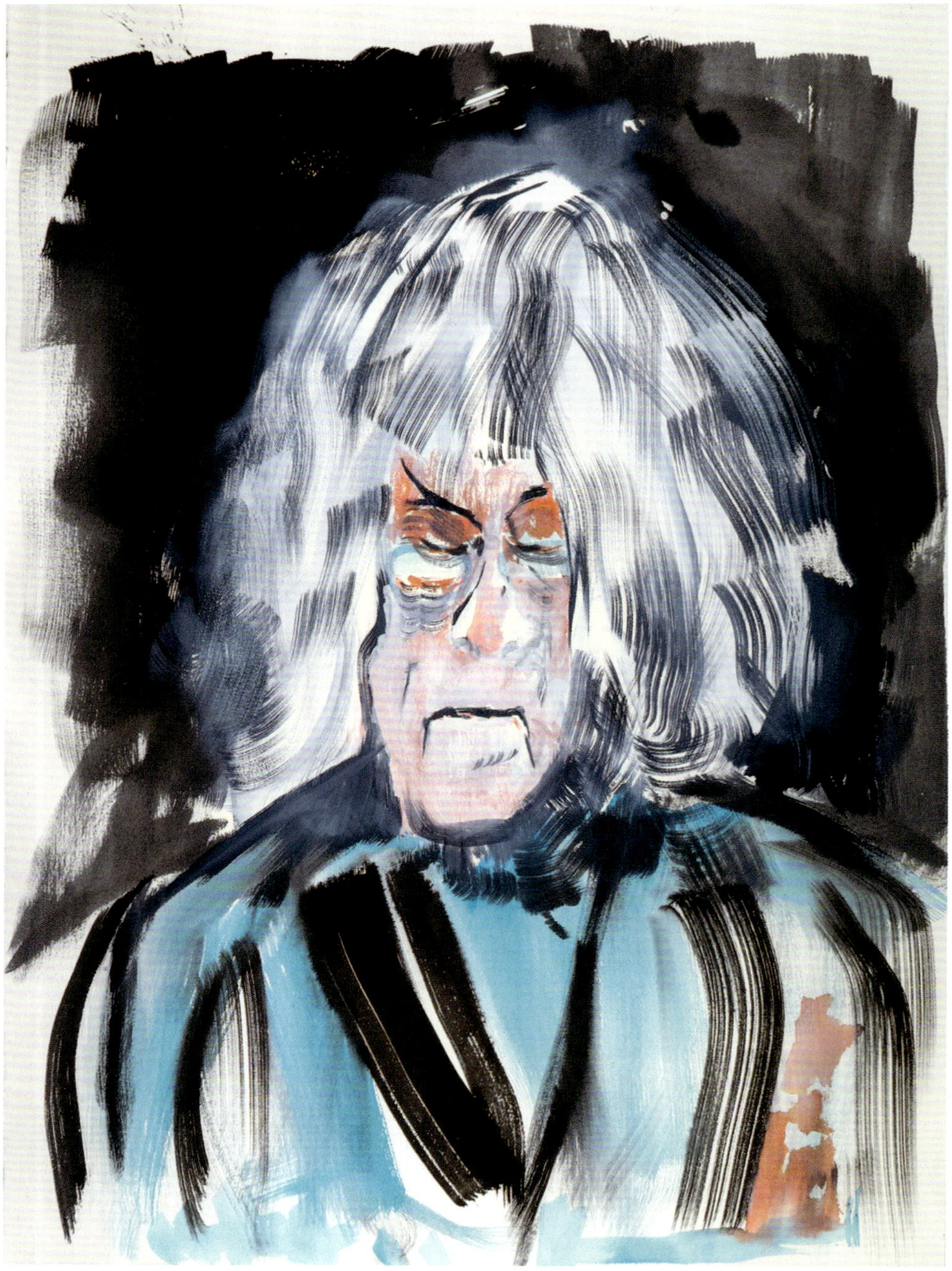

Terje Nicolaisen
Dag Solstad, 2017
Ink and watercolour on paper
760 × 560 mm

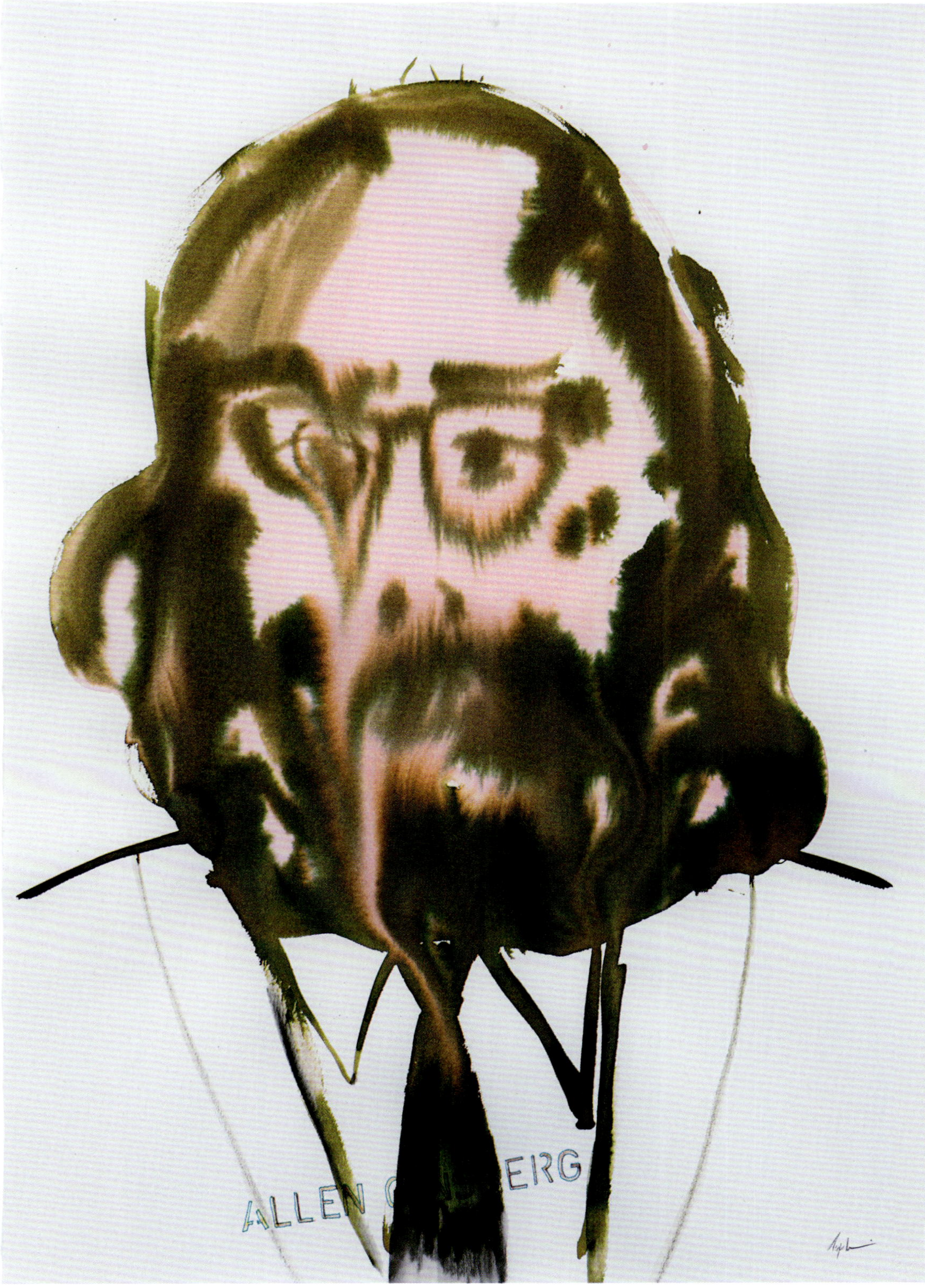

Terje Nicolaisen
Allen Ginsberg , 2007
Ink and watercolour on paper
1100 × 780 mm

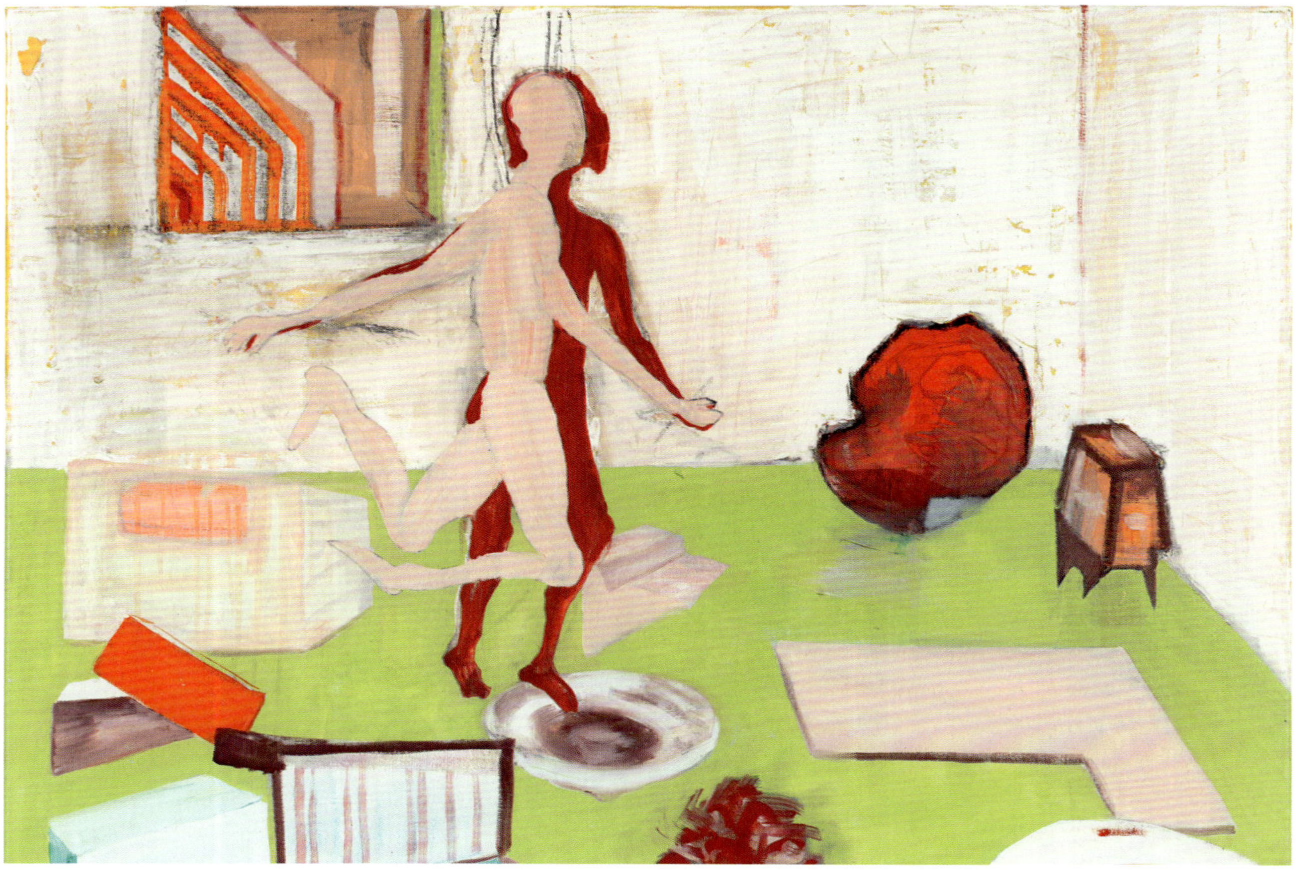

Terje Nicolaisen
From the Studio , 2016
Oil on canvas
80 × 100 cm

Nicolaisen chooses Munch

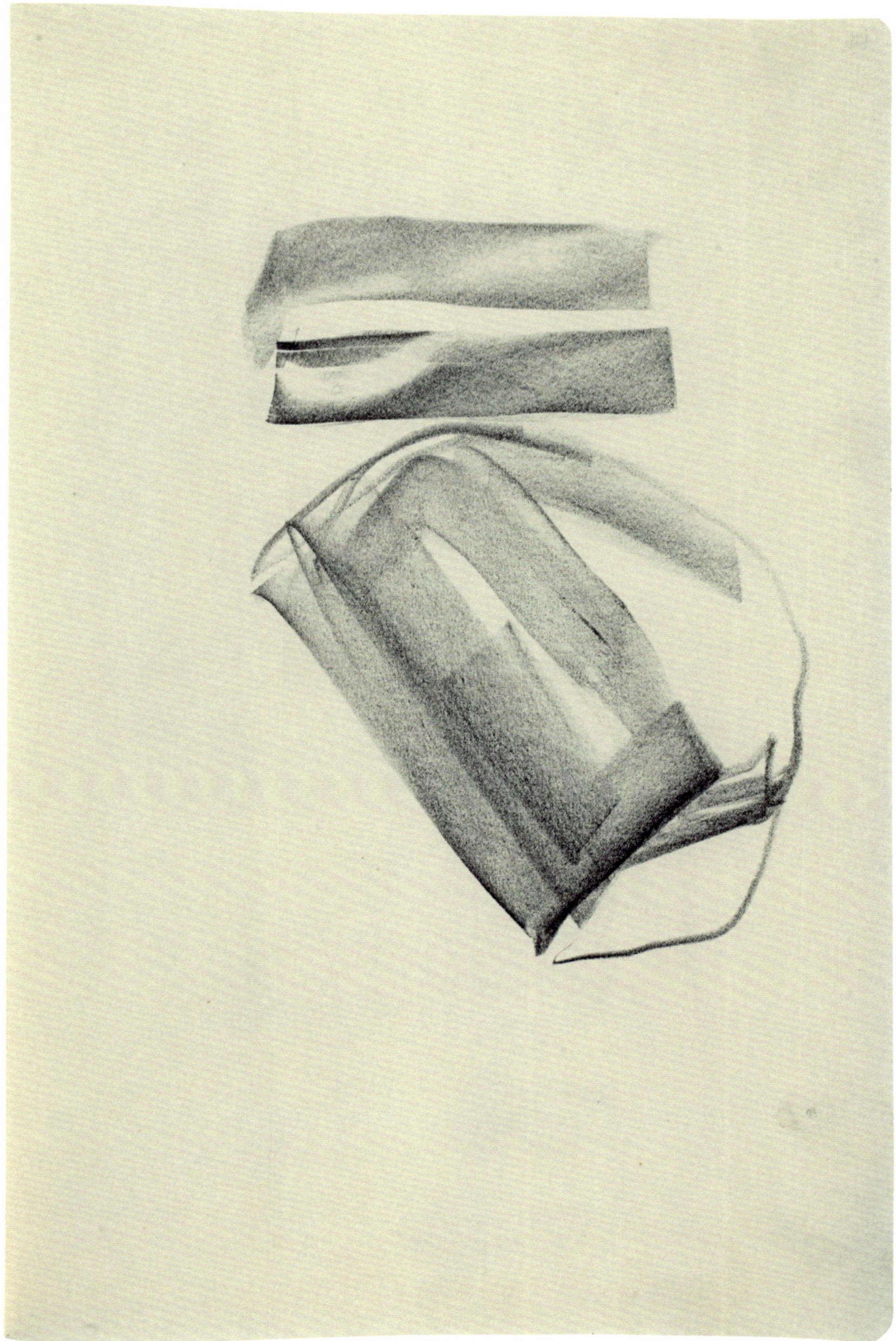

Unidentified Motif
1916
Crayon
355 × 253 mm

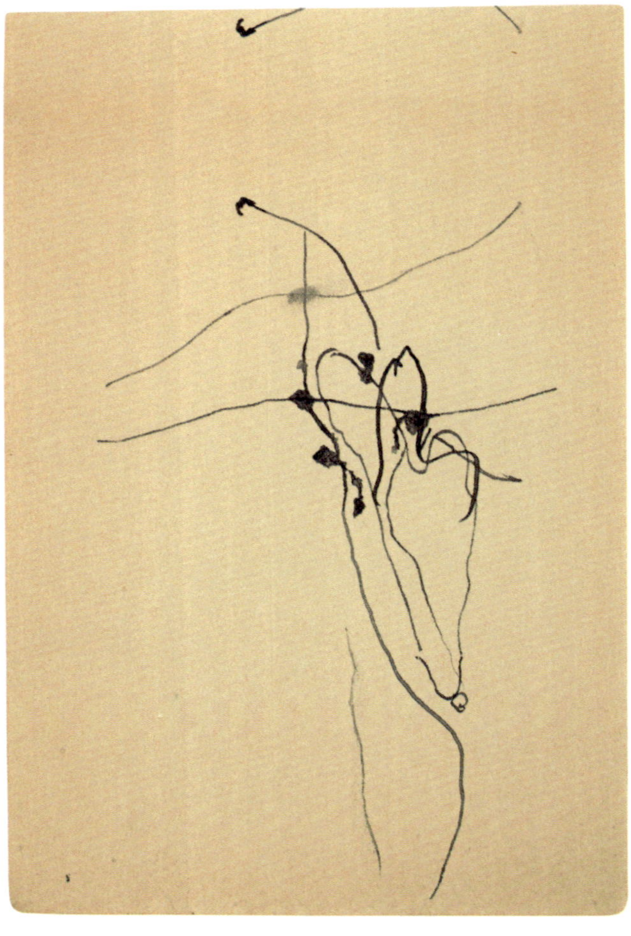

Doodle Drawing
1902
Pen
164 × 110 mm

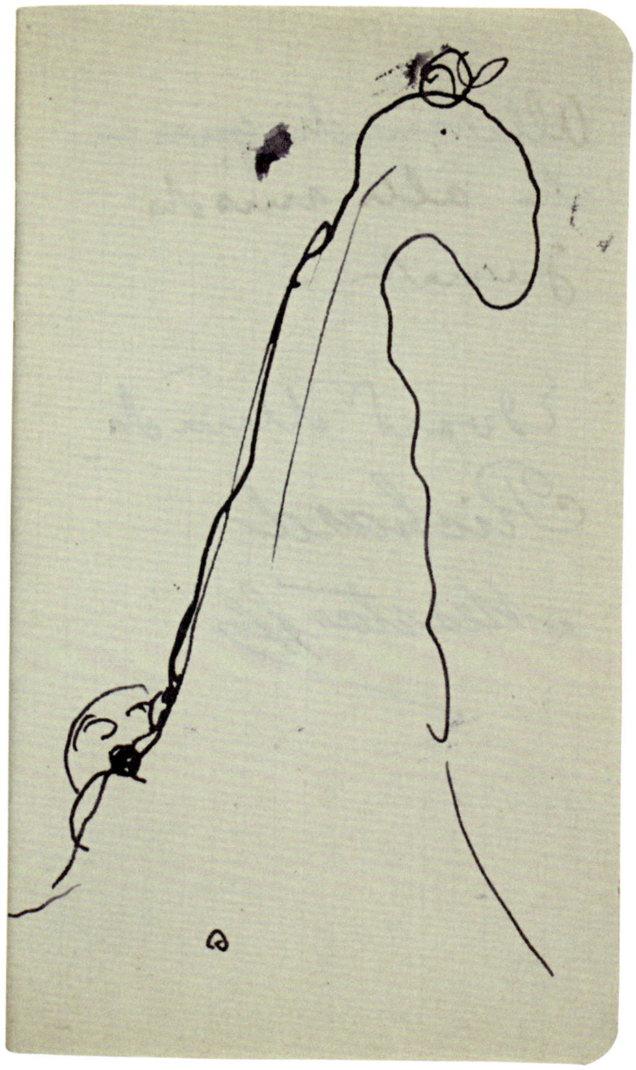

Sketchy Map of the Oslo Fjord
1904
Pen
137 × 80 mm

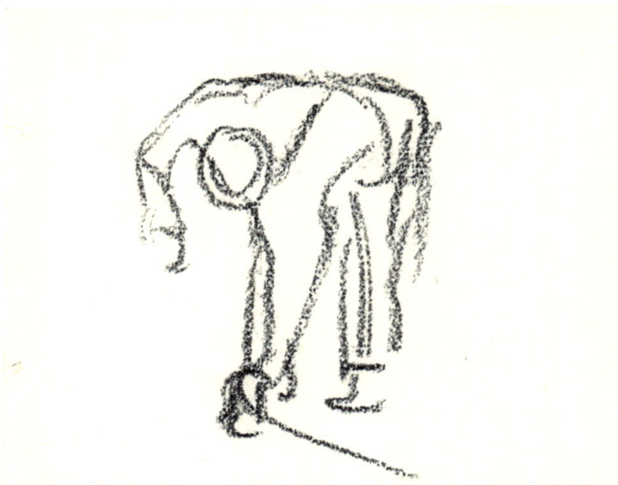

Man Bending Over
1929–30
Crayon
112 × 144 mm

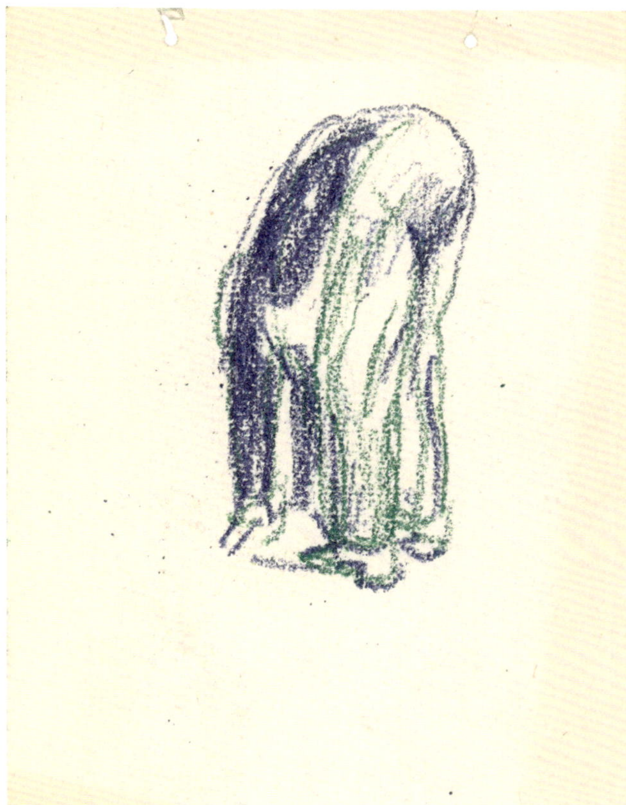

Man Bending Over
1929–30
Crayon
144 × 112 mm

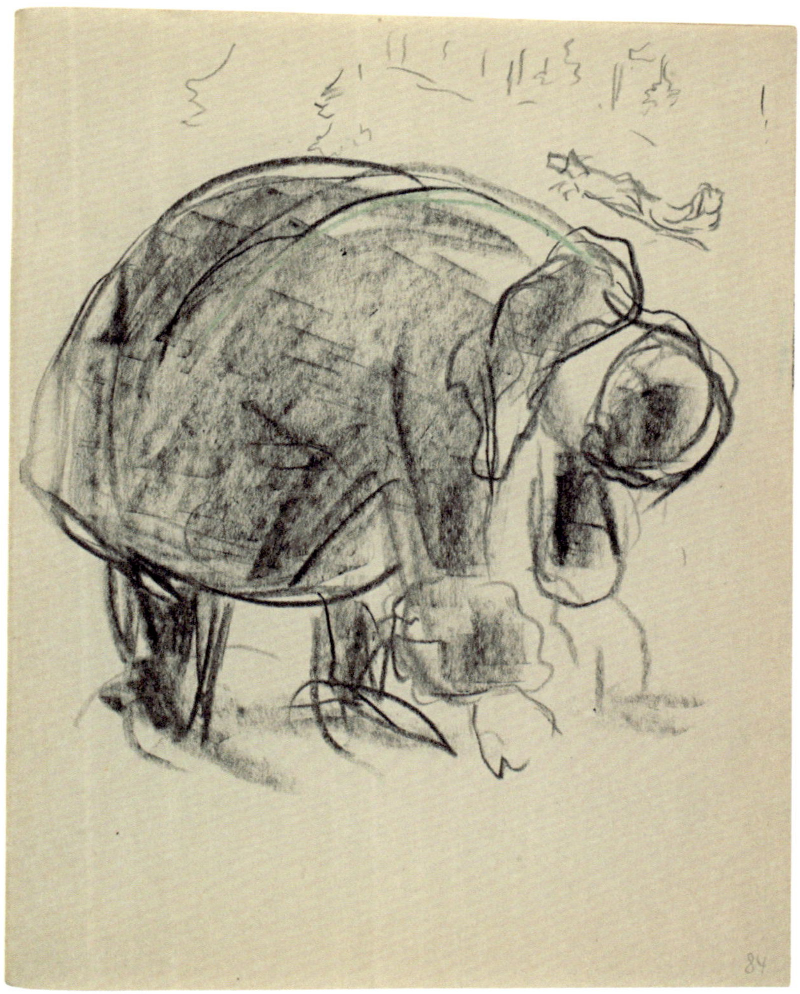

John Gabriel Borkman: Foldal in the Ditch
1928–30
Crayon
205 × 176 mm

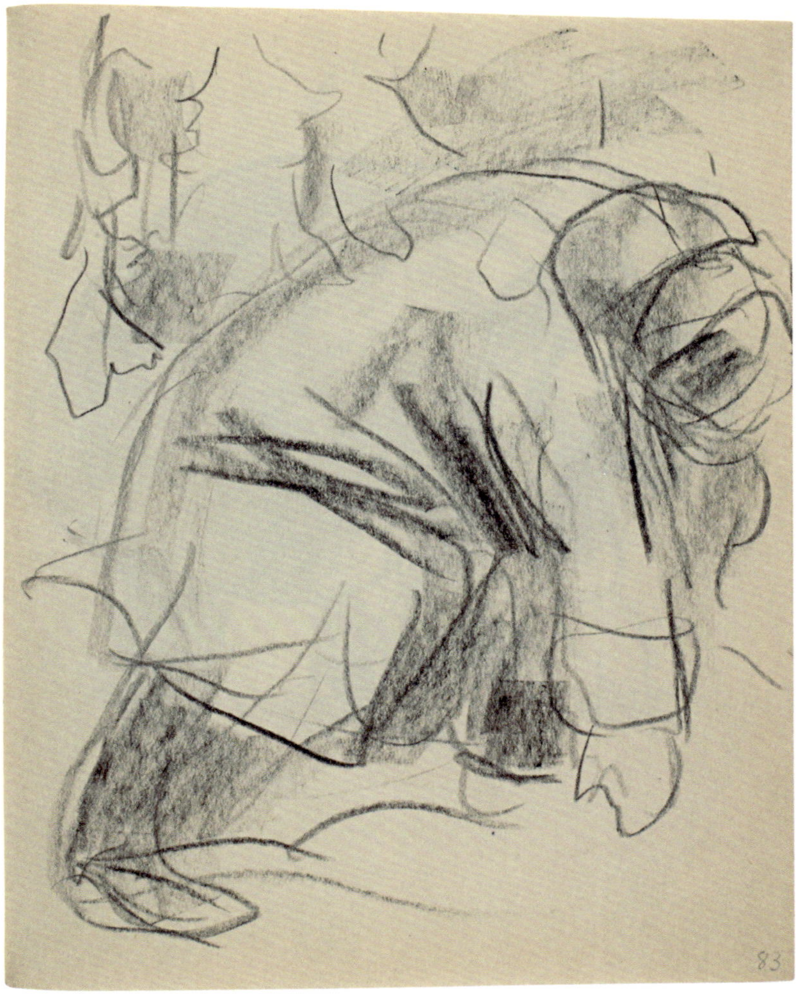

John Gabriel Borkman: Foldal in the Ditch
1928–30
Crayon
205 × 176 mm

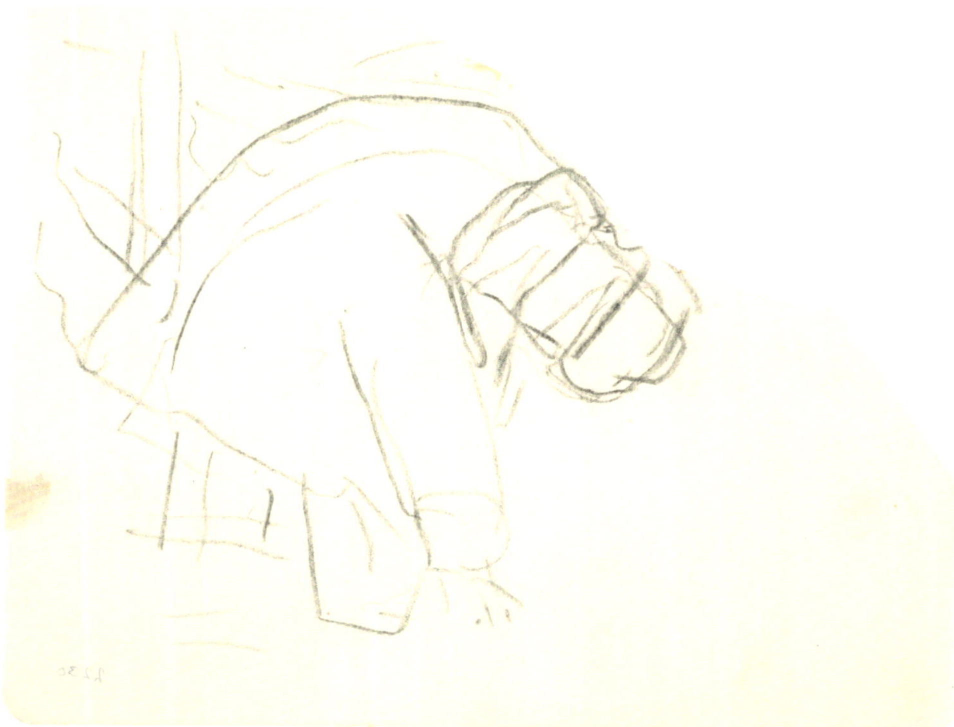

John Gabriel Borkman: Foldal in the Ditch
c. 1925
Charcoal
190 × 253 mm

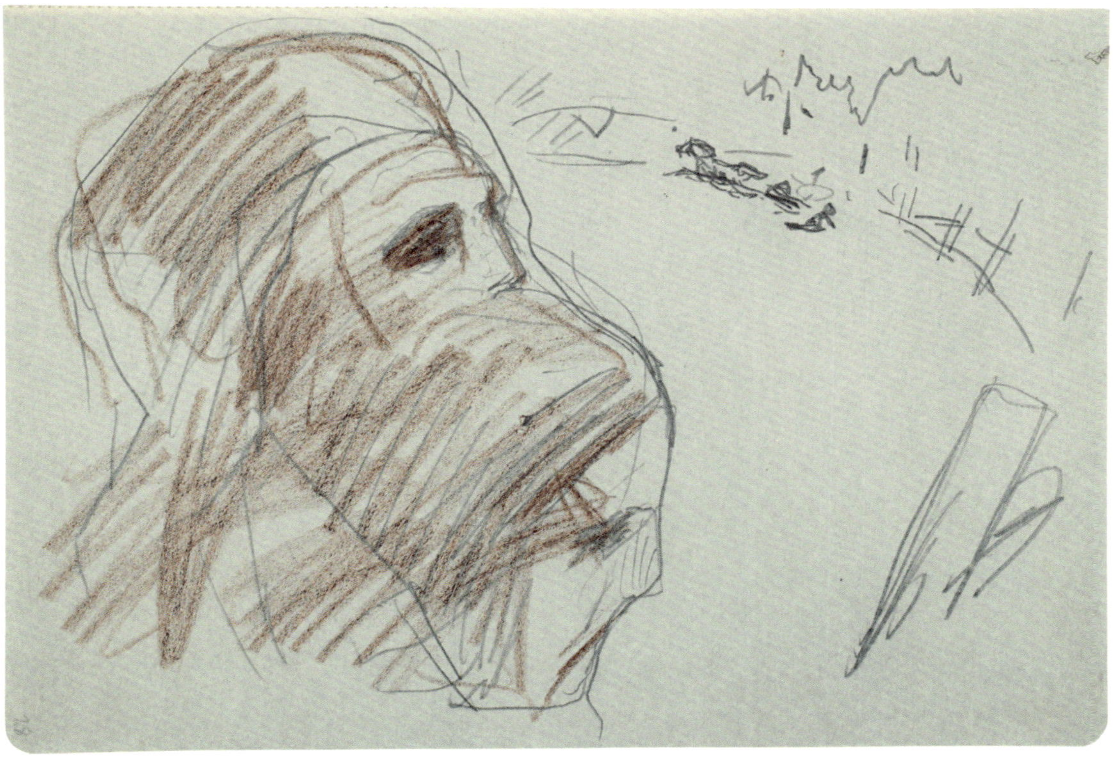

John Gabriel Borkman: Foldal in the Ditch
1914–15
Crayon and pencil
252 × 357 mm

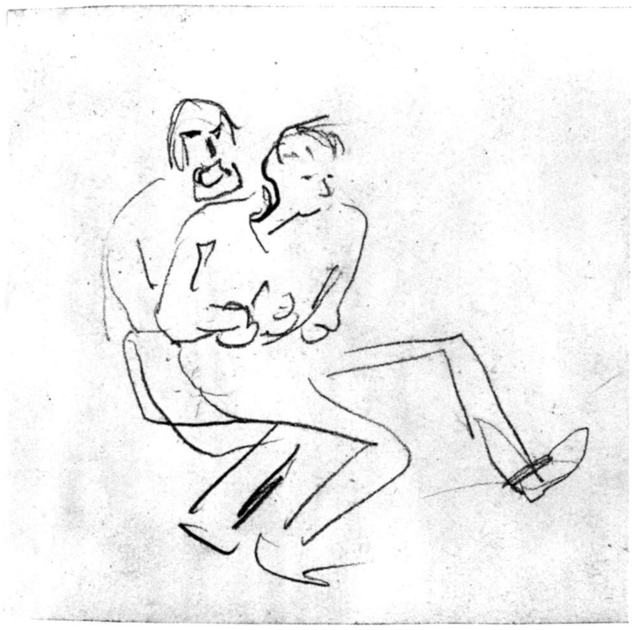

Two Men Fighting
1889
Pencil
177 × 134 mm (cropped)

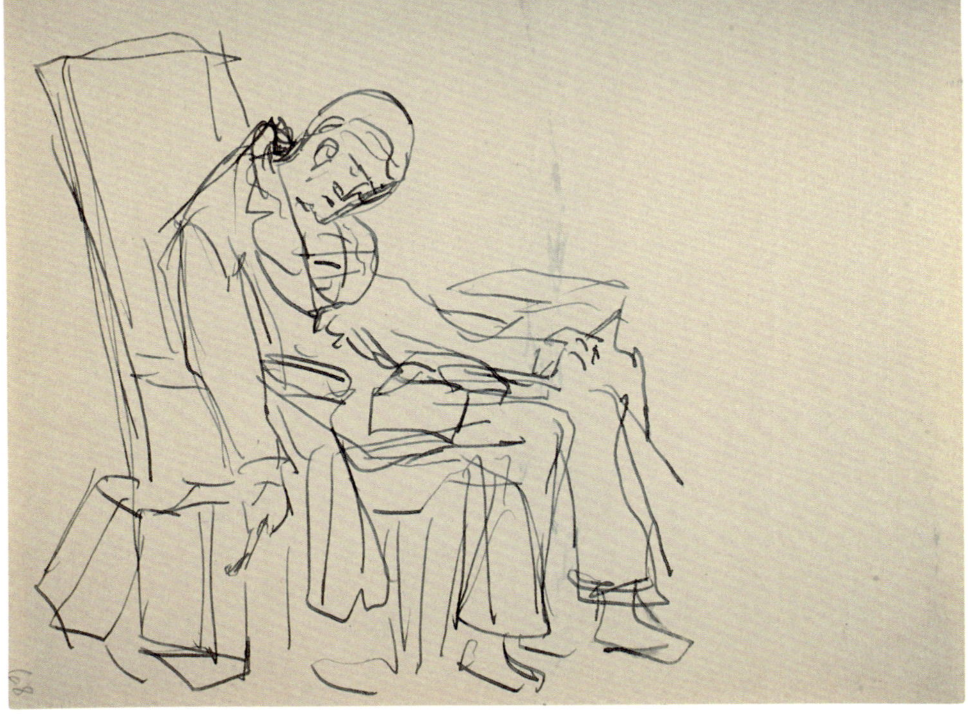

Falling Asleep in the Chair
1928–30
Pen
170 × 208 mm

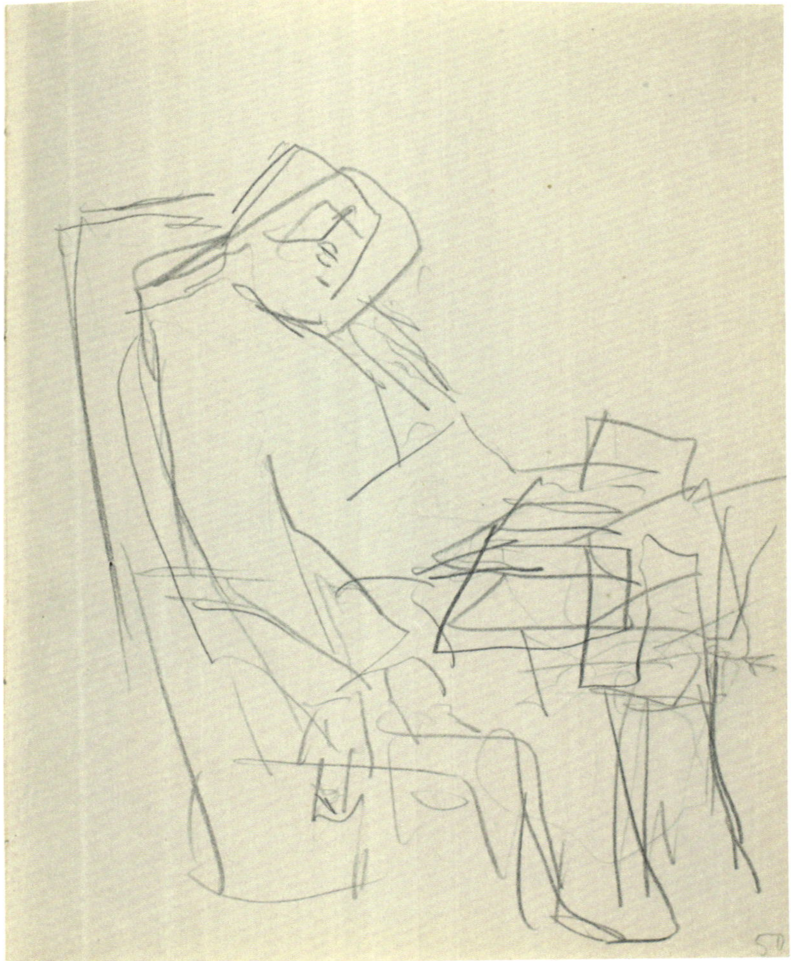

Falling Asleep in the Chair
1928–30
Pencil
208 × 170 mm

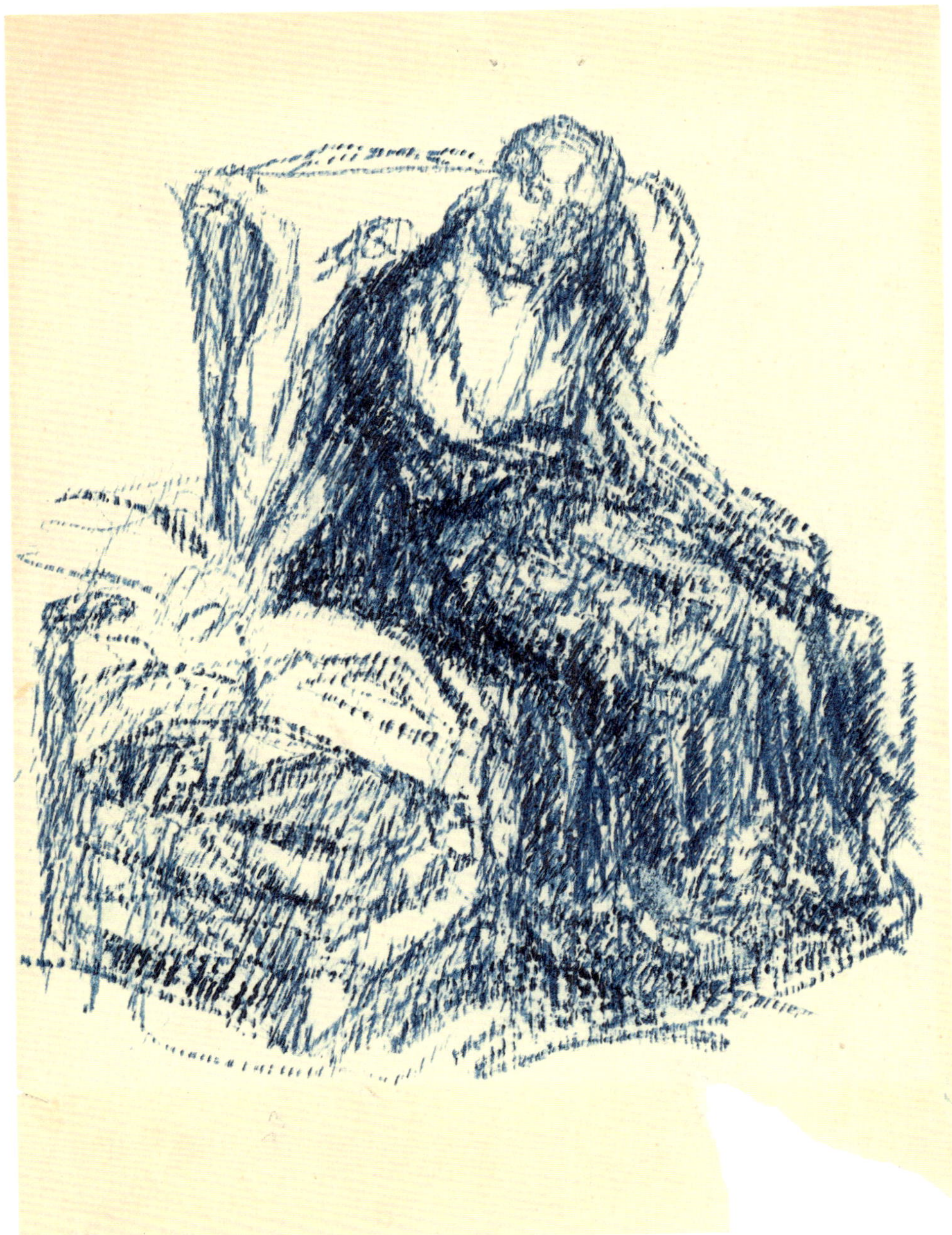

Falling Asleep in the Chair
1930–33
Crayon
290 × 223 mm

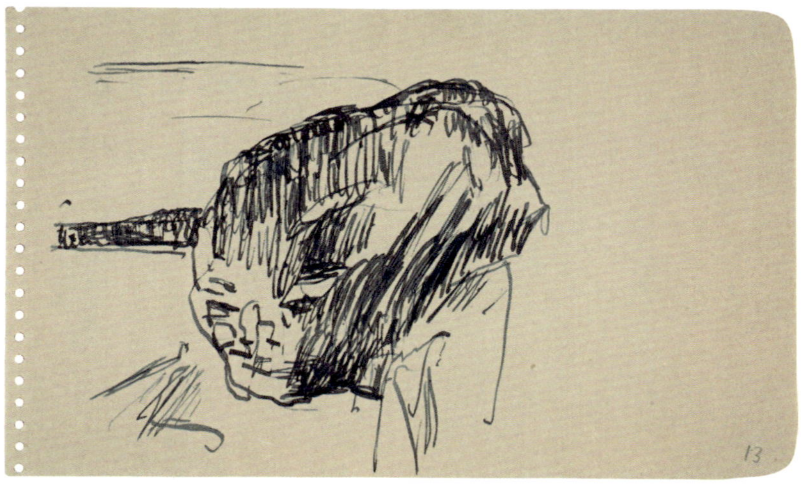

Landscape
1932–33
Pen
106 × 179 mm

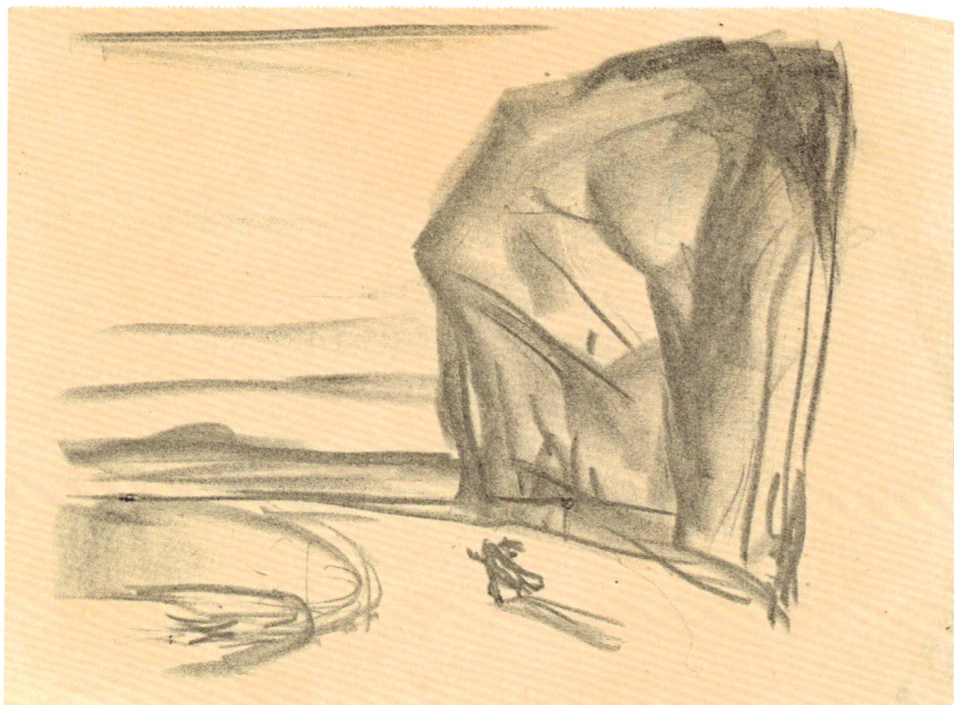

Original drawing for *Ragnarok: Two Escapees on the Beach*
1914
Crayon
199 × 266 mm

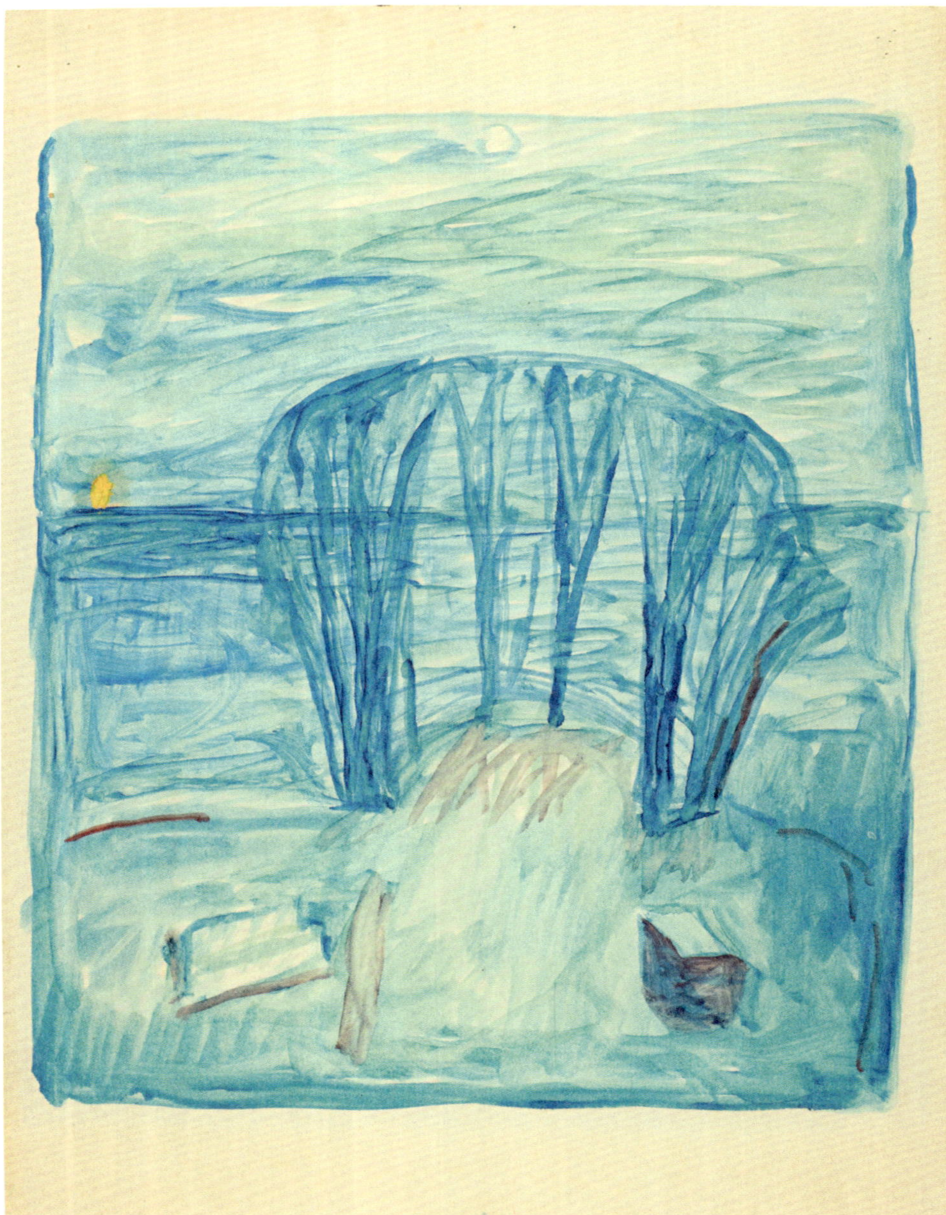

Explosion
1943
Gouache and oil
650 × 510 mm

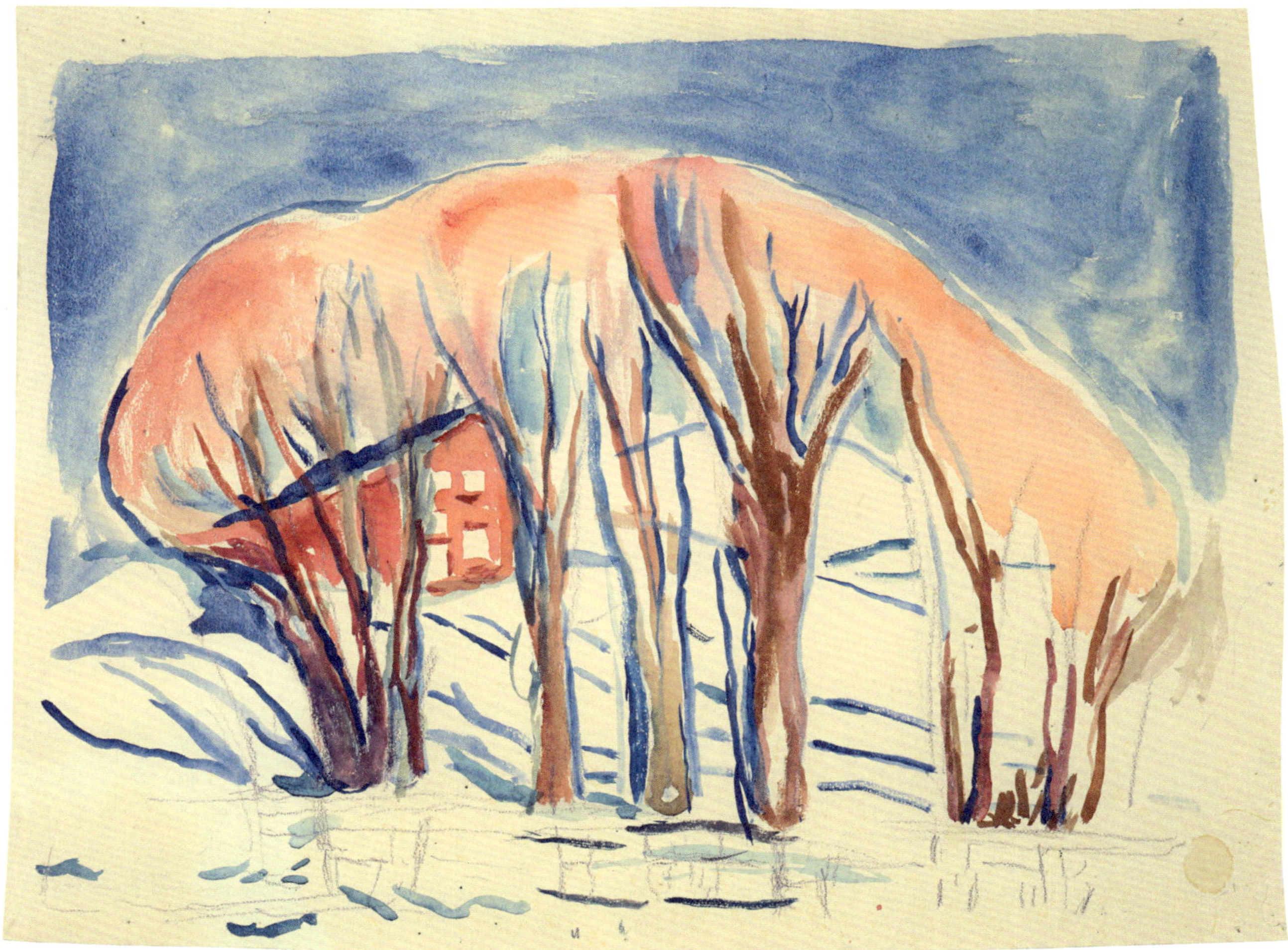

Winter at the Farmhands' Quarters
c. 1930
Watercolour, gouache(?) and crayon
425 × 575 mm

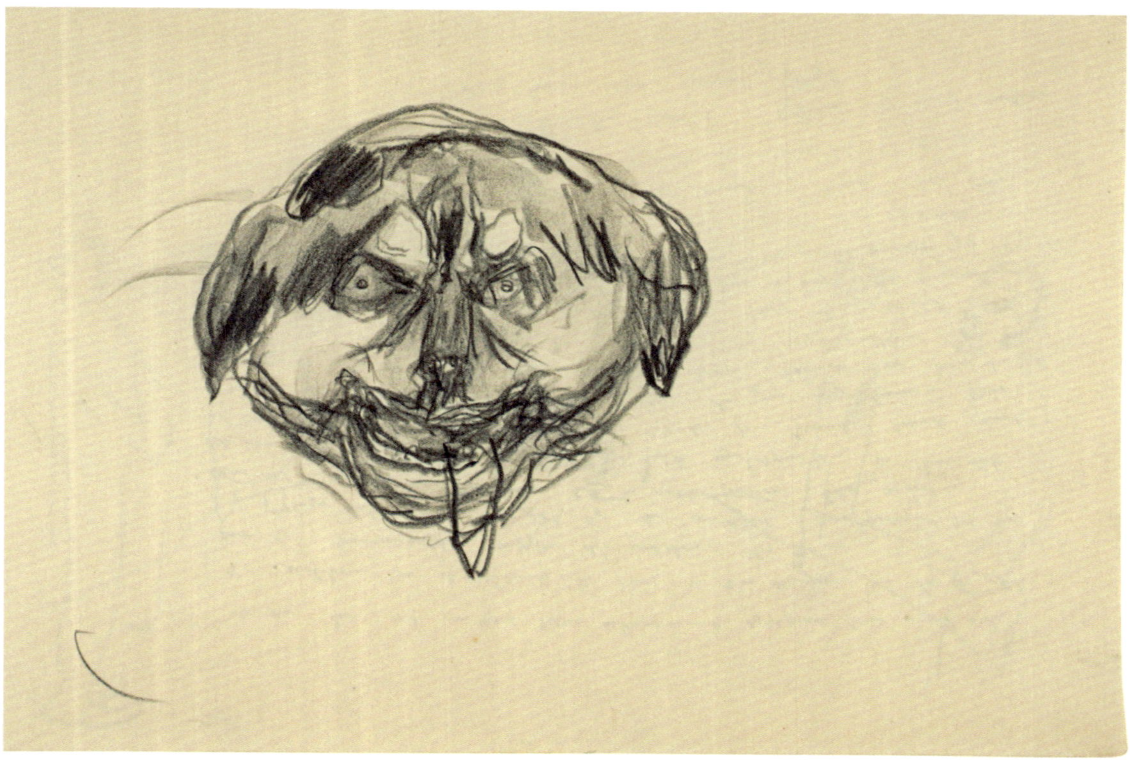

Gunnerud's Dog
1938–39
Crayon
267 × 410 mm

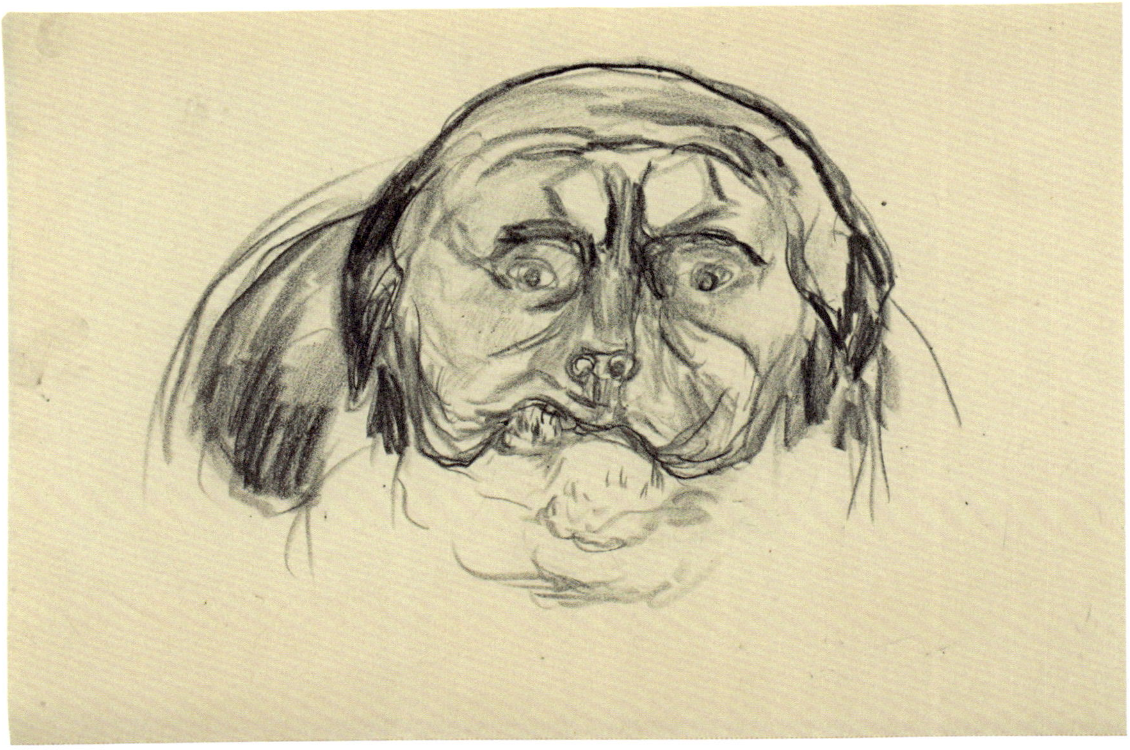

Gunnerud's Dog
1938–39
Crayon
267 × 410 mm

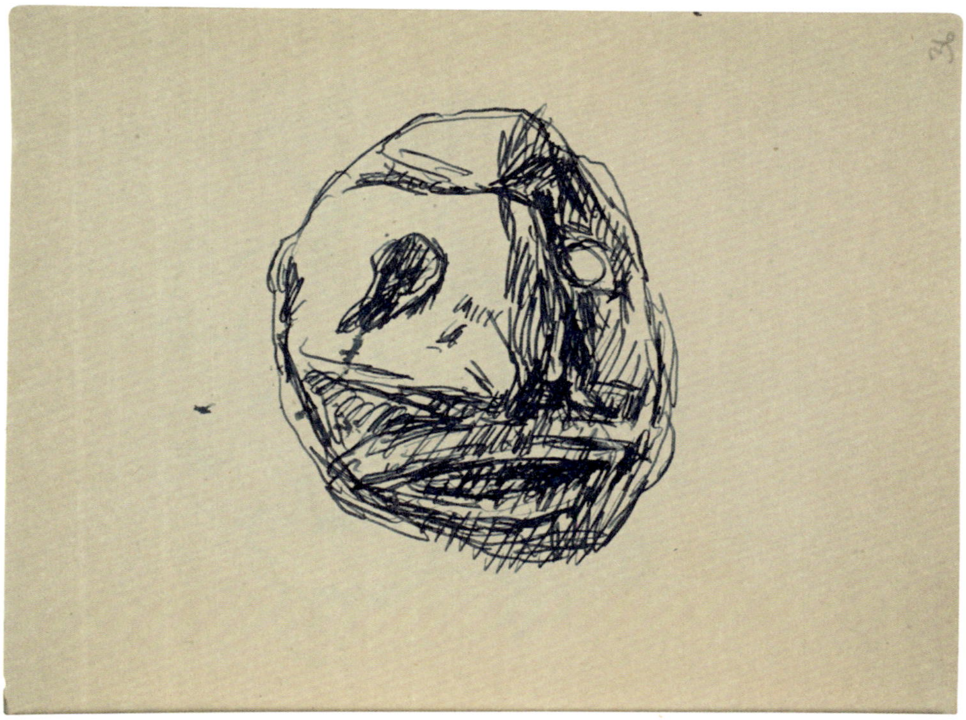

A Cod's Head
1938–42
Pen
103 × 136 mm

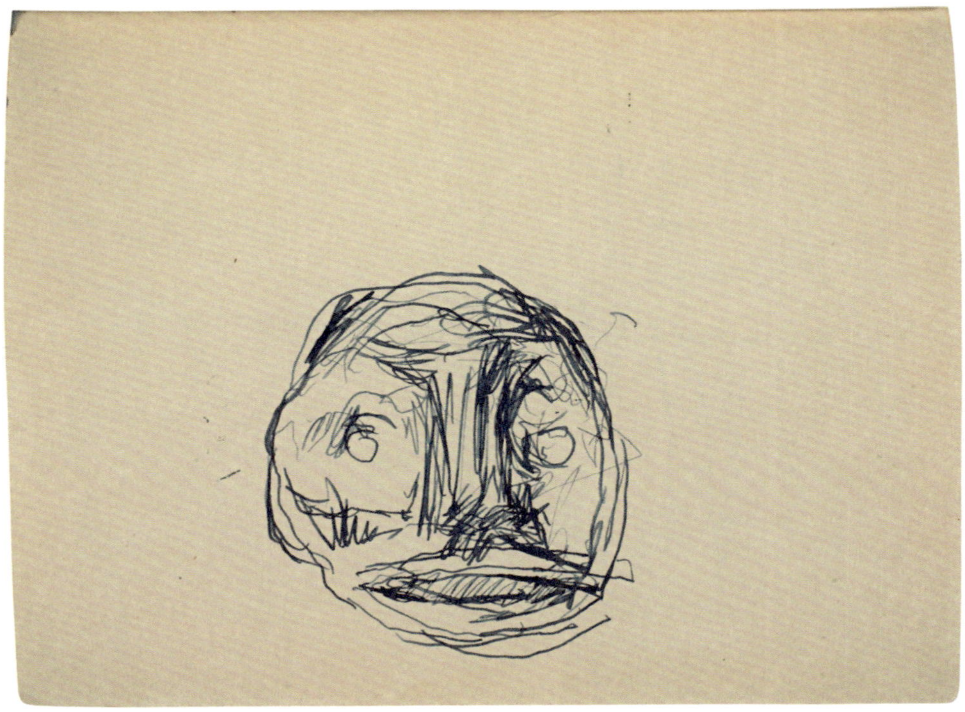

A Cod's Head
1938–42
Pen
103 × 136 mm

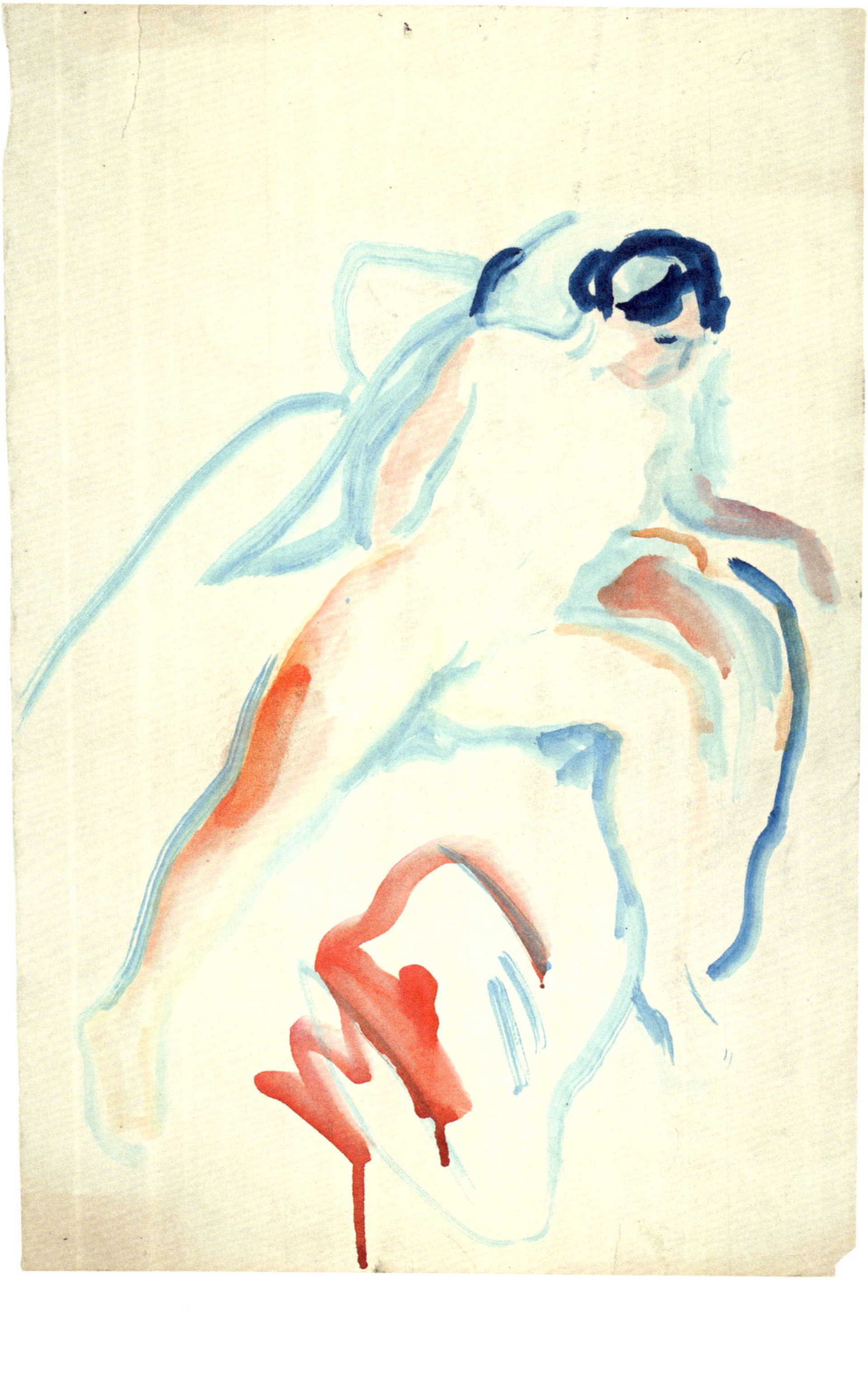

Female Nude on the Bed
1919–24
Watercolour
600 × 408 mm

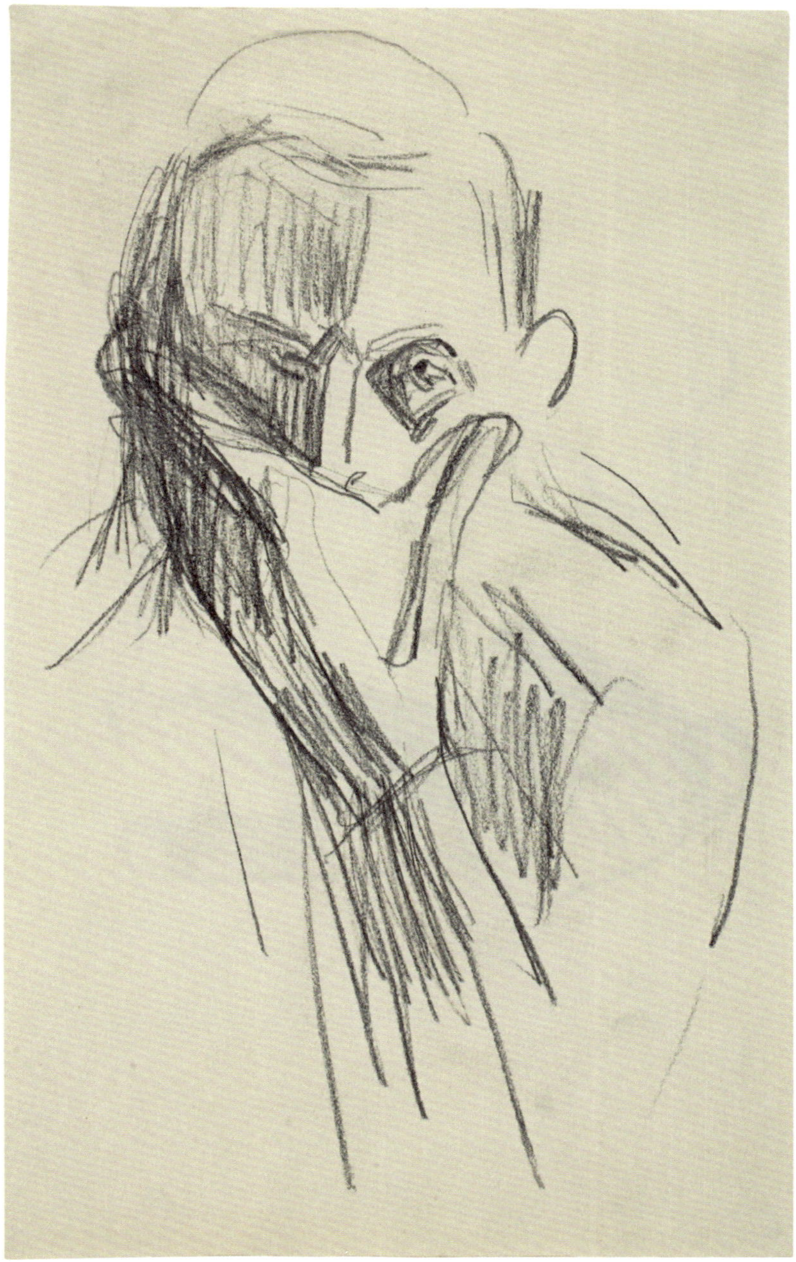

Portrait of a Man with Hand in Front of His Face
1914–15
Pencil
278 × 175 mm

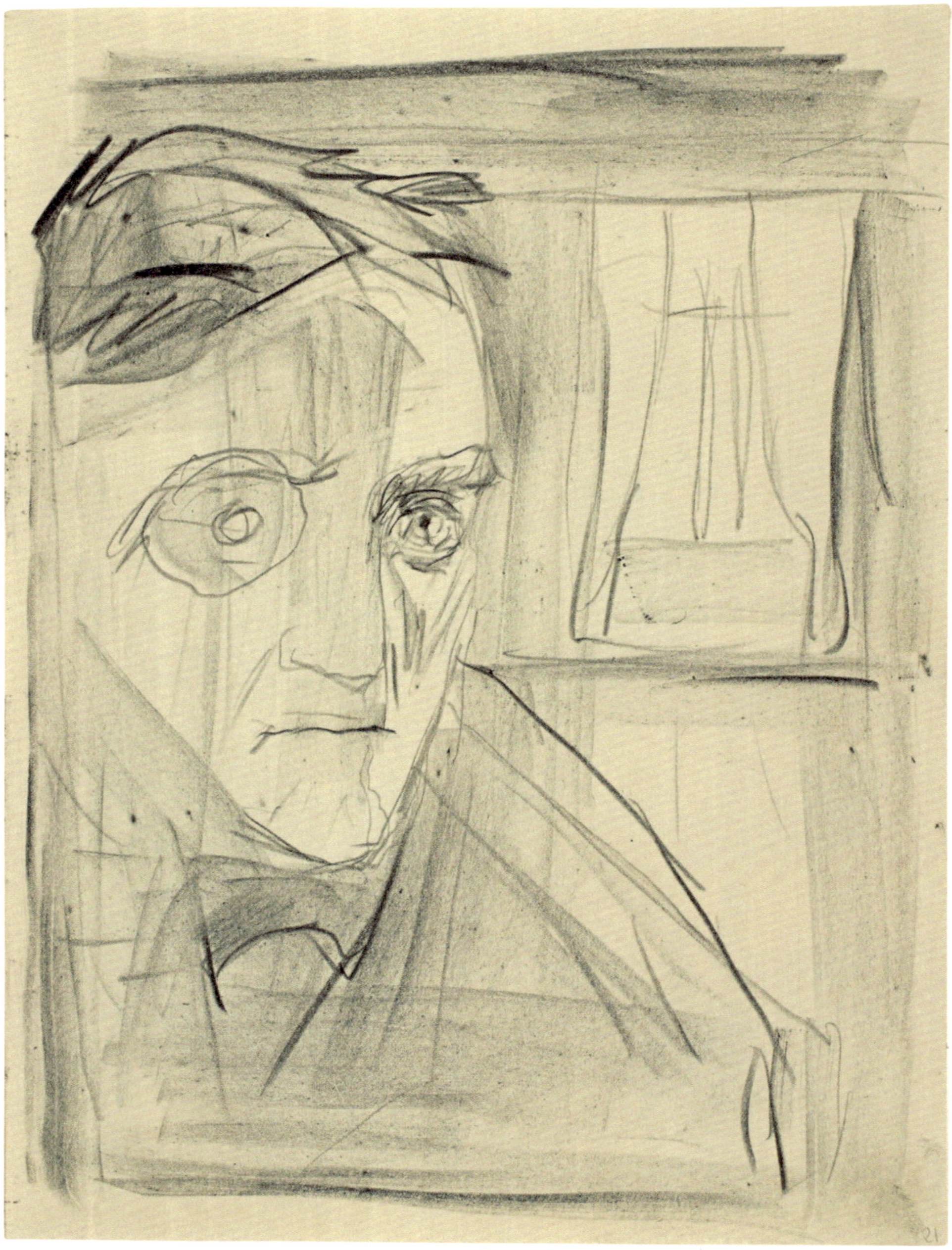

Male Head in Front of a Window
1916
Crayon
277 × 213 mm

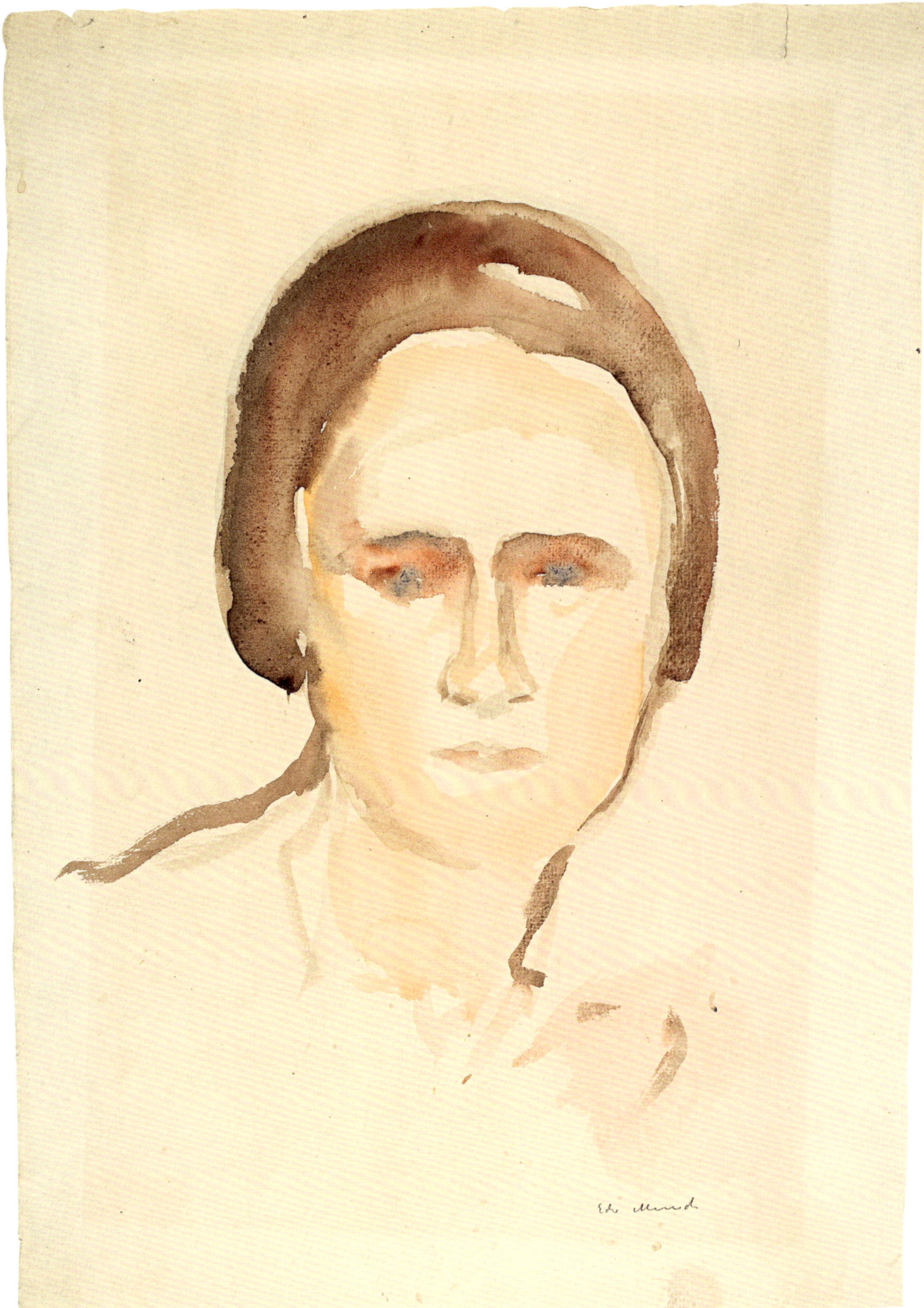

Female Head
1923–33
Watercolour
460 × 330 mm

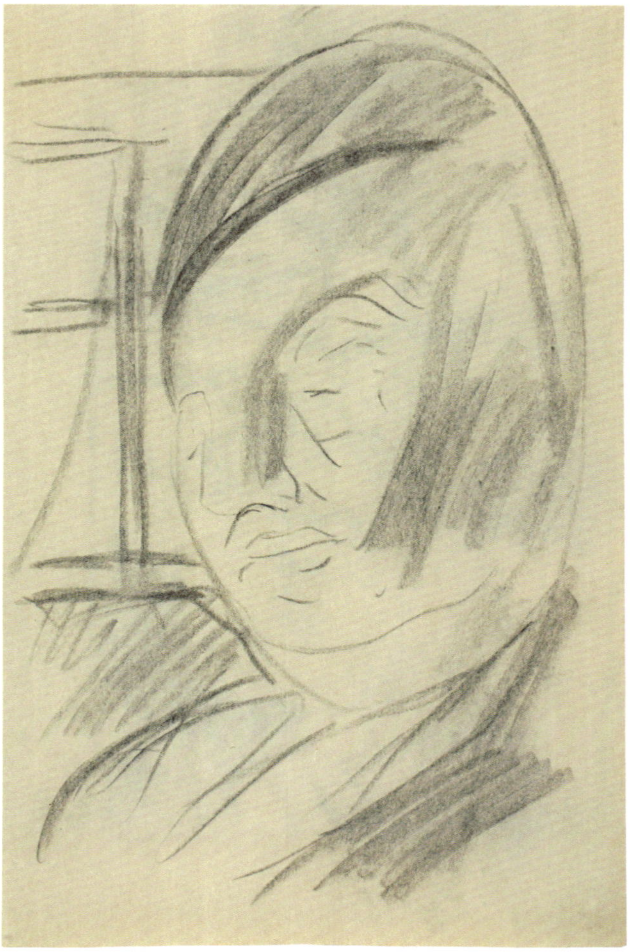

Male Portrait
1928–30
Crayon
410 × 267 mm

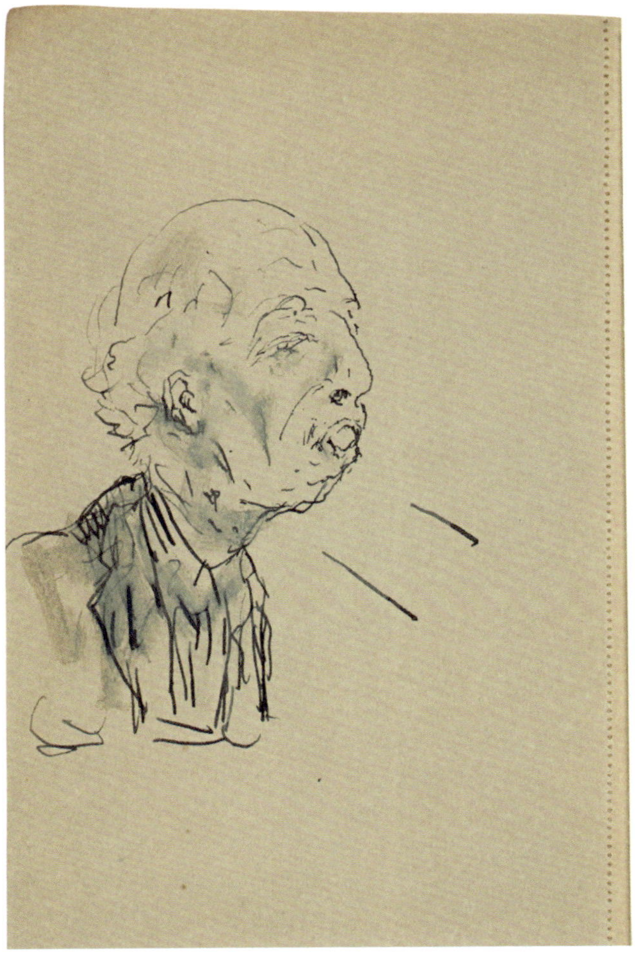

Male Portrait
1936–42
Pen and wash
203 × 130 mm

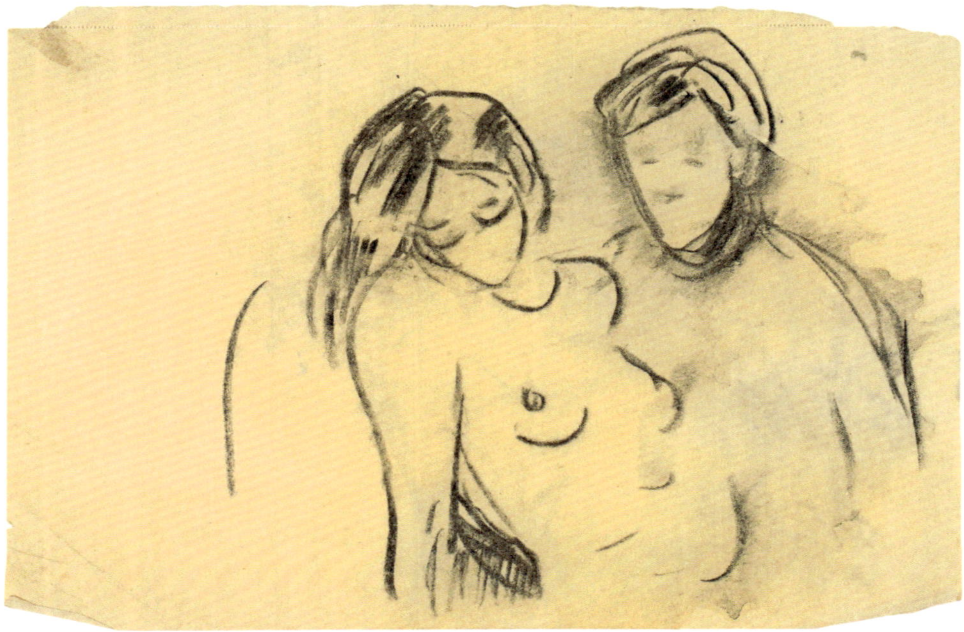

Two Nudes. Man and Woman, Half Figure
1912–15
Charcoal
269 × 409 mm

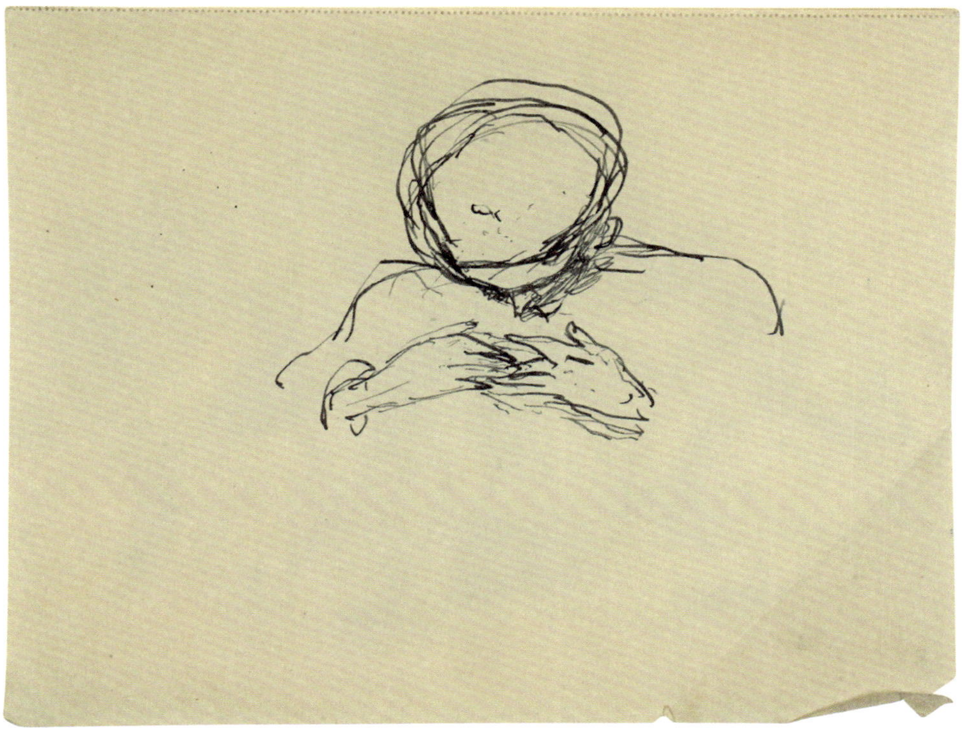

Handicraft
1927
Pen
210 × 268 mm

Modes of Thinking and Figuring

Nalini Malani interviewed by Mieke Bal

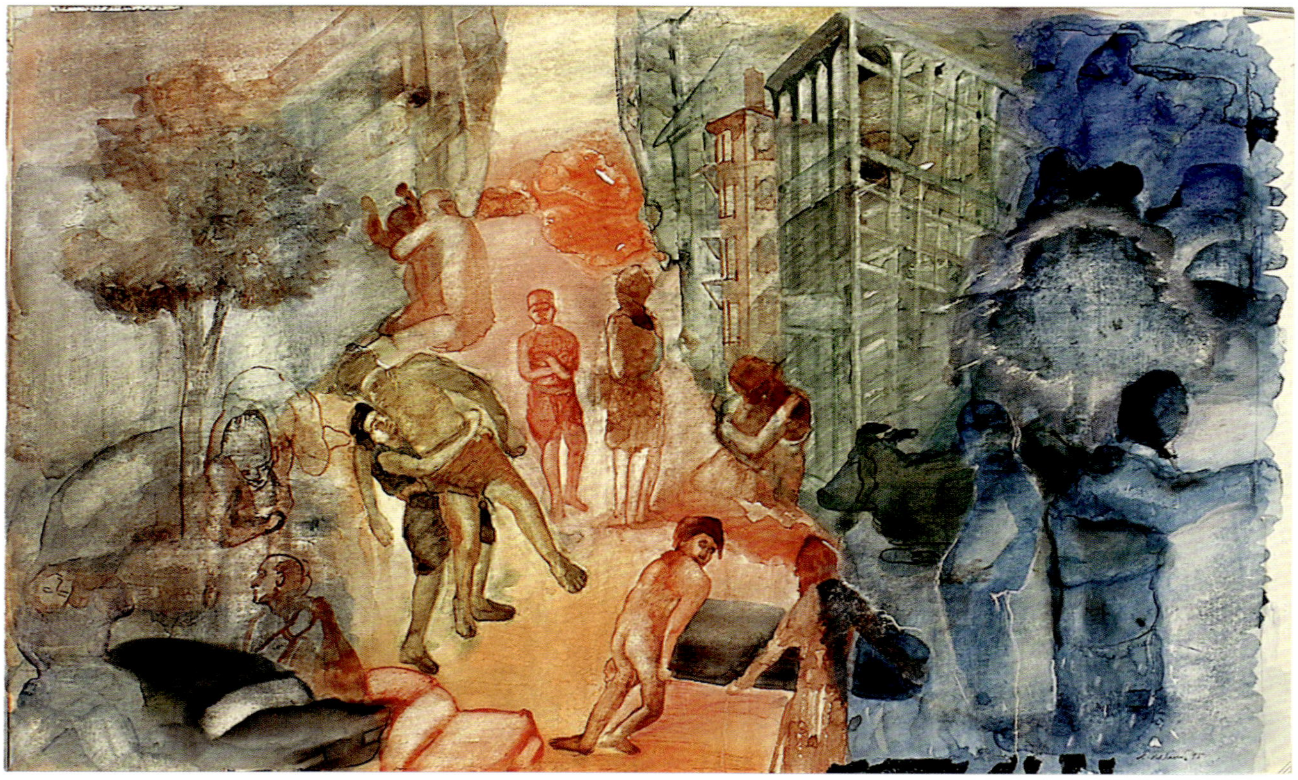

Nalini Malani
A Tree in Lohar Chawl, 1995
Watercolour on papier d'Arches,
76.5 × 127 cm

Nalini Malani works in several different media, but at heart she is a painter. She does not paint on canvas anymore, however. Reversed painting on acrylic and Mylar, animations on an iPad, charcoal wall drawings that she subsequently erases: experimenting with ever-new possibilities is her mode of working. Malani's subjects are historically anchored yet fictitious. Her interest in the political domain, her awareness of class divisions and, especially, her indictment of violence against women, keep her alert to burning issues in the world – contemporary as well as historical. The themes she has selected for this book all relate to such issues, without, however, addressing them directly; hence, propagandistically – an important common ground between her work and Edvard Munch's.

Bal From the 7700 drawings in Munchmuseet's collection you selected thirty. What was your first impression?

Malani What struck me was that wherever Munch was, perhaps travelling, perhaps in a restaurant, he needed to sketch something that he saw. In the later drawings it is more as though he recognised something in relation to his tormented inner life, of which he made a note. This small selection is based on what to me is unusual and different from the characteristic Munch. In these drawings I found elements that reminded me of my own work.

B What came first, the selection of the individual drawings or the themes that you have grouped them into?

M Somehow each of the selected works intrigued me from the first moment. To get a grip on what it was that fascinated me, I decided to group them, and came up with the eight categories: Absurd, Hieroglyphs, Proletariat, Puberty, Horror, Machismo, Death, and Witness.

B The thematic groups make total sense, even if we must assume Munch never saw his own drawings according to these categories. Was this your intention – to confuse the biographically-historically oriented Munch criticism a bit?

M Looking at this vast and unique collection of drawings, it gave me the opportunity to look at my own history with Munch and how my work as an artist relates to this. The selection and categorisation are a personal reflective intervention with no claim to academic values for the future. But it might give the reader of this book a different angle for reflecting on Munch's drawings.

B What do you mean by your own history with Munch?

M My education at the JJ School of Art (1964–69) in Bombay was based on the traditional British art school system. Munch's pictures were never shown, nor was his name even mentioned by any of my professors. I first saw a reproduction of one of his works on the cover of a book called *Lotte in Weimar* by Thomas Mann. Later I acquired a small Munch monograph from an outdoor book shop under the arcades of Bombay near Victoria Terminal Station. Munch's loose style of working in oil painting inspired me, as it was completely different from what was taught at JJ. When studying in Paris on a French government scholarship between 1970 and 1972, I saw many of Munch's lithographs. In the French left wing political and art scene in which I moved, there was an almost "anti-art" attitude, as it was considered bourgeois to make art for commercial purposes. Back in Bombay, in a time of nation building, besides the idealism there was the need to earn money and make paintings to survive. Munch's works became part of the inspiration for a new series of paintings called "His Life" made in the late 70s.

In one of them, *Grieved Child*, you see a young girl in a yellow dress running inside from the balcony. She has seen something outside which has made her anxious, but we don't know why she is screaming. Unable to understand an incident which belongs to the adult world, she runs inside expecting her family to shield her from it. Munch's famous work *The Scream* was part of the inspiration for a series of three paintings of a girl with these emotions. That is why I have included this iconic drawing, whereas the rest of the selection is more an intervention, a reflection of my own later work without any direct relation to Munch's art. M

I think your intervention is totally loyal to Munch's mode of working. We know that he approved when museum curators exhibited his paintings in new groupings that he hadn't planned; it inspired him to continue in the same direction, making new series where none had been intended. Your collection of six drawings under the heading "Absurd" is heterogeneous and each sheet holds a surprise. How do you see these images? B

The absurd, even in the political sense, has to do with life and therefore death. The gravity of death provokes a sense of absurdity. You go on with each day, knowing that the end is inevitable. There is an absurdity to life that has to be addressed. In attempting to answer this question artistically, one comes up with forms that are larger than life and refuse to be locked into a single interpretation. I often use an element of the absurd in my works, especially in the "reverse" paintings that I have made since the late nineties, where – related to our current political situation – I give new interpretations to the male gaze that dominates image history. M

The absurd might not enter Munch's paintings so often, but in his drawings, he allows his imagination and critique to wander along this road. Elements of the human body are disproportioned, like in *Portrait Sketch* (p.114), where the protruding teeth and starry eyes make the figure look absurd. The out-of-proportion forms become stronger in *Caricatures and a Drunkard* (p.115), and especially in the early drawing *Caricature: Old Man with Horns* (p.118) it becomes frankly bizarre. In *Figures and Animal*s (p.117) and *Caricatures* (p.116) only the faces have human features and the rest of their bodies have become animal. Yet, it is not possible to determine that they are "really" animals. *Caricatures* was made on the stationary of the Hotel Rohn in Warnemünde, where Munch stayed while he was painting. One wonders what the artist had in mind; whether this is a preparatory sketch for a painting, or just doodles he drew when he was waiting or was bored. The themes of observation and the semi-human return in the final sheet of this group, *Two People Eating Bread* (p.119). Although here, the observing creatures – naughty children? – with downcast eyes might be up to mischief, throwing stones down a wall, or does that interpretation sounds too absurd?

"Hieroglyphs" is a subject that you have worked on intensively and revisited again and again over decades, for instance in the series "Hieroglyphs of Lohar Chawl", related to the wholesale market for electronic goods in Bombay where you lived and had your studio from the late 70s until the late 90s (p.102). The two Munch images you present under the heading "Hieroglyphs" seem to be related, while remaining both strange and very different. Can you explain the heading? B

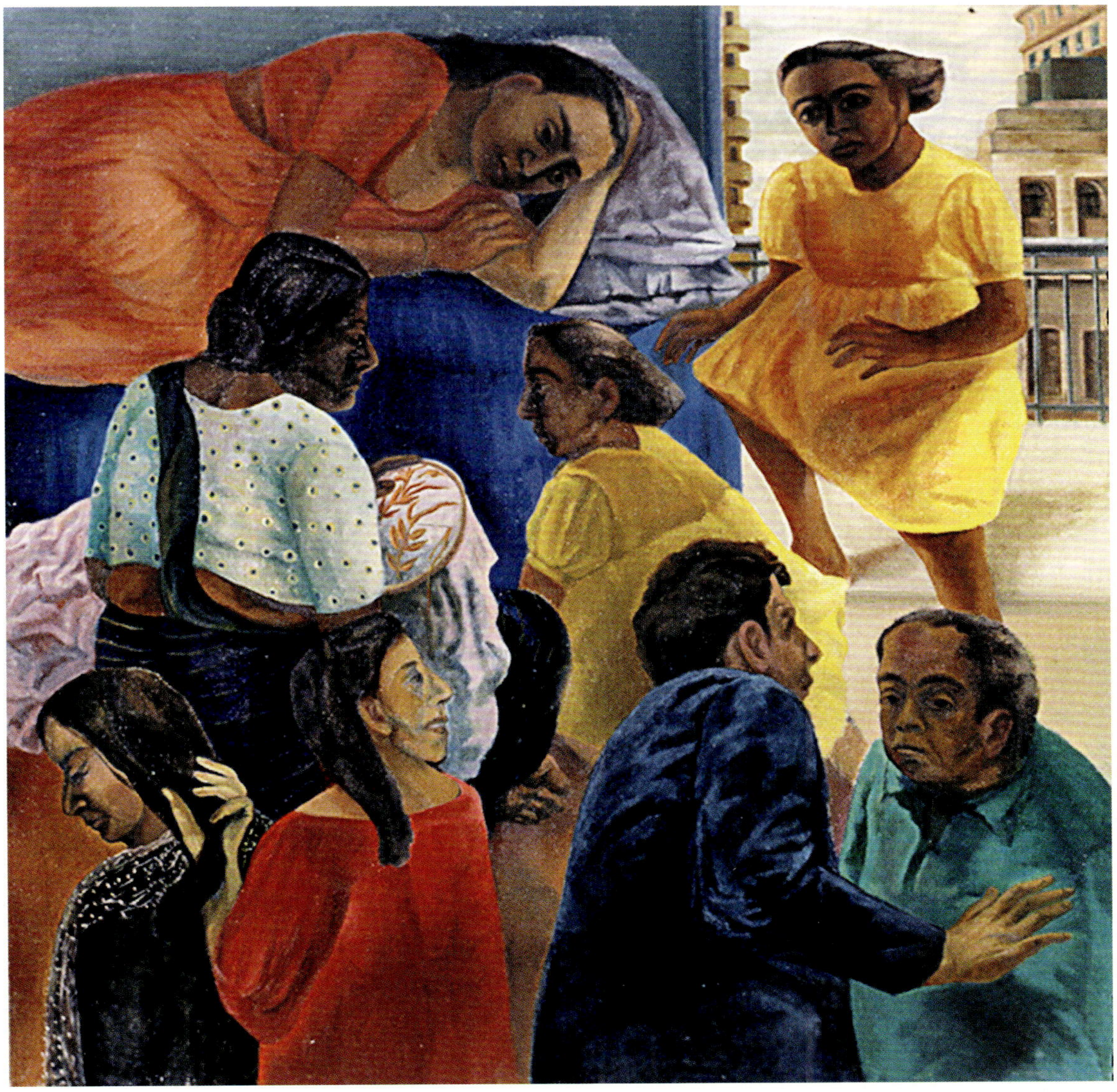

Nalini Malani
Grieved Child from the series "His Life", 1981
Oil on canvas
122 × 122 cm

For me, hieroglyphs are something that you can't decipher. A language that escapes you, that bars you from entering it. Hieroglyphs are between writing and drawing. The letters are depicted by figuration. This quality makes hieroglyphic texts apt means for thinking about media. This very early drawing by Munch from 1874, when he was eleven years old, reminded me of the language of hieroglyphs and its similarity to comics (p. 120). It depicts a girl and a bird, with seven drawings continuing the story on the backside of the sheet. The multiplicity of the frames and the repetition of colours – especially the blue that defines the composition – suggest continuity between events and figures. Clearly, in these drawings observation again merges with fantasy. M

These drawings are quite remote from the next group, the three depictions of labour that you have titled "Proletariat". B

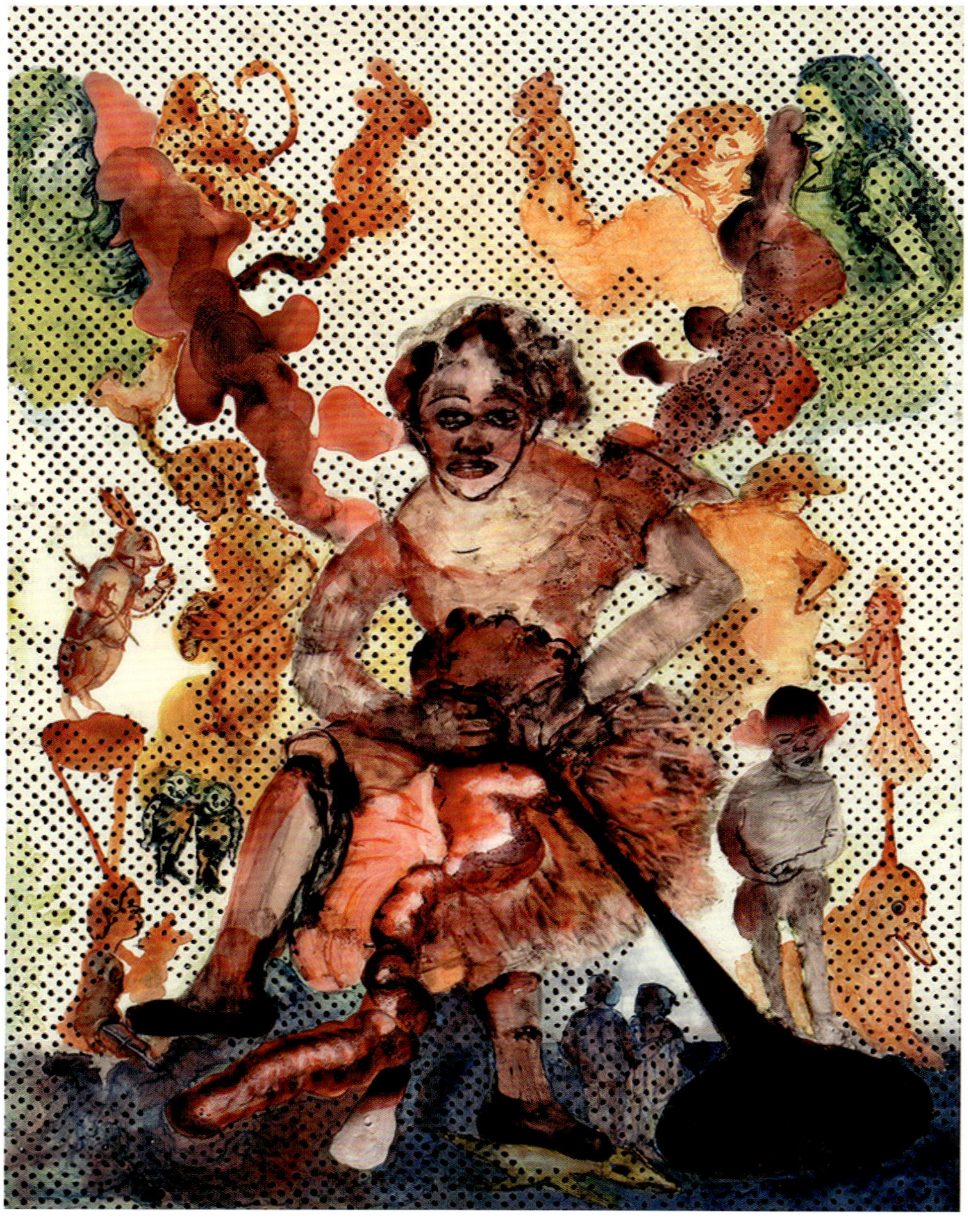

Nalini Malani
Living in Alicetime: Broken Alice II, 2005
Watercolour, acrylic and enamel reverse painting on acrylic sheet
152.5 × 122 cm

M

"Proletariat" is another recurring topic in my work – the working class that builds cities and maintains everyday life. A city might be the dream of an architect or a politician, but in the end it is the proletariat that builds the grand mansions brick by brick. The establishment in a blatant capitalist state, towards which many countries are moving, uses them and, when they are no longer functional, throws them out.

In the drawings *Construction Work* and *Bricklayer* (p.122–123), the hard-working men hardly have time to look up at the others and at the world. In the drawing *War Invalid: The Beggar* (p.124), the person walking on crutches has a broken body; he did not even get a chance to build up his country after the war. In my drawings of the working class in Lohar Chawl, I remember well how I felt held back from sketching their lives as it was an invasion of their privacy. I worked from memory. I could not stand in the street observing, and then depicting these people. That would be an intrusion. Yet, not depicting them at all would be a censoring of an unjust social reality. Therefore, I also started my ongoing series of "Wall Drawing / Erasure Performance" in 1992; erasing as an avoidance of fixating. Here, the workers of Lohar Chawl entered with *City of Desires*, the elite space in south Bombay where I drew for two weeks on the walls of a gallery while it was open to the public.

B

Yes, I remember that dilemma from Adorno, who first said that making art after the Holocaust was inadmissible, but then retracted it in *Aesthetic Theory* because suffering cannot be censored away. Between avoiding voyeurism and censoring, there is no really good solution. But Munch's and your decision to replace observation with recall seems the best solution. How does this relate to the nudity in the three-sheet group you call "Puberty"?

M

Well, yes, in the famous puberty paintings Munch empathises and perhaps romanticises the dilemma of entering adulthood. That moment, that in-between phase that is full of confusion. In my work a young girl often appears innocently skipping rope, but also watching the world and herself change as in *Broken Alice II* (2005), from the series "Living in Alicetime", where we see Alice after Lewis Carroll's version of the story, growing up and experiencing her first menstruation. In Munch's *Seated Female Nude* (p.125) and *Seated Female Nude with Hands Holding Her Knees* (p. 126) you still see the innocent girl. Besides the subject, these drawings attracted my attention because of the bright colours and transparency of the watercolours. They reminded me of Kalighat, an early 20th century Indian painting style in which volume is not depicted but suggested by shallow shadows, constituted by something between line and plane. I frequently use that style myself, to bring the past into the present, as Kalighat is for me the start of modernism in India. A modernism that did not reach its full potential, leaving us in the current situation of growing sectarian conflicts where constitutional rights are curtailed on religious grounds. The third drawing, *Omega Weeping* (p.127), is very different. The sadness of the figure's eyes speaks volumes about her inhibition, her shame of being confronted by voyeuristic spectators. Her expression reminds me so much of the gang rapes in India, where freedom and innocence are lost for a lifetime, even ending in murder. This is something that deserves our utmost attention and effort to counter. I have made an animation project on the topic, which was presented as a 60-meter high projection on the Taj Tower in Bombay as a public statement on 8 February 2020 (p.111).

The eight groups are intricately related thematically, so that they become artistic modes rather than semantic themes. This becomes clear with the next one, the six sheets of the group "Horror". How do you see horror here? B

Horror can be of two kinds, one you feel in your own mind, in your own imagination, and the horror that come from outside. The effect of horror is presented in combinations of fantasy, observation, and the shame of both voyeurism and exhibitionism. The drawing *The Veil* (p.133) says it all. The woman covers her mouth, as if she cannot speak. But she covers it with her hair, which confuses our intercultural world. From antiquity until today, women's hair has been the object of taboo. Lifting her hair to cover her mouth unveils her body, and thus, to the prudish eye, the gesture would defeat its purpose. In *The Veil* and *Sketch for Theatre Programme Peer Gynt* (p. 132), ironically, a neatly dressed, coiffed and hatted woman also covers her mouth, but now with the ornamental gauze of her puffed sleeves and collar. Strange but meaningful for my series, this woman's breasts are also visible – fantasy enters, after all. M

I couldn't help myself from including in this group a drawing from 1893, full of intense colouring, where we recognise Munch's most famous painting, *The Scream* (p.131). Munch's favorite combination of yellows and blues seems almost monomaniacal here. The hastily applied lines and strokes make us imagine the furiously drawing artist, pressing hard on the pencil. And if the horror is in any doubt, the prophetic skull which the figure is covering with his hands is clearly already dead. A related expression may be found in his typical group portraits with wide open-eyed figures like *Grenadierstraße in Berlin after the War* (p.130), *Anxiety Motif* (p.129), and *Caricatured Figures* (p.128). In *Grenadierstraße in Berlin* the three large figures in the foreground all have remarkable eyes: turned inward, yet affected by what they see. What makes this drawing so gripping is the ignorance of the viewer regarding the spectacle that so horrifies these three men. Instead of being co-horrified, we can only postulate empathy. And this, perhaps, is what makes the visualisation of horror so important.

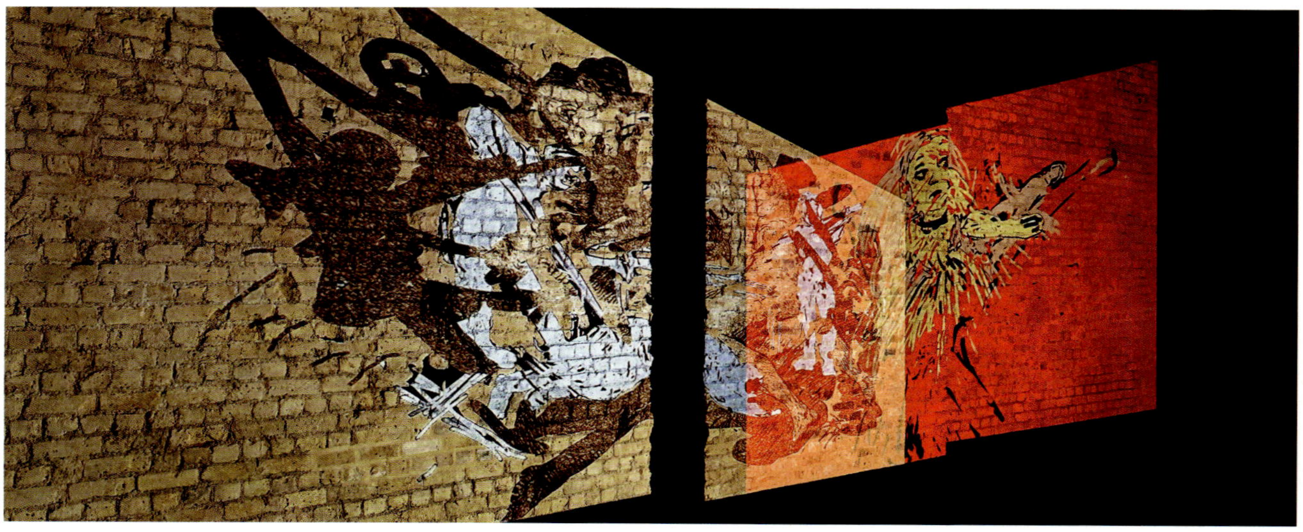

Nalini Malani
Can You Hear Me?, 2018–20
Animation chamber, 9 channels, 88 iPad animations, sound

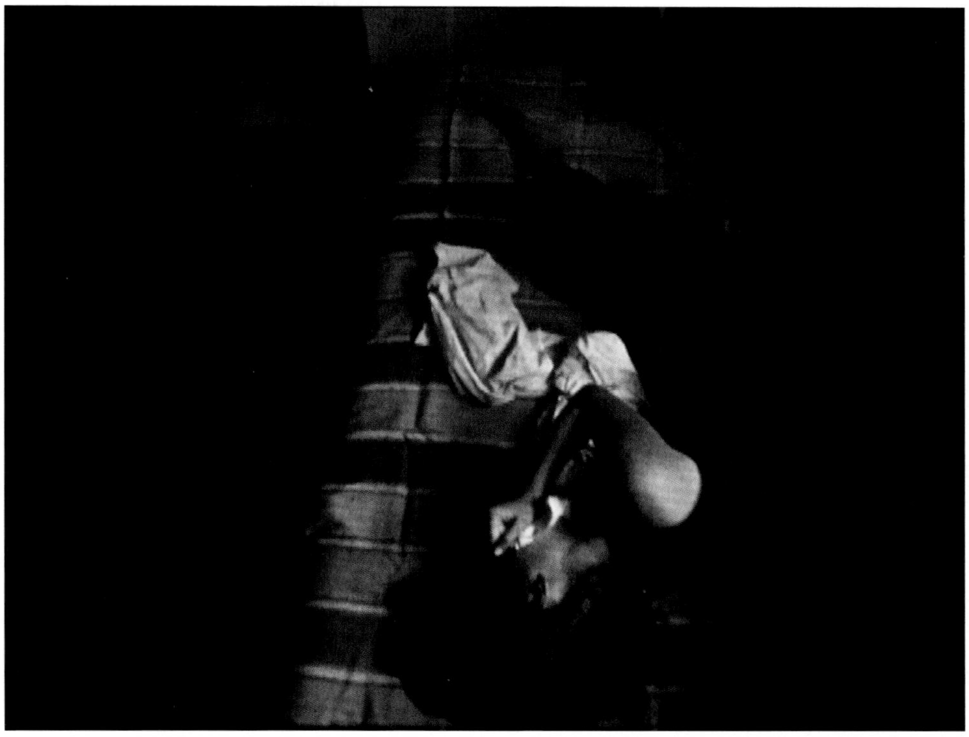

B In the next group, called "Machismo", the first of the five drawings could just as well be part of the "Horror" series, don't you think?

M Machismo has to do with the Alpha Male. To talk about it in sympathetic terms, the machismo is a denial or denigration of his feminine side. It includes male misbehaviour as well as ludicrous arrogance. But also dreadful assaults, which can cause horror. In a wider sense, machismo has been addressed in all of my art, from the early films like *Onanism* (1969) to my recent iPad animation *Feminine Masculine* (2018), in which I quote Veena Das: "There are feminine regions of the self that reside in both men & women". In Munch's drawing *The Afflicted Eye* (p.136), there is a gigantic bird attacking a woman, who pulls back from the aggressor. In *The Splitting of Faust* (p.134), the arrogant looks of the two standing men tell us they are not interested in the woman next to them. It seems they are denying the woman her existence – hence the two red stripes over her face, as an effacement. Similarly, the two next drawings, *Standing Woman* (p.135) and the much earlier work *The Hands* (p. 137), show women alone. The one with eyes of shock and disappointment, the other, younger, turning her head away from the grabbing hands. In *Standing Woman*, the woman looks distraught, whereas in *The Hands*, she could be interpreted to mock the machos. Finally, in *Woman with a Samoyed* (p.138) the woman is harassed not by hands but by heads, looks, as if the entire space is filled with horny blokes. She seems neither amused nor distraught; neither coquettish nor angry. Perhaps she is just indifferent, disinterested, which is the worst blow such men can get.

B How do you go from this to the theme of "Death"?

M Well, after all these different gazes, from voyeuristic to aggressive, from indifferent to empathic, images of death form the closure to an increasingly disturbing series. Death is ambiguous: dying is not the same as being dead. I see death in a non-religious way. I think of myself as part of nature – just as nature grows, it has to die, like us. The moment of birth is also the inexorable day by day movement towards death. Death: the inevitable.

Nalini Malani
Onanism, 1969
Digitalised 16 mm b/w reverse stock film, no sound
3:52 min

In the drawing *Peer Gynt, Mother Aase's Death* (p. 141), the very thin, barely visible lines that make up the skull reveal the state of the person in the bed. This is another form of that anti-voyeuristic delicacy. The witness, the person above who is there but cannot see the dead/dying woman, is surrounded by a substantial shadow that has the tones of sadness. M

In *Autopsy of a Male Body* (p. 140), a coloured corps fills the space obliquely, as if it does not quite fit. This image is impressive because of that space-filling quality: death takes over; in the face of death, nothing else matters. The third drawing, *Kiss of Death* (p. 139) in thick black ink, is entirely symbolic. A drowning woman, and Death impersonated. Is this figure of Death grabbing his prey, about to pull her under the water, or trying to save her? Ambiguity all over.

As an epilogue I propose an eighth category, "Witness", with two works that are quite unusual in Munch's oeuvre – drawings on photographs. They reminded me of my early collages from the late 60s/early 70s, the same time as I made my experimental films and cameraless photographs. The photographic reality serves, indeed, as the witness we have seen all along in my selection. In the postcard to Thorolf Holmboe (p. 142), between two young girls on skis, a third person appears, looking at the viewer. Intruding into their space, the stern-looking man is drawn with doodle-like, elliptic rounds that emphasise his lack of reality. In the postcard with two hanged men (p. 143), the tree branches serve as gallows in a sleeping city. We are witness to something that is not there in the reality of the photograph, but rather more like projections from within us.

Both these drawings have an exact date. Connecting works to specific dates is something I do in my recent animations made on my iPad, which I call *Notebooks* and are exhibited in an installation format as an animation chamber (p. 108). These works are a direct reaction to what I see or read, and my animated figures are superimposed on text or image quotes, just as in these postcards.

So, you selected drawings that do, address and achieve something, rather than plain themes? B

Yes, you can call them modes of thinking and figuring rather than themes. M

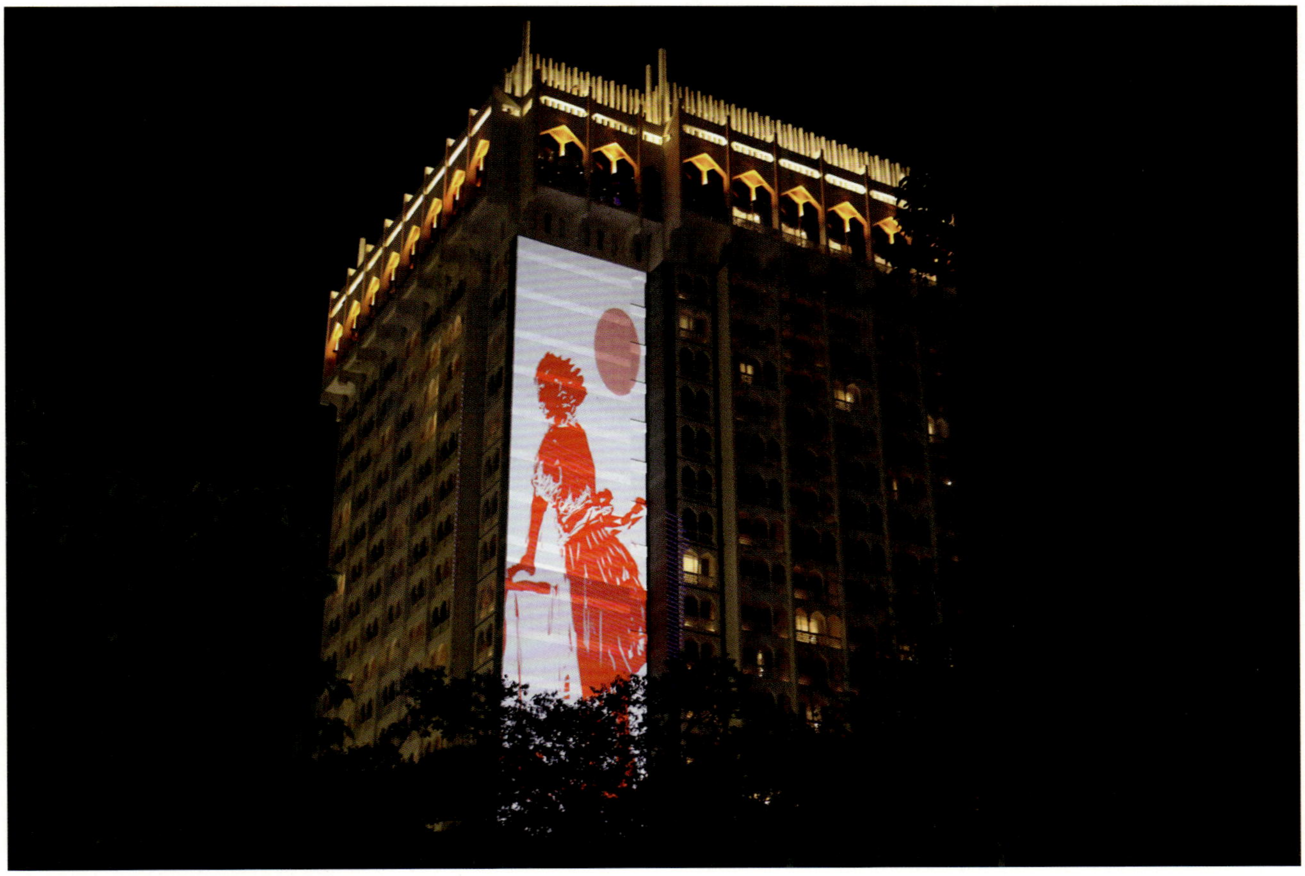

Nalini Malani
Can You Hear Me?, 8 February 2020
iPad animations, sound
60 × 13 meters

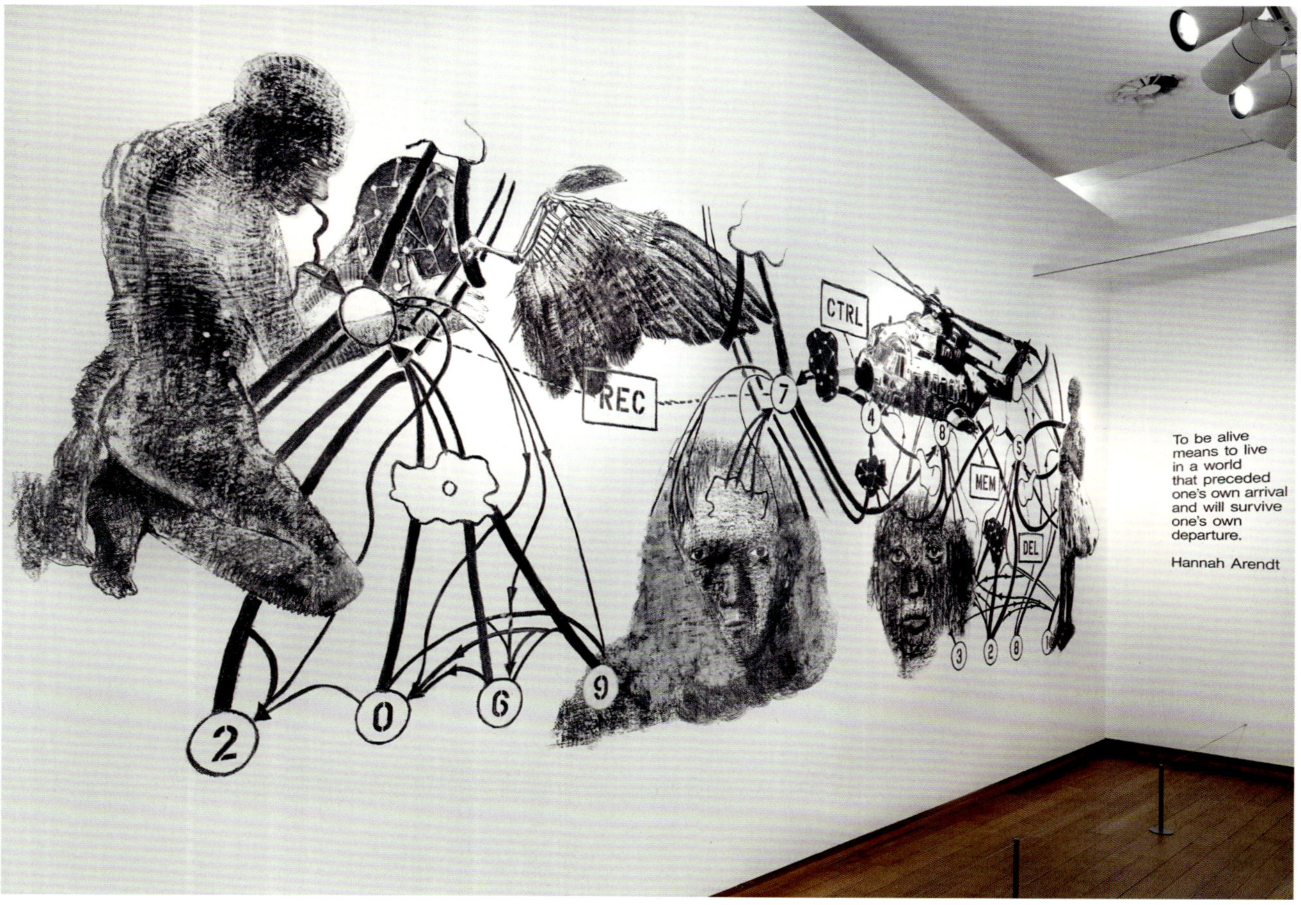

Nalini Malani
City of Desires, 1992–2017
Charcoal Wall Drawing / Erasure Performance

Malani chooses Munch

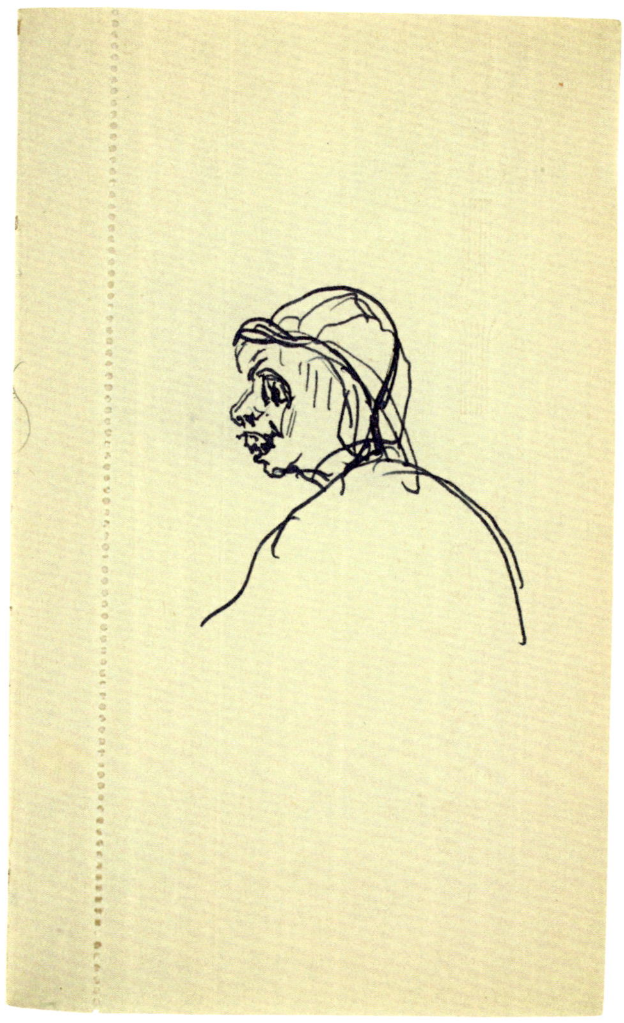

Portrait Sketch
1928–29
Pen
158 × 98 mm

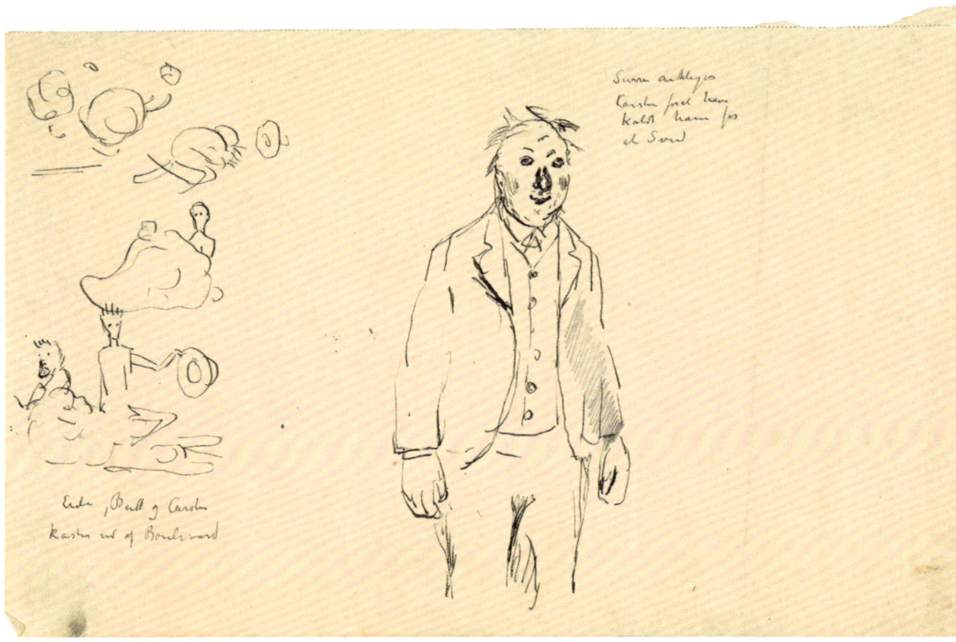

Caricatures and a Drunkard
1911–15
Pen and pencil
269 × 408 mm

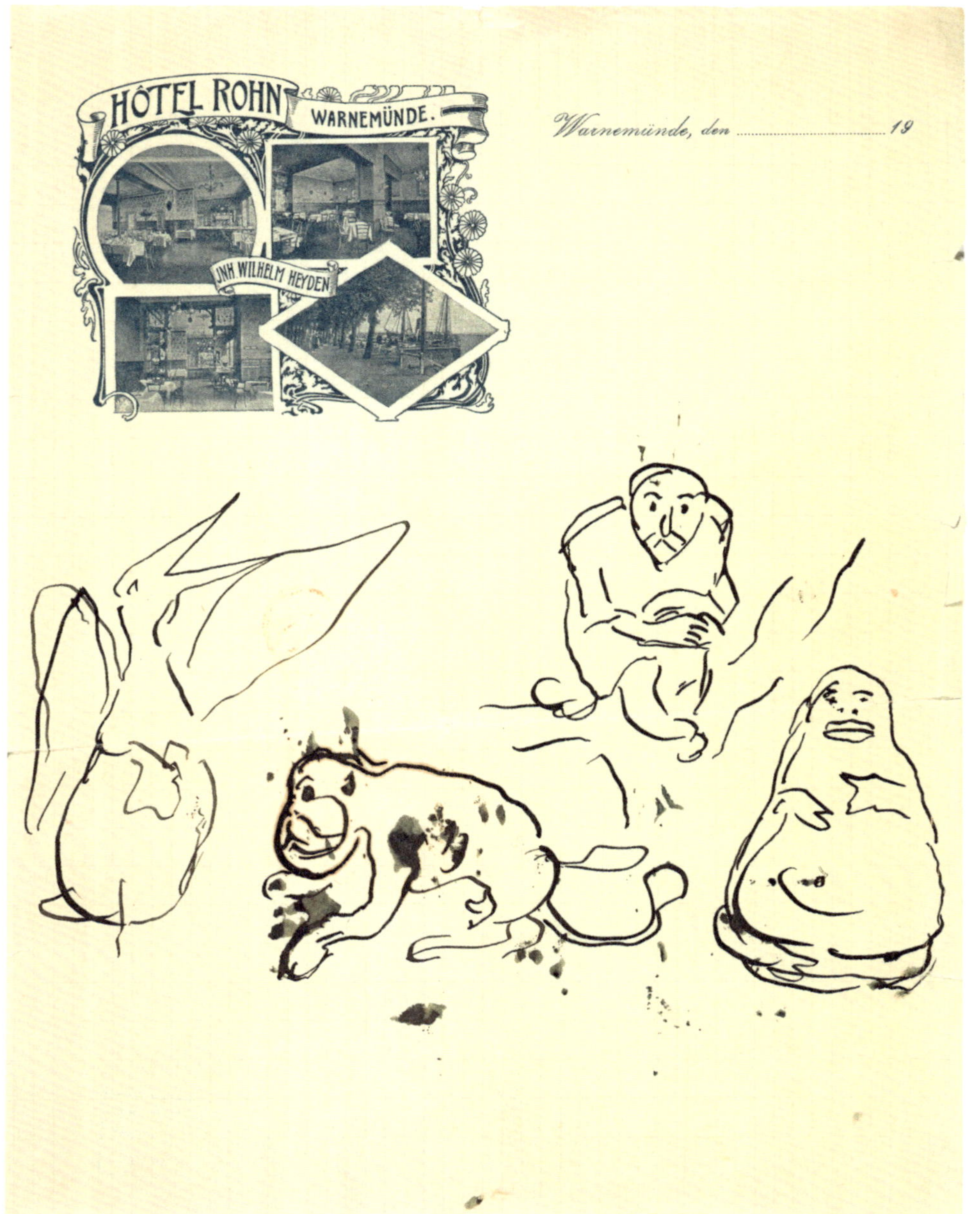

Caricatures
1907–08
Pen
280 × 222 mm

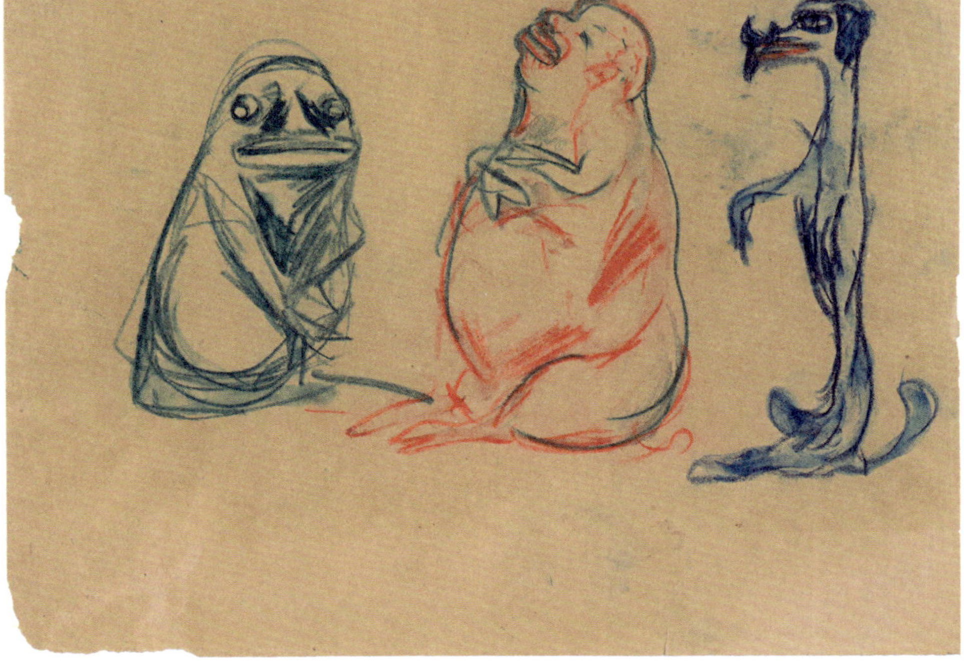

Figures and Animals. Bødtker, Heiberg and Toad
1908–09
Crayon and pastel
337 × 439 mm

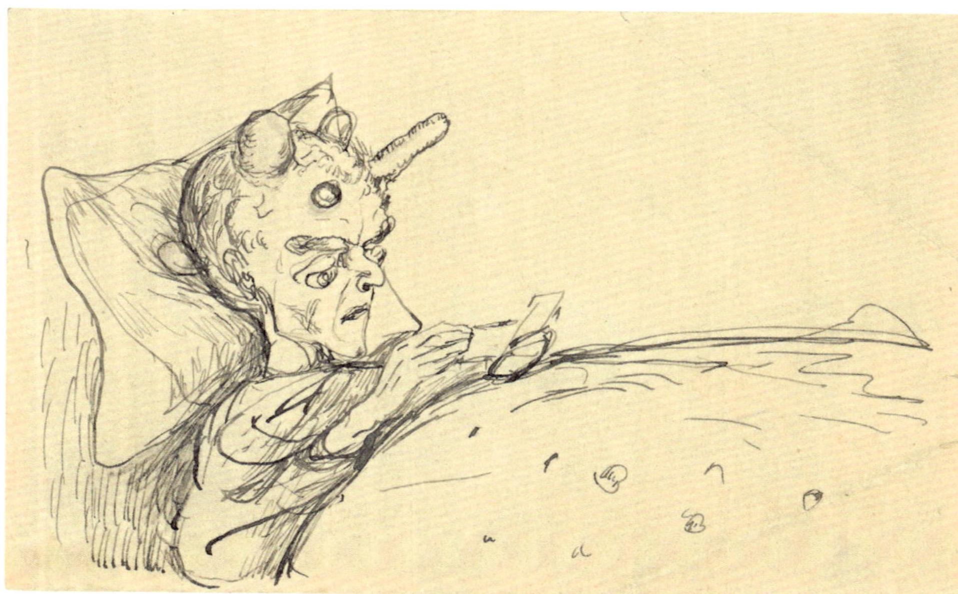

Caricature: Old Man with Horns
1899–1900
Pen
110 × 180 mm

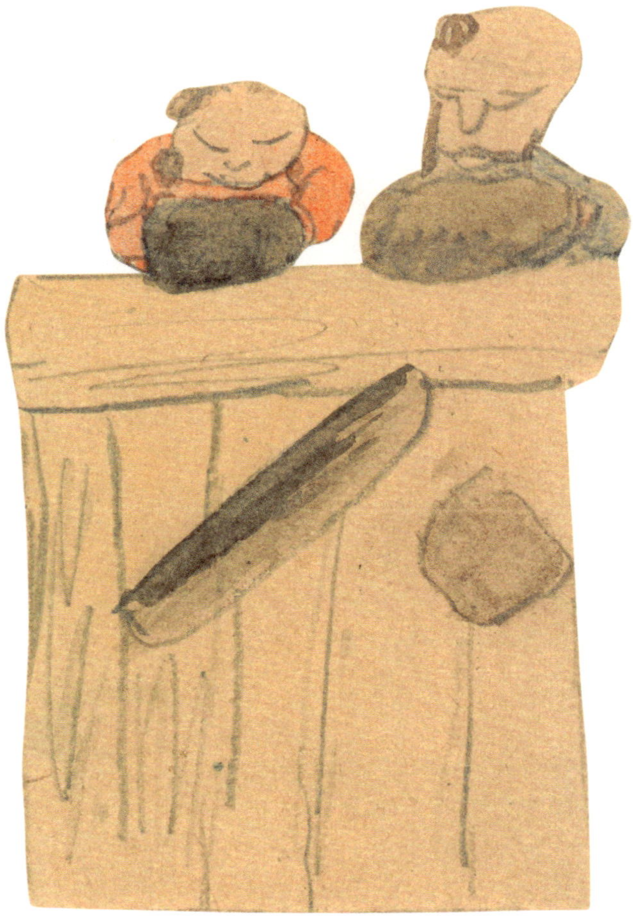

Two People Eating Bread
1874–76
Watercolour and pencil
82 × 57 mm

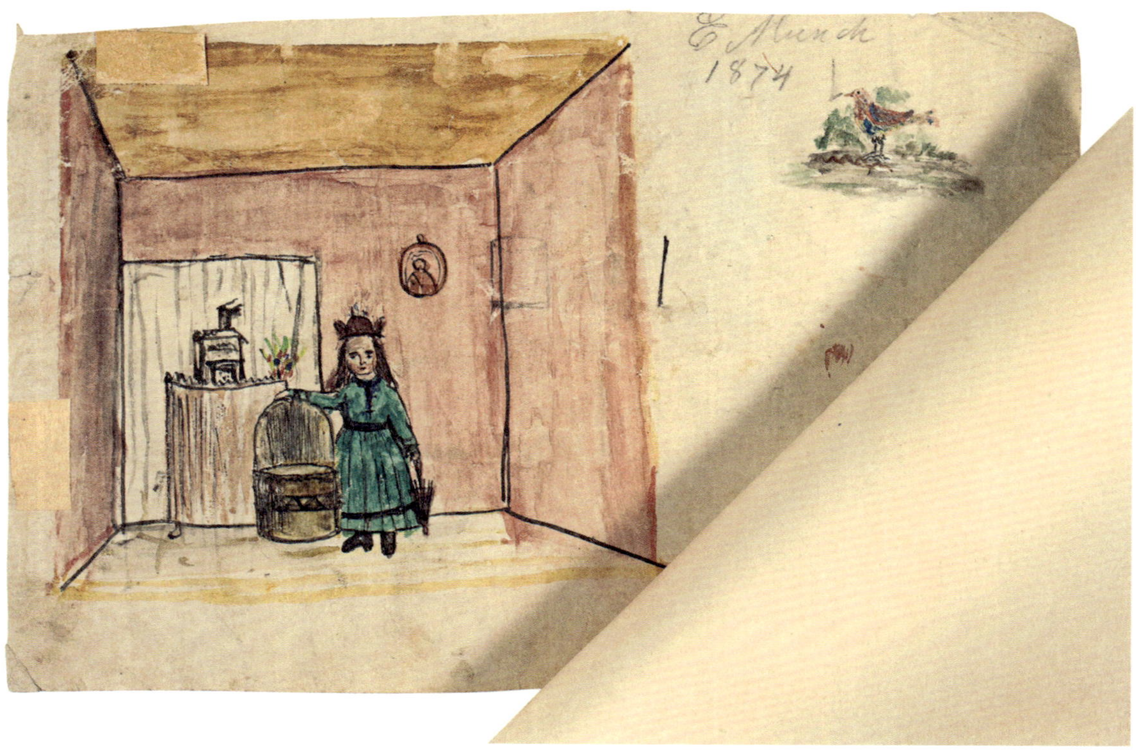

Interior with Girl and *Bird*
1874
Watercolour and pen (left motif), watercolour (right motif)
98 × 110 mm (left motif), 19 × 37 mm (right motif)

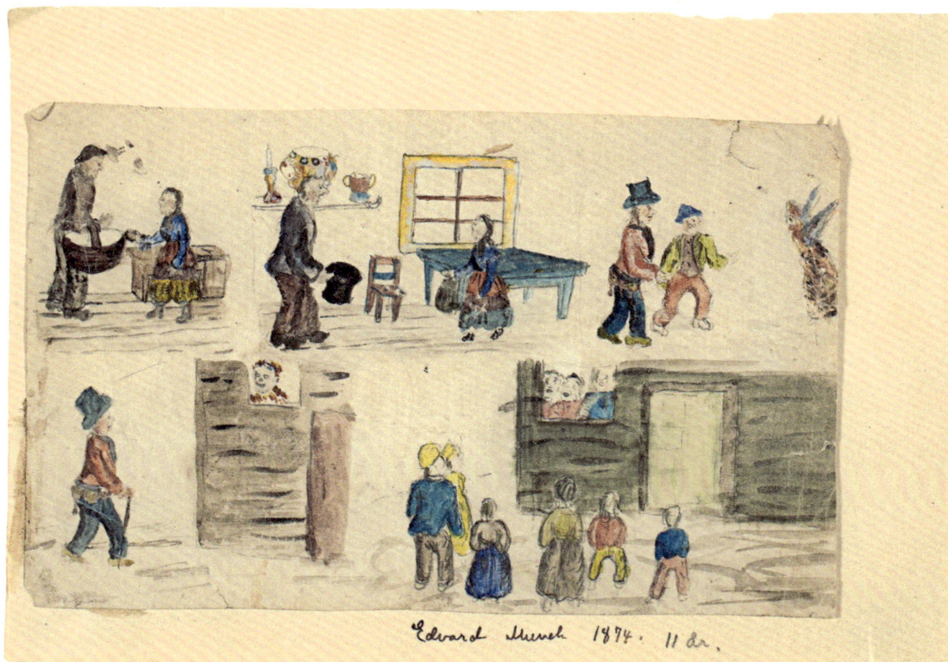

Five Illustrations
1874
Watercolour and pencil
122 × 193 mm

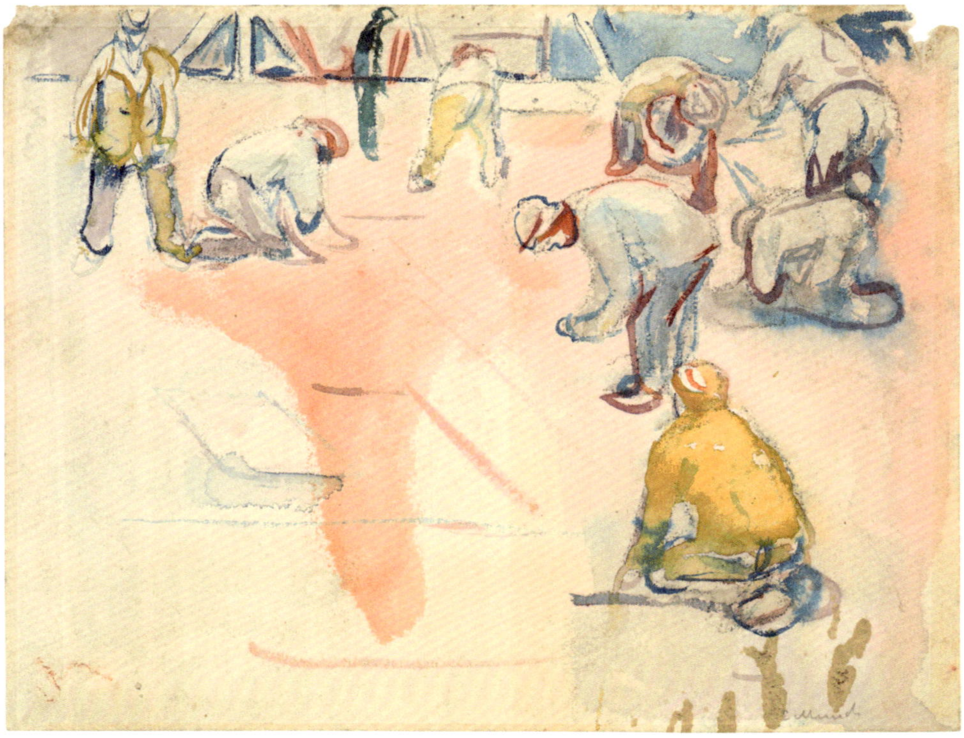

Construction Work
1929
Watercolour and charcoal
300 × 395 mm

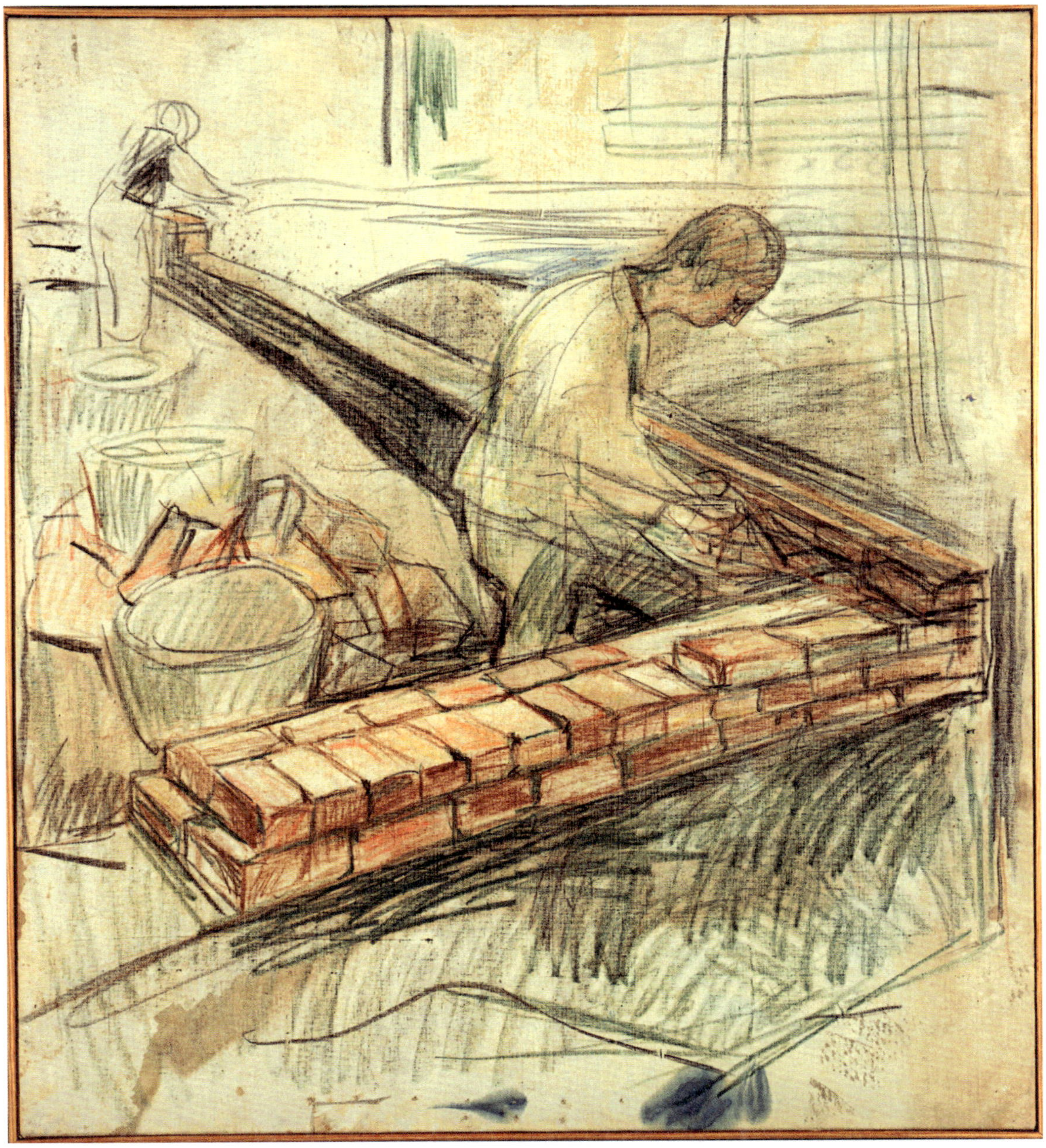

Bricklayer
1929
Crayon on unprimed canvas
85,5 × 78,5 cm

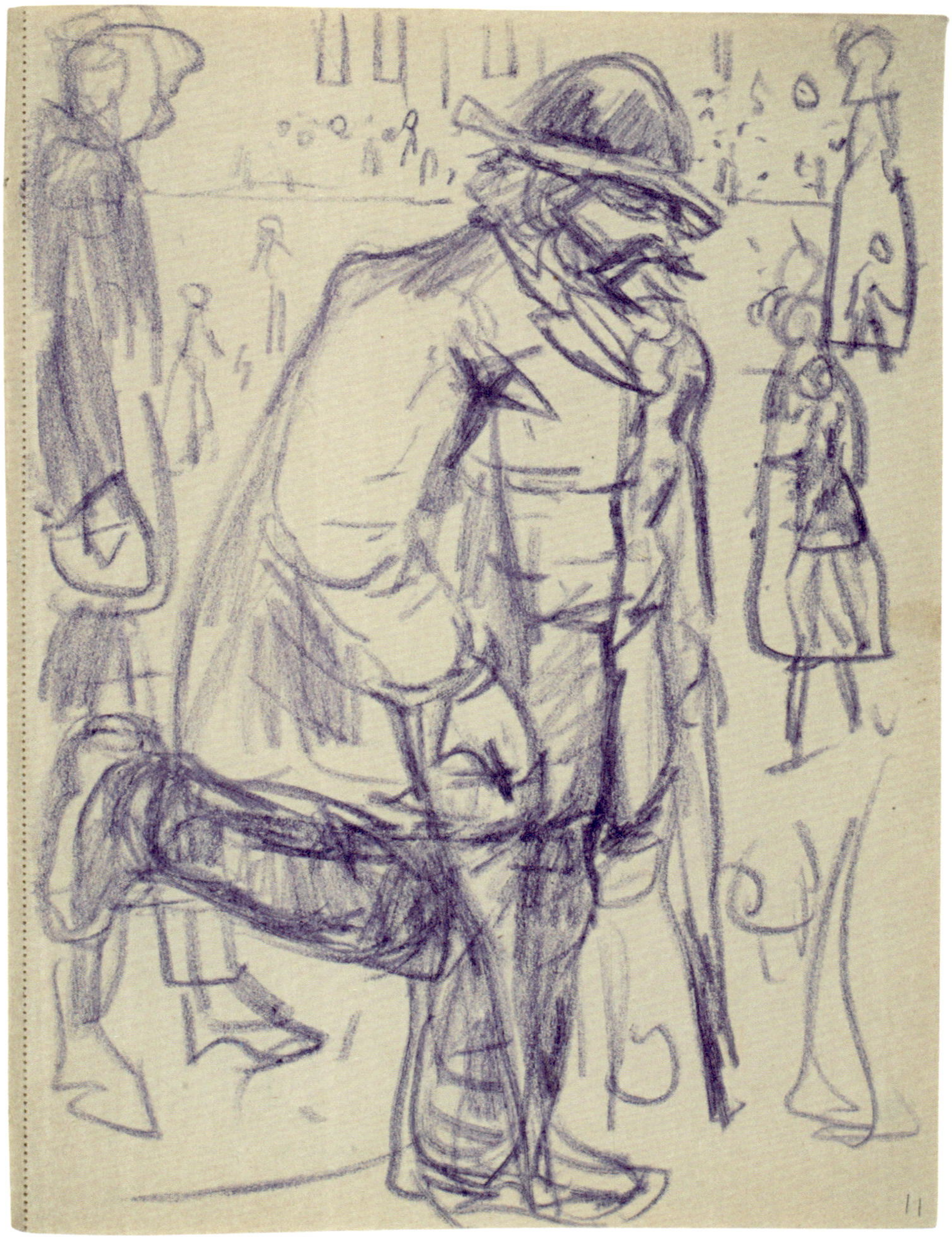

War Invalid. The Beggar
1916–18
Crayon
266 × 208 mm

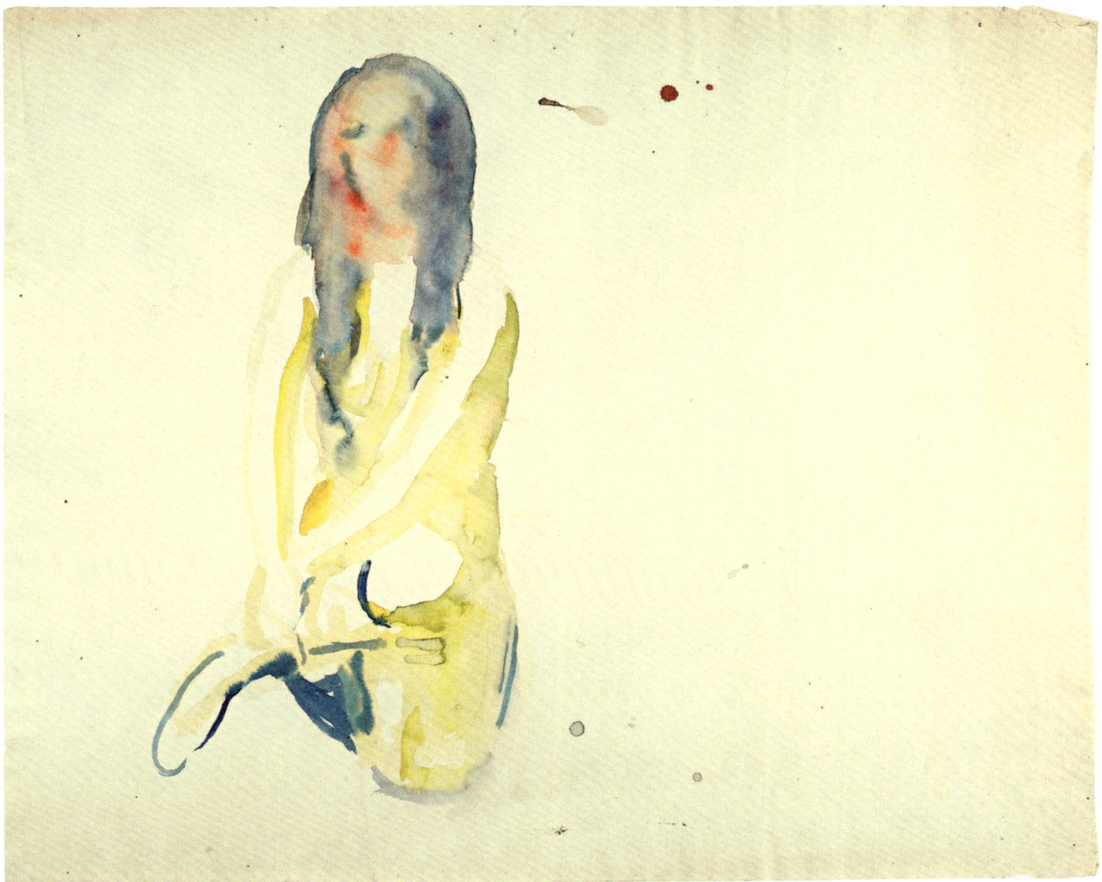

Seated Female Nude
1912–17
Watercolour
490 × 614 mm

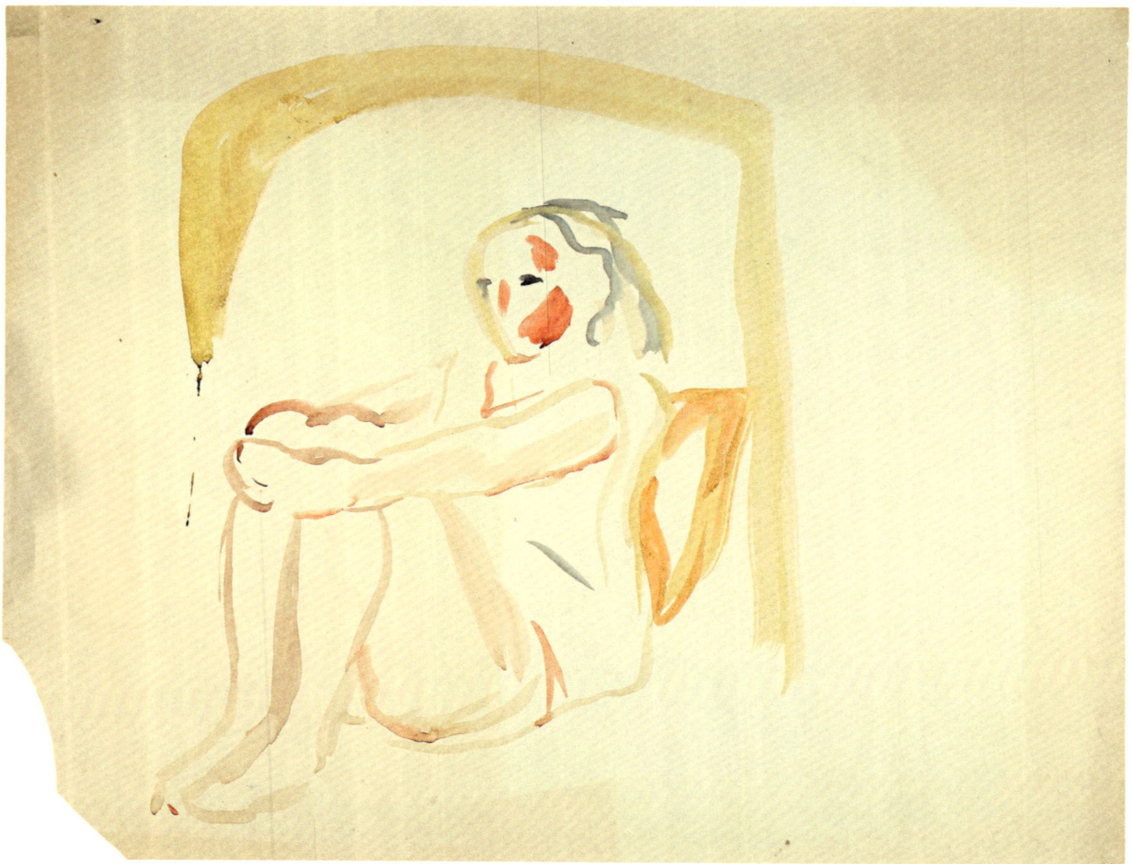

Seated Female Nude with Hands Holding Her Knees
1918–22
Watercolour
497 × 637 mm

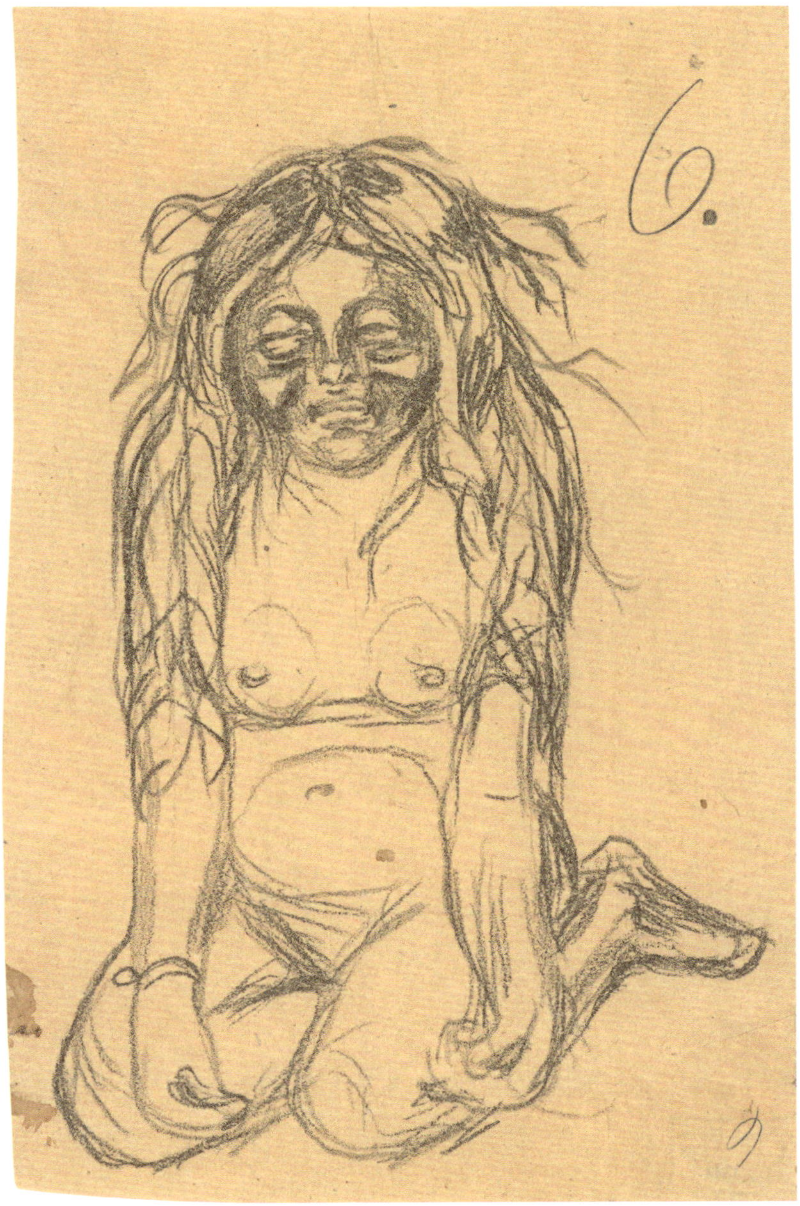

Omega Weeping
Original drawing for the lithograph *Omega Weeping*
1908–09
Crayon
312 × 205 mm

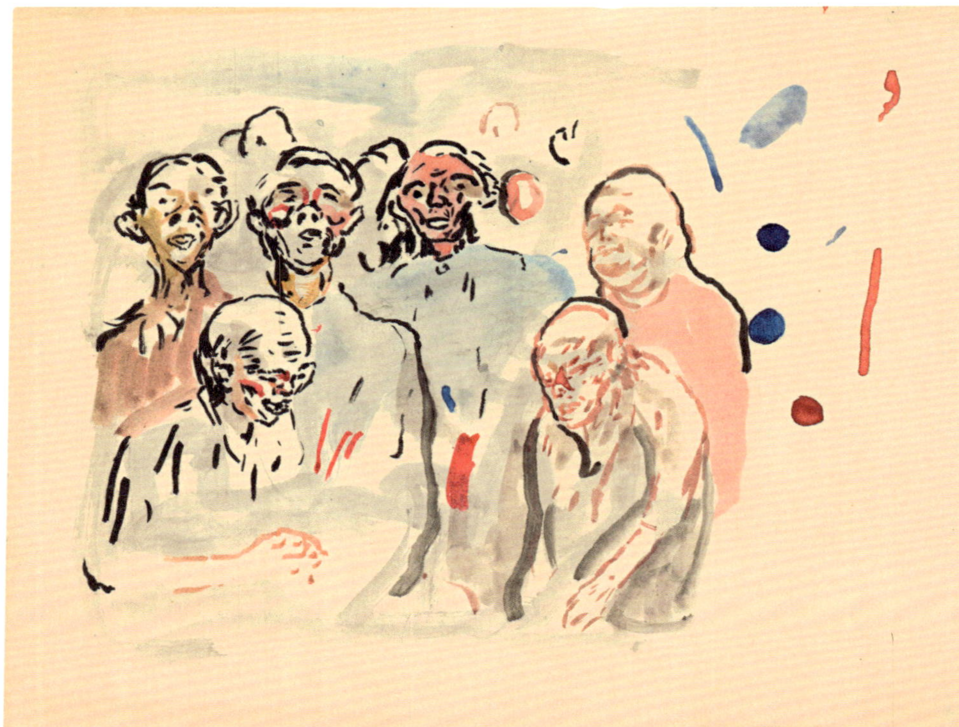

Caricatured Figures. Peer Gynt(?)
1932–34
Brush and watercolour
270 × 353 mm

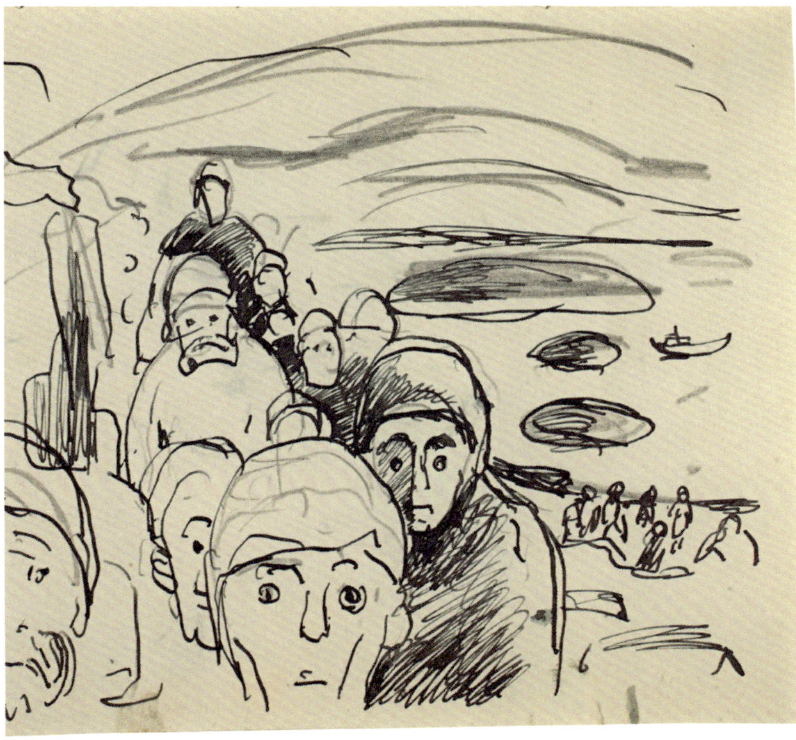

Anxiety Motif
1928–30
Pen and pencil
170 × 208 mm

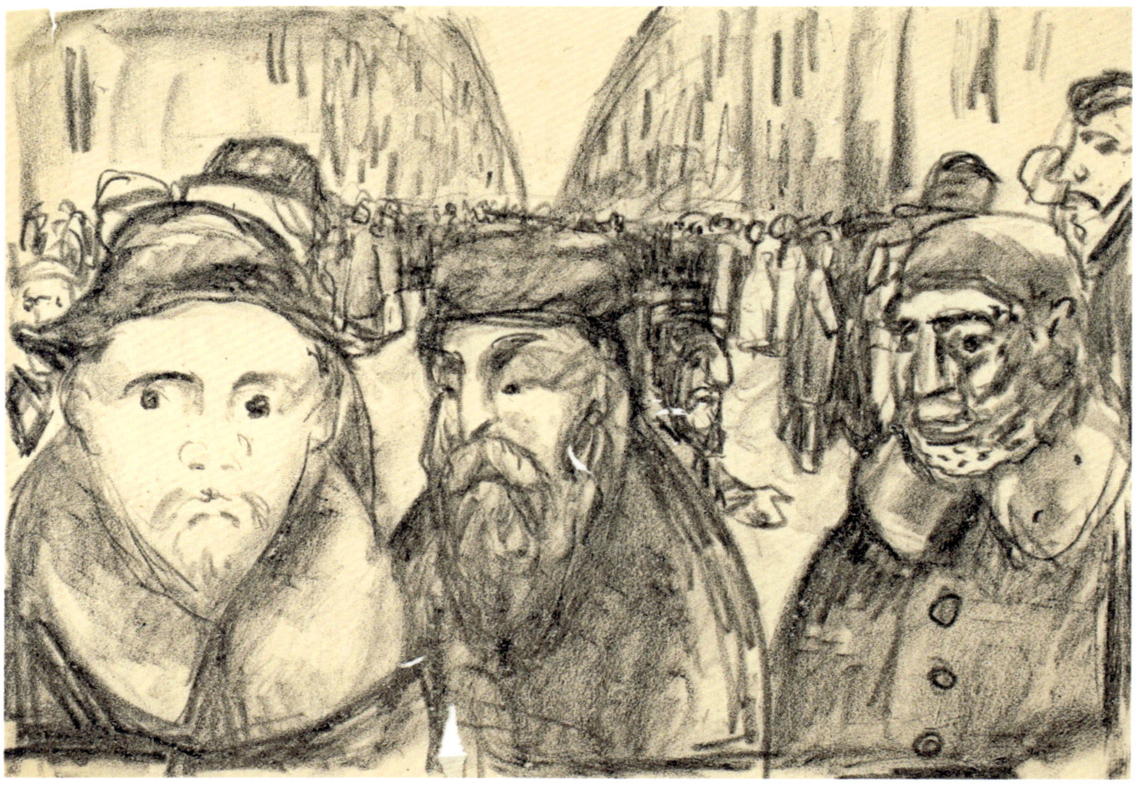

Grenadierstraße in Berlin after the War
Original drawing for the lithograph
Genthinerstraße in Berlin after the War
1920–21
Crayon
270 × 401 mm

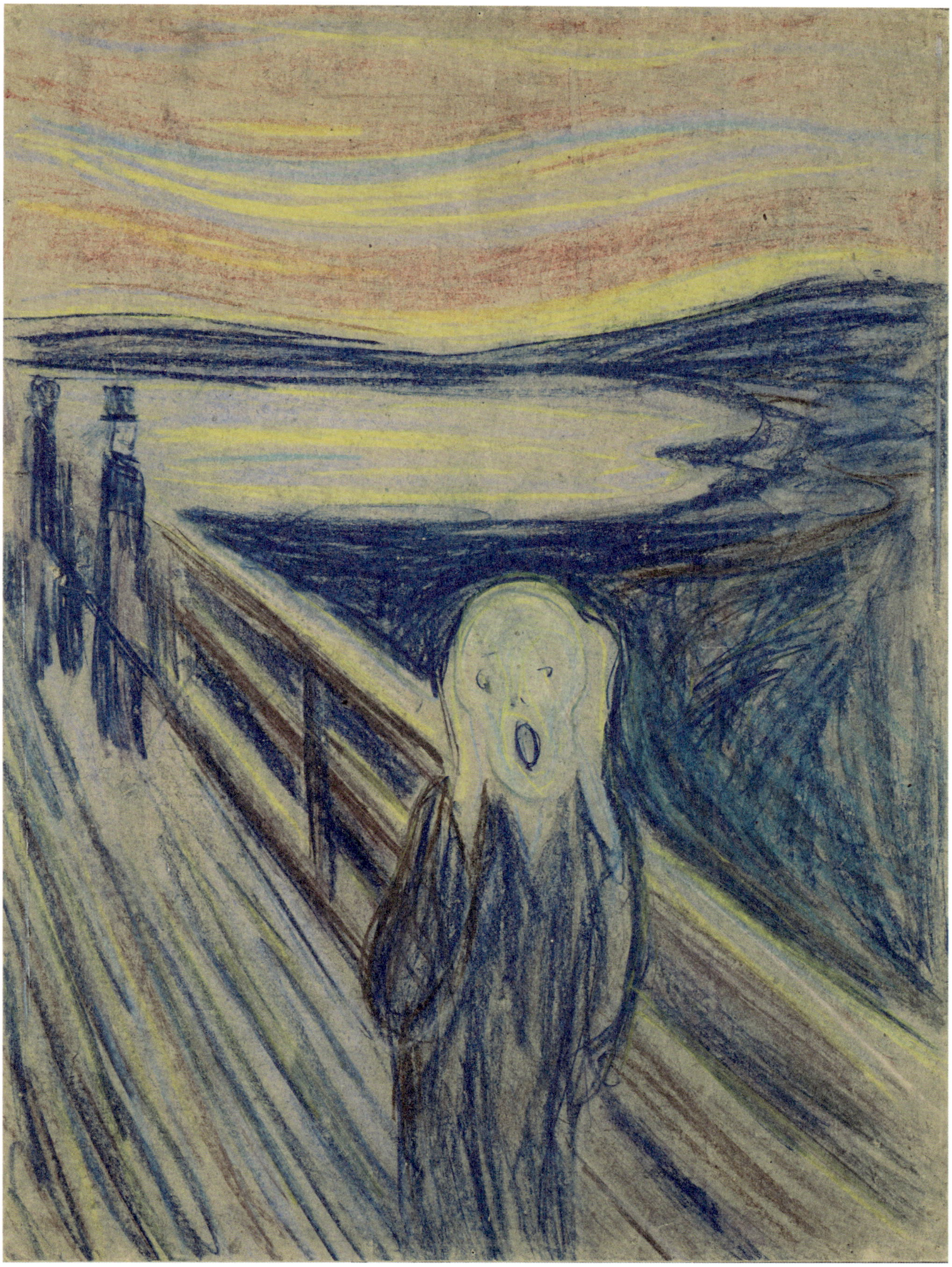

The Scream
1893
Crayon on unprimed canvas
74 × 56 cm

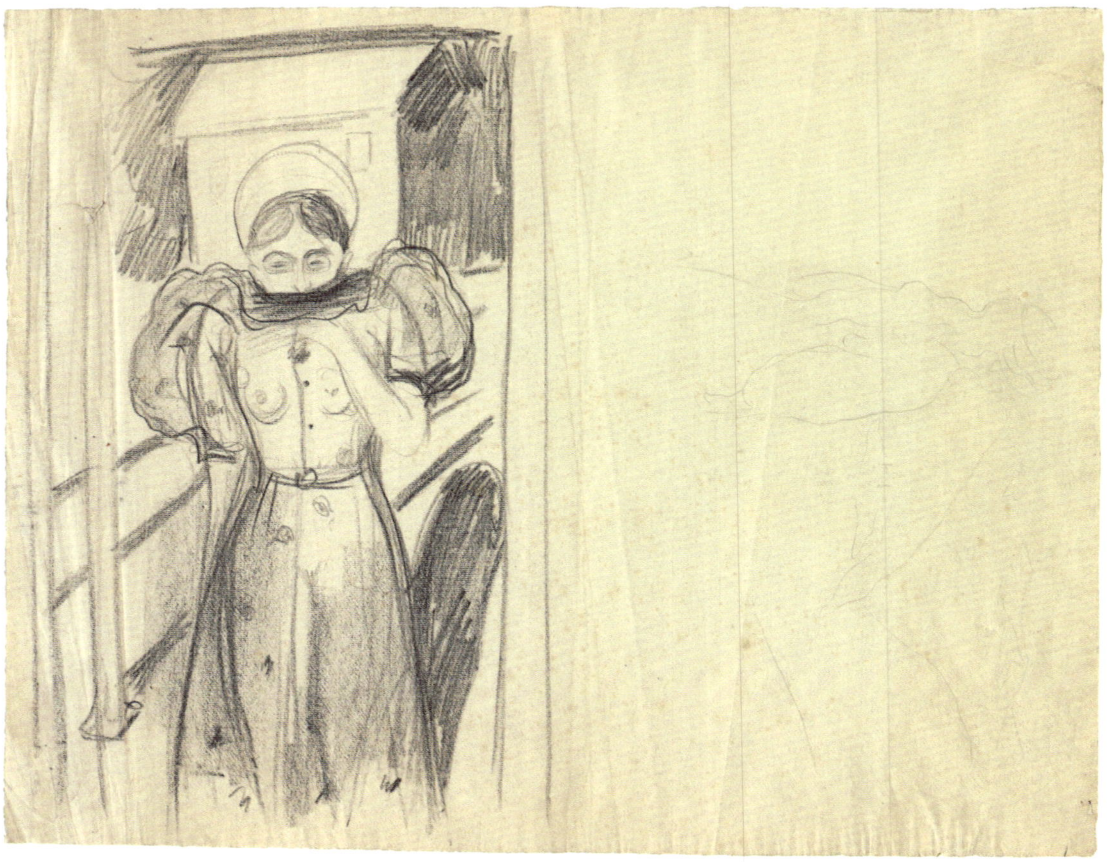

The Veil and *Sketch for Theatre Programme for Peer Gynt*
1896
Crayon (left motif), pencil (right motif)
472 × 618 mm

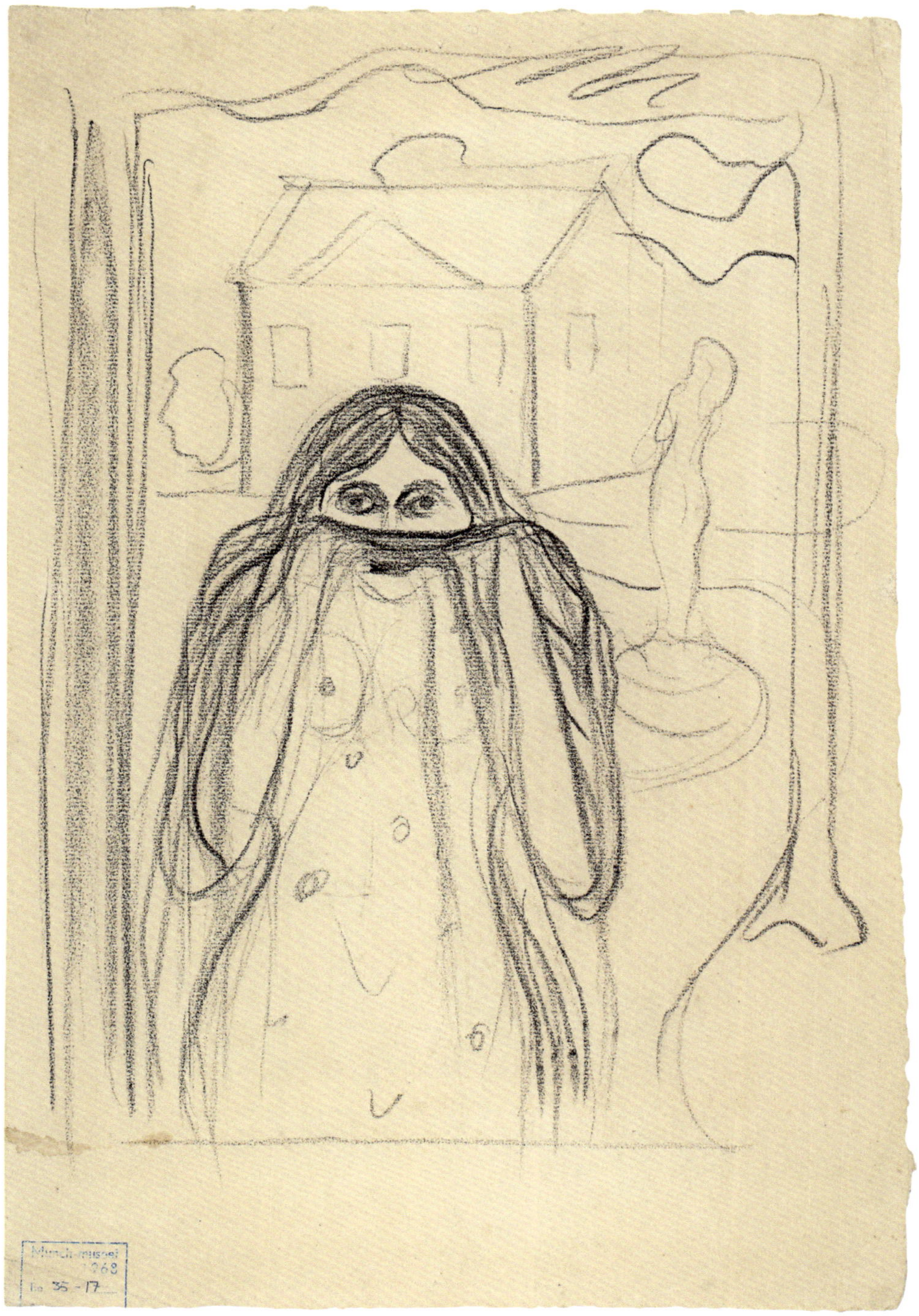

The Veil
1896
Crayon
448 × 315 mm

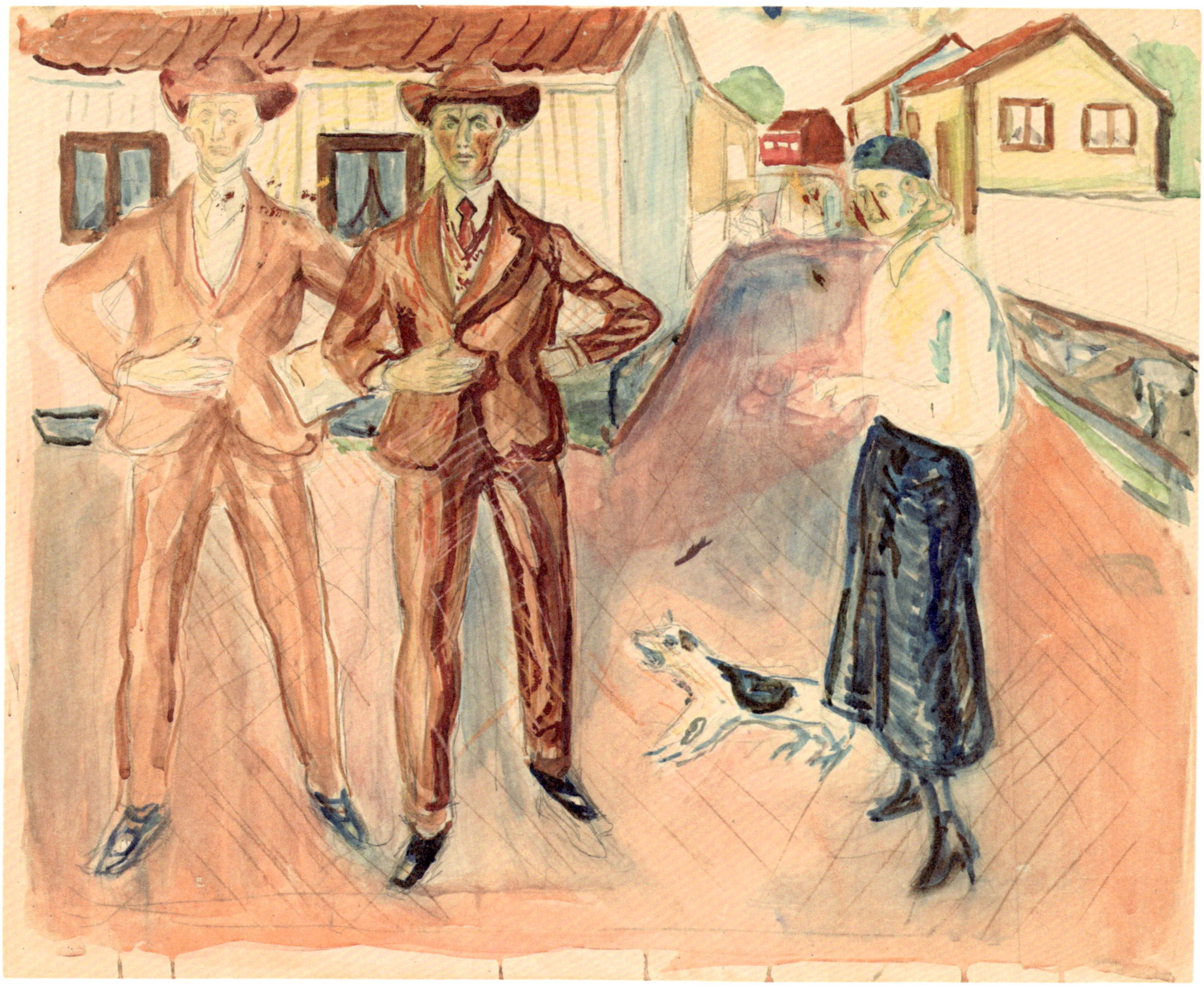

The Splitting of Faust
1932–35
Watercolour, gouache, pencil and crayon
700 × 860 mm

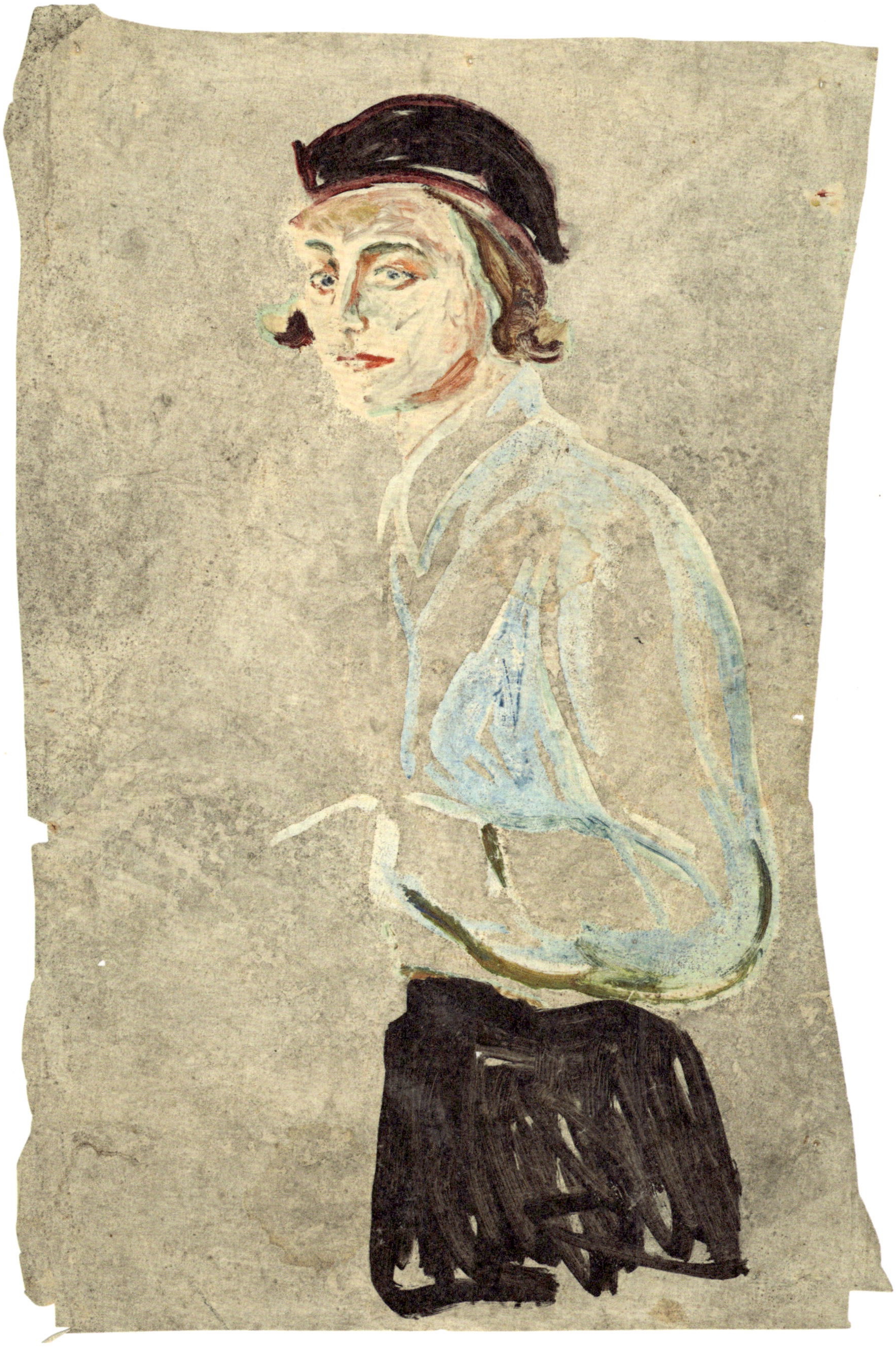

Standing Woman
Study of detail for *The Splitting of Faust*
1932
Gouache on canvas
90 × 60 cm

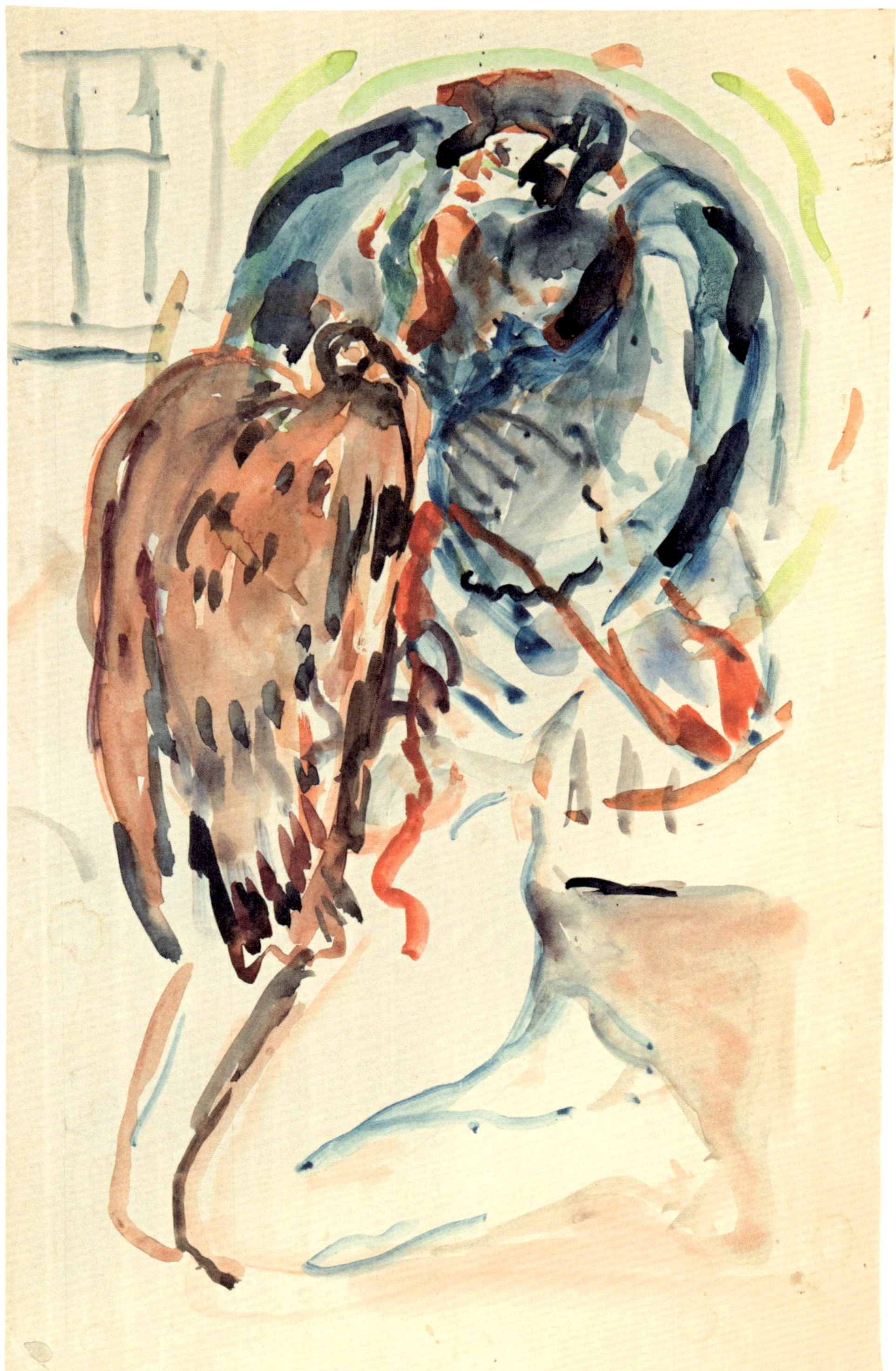

The Afflicted Eye. Kneeling Female Nude with Eagle
1930
Watercolour
500 × 322 mm

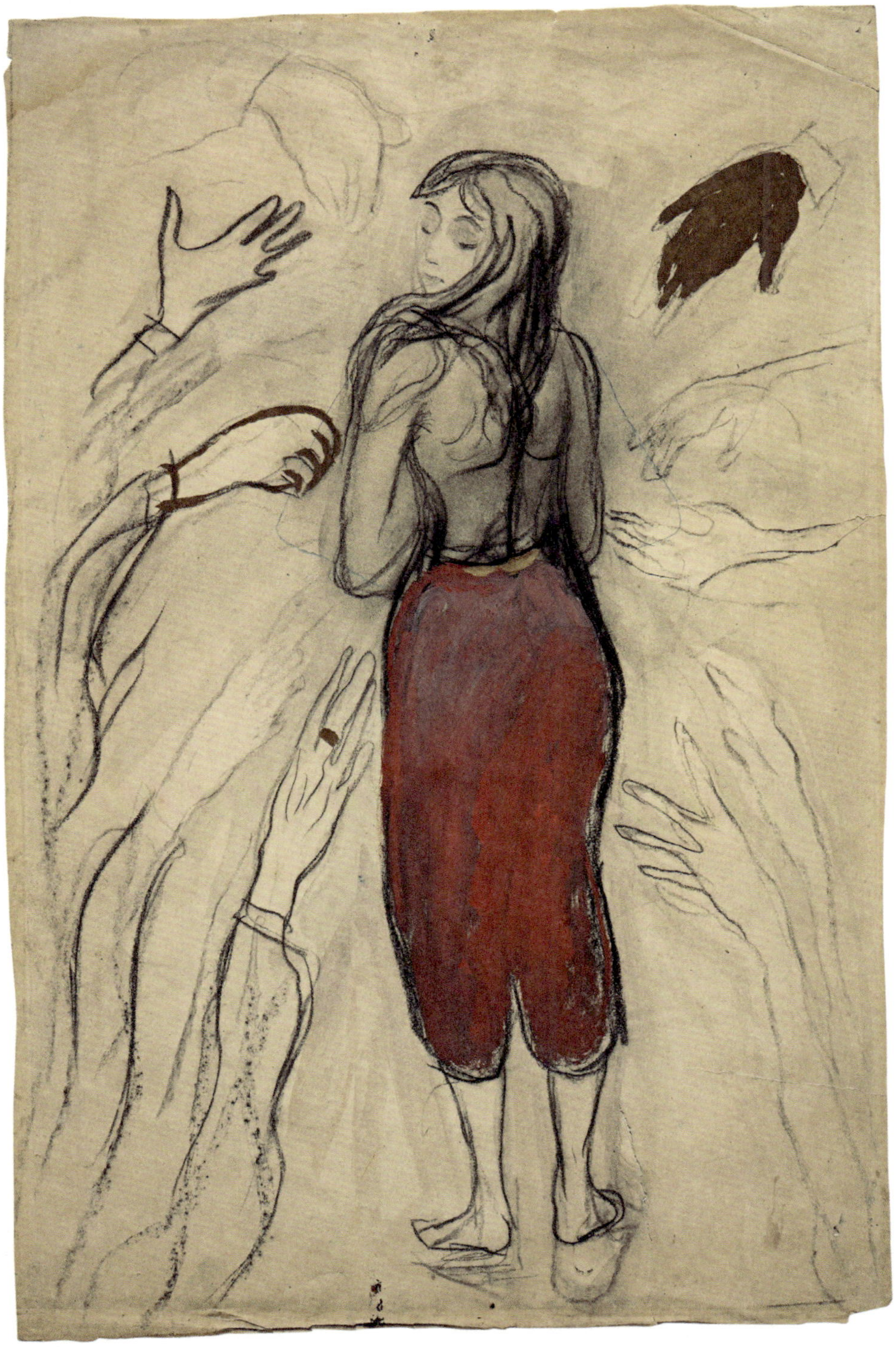

The Hands
1893
Charcoal, gouache and crayon
679 × 452 mm

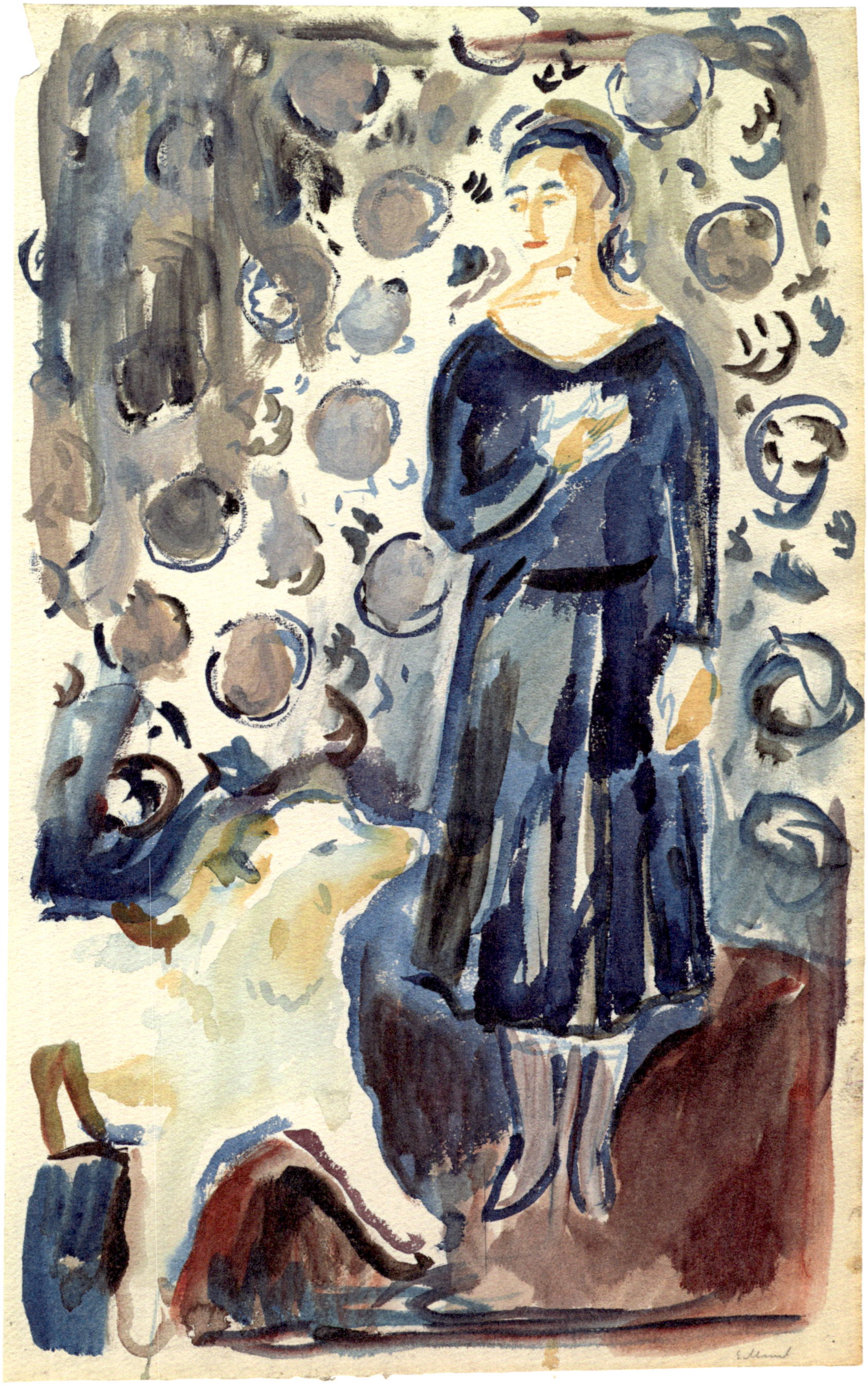

Woman with a Samoyed
1929–30
Watercolour
679 × 424 mm

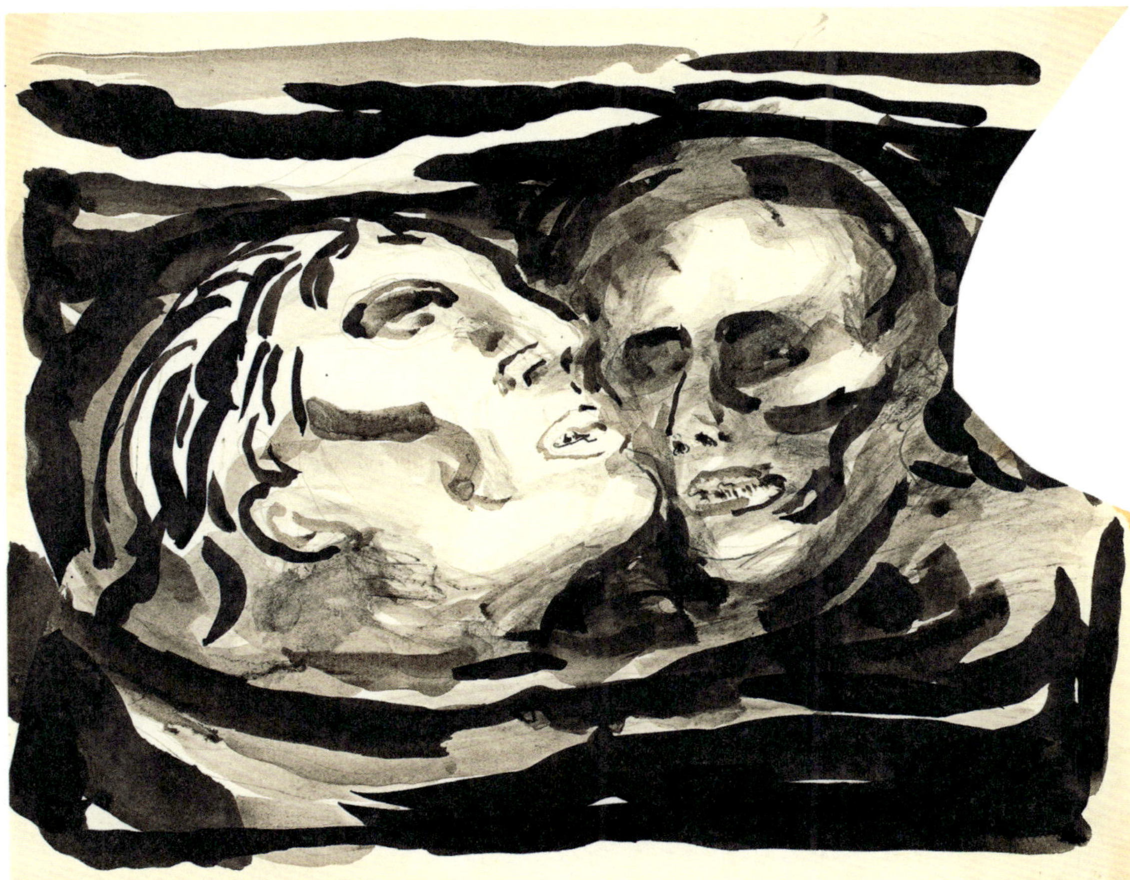

Kiss of Death
1933
Brush and pencil
219 × 282 mm

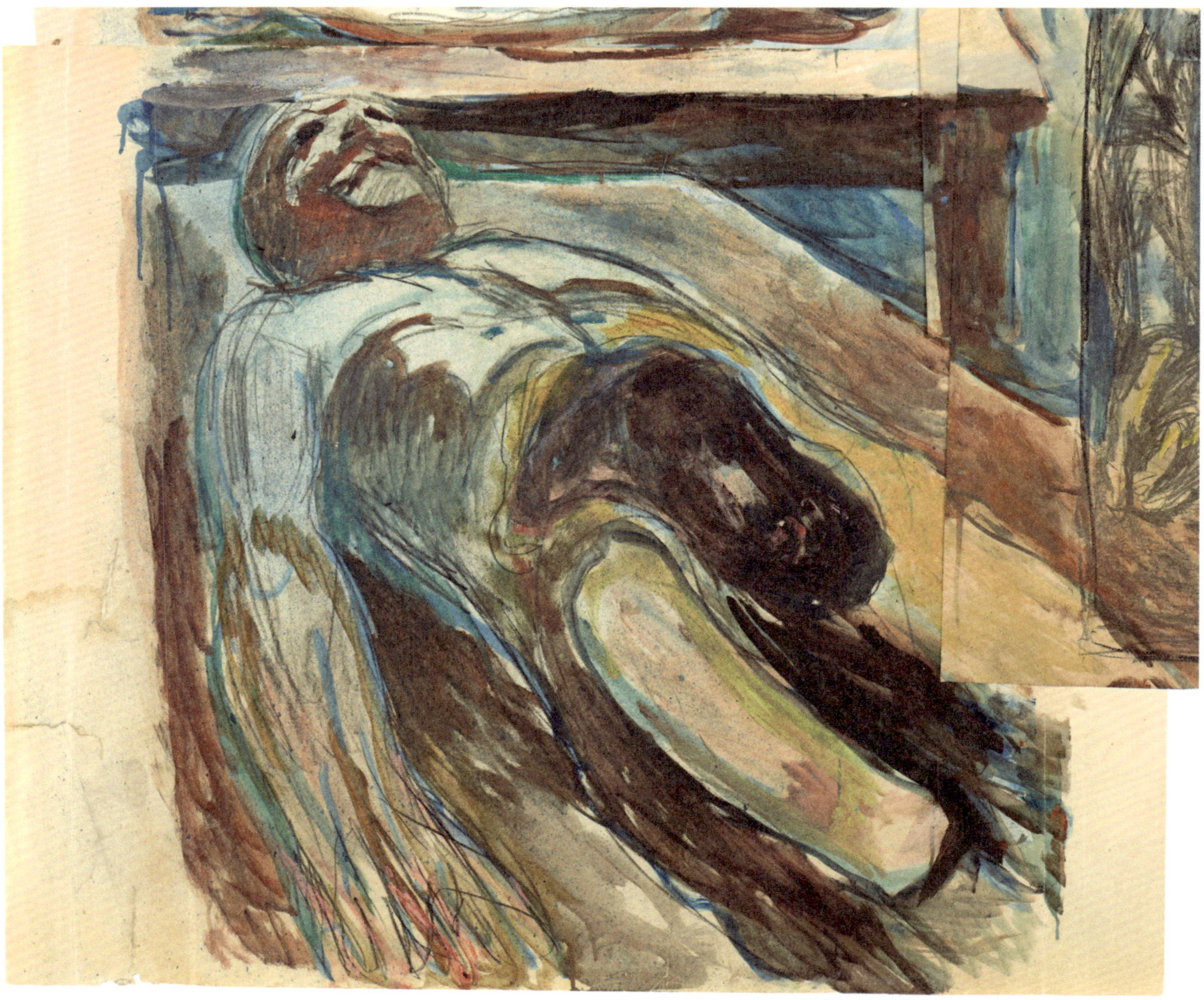

Autopsy of a Male Body
1928–32
Watercolour and charcoal
703 × 865 mm

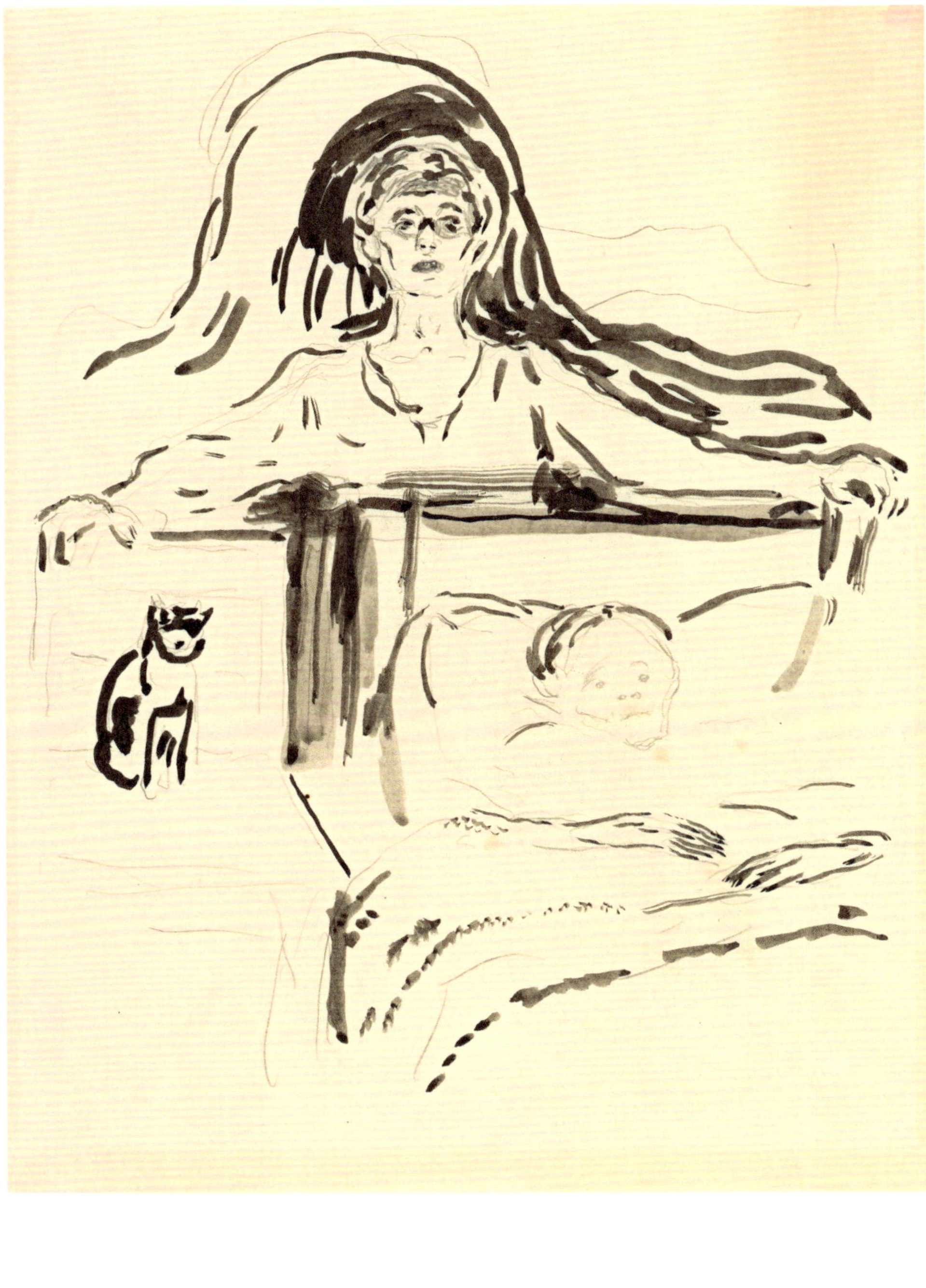

Peer Gynt: Mother Aase's Death
1933
Brush and pencil
282 × 220 mm

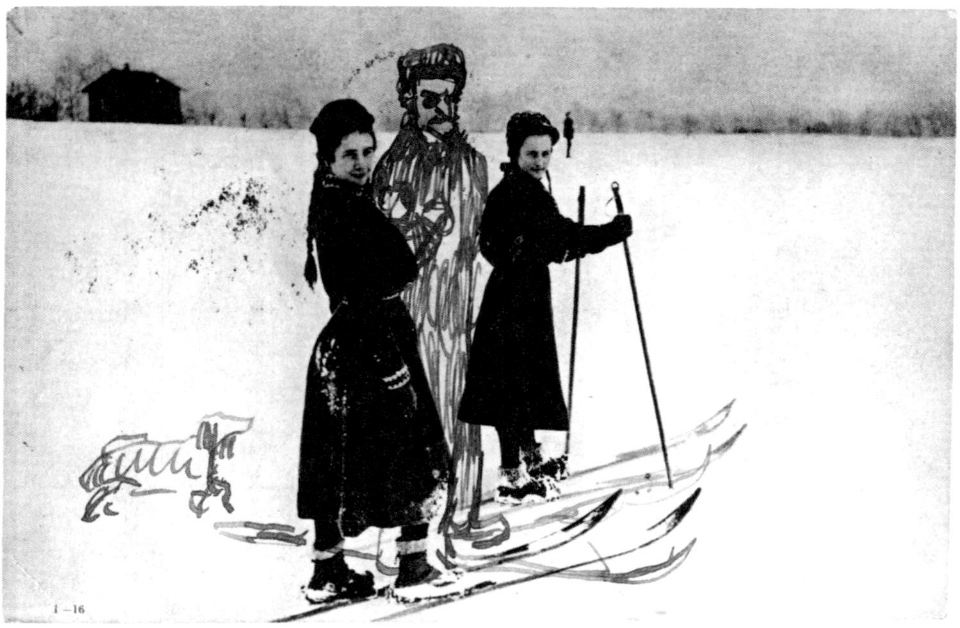

Edvard Munch's drawing of a man on skis and a dog, added to postcard of two women on skis; sent to the artist Thorolf Holmboe as a New Year's greeting on 9 January 1912

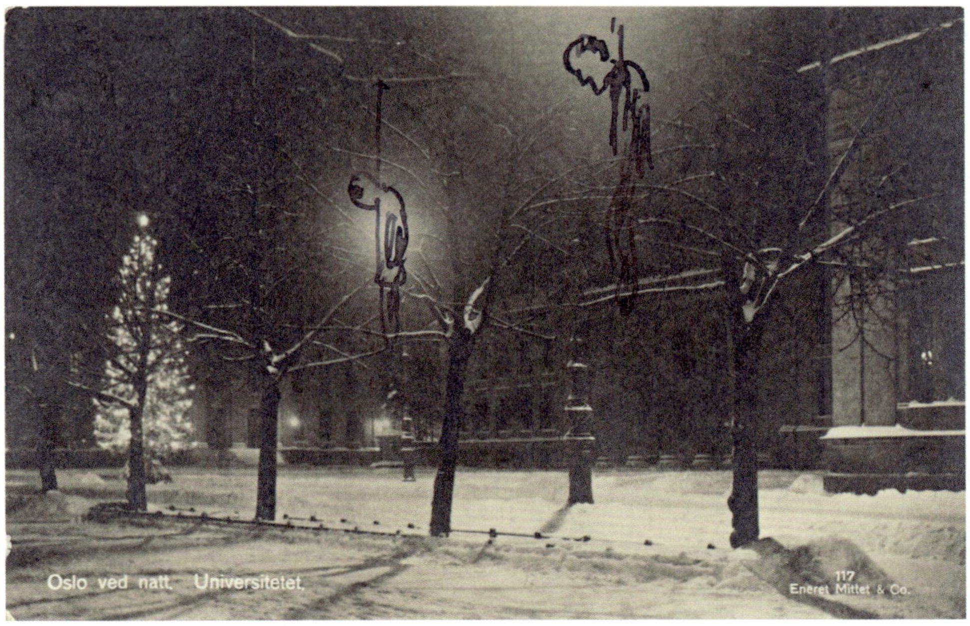

Edvard Munch's drawing of hanged men added to postcard of "Oslo by Night. The University"; sent to the artist Thorolf Holmboe as a New Year's greeting on 31 January 1926

There is No Longer Any Need for Landscapes

Georg Baselitz
interviewed by Jon-Ove Steihaug

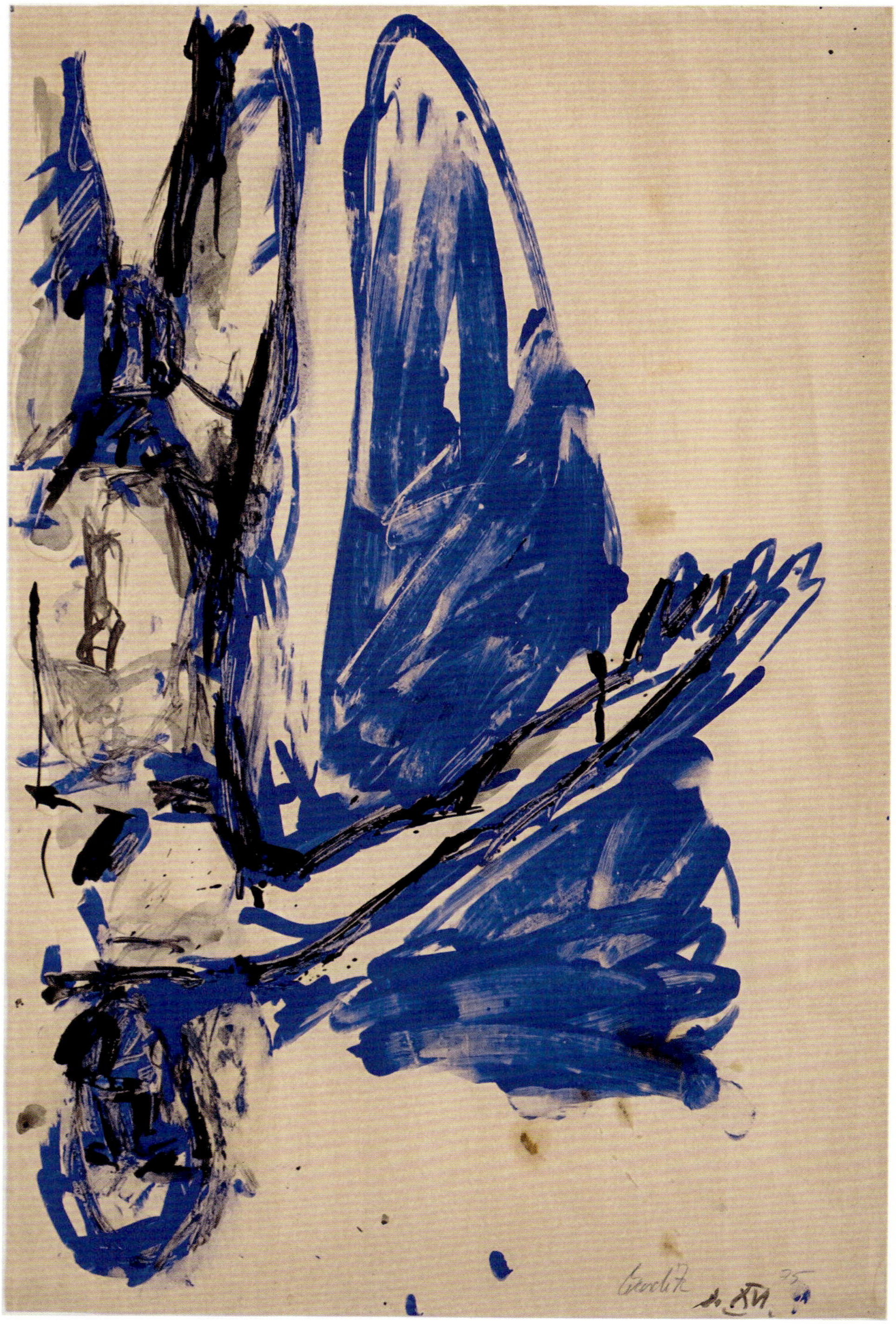

Georg Baselitz
Triangle between Arm and Torso, 1975
Gouache and oil on paper
56 × 40.7 cm

Georg Baselitz grew up in what, from 1949 to 1990, was called GDR or East Germany, and became interested in artistic outsiders such as Antonin Artaud and Carl Fredrik Hill early on. Included among these artists was Edvard Munch. As with Munch, the human figure has remained the most important motif in Baselitz' art. And like Munch, he has also worked concurrently with painting and printmaking, in particular etching, woodcut, linocut and lithography. This interview was done in Baselitz' studio in the vicinity of Ammersee, a half-hour ride from Munich, where he also lives.

Steihaug

Edvard Munch is an artist who has accompanied you for a long time, and whom you also refer to explicitly in a number of works throughout the past forty years. What kind of relationship do you have with Munch and his art?

Baselitz

Strangely enough, I made a few small drawings that resemble Munch's early on – I think it must have been around 1958. Why Munch? Well, because young artists need information; they must be acquainted with both contemporary art and the art of the past, and that information was not available to us in GDR. I had no knowledge of either Klee, Kirchner, Schwitters or Bauhaus. All the same, I must have seen Munch's pictures. I think my father had a calendar with his pictures. He had also seen the exhibition *Entartete Kunst* in Dresden, where several of Munch's works were shown.[1]

Yesterday I found an interesting quote by Goebbels. In the newspaper Tidens Tegn, in honour of Munch's 70th birthday, he wrote: "Edvard Munch's works arise out of the Nordic-Germanic earth and speak to me of the profound gravity of life. His pictures, the landscapes as well as the human representations, are full of profound passion. Munch struggles to grasp nature in all it[s] truthfulness and holds it tight with ruthless disdain for all of the formal academic traits in painting. As a powerful independent spirit – a legacy of Nordic culture – he liberates himself of any form of naturalism and reaches back to the eternal groundwork of folk art."[2]

S

This quote is from 1933?

B

Yes. The Nazis made several attempts to reinstate Munch into their cultural politics after that. Unlike Knut Hamsun, he rejected their overtures. And it was in that connection I saw Munch's art for the first time.

S

And since the beginning of the 1960s Munch has shown up repeatedly in your works. What is it that has continued to interest you throughout all these years?

B

I am actually not interested in academic art history, but am in search of art that I feel an affinity with. For me, the border between North and South is more important than the one that exists between East and West. Although like Scandinavians I set great store by Italian art, it has always been Nordic art that has provided my own work with the most energy. At the same time, I also have a strained relationship with pathos, and when as a German you have a problem with pathos, then you have a big problem! My entire life I have attempted to swim against the current and associated myself with people who were quite unknown, such as Carl Fredrik Hill and Ernst Josephson.

What made Munch interesting was precisely that he took another path. Although he was of course important for art historians, there weren't many artists who were preoccupied with him when I was young. All of the art movements in Germany were about politics, about socialism or communism, but I have never heard Munch say anything about being for a world revolution.

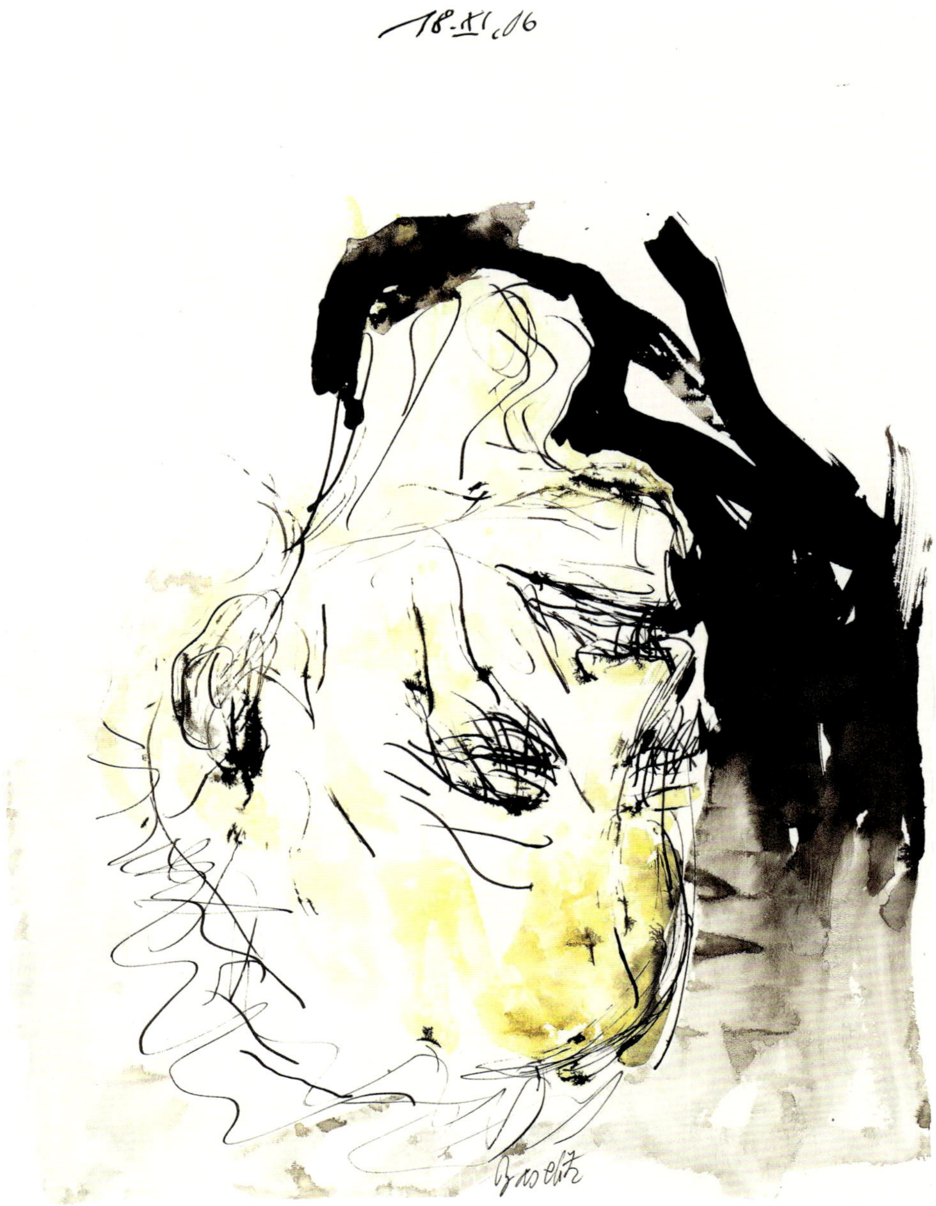

Georg Baselitz
Untitled, 2006
Pen, watercolour and ink on paper
65.4 × 50.5 cm

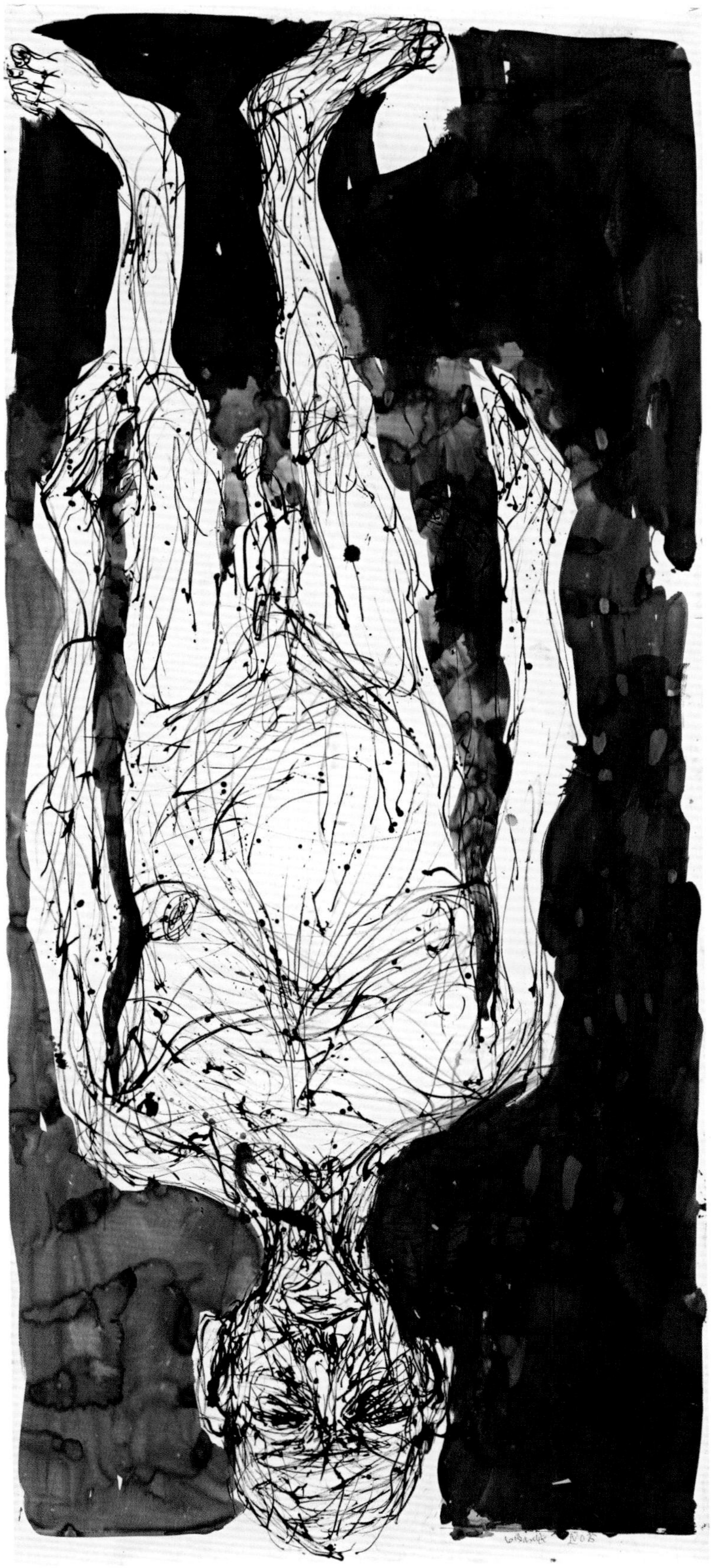

Georg Baselitz
Untitled, 2015
Pen and ink on paper mounted on canvas
331 × 148.5 cm

Around 1982 you painted Munch together with members of the German artist group Die Brücke. Why did you place him together with them? S

He was actually the main person in the group! B

Nevertheless he did not even respond when they invited him to exhibit together with them around 1906? S

Well, why should he? He was proud, and I believe that is a typical Nordic trait. Ernst Ludwig Kirchner was also proud, but Munch was even more so. When I placed him together with the Brücke artists, it was actually as a substitute for Max Beckmann, whom I dislike. B

In West Germany Expressionism experienced a kind of revival during the 1980s among very young artists, often called the "junge Wilden" ("Young wild ones"). Was your painting from the early 80s associated with this movement in any way? S

No, the "junge Wilden" were not really aware of the German expressionist tradition; they attempted to paint like Kirchner, but didn't have any real understanding of his art. For me, it had to do with the feeling that I had forgotten something. It had to do with the lack of knowledge about who artists like Kirchner were. One day in the mid-1970s, when I was a professor at the art academy in Karlsruhe, I went into the museum to have a look at Emil Nolde. I immediately became greatly excited. His paintings were utterly insane! Before that I had actually rejected Expressionism. B

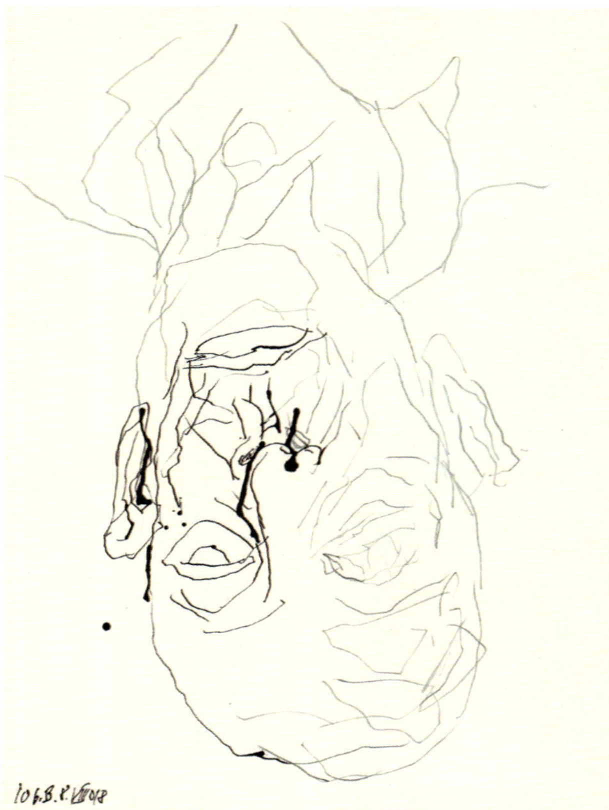

Georg Baselitz
io, 2018
Pencil and pen on paper
66.4 × 50.4 cm

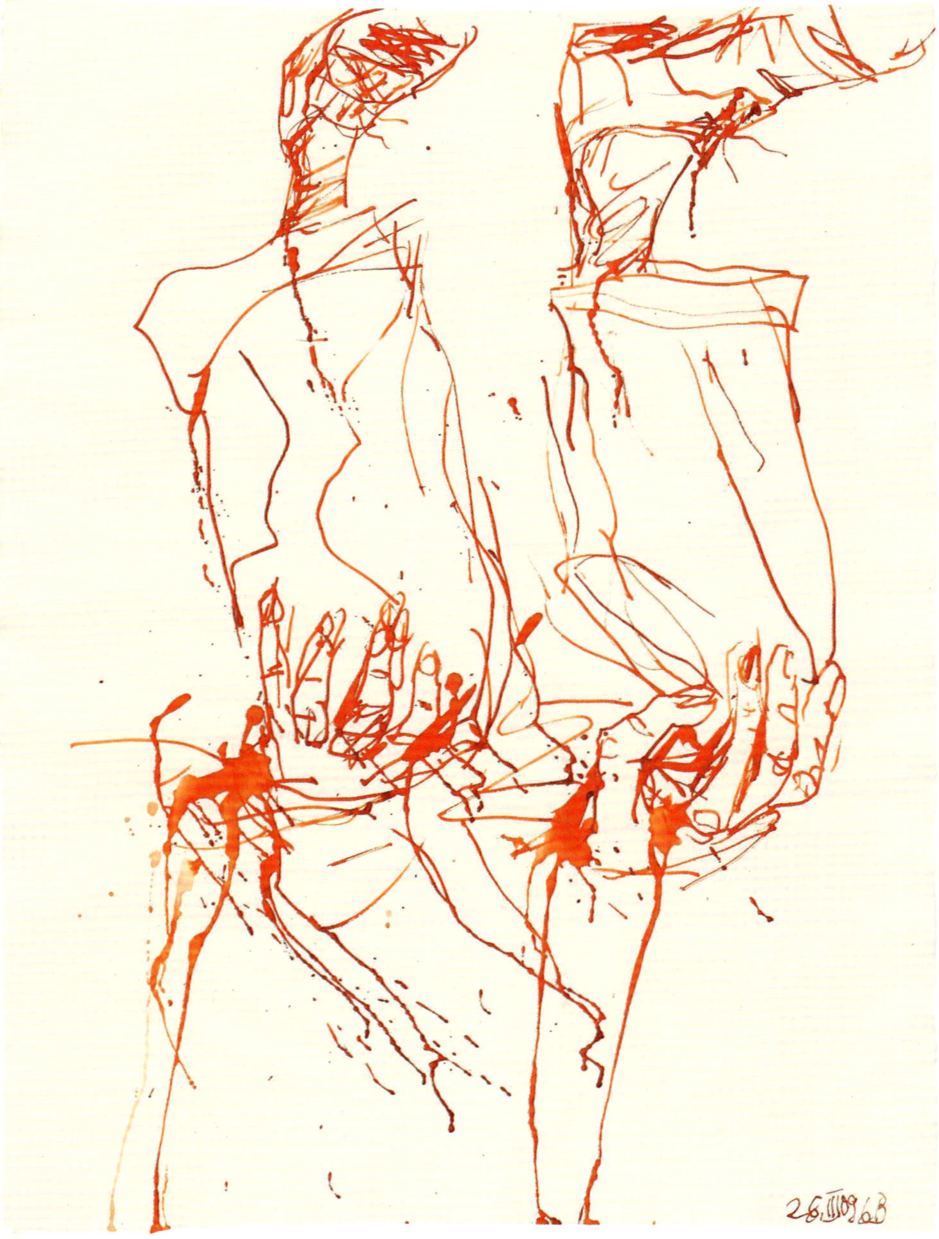

Georg Baselitz
Blue North, 2009
Pen on paper
67 × 50.8 cm

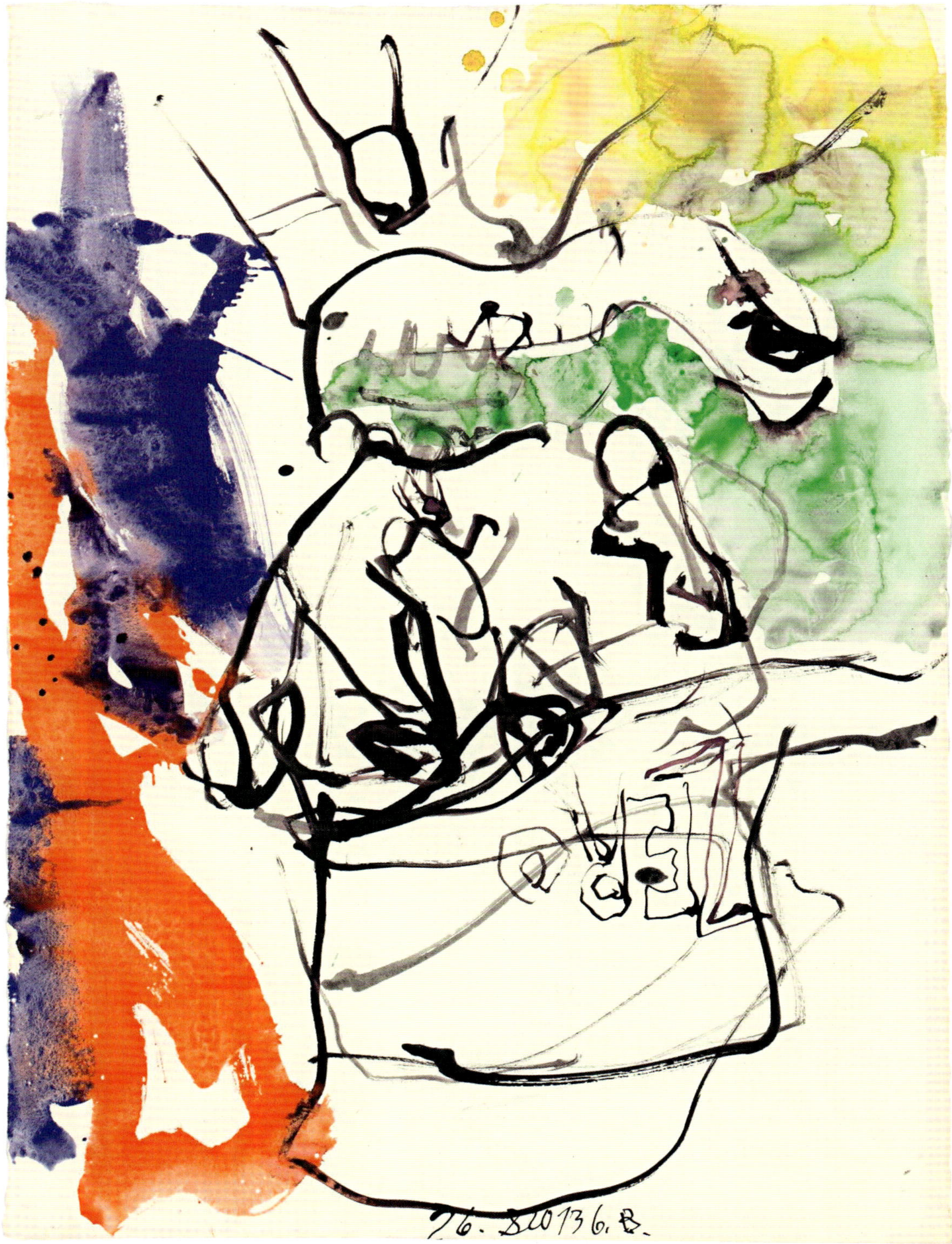

Georg Baselitz
Untitled, 2013
Ink wash and watercolour on paper
66 × 50.4 cm

S We have invited you to make a selection of Munch's drawings, and you have only chosen self-portraits.

B Yes, and there is a natural explanation for that. I have always been interested in self-portraits. Kirchner made self-portraits from first to last, and one can thus see the passing of time and the process of maturing and aging in his pictures. In Munch one can see how he develops his skills as a painter and draughtsman, and at the same time he has depicted physical decline as almost no one else. In that case, it would have to be the self-portraits Otto Dix made after he had a stroke.

I feel that I am doing the same thing now that I have become old. You no longer direct your gaze outwards; there is no longer any need for landscapes. This hermetic aspect of art I think is interesting. So for me the most significant pictures by Munch are not *Starry Night*, *The Sick Child*, *Jealousy* or *The Death of the Bohemian*, although they are fantastic. The most important thing is the development one can see in the series of self-observations, which continue all the way up to Munch's death.

S How have you treated the increased vulnerability and awareness of death that comes with age in your works?

B This is a theme that continues to interest me. Strangely enough I have worked more than usual in recent years. By that I mean that I work with increased intensity and greater pleasure than before. Age has given me greater freedom and made me less dependent on having to relate to new information. At the same time I have totally lost interest in depicting myself. I experience that my works are now more about reflecting a state of being rather than depicting myself. What I think about instead are other artists whom I like, and whom I cite in my pictures – whether it is their forms, textures, formal aspects, handwriting or style.

S You have often painted and drawn yourself together with your wife?

B When I visited the National Gallery of Art in Washington D.C. and saw Jacques-Louis David's portrait of his wife, I was very moved. You can see right away that it is David who is the artist, and yet the portrait is devoid of any pomposity. What one sees is a woman who was loved. After that I have come to the realisation that every artistic career has a private and a public side. In my own art it feels as though the public side has completely fallen away. As an artist I have always been interested in my close family, and among them my wife has the most important and noticeable role. But I have also painted dogs. [Baselitz laughs.] I have continued to paint them; perhaps their number has increased over the years.

S Did you find any surprises among Munch's drawings?

B Many of them I have not seen before, but the last of the self-portraits he drew surprised me in particular. There are some in which Munch appears proud; in others he appears sick and miserable. Such as this seated self-portrait, it is quite ruthless. The body is bluish-white and the head is red, while the beard has turned grey (p. 169). Picasso incidentally made some self-portraits in which he nearly resembles a skeleton and almost looks like he has lost his mind, with large, glaring eyes. Munch, on the other hand, retained all of his abilities until the very end. He just became more relaxed.

Can you say anything more about the selection in conclusion? S

I have not considered whether the drawings are beautiful or good. That has never interested me. I have tried to limit the selection to include simple drawings, without any artistic tricks. I wanted to show how someone has attempted to depict something – a person – with simple means. It is of course a bit strict in a way, and others would surely go after other criteria. I really don't have anything more to say about it. B

1 *Entartete Kunst* was a Nazi organised propaganda exhibition, whose aim was to ridicule so-called "degenerate" art, which encompassed a number of different trends within experimental modernistic art. The exhibition opened in Munich in 1937, at the same time as *Die Große Deutsche Kunstausstellung*, an exhibition showing artwork that was approved by the regime. In occupied Norway a similar exhibition was shown in the National Gallery in 1942, under the title *Kunst og ukunst*, but here Munch was placed among the "approved" artists.

2 Joseph Goebbels, "Det nye Tyskland hilser Edvard Munch", Tidens Tegn, 12 December 1933. Goebbels' text was printed among several surveys in honour of Munch's 70th birthday.

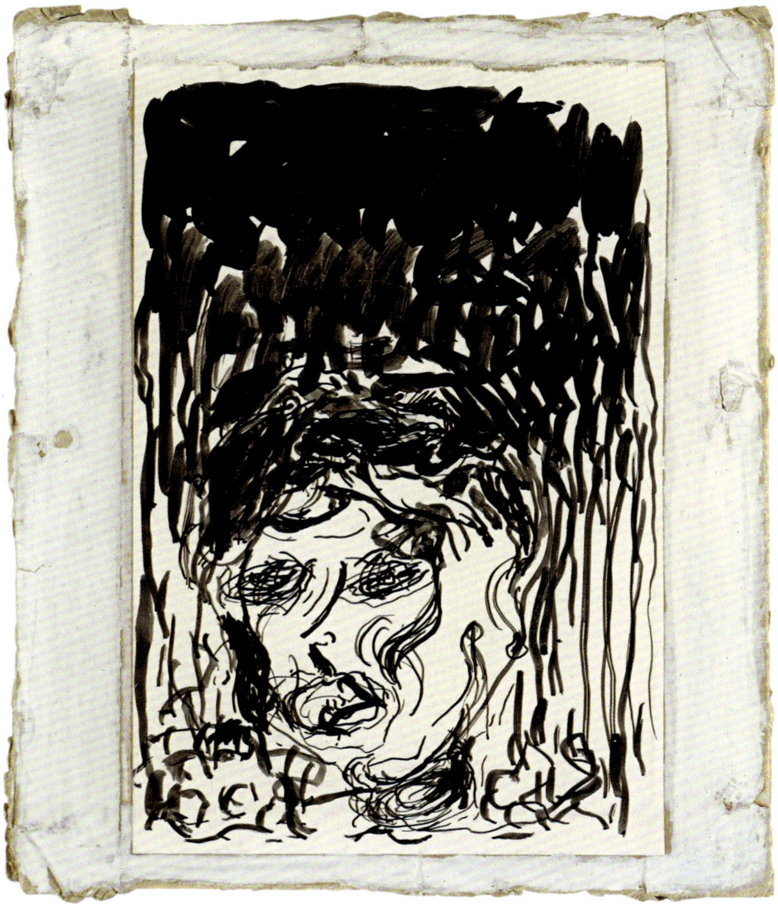

155

Georg Baselitz
Head (Munch), 1960
Pen and ink on paper, and opaque white on cardboard
15.5 × 10.4 cm

Baselitz chooses Munch

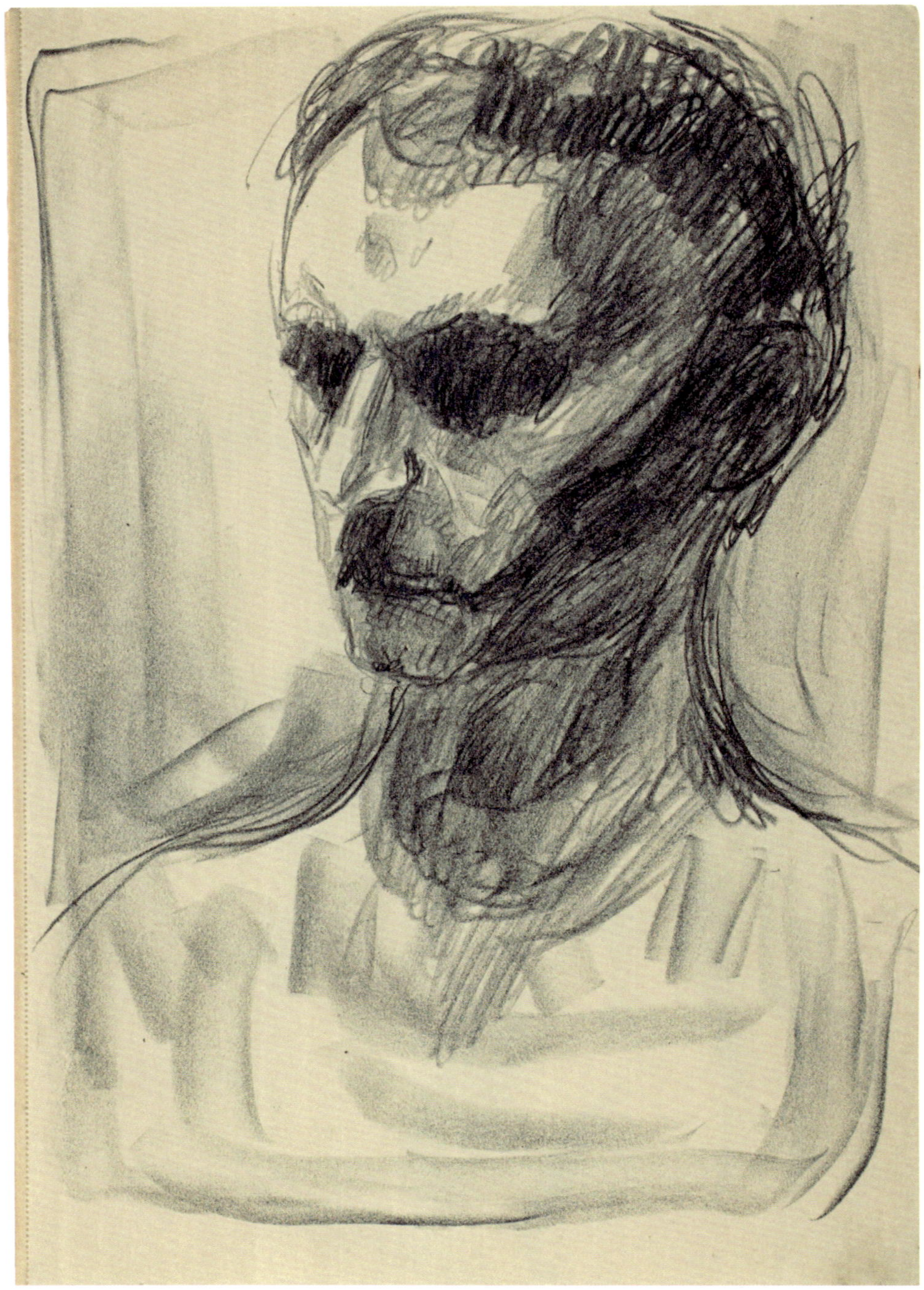

Male Head. Self-Portrait(?)
1913–15
Crayon
400 × 281 mm

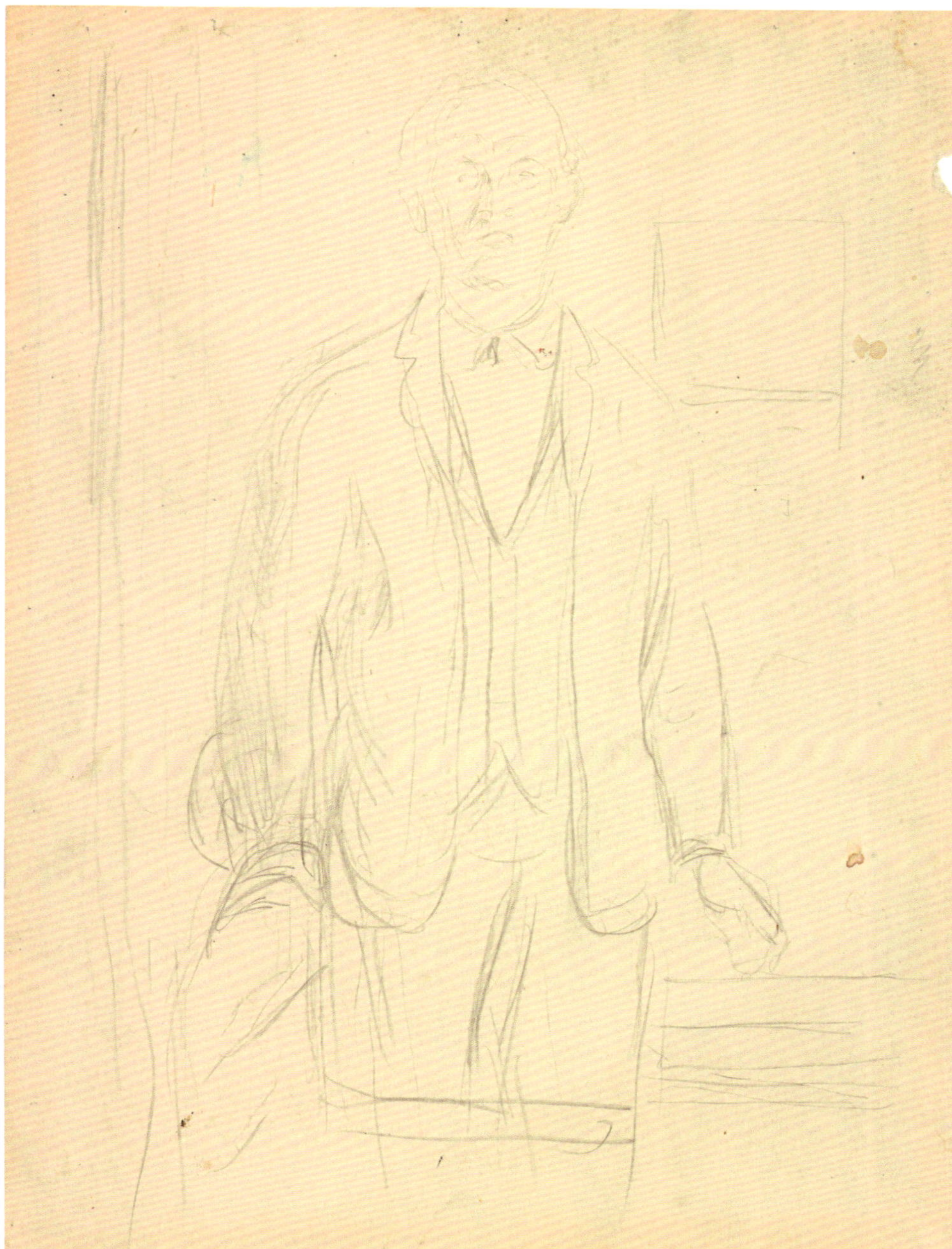

Sketch for *Between the Clock and the Bed*
1940–43
Charcoal
652 × 498 mm

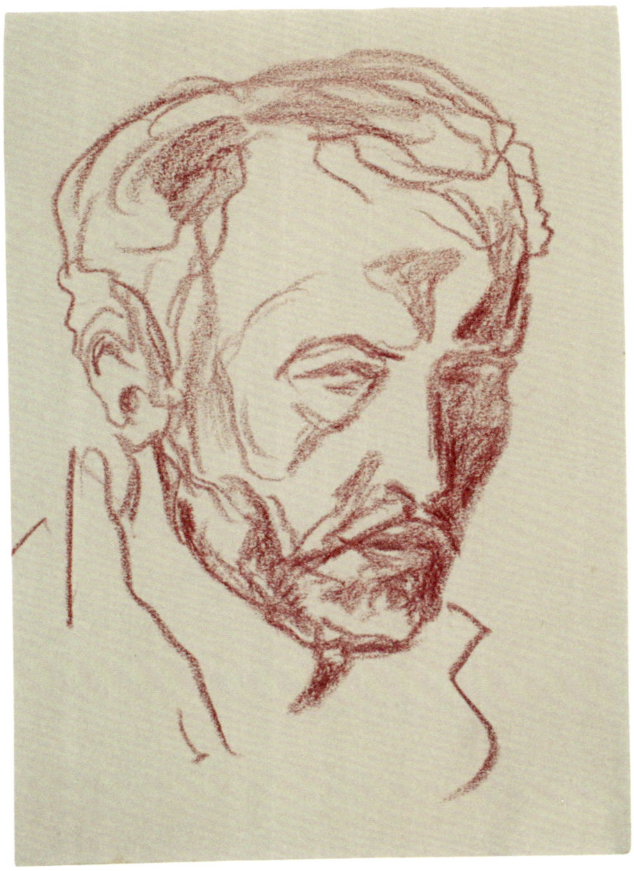

Self-Portrait
1919
Crayon
184 × 132 mm

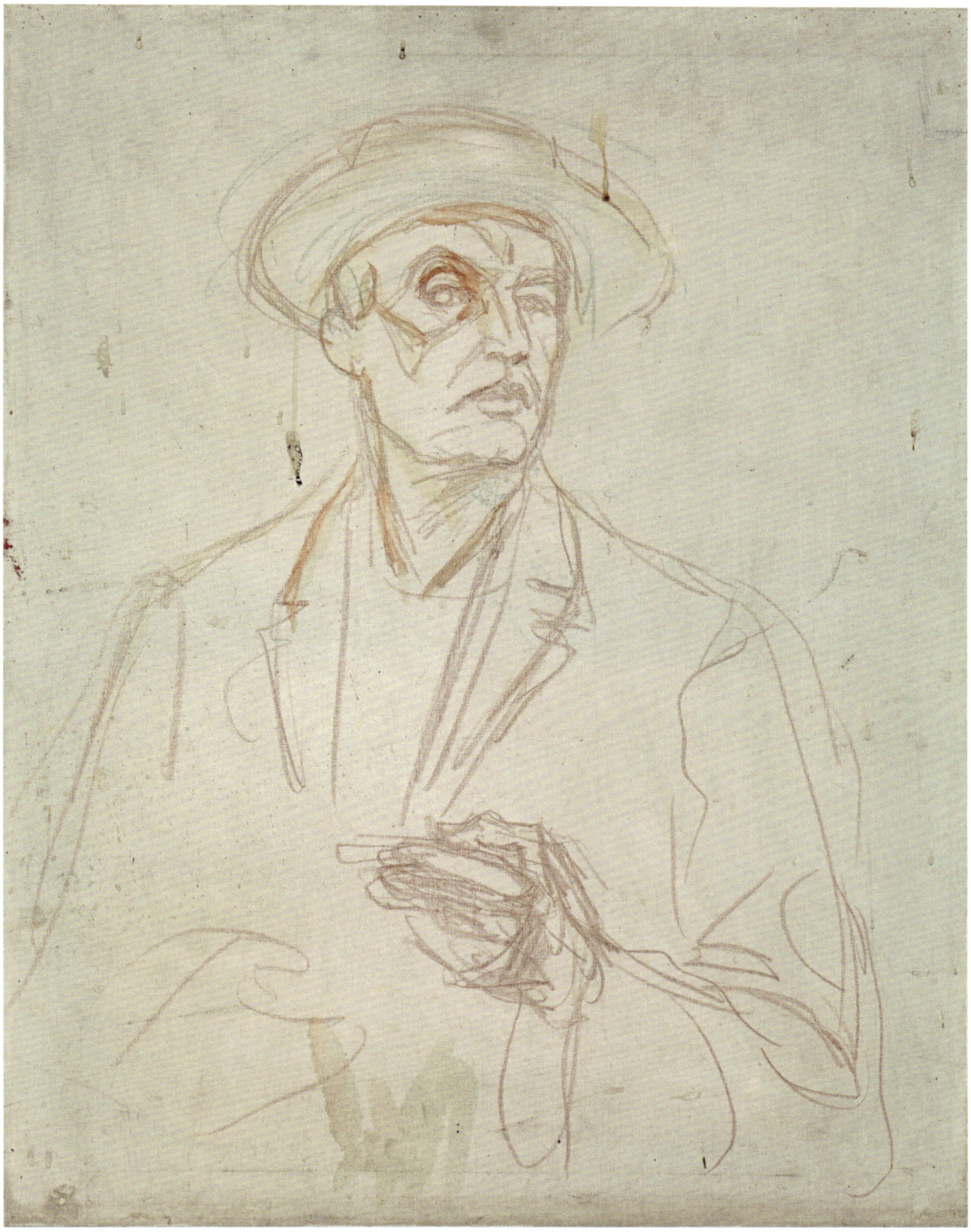

Self-Portrait with Afflicted Eye
1930
Charcoal, oil and crayon(?)
90 × 72 cm

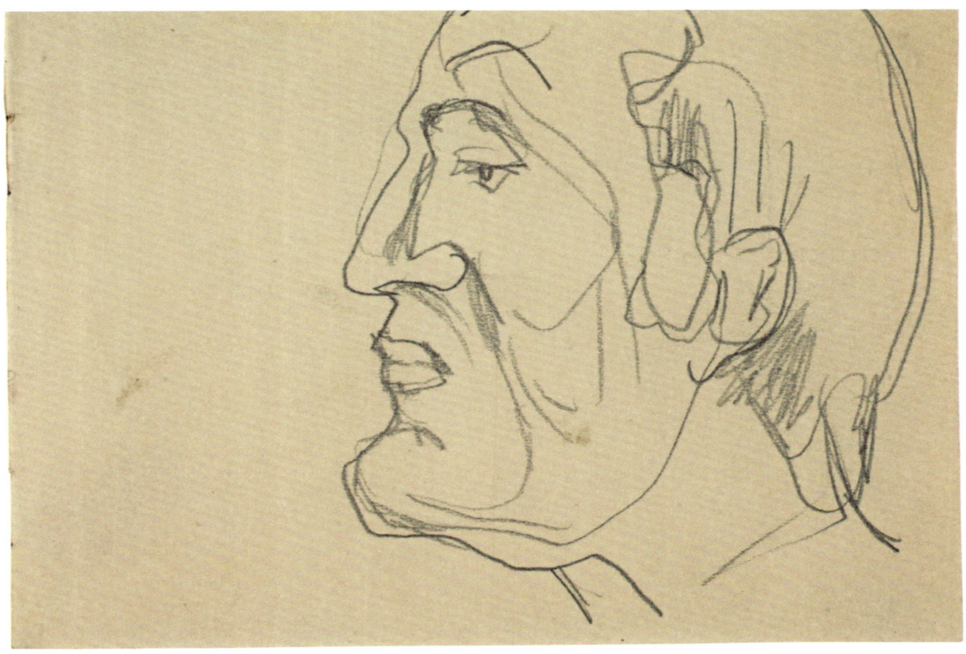

Self-Portrait in Profile
1918
Pencil
128 × 163 mm

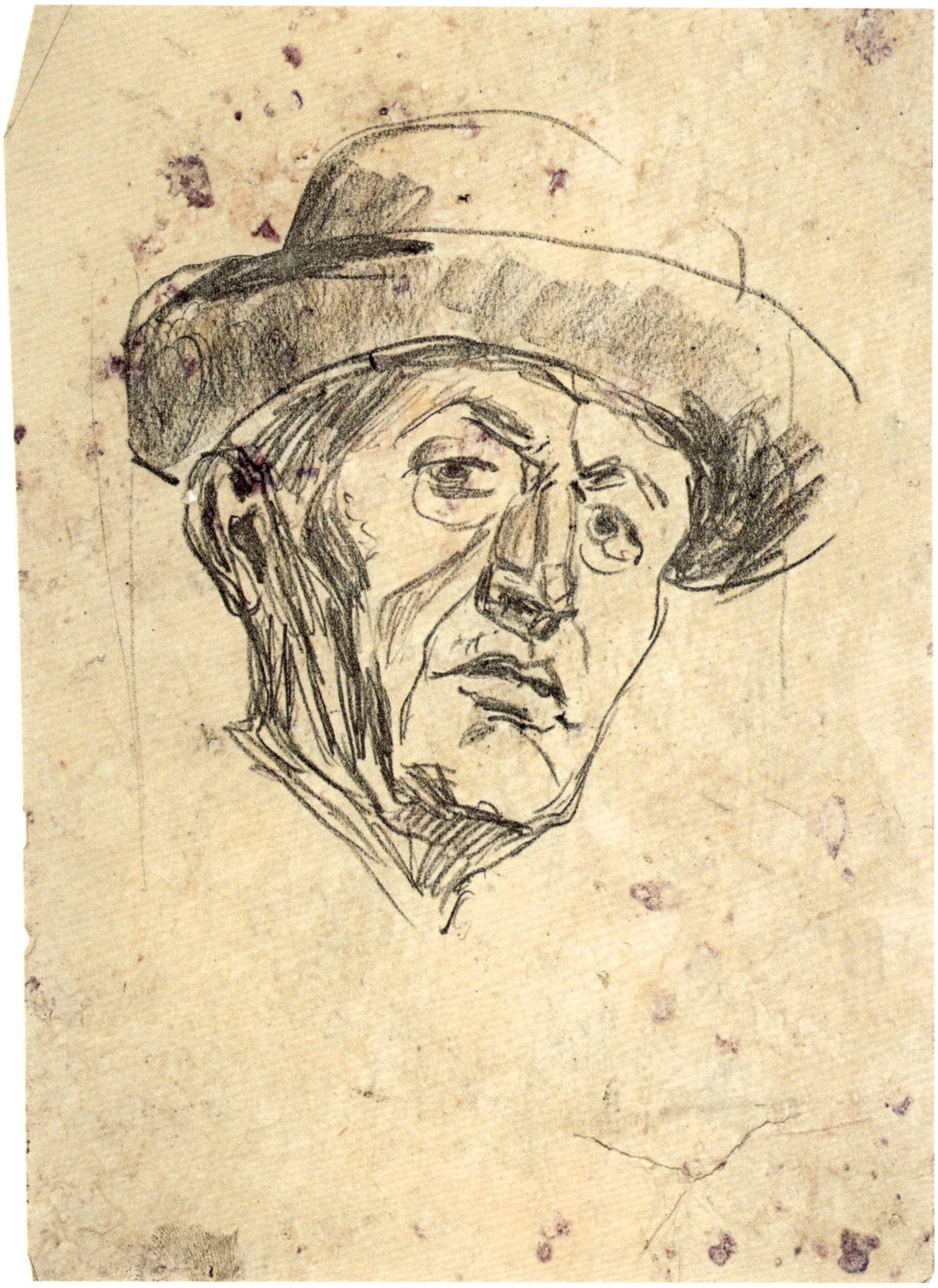

Original drawing for *Self-Portrait with Hat I*
1927
Crayon
328 × 220 mm

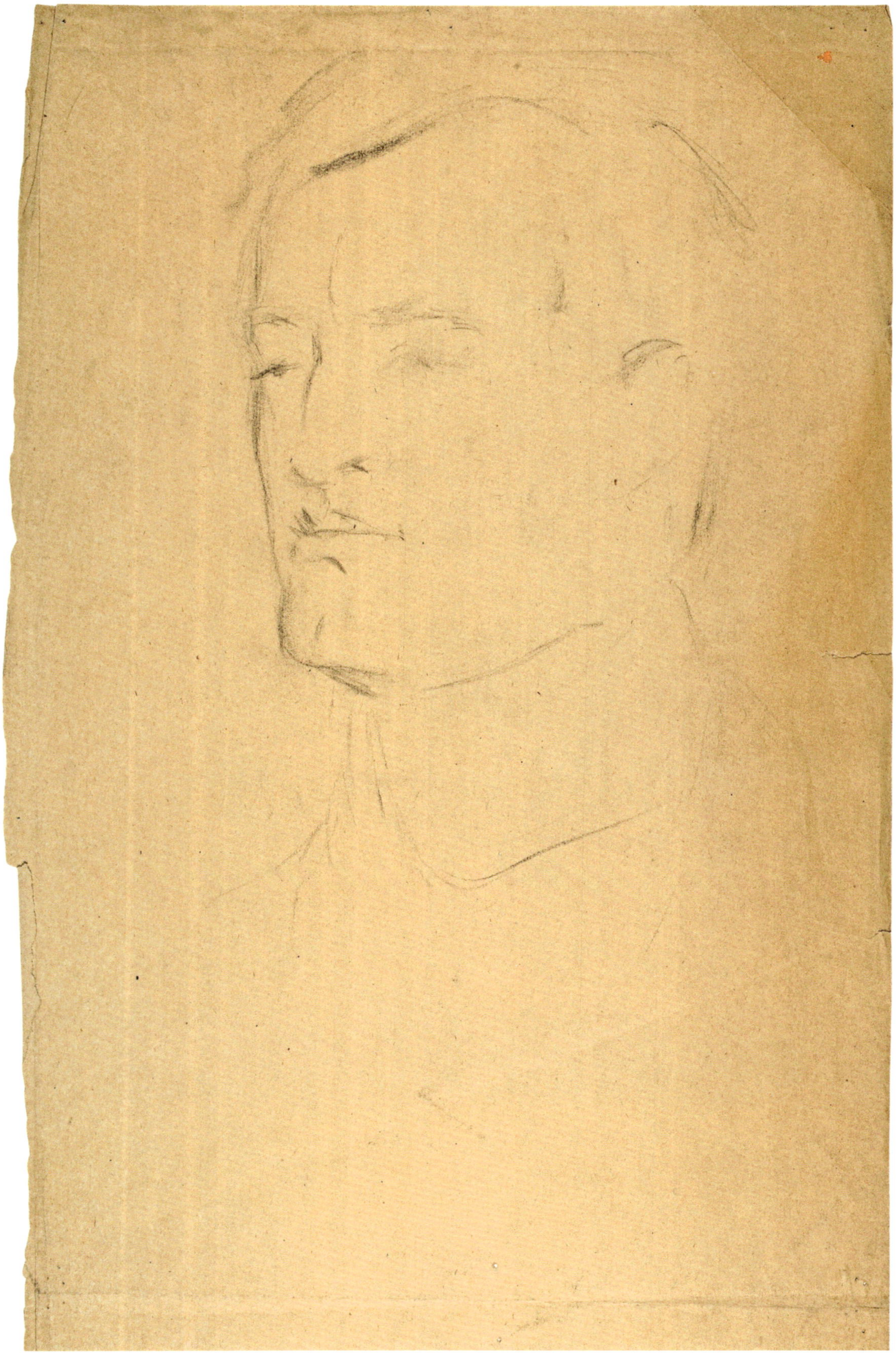

Self-Portrait
c. 1905
Charcoal
564 × 346 mm

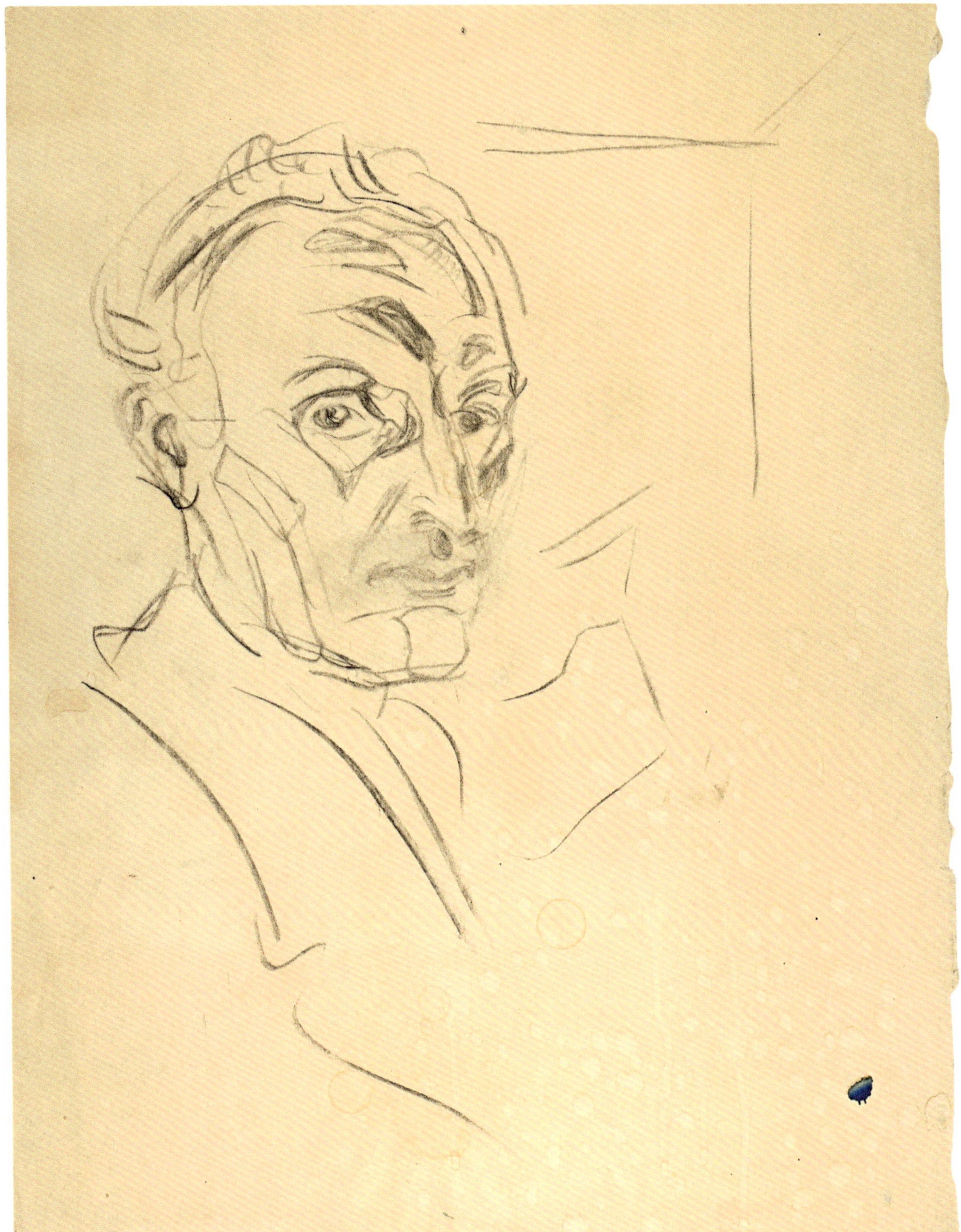

Self-Portrait
c. 1925
Charcoal
598 × 462 mm

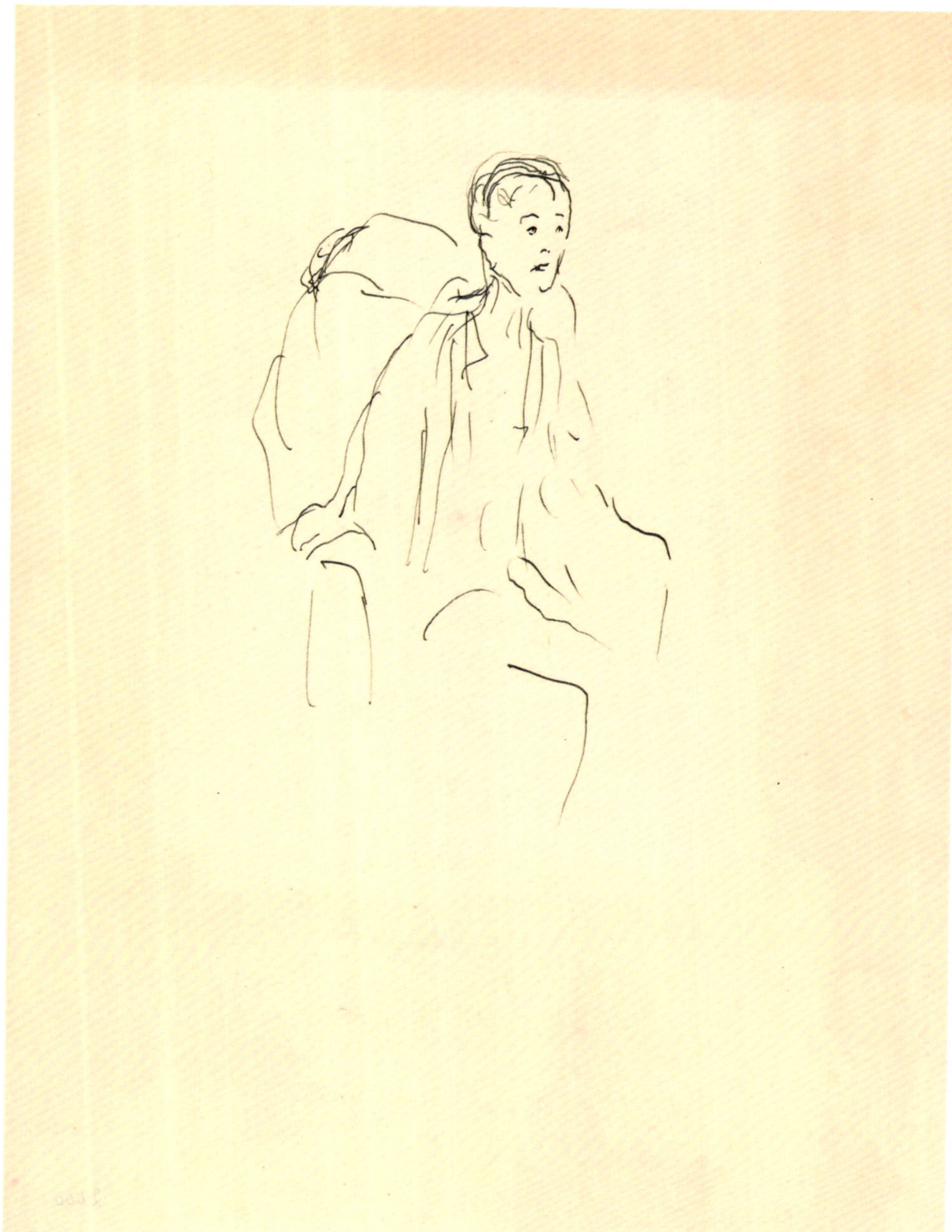

Rising from the Chair
1932–34
Pen
292 × 224 mm

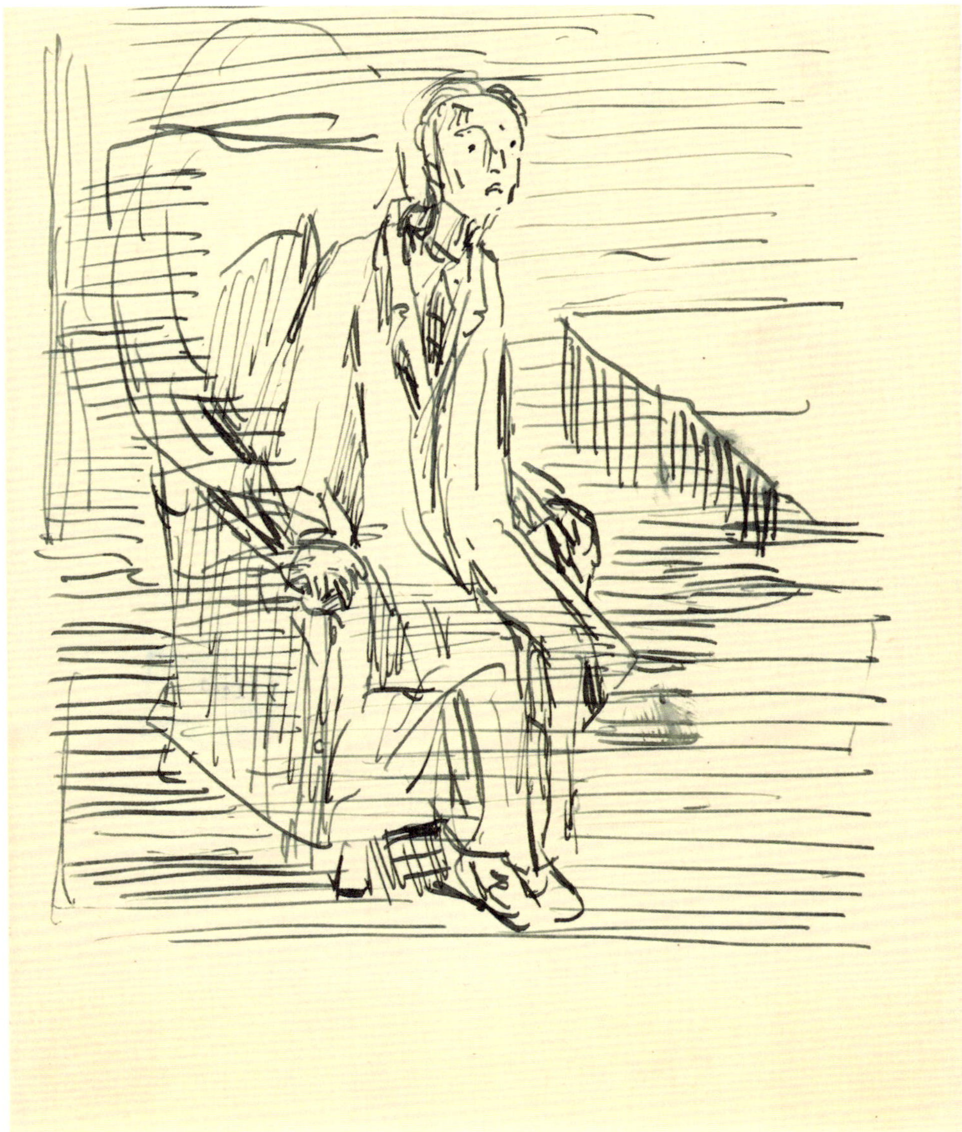

Rising from the Chair
1932–34
Pen
275 × 216 mm

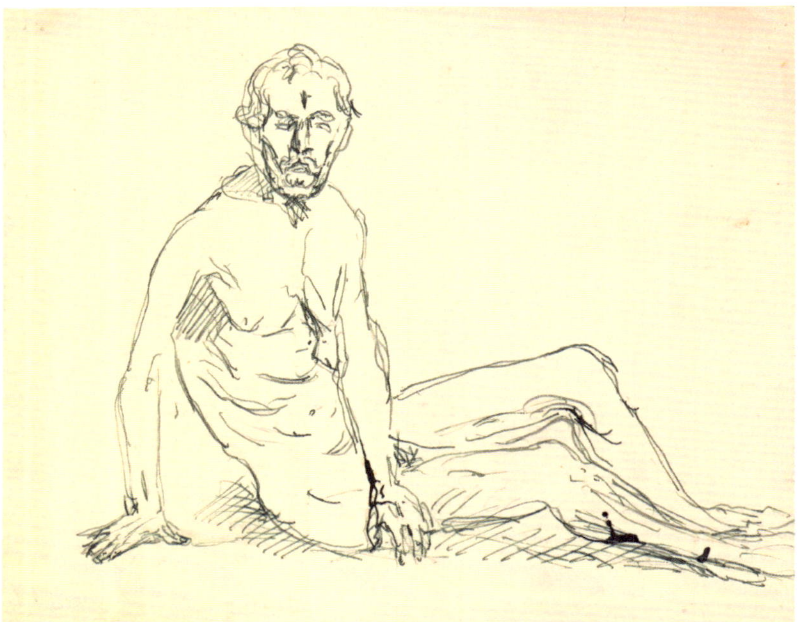

Seated Male Nude. Self-Portrait
1933–34
Pen and pencil
216 × 275 mm

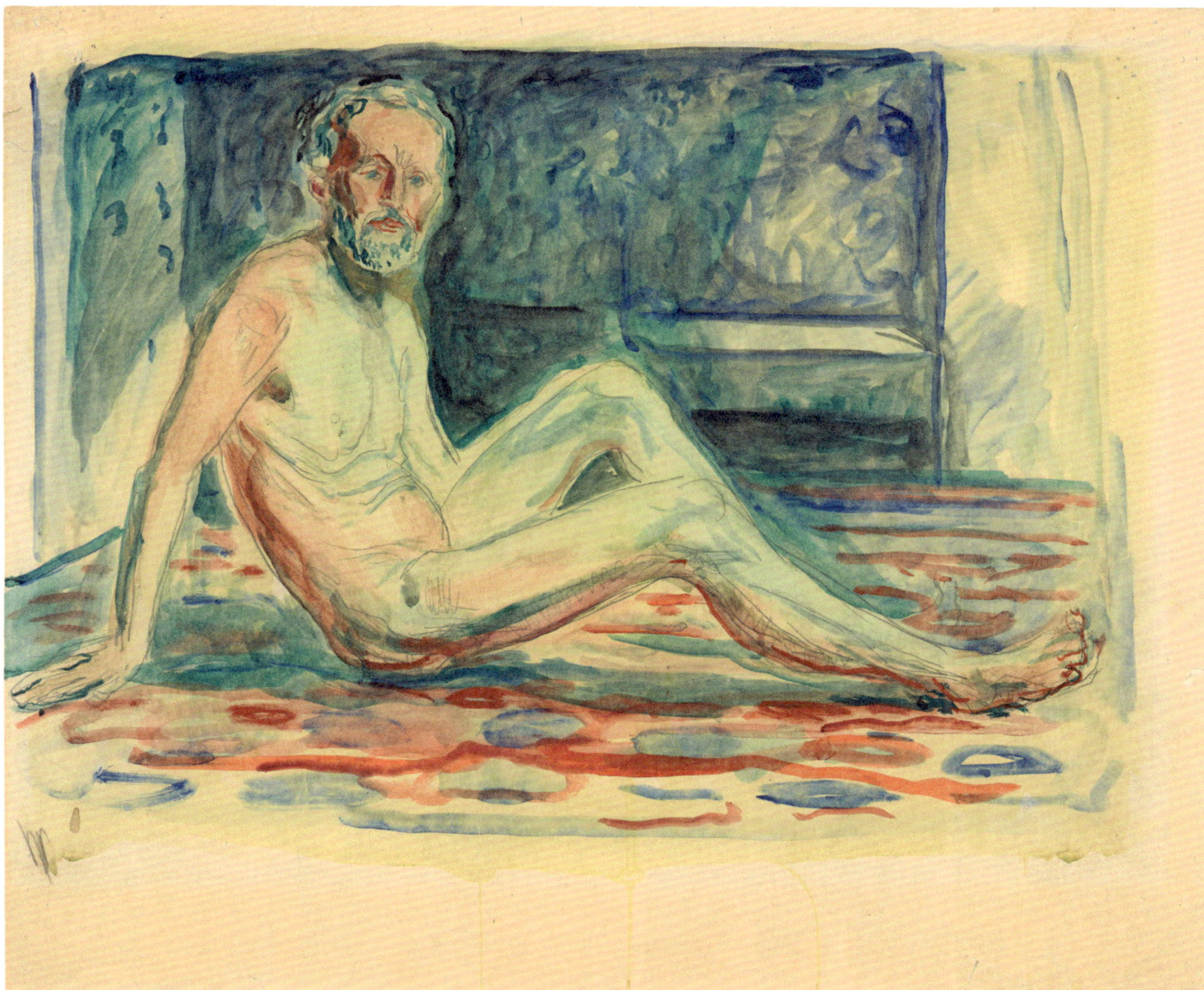

Self-Portrait, Sitting on the Floor
1921–35
Watercolour and pencil
700 × 862 mm

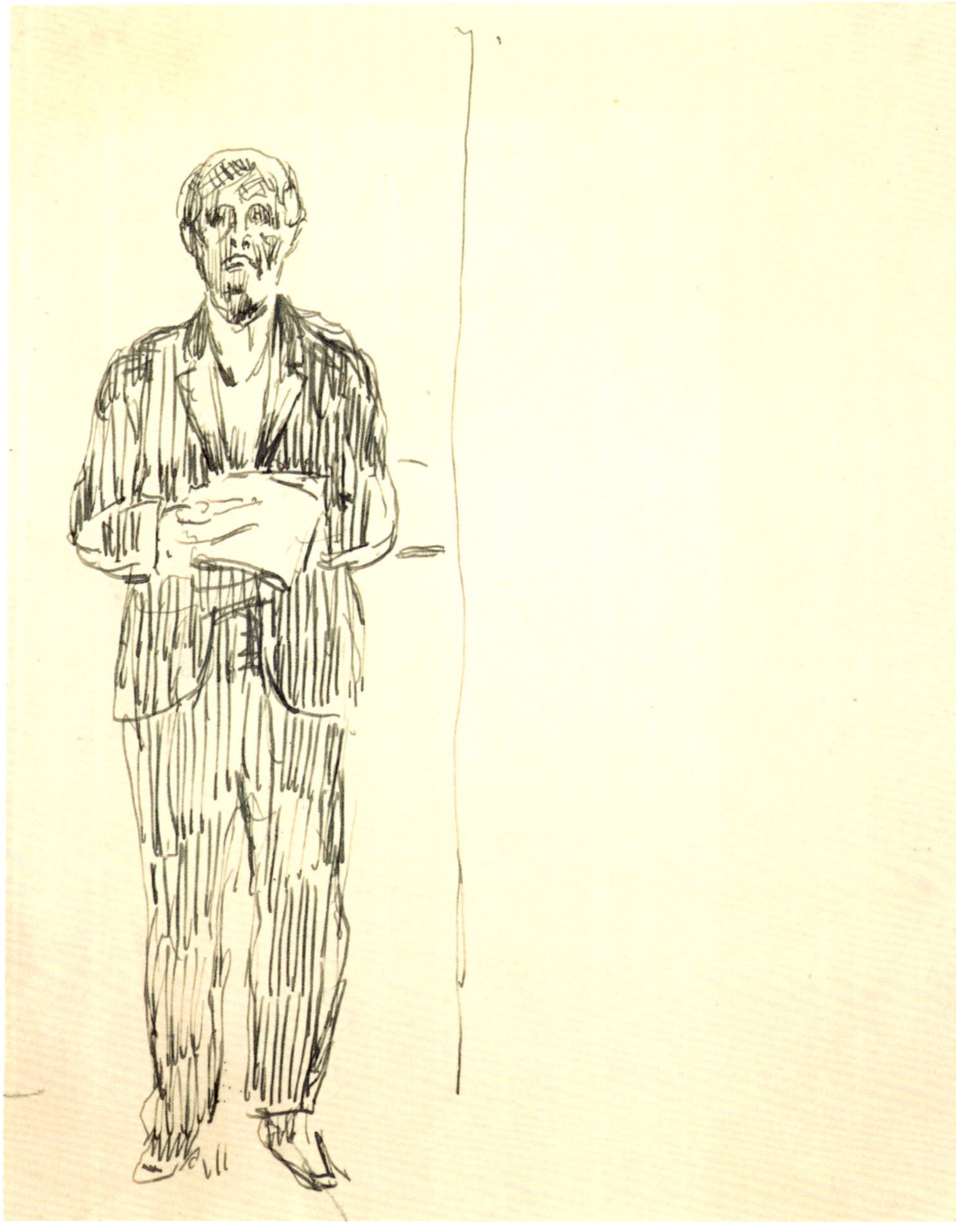

Self-Portrait, Standing
c. 1940
Ink
279 × 220 mm

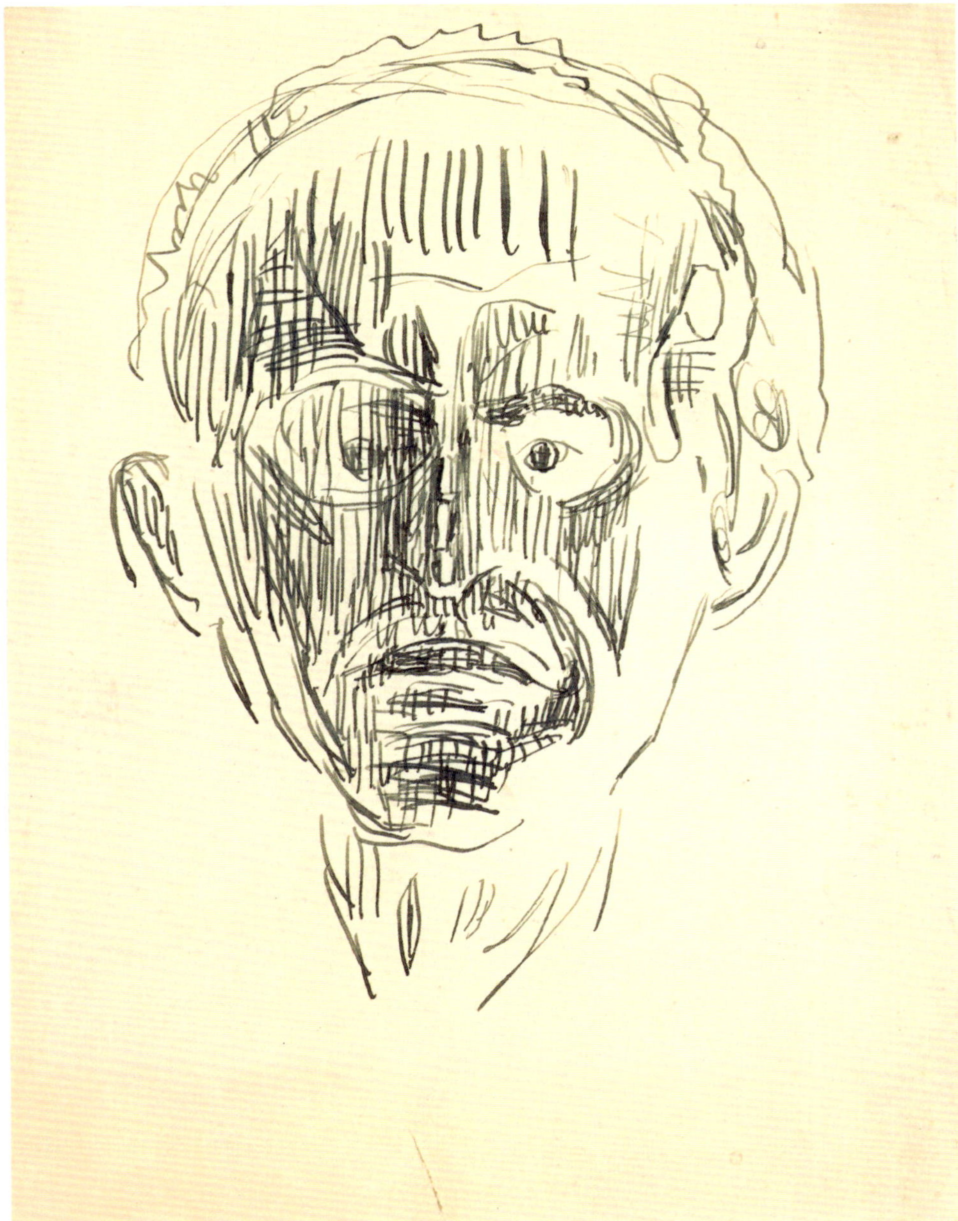

Self-Portrait
c. 1940
Pen
276 × 215 mm

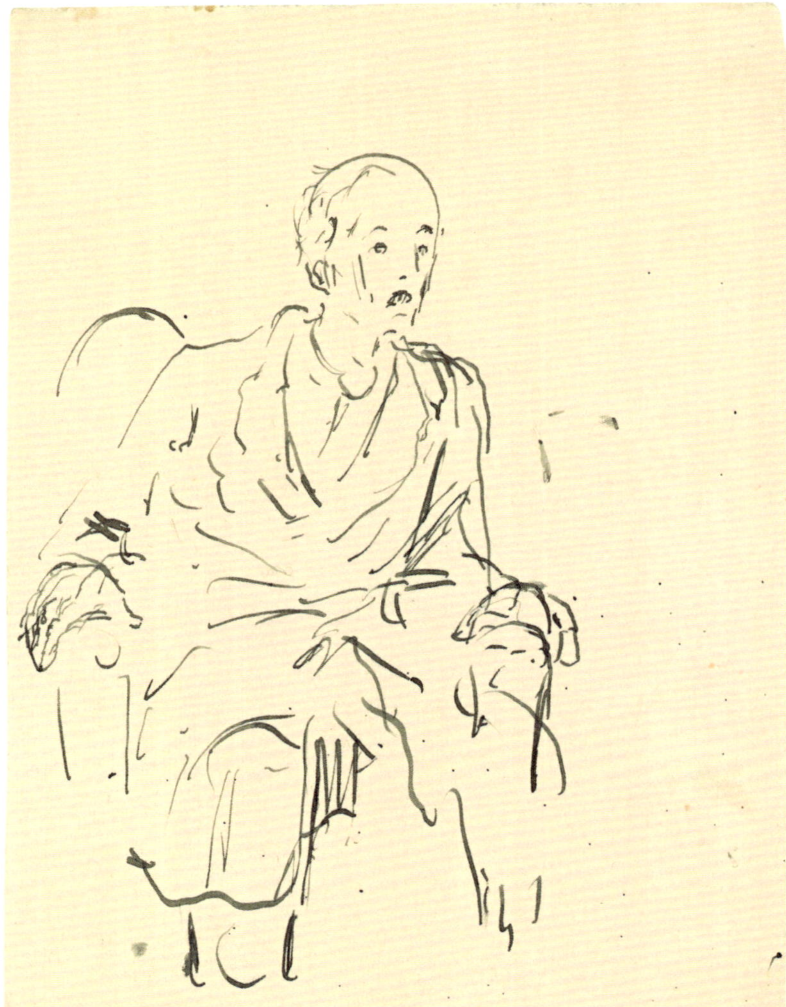

Rising from the Chair
1932–34
Pen
226 × 175 mm

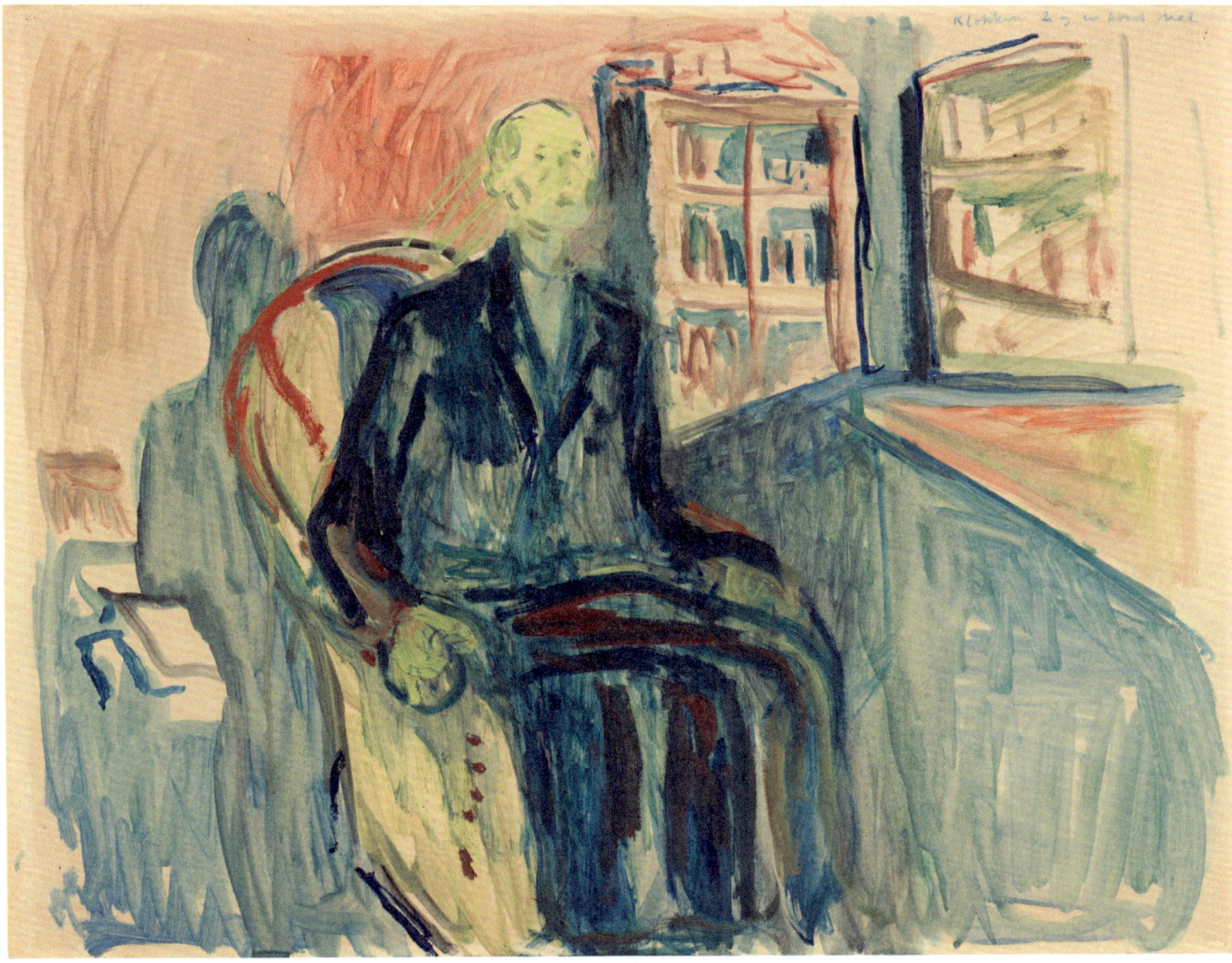

Self-Portrait. Quarter Past Two in the Morning
1940–43
Watercolour and gouache
302 × 500 mm

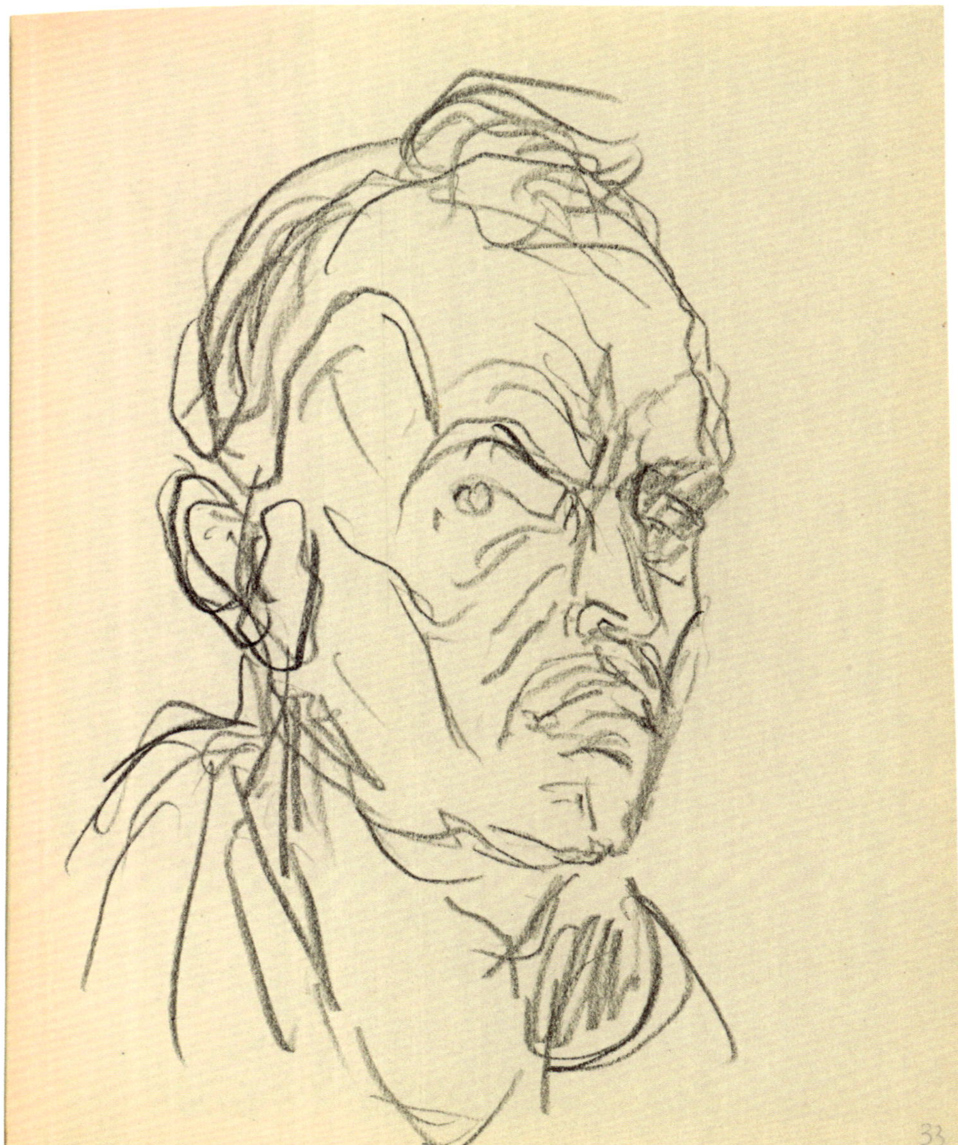

Self-Portrait
1920–30
Crayon
205 × 176 mm

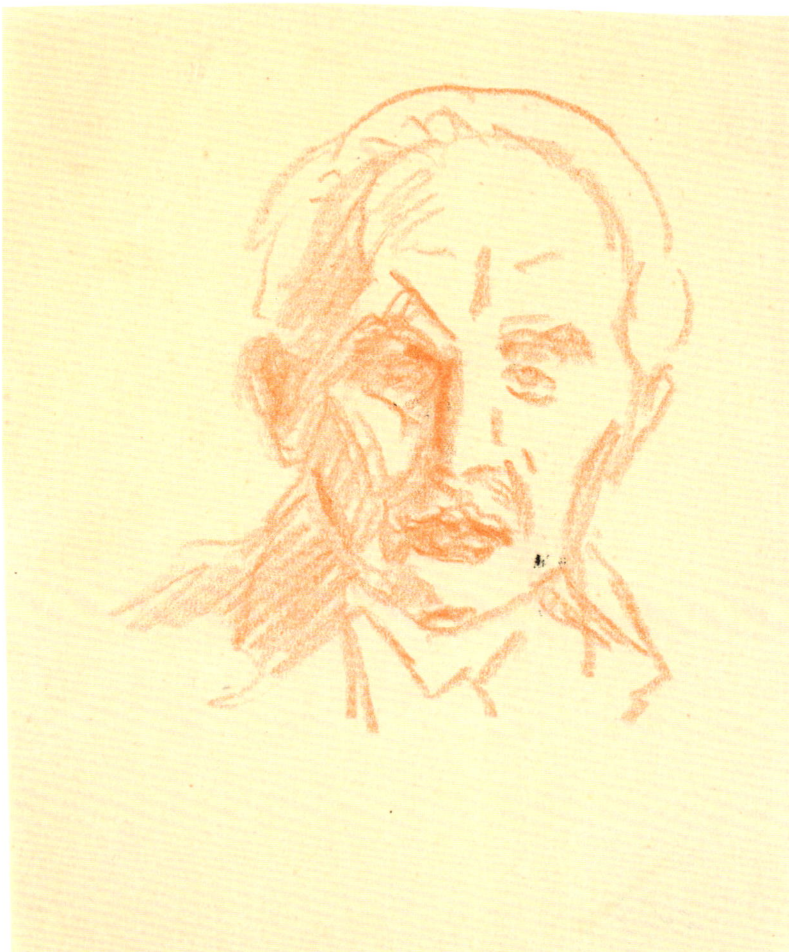

Self-Portrait
c. 1935
Crayon
142 × 115 mm

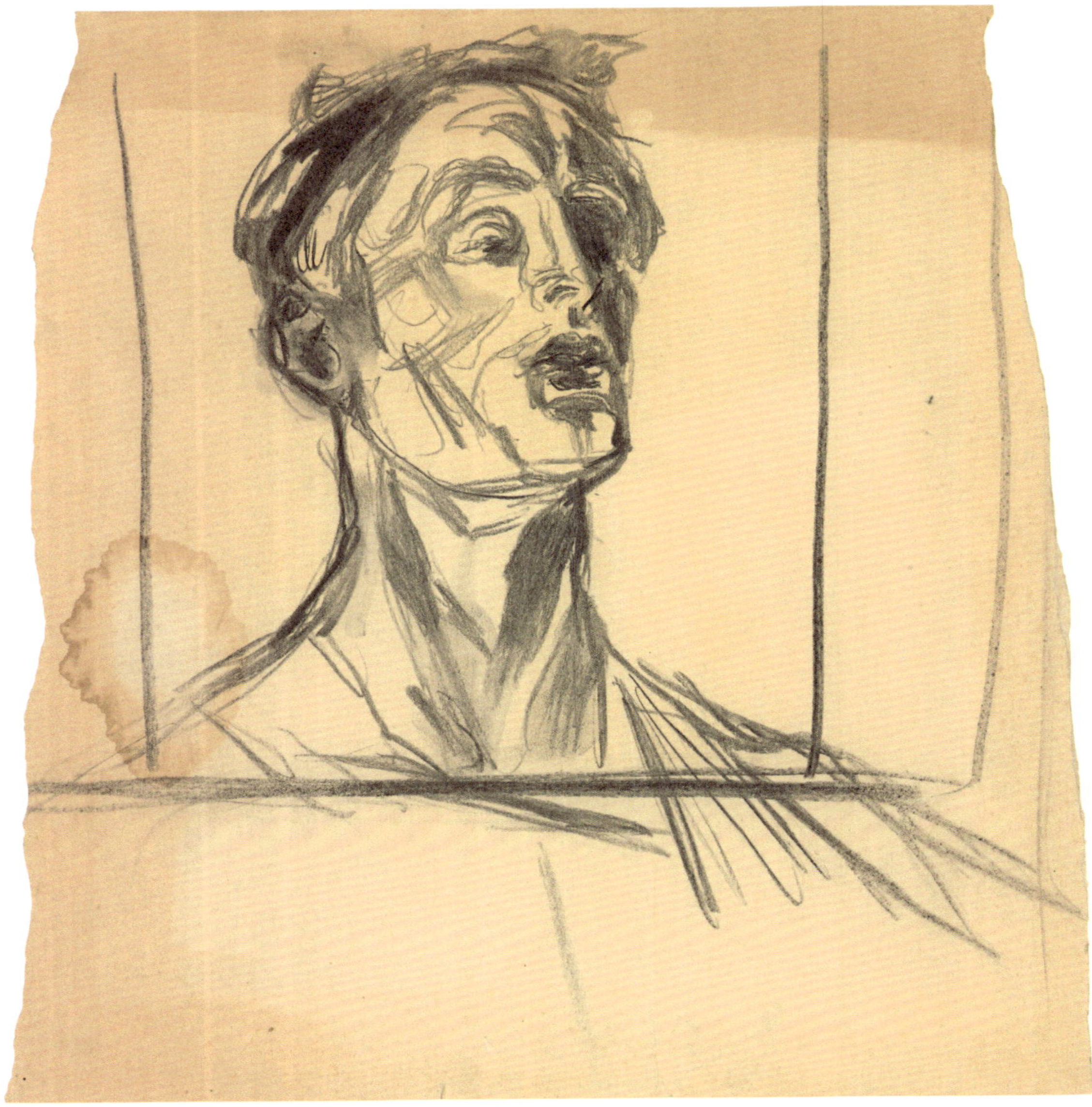

Self-Portrait
c. 1915
Charcoal
600 × 600 mm

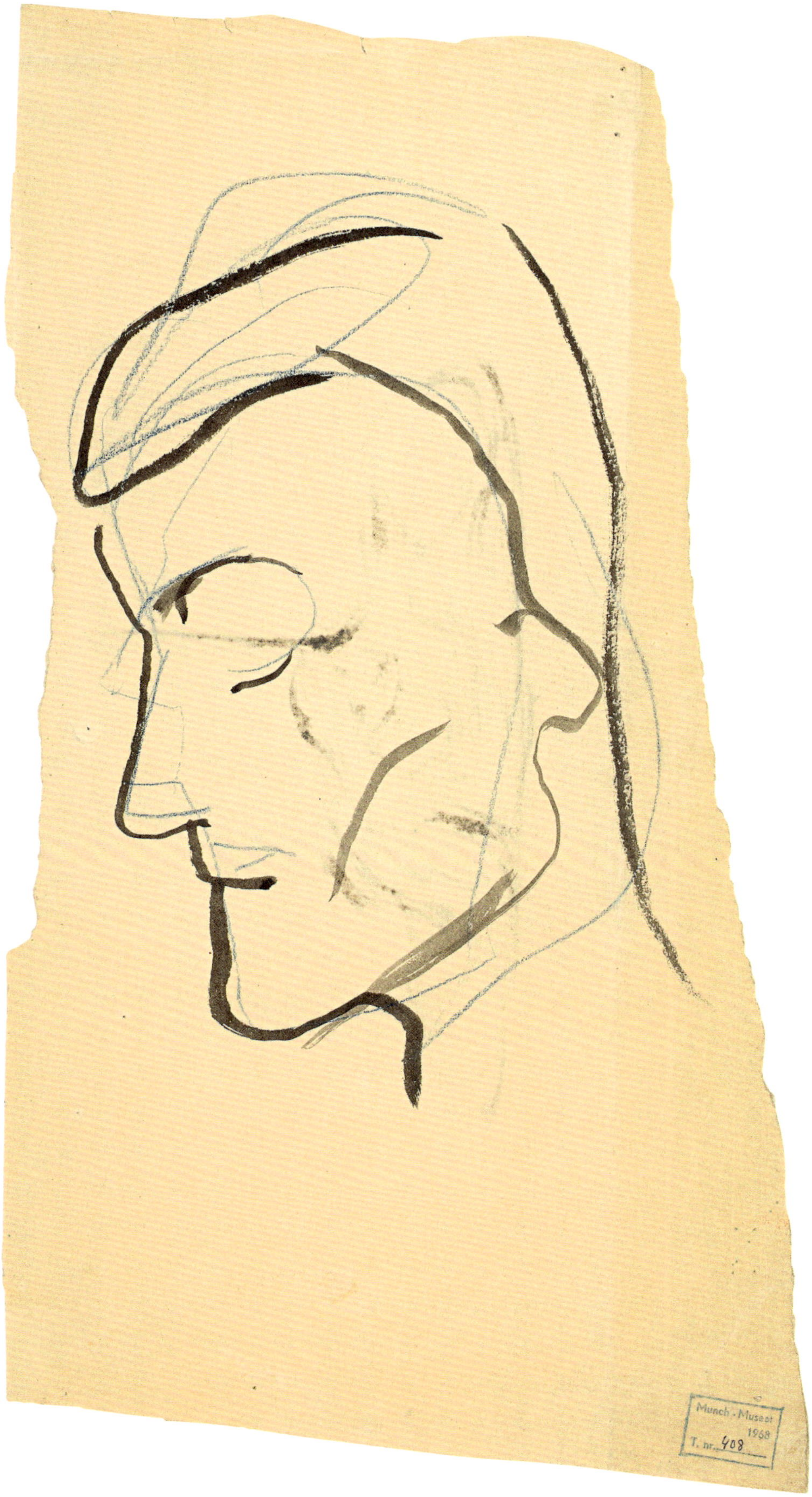

Male Head
1896
Brush and crayon
445 × 225 mm

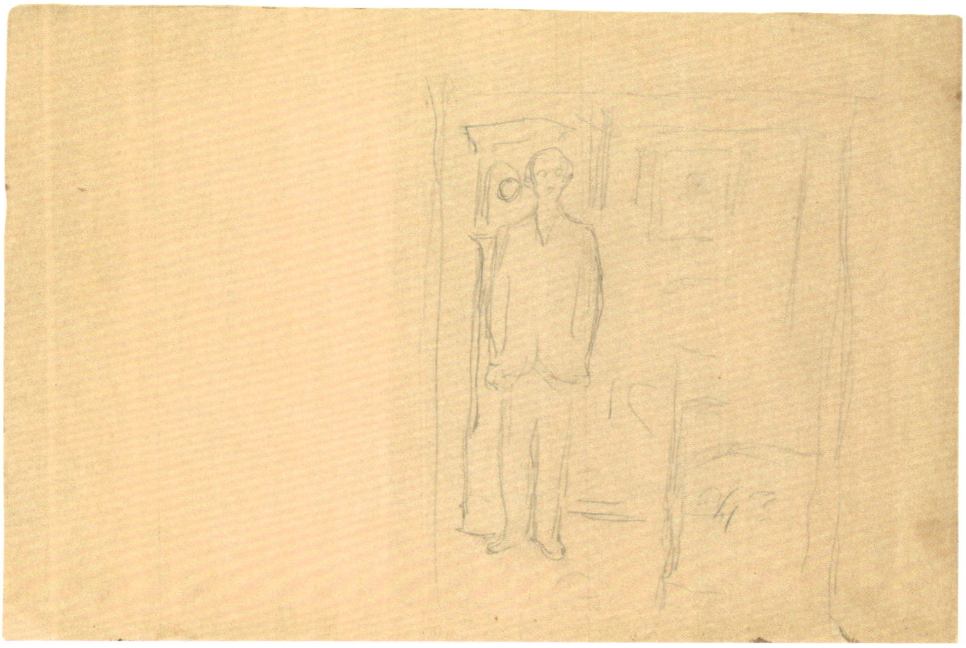

Sketch for *Between the Clock and the Bed*
1940–43
Pencil
241 × 322 mm

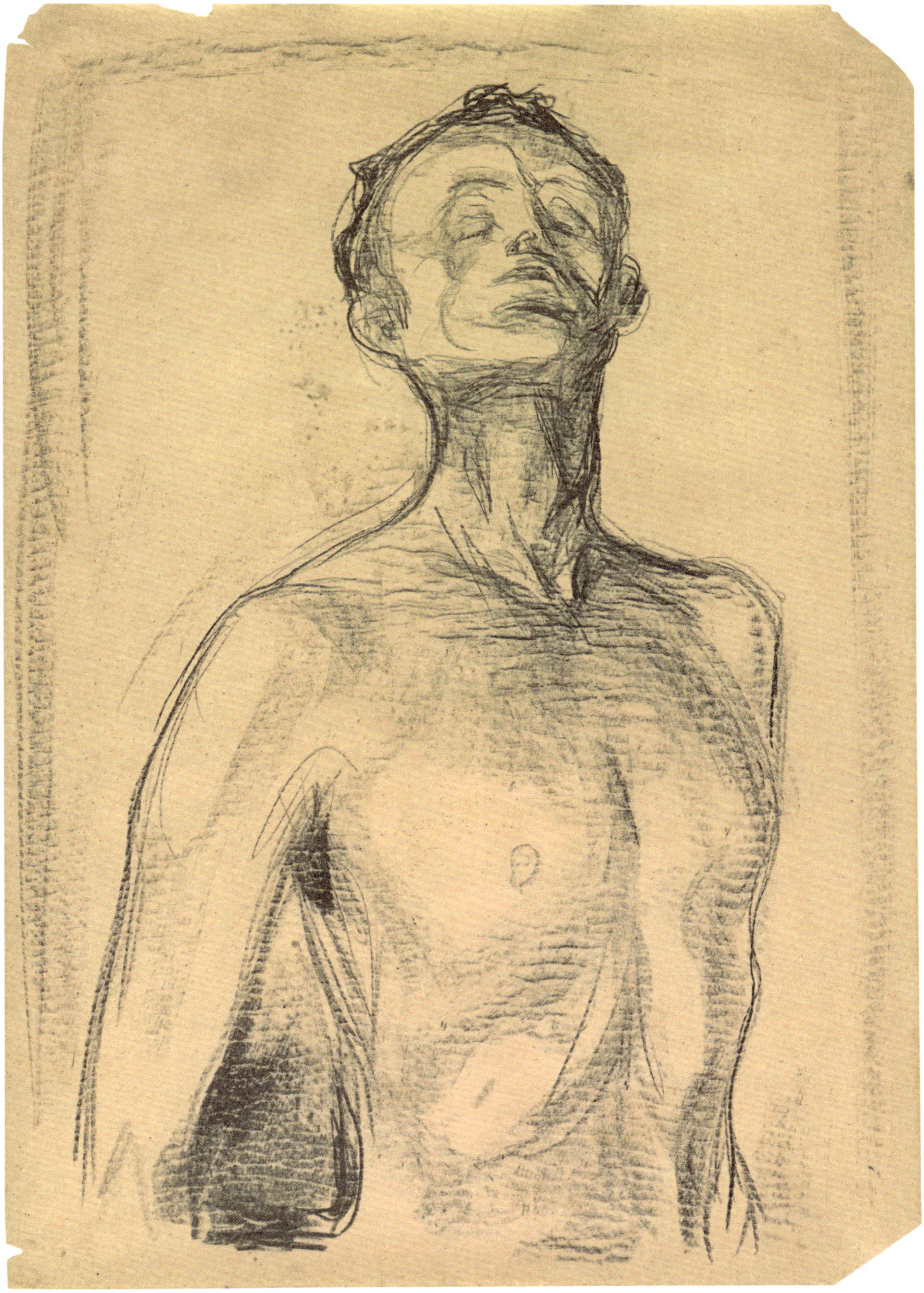

Self-Portrait
c. 1915
Crayon
675 × 483 mm

True Drawing is Like a Heartbeat

Tracey Emin
interviewed by Jon-Ove Steihaug

Tracey Emin
The Truth is I wanted you, 2019
Acrylic on canvas
182.6 × 214.3 cm

Tracey Emin has for many years and in many contexts talked about Edvard Munch's significance for her as an artist. She was able to elaborate on this interest in the exhibition *Tracey Emin / Edvard Munch. The Loneliness of the Soul*, shown at the Royal Academy of Arts from November 2020 to August 2021 and subsequently at MUNCH. She is also the artist behind the nine-metre-high bronze sculpture *The Mother*, a tribute to Munch, outside the museum's new building in Oslo's harbour area Bjørvika. This interview took place via telephone in the midst of the Corona epidemic in June 2020.

Steihaug — You have been looking closely into Edvard Munch's art while working on *Tracey Emin / Edvard Munch. The Loneliness of the Soul*. What new things have you discovered while going through the museum's collection?

Emin — Actually, I didn't find anything really new. I have been looking at Munch's work all my life, since I was seventeen. He is my favourite artist, always has been, ever since I was a teenager. But having looked at all the paintings, all the watercolors, all the drawings, my opinion of him is more qualified. I think now that he was even more sensitive, had more anxiety, was more tearful and more brokenhearted.

S — Although many of the drawings in your selection date from the 1880s and 90s, they are quite diverse. What is the main thread in your selection, would you say?

E — The main thread is that I wanted really good ones. I didn't choose to curate them thematically and I didn't go for the Munch classics. I went for the ones that I thought were really, really good, and I chose some of his poems and his writings, because I think most people don't know about them. His watercolour poems are so heartfelt and sensual and so sad.

S — You have also chosen several female nudes?

E — Munch painted loads of women, and many of them are archetypes; Madonnas, Medusas, femme fatales, she-devils. What he has to say isn't directed towards women, it is directed towards love and nature, and the understanding of everything, like the cosmos. Whereas if you look at the way men are portrayed in his work, some may be archetypes of himself, but all in all the male figures in his work are so much more erotic, so much more sexual; they almost have this gay male sex thing. Having said that, the reason I chose these drawings is simply that they are very poetic, very expressive, but above all, they are really, really good. Take *Standing Female Nude* (p. 209). That is just a fantastic drawing; it's anatomically correct, while there's also an edge to it. The sensuality, the sexuality, the way her breast is perched. The way her clothes are hanging around her knees, you know, her hair is down and loose. You can tell it is Munch, but mainly it's just an incredible drawing by a very accomplished artist.

S — You have picked another nude from around the same period as well, *Female Nude from the Waist Down* (p. 214).

E — It's such a strange study. It isn't very sexy; her legs and vagina are closed. But also, there are these details of the vagina; he is really looking, really trying to concentrate on what he sees. Otherwise his depictions of women's genitalia are kind of messy, as if he didn't really know what he was talking about.

S

Among the nudes in your selection, there are also a couple Munch did when he was in his fifties and had settled permanently in Norway. He seems to have turned to working with models with new intensity in these years; at times he would have a model come over nearly every day, like a regular drawing exercise.

E

What's great about these model drawings is that even as an established artist he decided he still had to understand the craft of drawing. It's the same with me. Every seven years or so I take drawing classes and go back to drawing models. Because although I know what the human body looks like, I forget about its real weight, and end up drawing something like a pastiche or parody of my own drawing. Another thing that I find interesting is that when you look at Munch's model studies, you can see that he wasn't trying to seduce them, he was really just drawing. It's not like other male artists at the time, who all fucked their models.

S

Moving on to one of Munch's more famous and iconic motifs, you have selected a drawing he most probably did around the same time as he was painting his work *Madonna*, or as it was called when exhibited for the first time, *Kvinna som älskar (Loving Woman)*. It is a very beautiful rendering of a reclining woman (p. 221). The female figure and female sexuality have also been an important theme in your work.

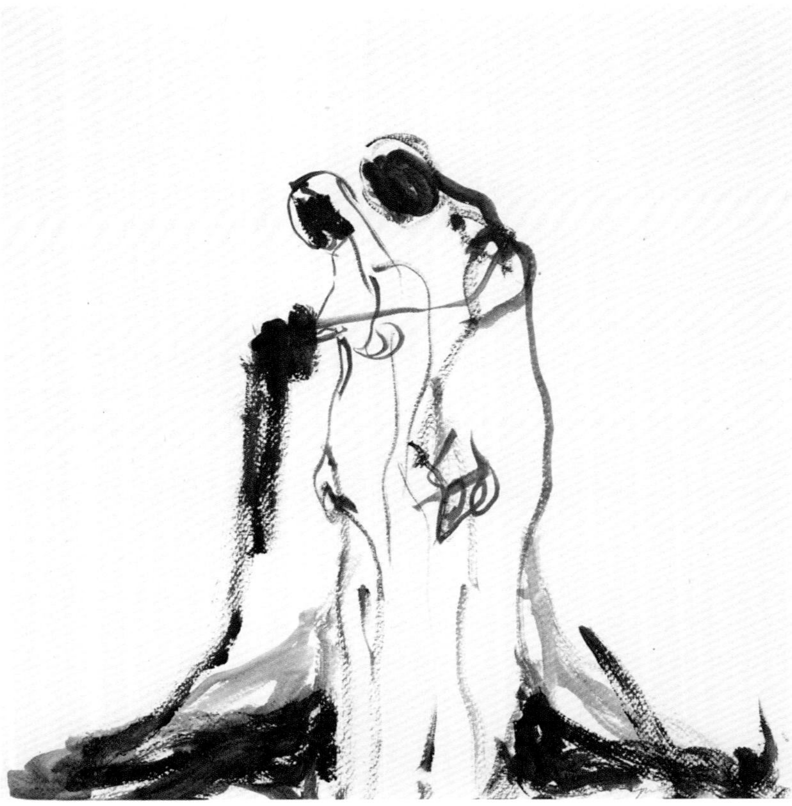

Tracey Emin
I love you, 2015
Acrylic on paper
35 × 35 cm

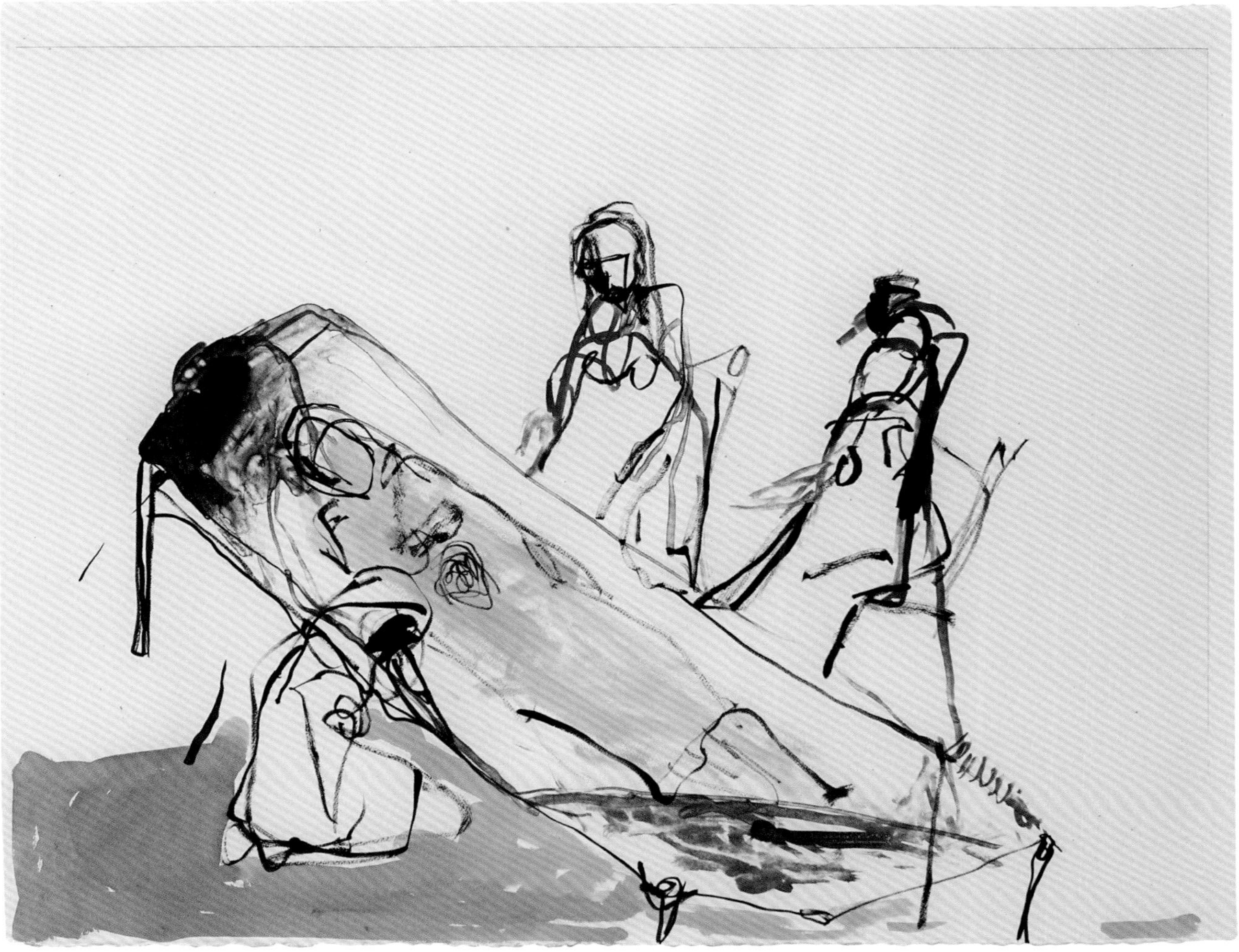

185

Tracey Emin
Mother 6, 2017
India ink hand painting on lithograph
76.5 × 103 cm

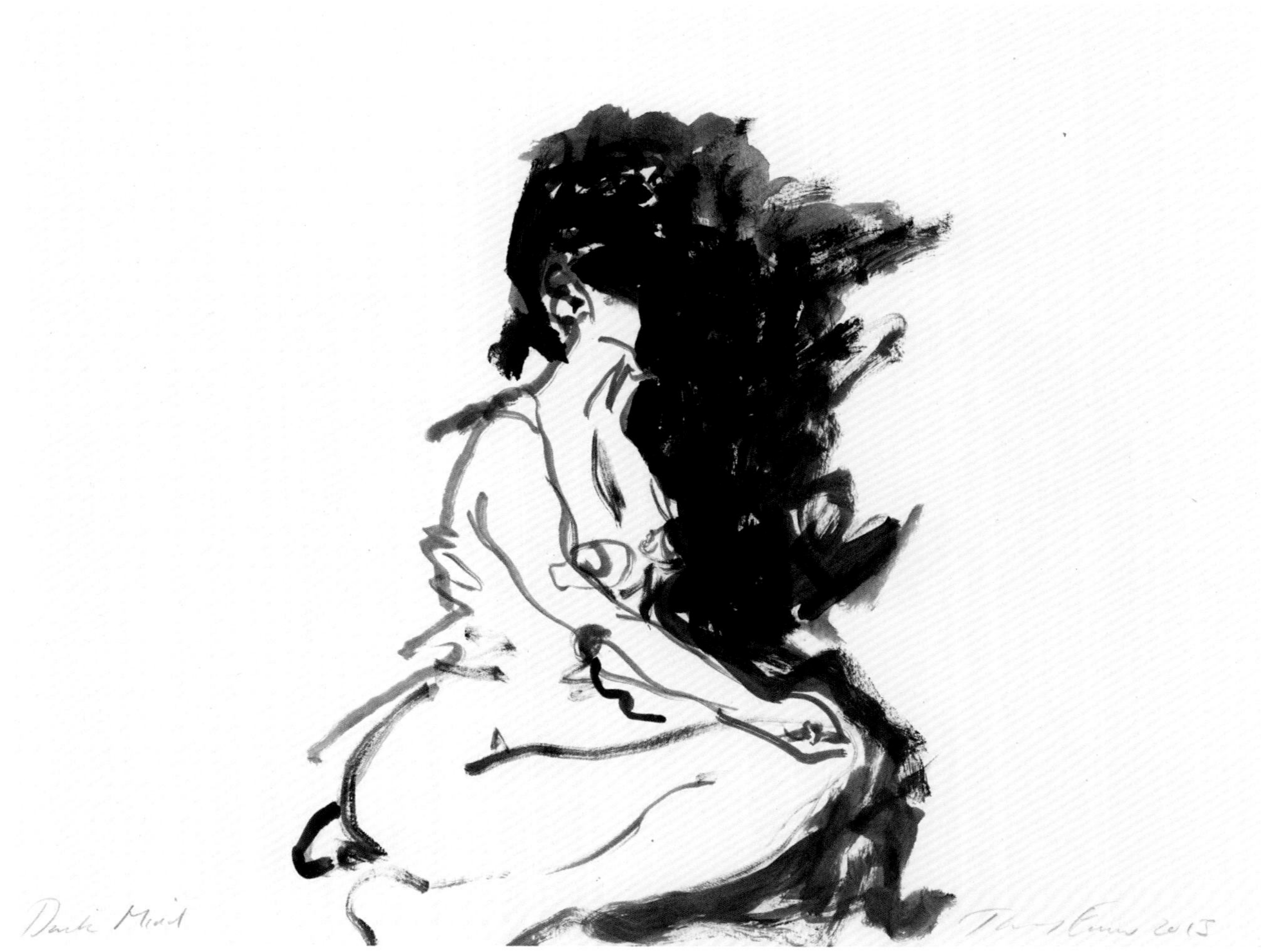

Tracey Emin
Dark Mind, 2015
Gouache on paper
30.5 × 40.6 cm

E Well, I am female, so that's me, isn't it? That's what I meant when I talked about Munch's archetypical women. It wasn't like he was drawing his friends or his lovers or whatever; he was illustrating his ideas. But in this sketch, the woman looks real, doesn't she? I think he probably knew who she was. She's got nice tits, and she doesn't look typically Norwegian. She definitely has a different ethnic background, and I find that quite interesting. The other thing I learned by going through the archive at Munchmuseet, was that he was looking at other artists; they were the artists who would have been successful at the time, in Vienna, Paris, or Berlin. So at that time, he would be looking at Gauguin and ... who else?

S Degas, perhaps?

E Yes, exactly.

S There are some more burlesque motifs as well in your selection, with a sitting woman hugging a bear, relating to his later lithographic series "Alpha & Omega".

E We know how much Munch loved animals. I think he looked for excuses to draw and paint them. These two, titled *The First Human Beings: The Woman and the Bear*, are so sweet and innocent (p. 195 and 210). You've got the metaphor of the bear, the primal beast and all that kind of thing, but these drawings are not about that. I think they started with a doodle which looked like a bear, and then he put the other figures in. In my selection, I've got a few of those that must have started with him playing around on the paper, without any clear idea of a finished work, and then it went off into something else, like "Alpha & Omega".

S And then there are three drawings related to crucifixion ...

E Every Easter I paint or draw crucifixes. The last years I've done some really large crucifix paintings. To me, these Munch drawings are so beautiful, especially the one of the country road (p. 203). It's just exquisite. Perhaps it really isn't about crucifixion, but more about a place to stop, about surrender. More like an ex-voto, a place to contemplate.

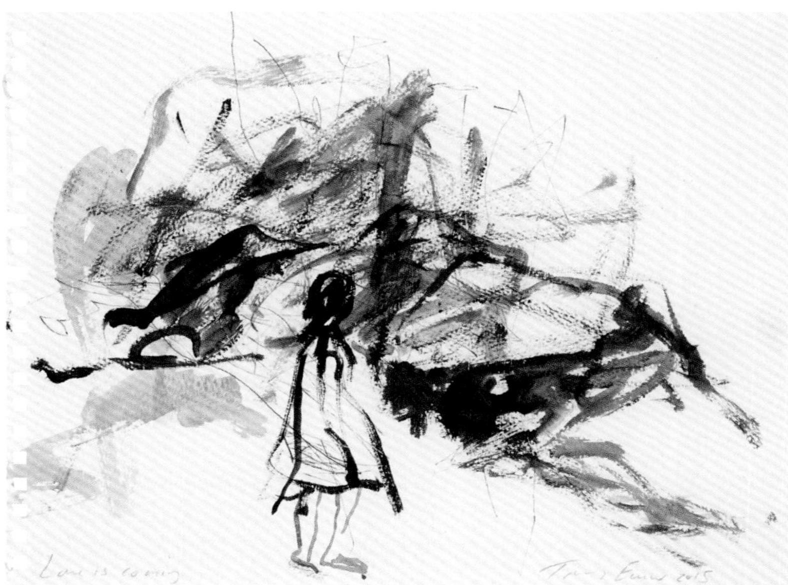

Tracey Emin
Love is coming, 2015
Gouache on paper
28 × 38 cm

Another recurring motif in your selection has to do with metabolism. What is it that interests you here? S

I think it's about transference and the psychological movement of things within his work. Munch doesn't draw pictures. Rather, there is an alchemical movement of the mind, like a shifting of things. The metabolism is a clear illustration of this. E

Exactly, these motifs relate to questions about the cycle of life. Do you feel that these ideas are still relevant? S

I think that Munch, right now, is really deeply needed; he is very much an emblem for the times we are living in. Maybe 20 years ago, people couldn't see it because things move in and out of fashion in waves. Now Munch is at the top of his wave. People want to be touched by emotion, to have their feelings shared. They don't want to accept that having an emotional strain is a weakness. It's part of life, it's part of humanity. In fact, the more open you are about your weakness, the stronger and the more well-defined you will be as a person. E

In what ways do you think that Munch's drawings touch on your own practice? S

It doesn't! I draw so differently from Munch. His drawings have quite a heavy line, they're very graphic, although there are some exceptions to this in my selection. If there is a similarity, it's in the letters that I send to people. They are quite similar to Munch's loose pages and sketchbooks. I've got thousands of drawings; it's a way for me of expressing myself, almost like handwriting; it's like a fast way of emptying myself. So Munch has these drawings, but also these works on paper that are just from his mind, just his language which he is expressing. Whereas in Munch's big paintings, he had classic subjects. And I don't pick those classics, thinking "I am now going to paint Oedipus and do my own version of that subject"; it isn't like that. I do a drawing, and go, "fuck, that really looks like Oedipus!" E

Even when Munch drew imaginative scenes, he was still relying on studies of things he had seen in the world, whereas you seem to draw more purely from memory or imagination. S

It's interesting, over the last three months, I've been doing drawings of my house. E

That's something quite new for you, isn't it? S

Yes, it's completely new. It's very odd. The drawings of my house look like something from the *Twilight Zone*, like something sketched from a dream world. And I've got another 20 years, haven't I, so who knows what's going to happen. I was making work like this when I was very young, about how I felt, and I was writing all the time. So when I came across Munch, it was like meeting a kindred spirit, a friend, someone I could talk to, someone who understood me. Back when I was a student in my twenties, I did so many wish cards and graphic works, and I was so influenced by Munch – it was like a homage to him. I wrote my thesis on Munch. I was in love with him, and by that I don't mean that I thought he was a really good artist – I was actually in love with him. I think we would like each other; I think we would get really drunk together; I think we would do seances together; I think we would talk to the dead together. Perhaps we wouldn't have been lovers, because I don't know how much of a lover he was. I recently said to Jonathan Jones, the art critic, that Munch was really sexy. And Jonathan said, "You don't say that about an artist." Well, people say that about me, so why not? E

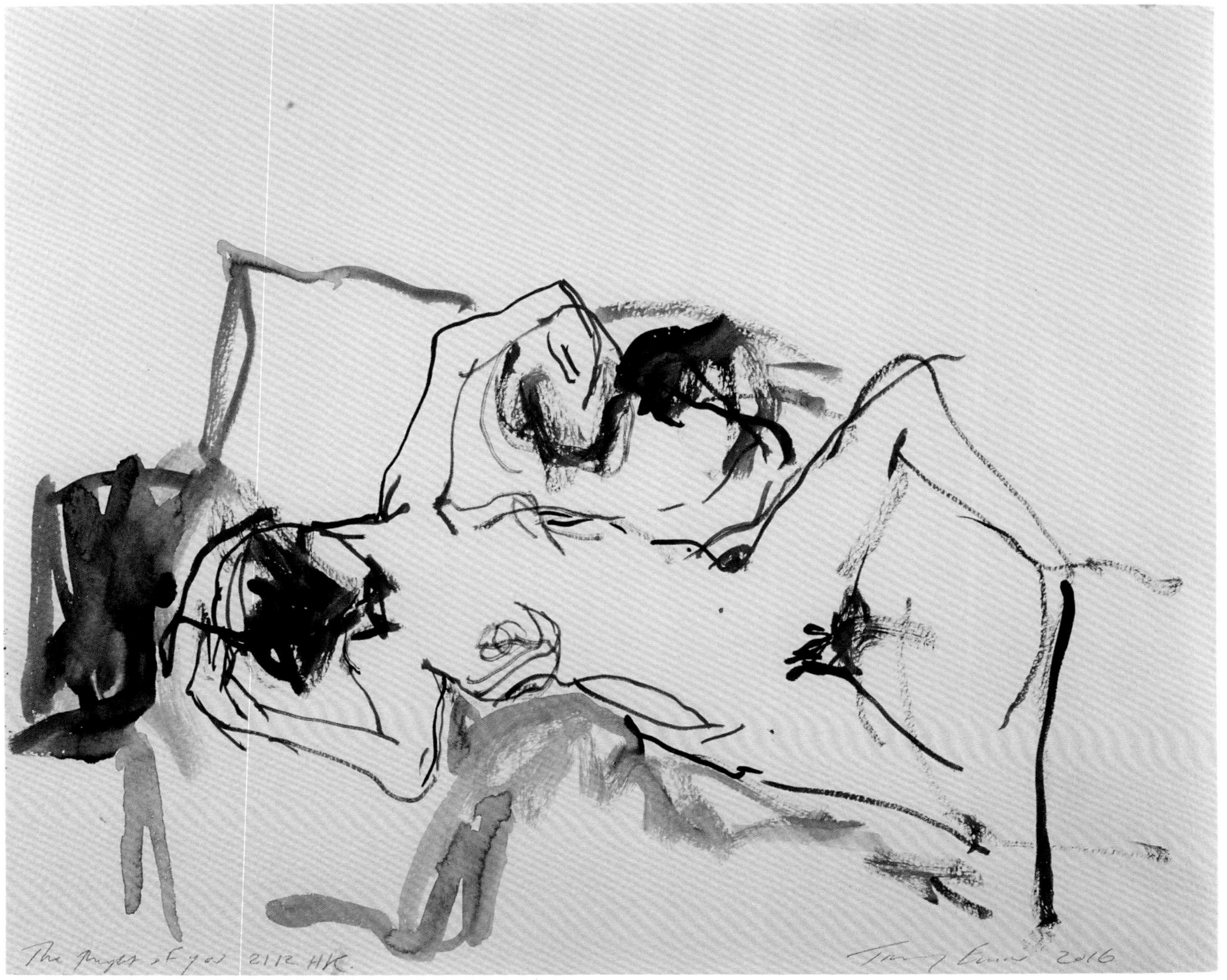

Tracey Emin
The thought of you 2112 HK, 2016
Gouache on paper
40.5 × 50.8 cm

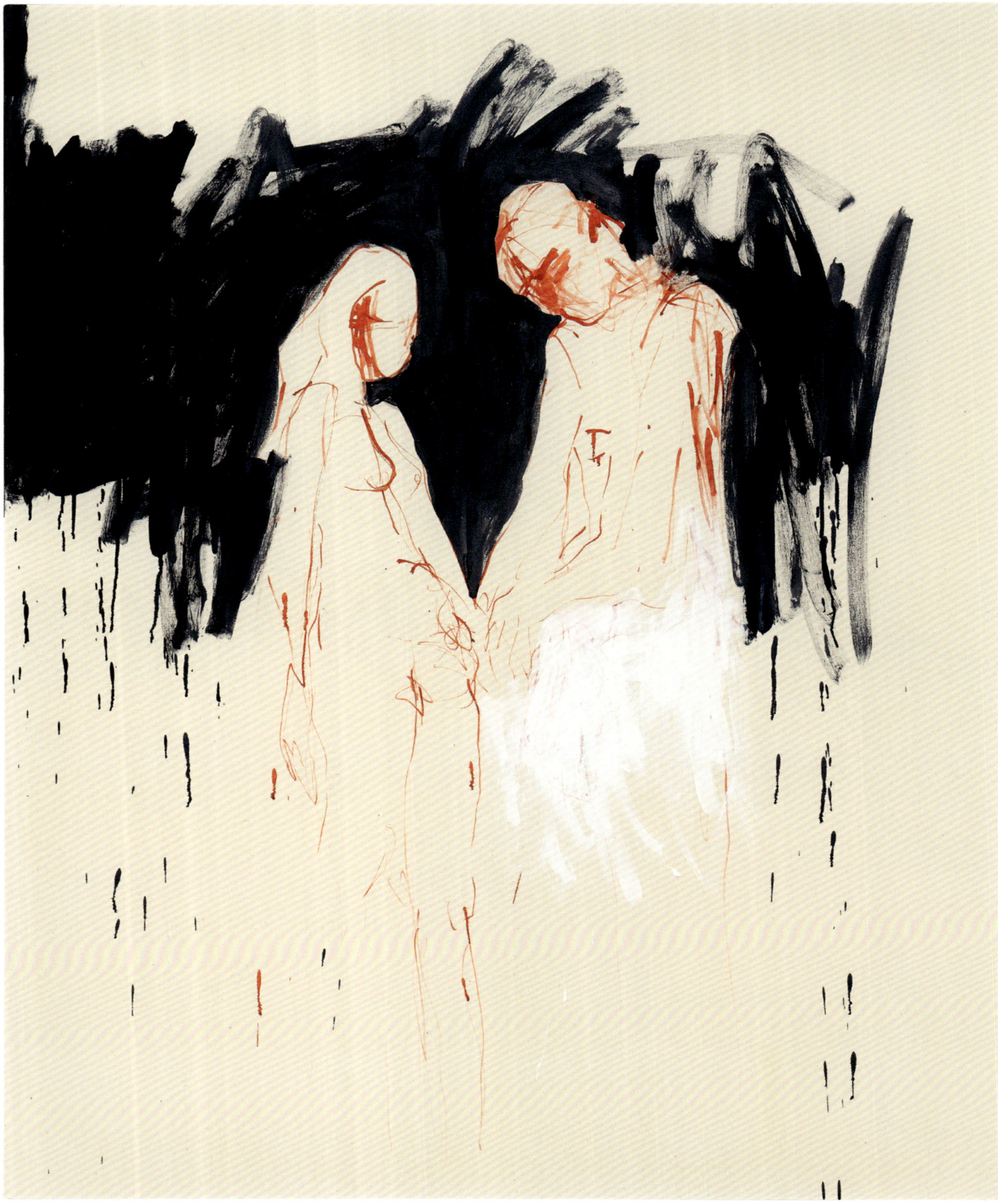

Tracey Emin
I said I would say goodbye, 2019
Acrylic on canvas
182.1 × 152.2 cm

S If we could briefly touch upon the large sculpture you have made called *The Mother*, which is to be placed outside the new MUNCH: do you find that there are connections between drawing and sculpture?

E Sculpture is really interesting, because I don't really have much control of what I do. I work with sculpture for about two months each year. These are periods when I can't draw, when I can't paint; when I can't see, almost as if I were blind. And so I just feel. The work is done purely through my hands. I don't look at the clay. It's like, bang, bang, bang – it happens really fast. It's like an automatic physical response.

S Is that the way you understand drawing as well, as a kind of physical and direct mark-making?

E I've always drawn. Even when I destroyed my paintings, which I did twice when I was young, I kept my drawings. So yes, the mark-making was always important to me. Here's what I think about drawing, I think that drawing comes from the heart and the soul. What happens is, the heart pumps, the blood comes down through the heart, through the arm, through the hands, out through the hand, the eyes see, it comes in, it goes through the blood, through the heart, the arms, through the hands, out of the hands and on to the paper, and it's got an electric pulse, it's like a heartbeat, that's what true drawing is. The other thing about drawing, is that it is intensely personal. It's like masturbating. It isn't a shared thing. It's got nothing to do with anyone else, it's deeply personal, something which takes place between the artist and the paper. It's a solo pursuit.

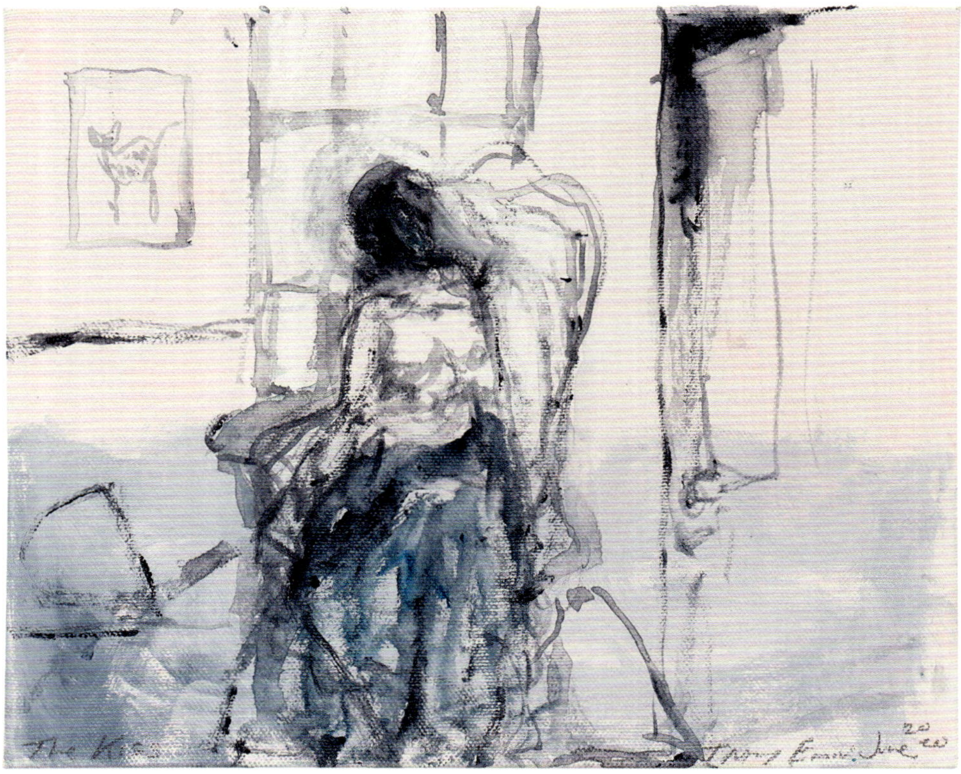

Tracey Emin
The Kiss, 2020
Acrylic on canvas
20.3 × 25.4 cm

Emin chooses Munch

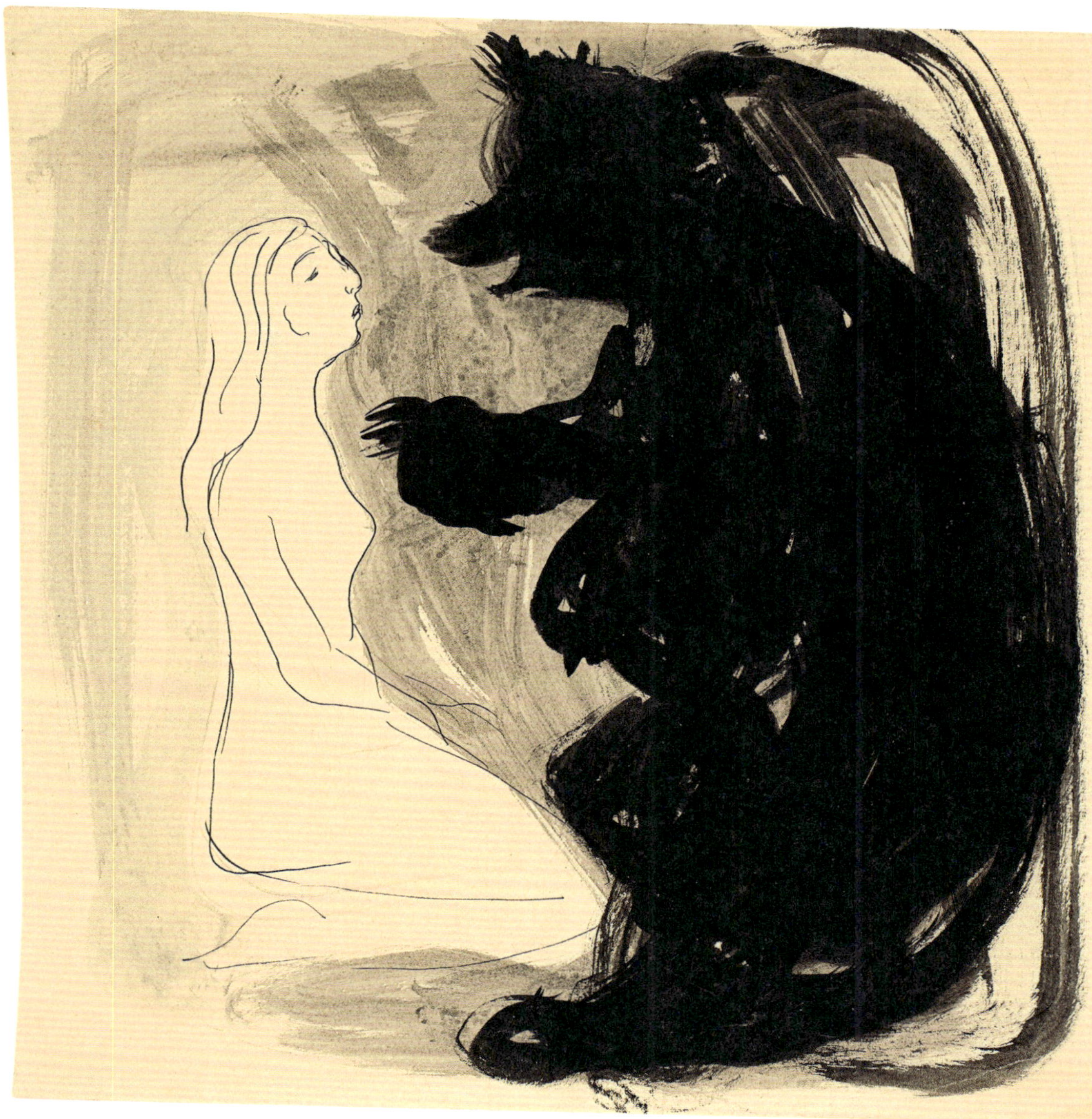

The First Human Beings: The Woman and the Bear
1895–96
Pen, brush, wash and charcoal
322 × 324 mm

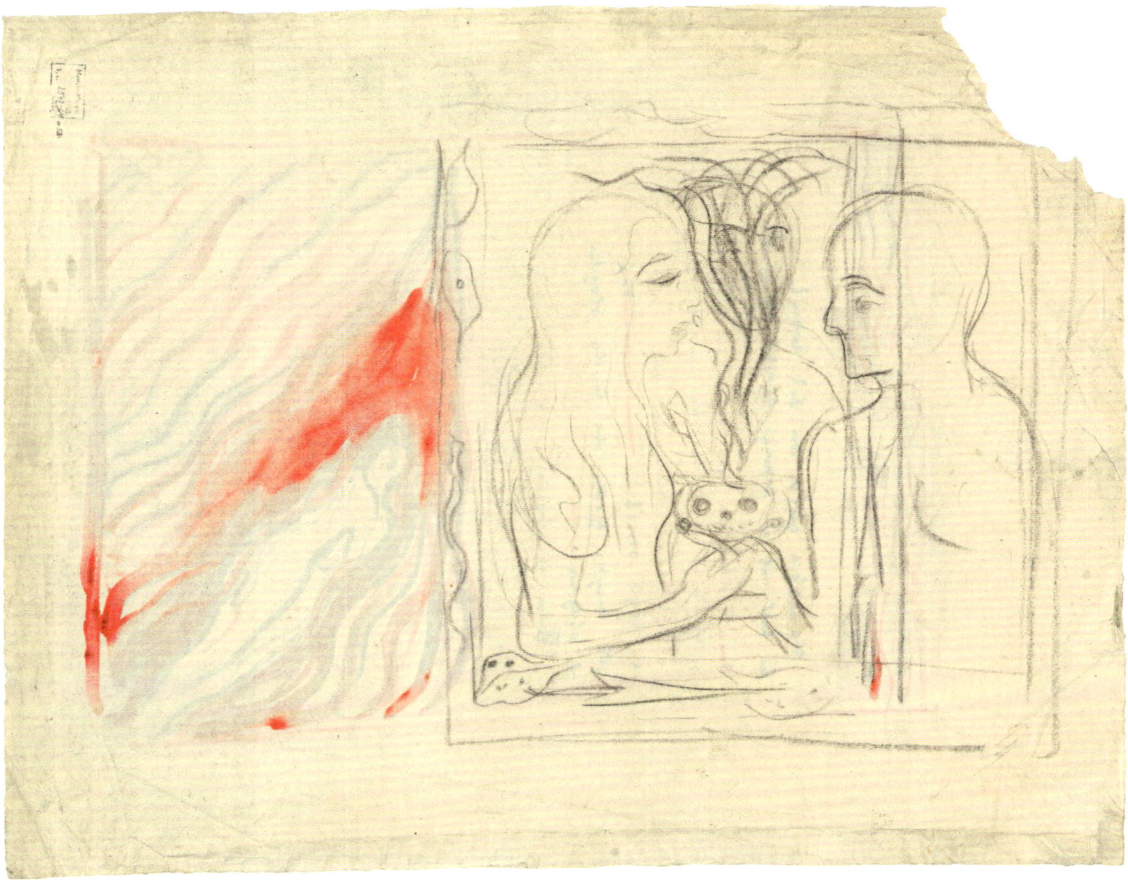

Metabolism
1896–98
Gouache and pencil
473 × 618 mm

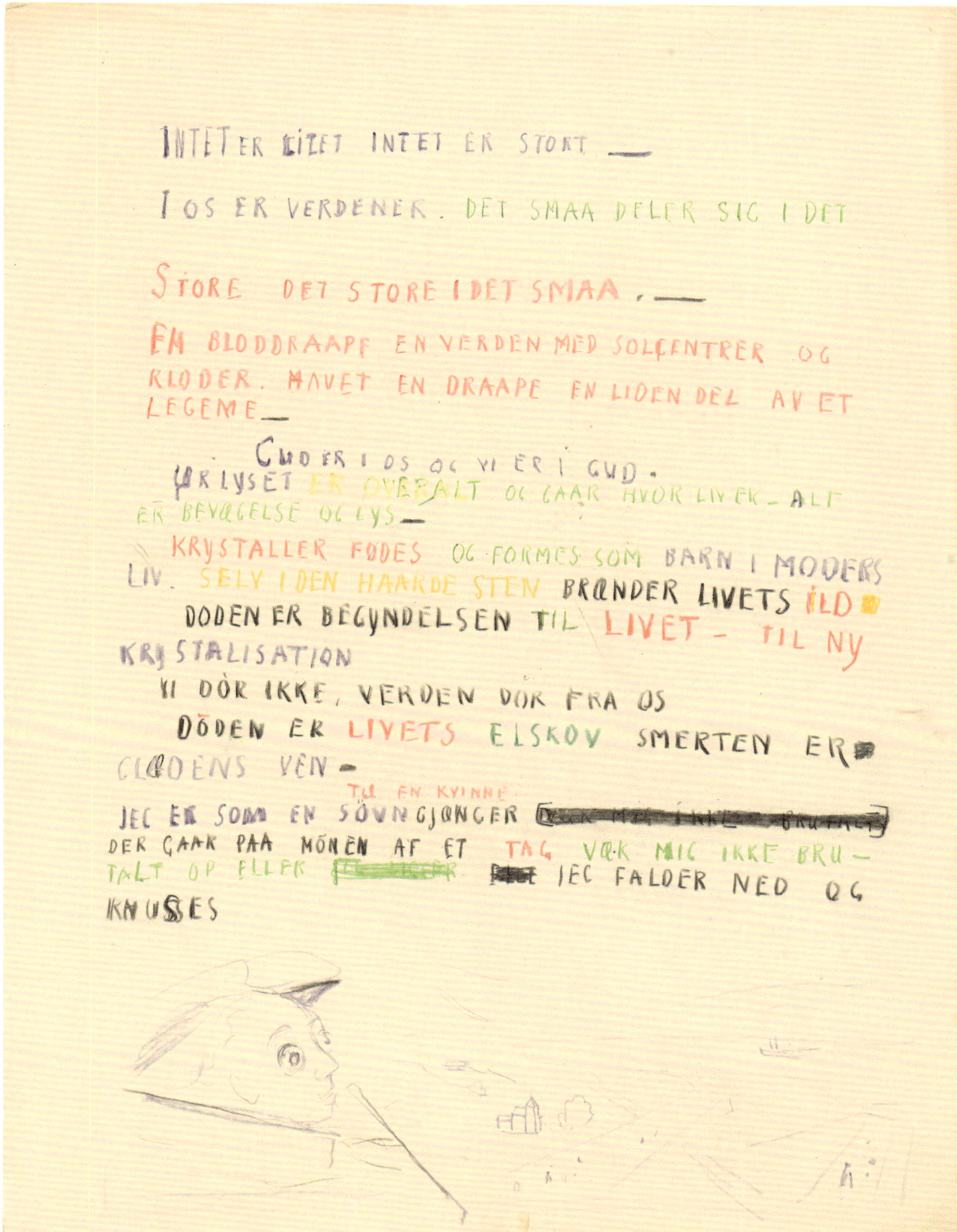

"Nothing is small nothing is great"
c. 1930
Crayon
649 × 501 mm

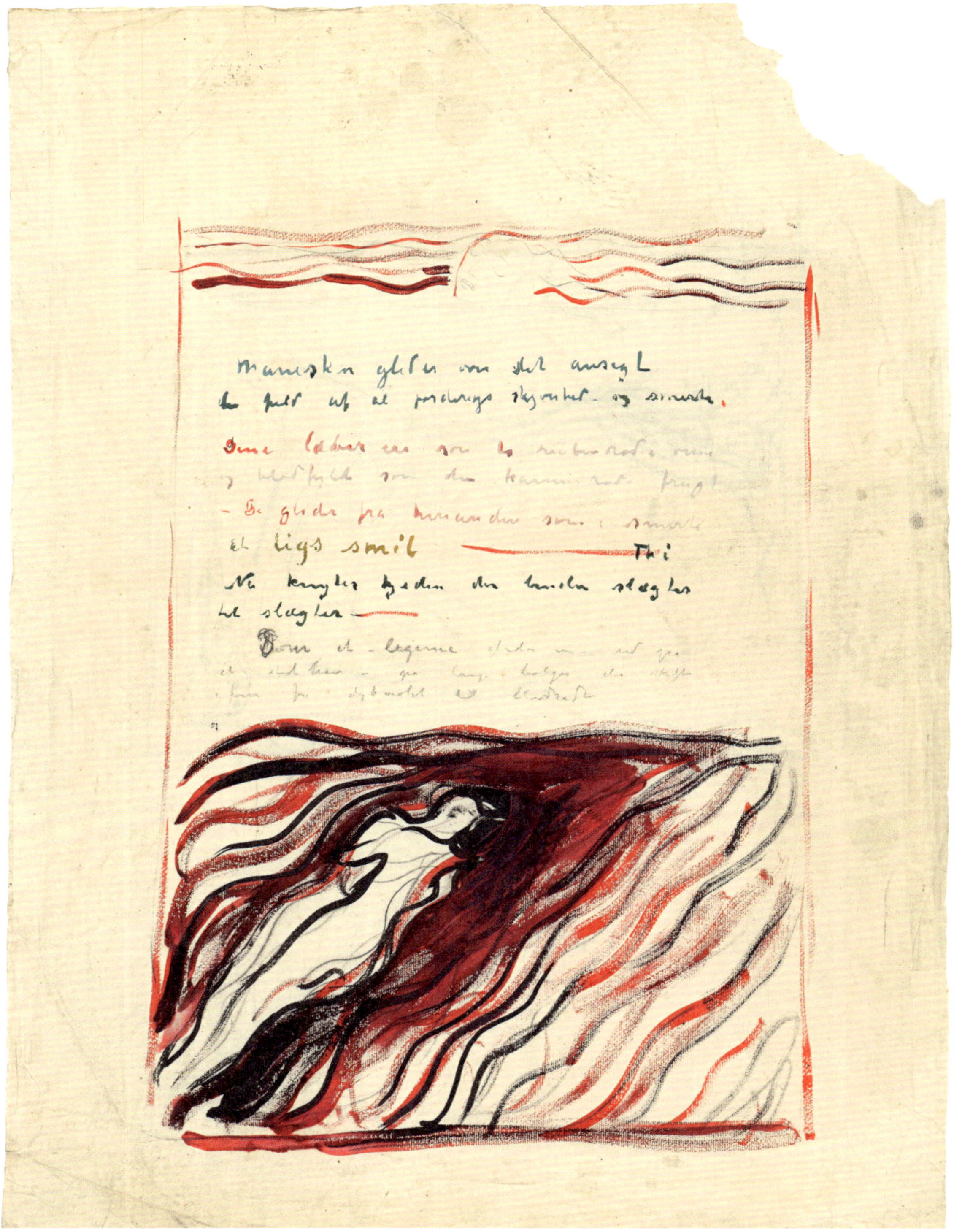

The Wave
“Moonlight glides across your countenance”
1896
Gouache and pencil
618 × 473 mm

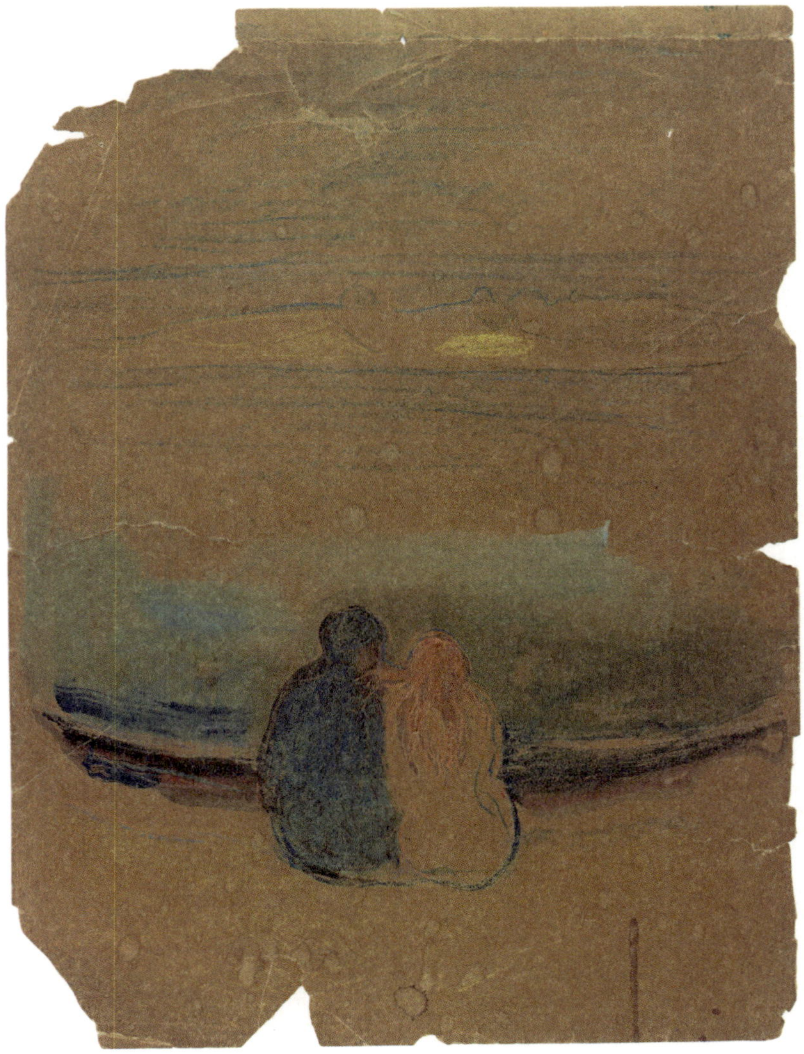

Alpha and Omega
1908–09
Watercolour, pastel and crayon
640 × 496 mm

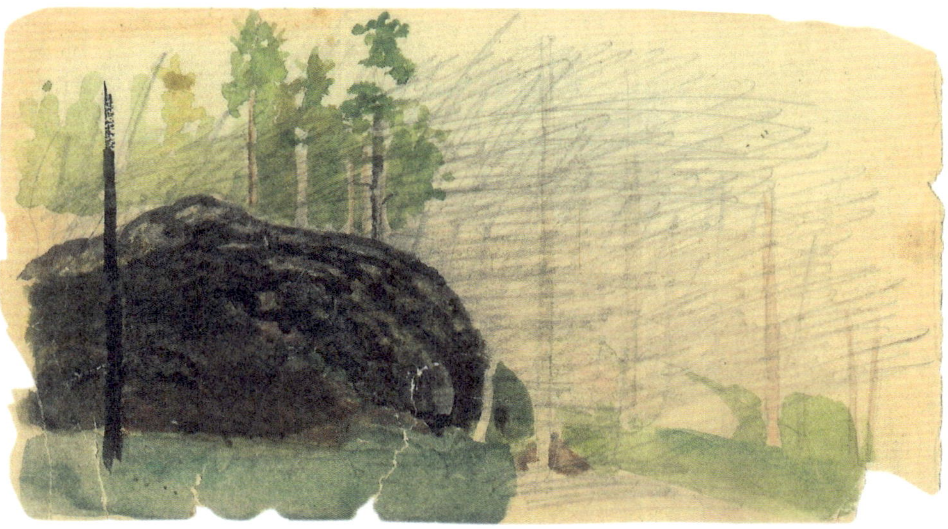

Landscape
1881
Watercolour and pencil
113 × 270 mm

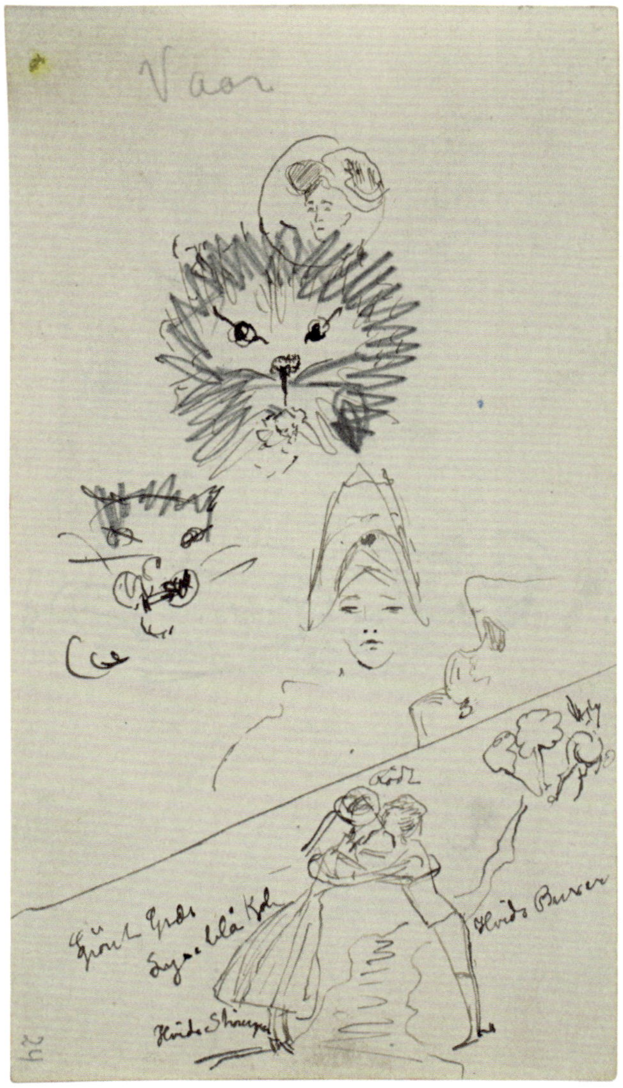

Sketches of People with Animals and *Couple Kissing*
1886
Pen and pencil
154 × 87 mm

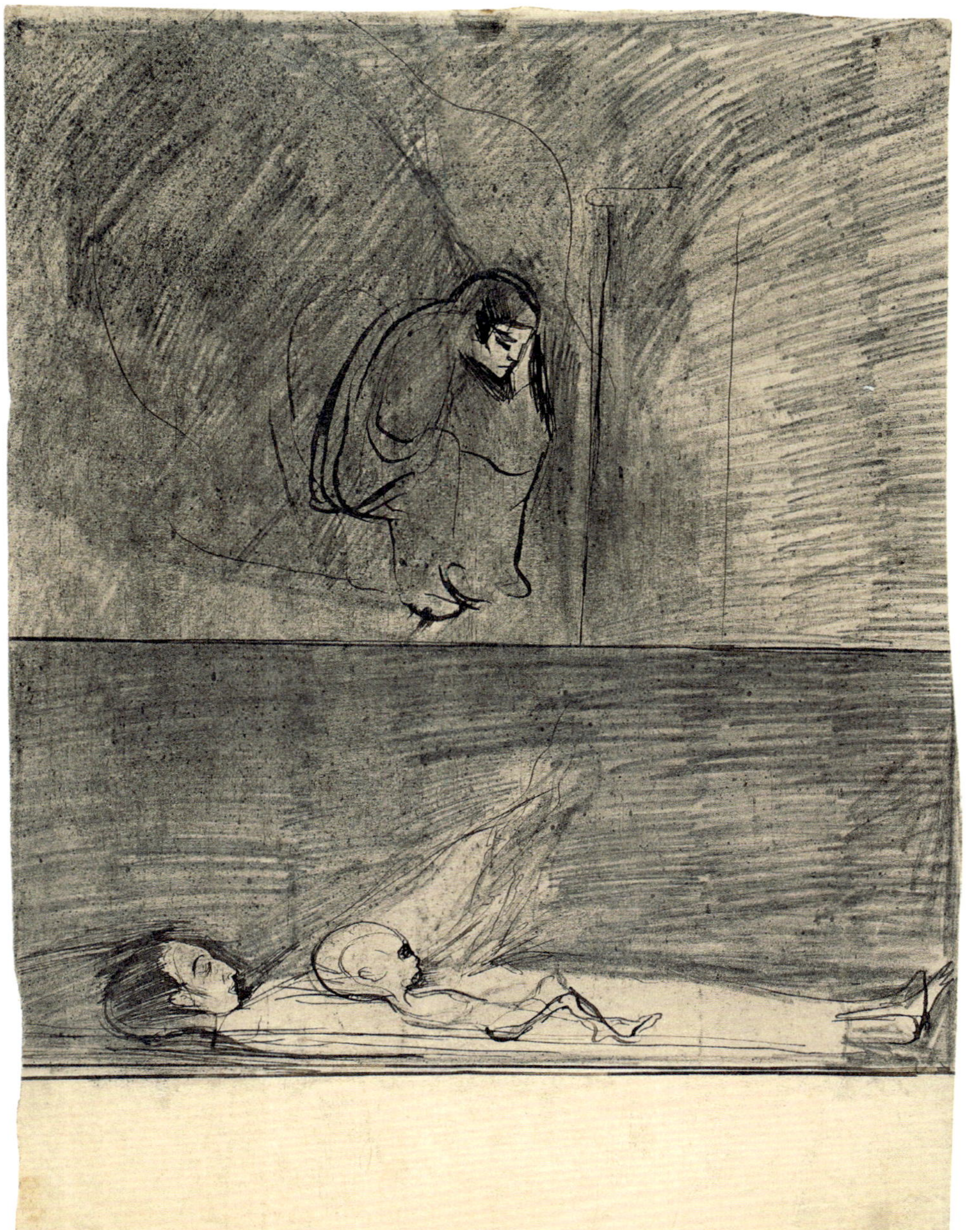

Seated Man and *The Dead Mother*
1890–94
Pencil and pen
350 × 263 mm

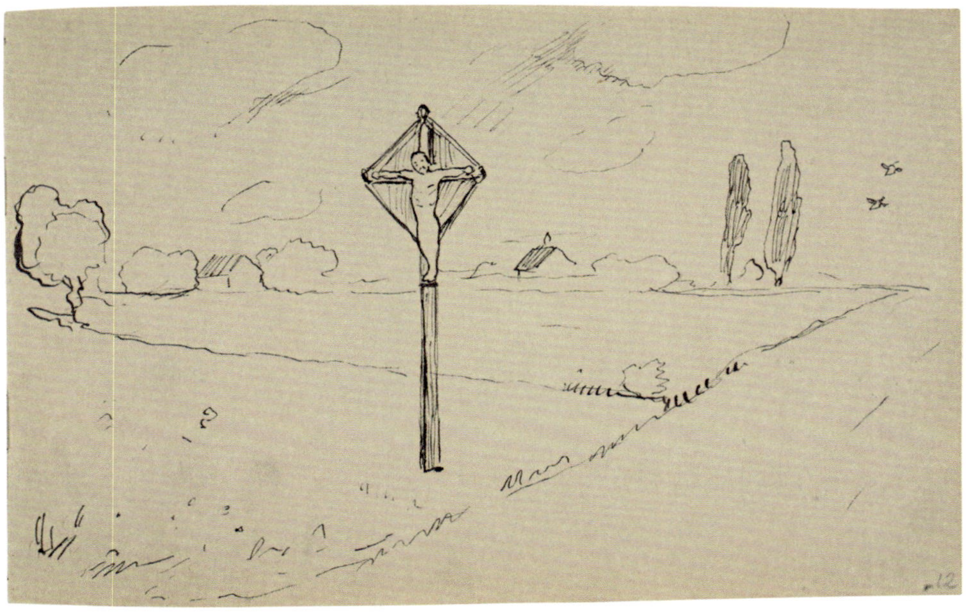

Crucifix on a Country Road
1905
Pen
148 × 229 mm

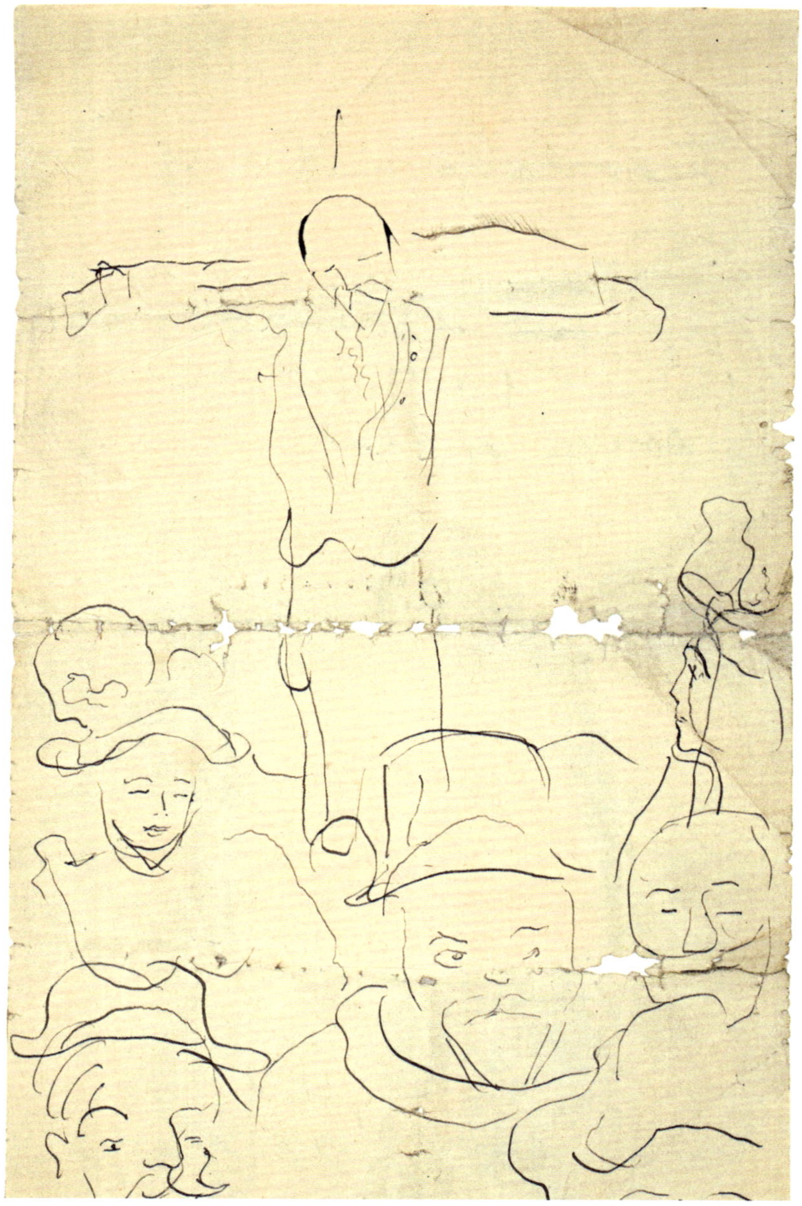

Crucifixion
1890–1900
Pen
260 × 208 mm

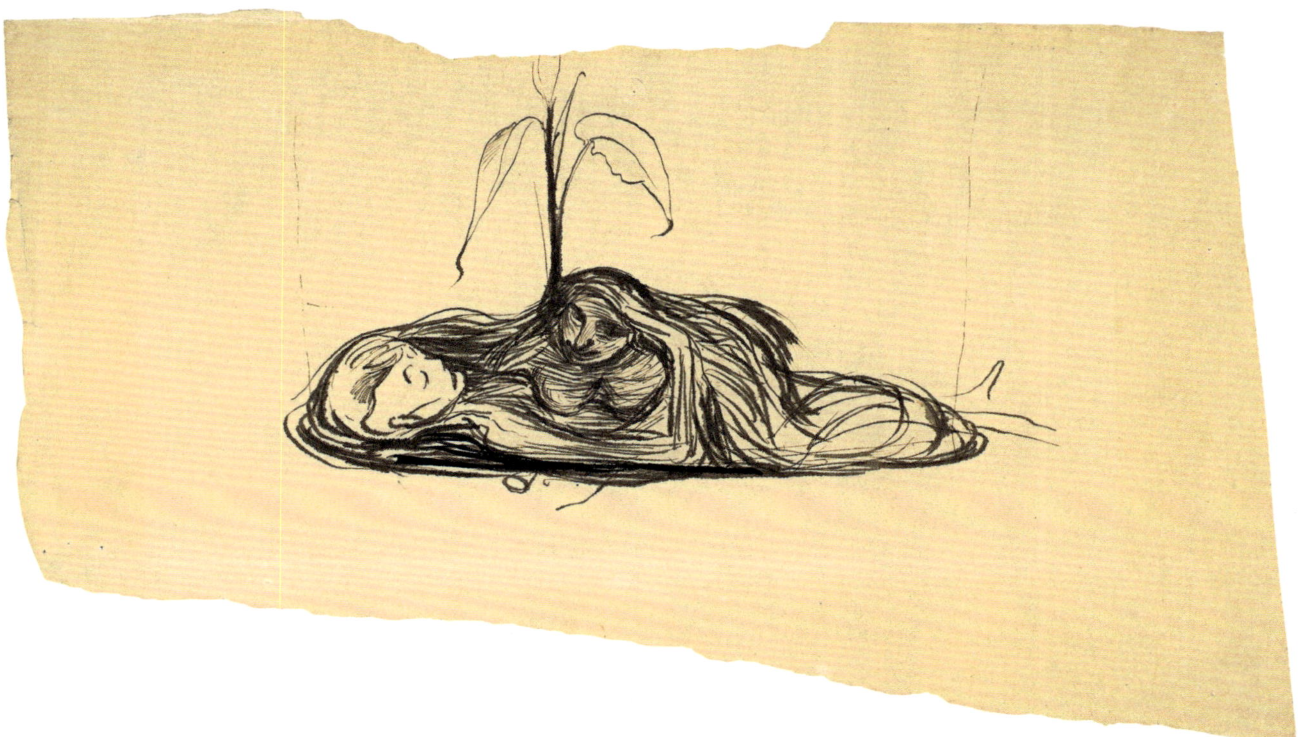

Sketch for *Metabolism*
1896
Pen
225 × 445 mm

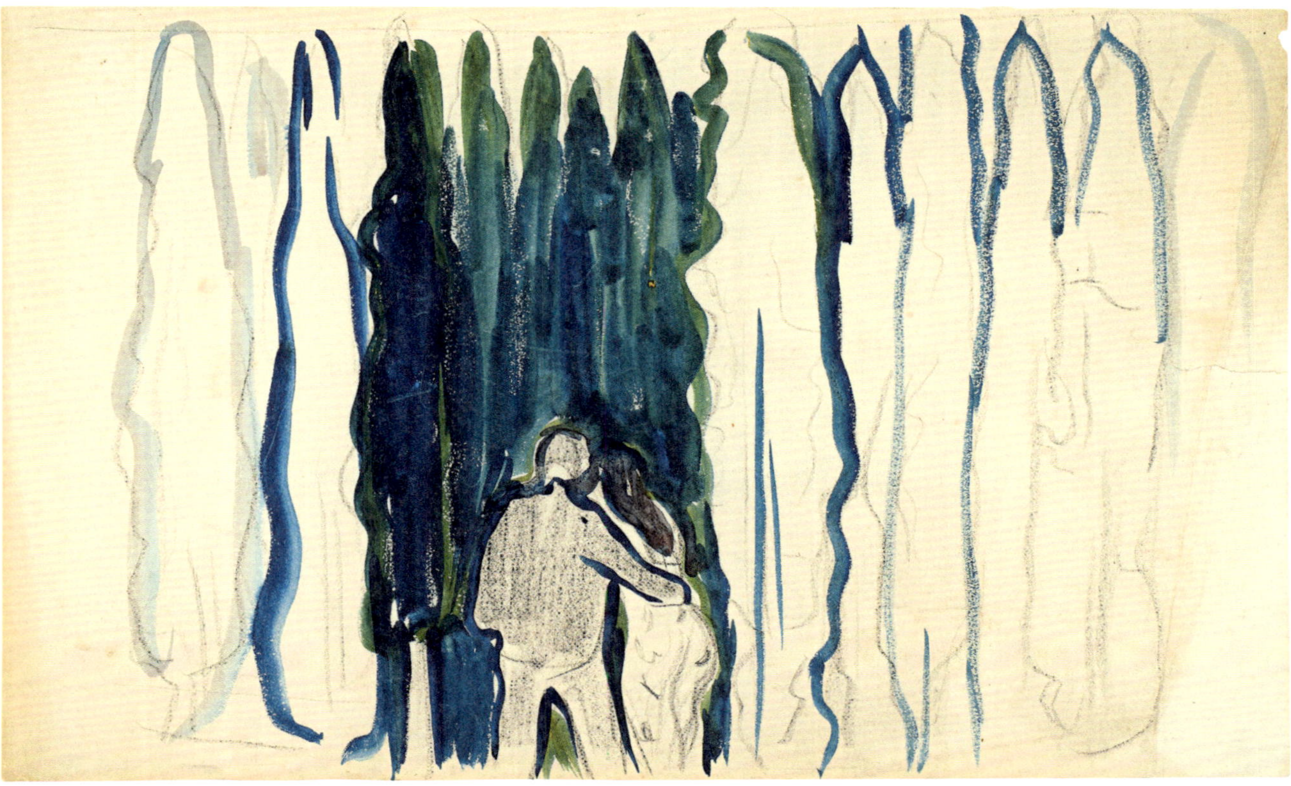

Towards the Forest (The First Human Beings)
1896
Watercolour and crayon
302 × 500 mm

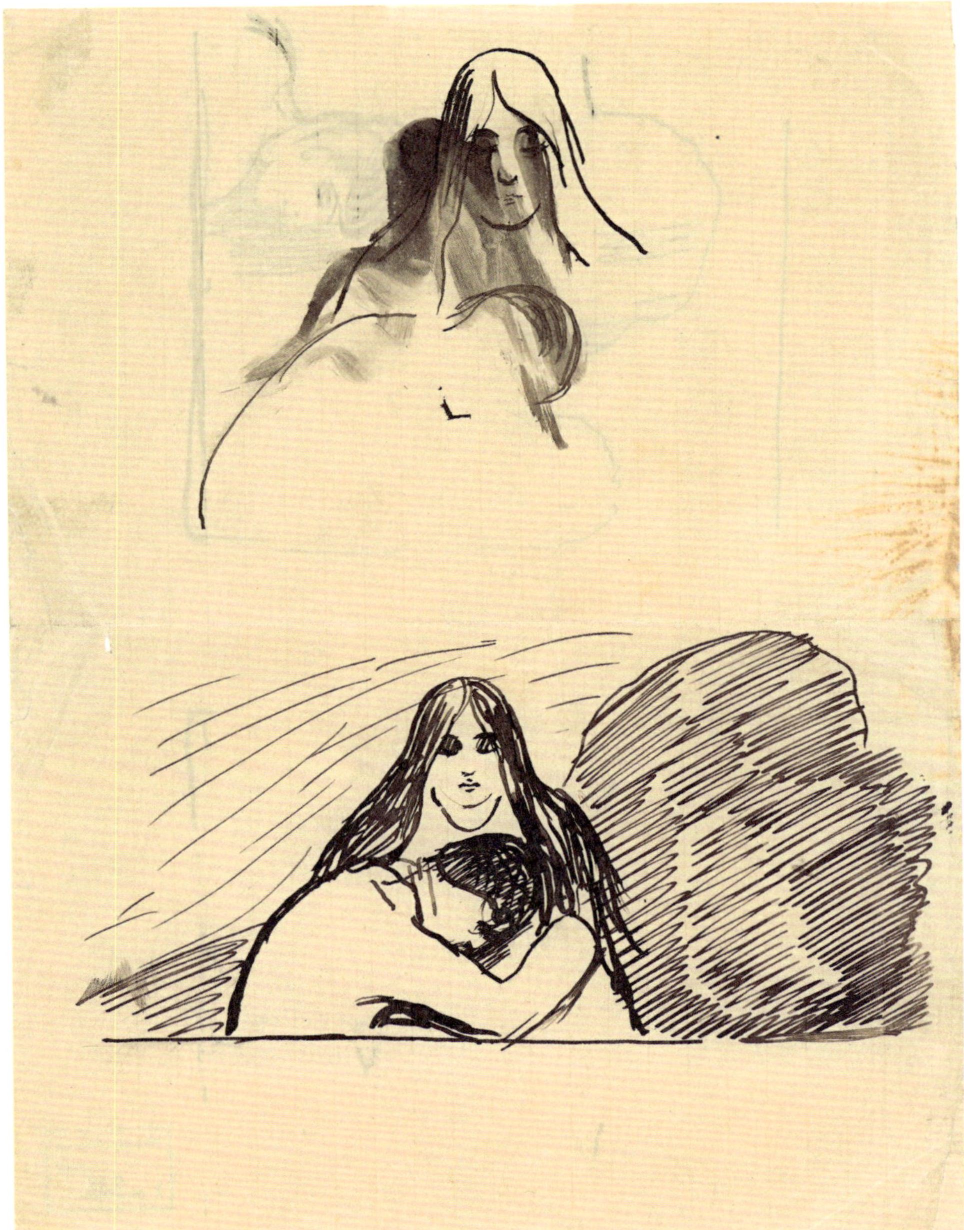

Two Sketches for *Vampire*
1892–93
Pen
284 × 220 mm

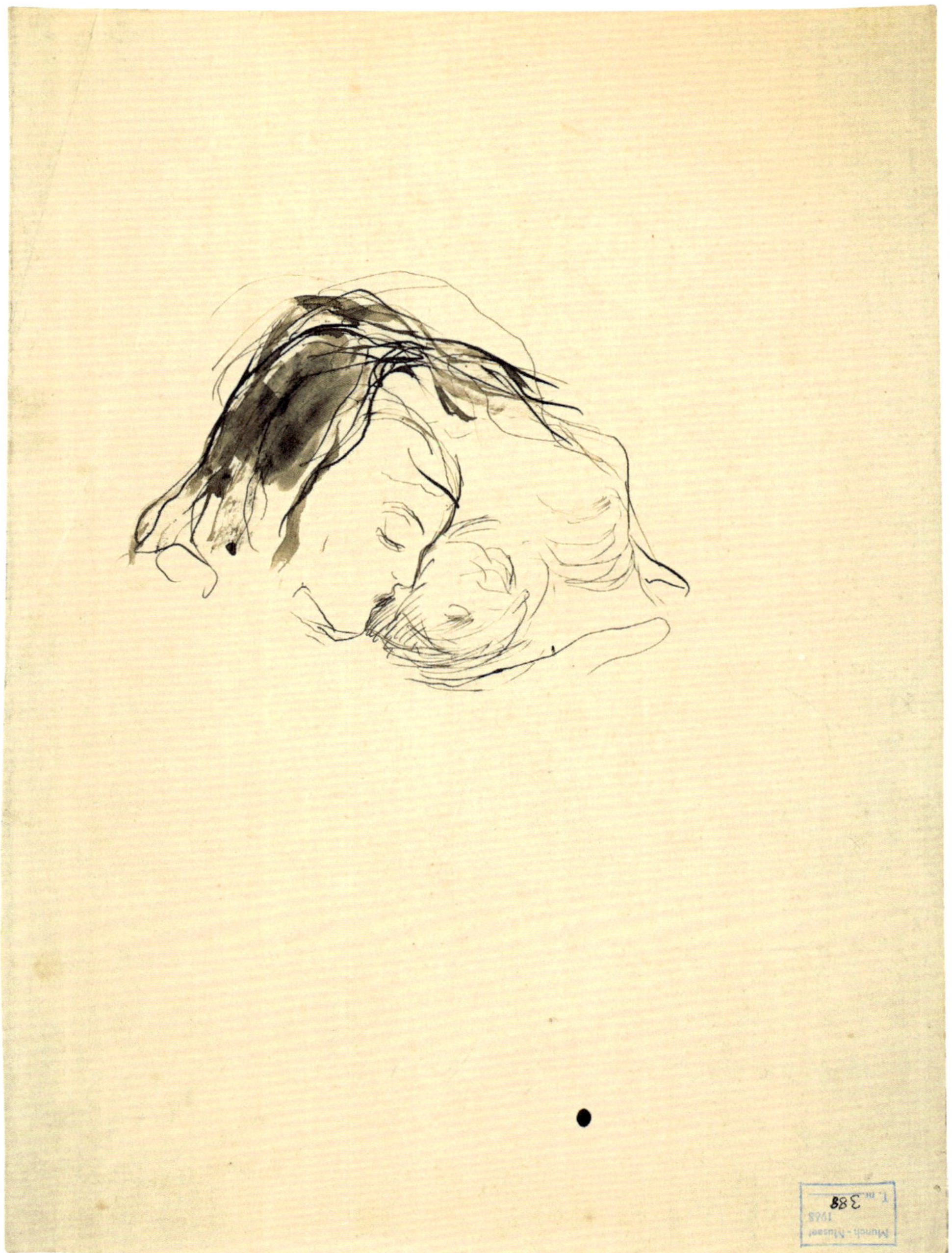

Man's Head against Woman's Breast
1890–92
Pen
384 × 290 mm

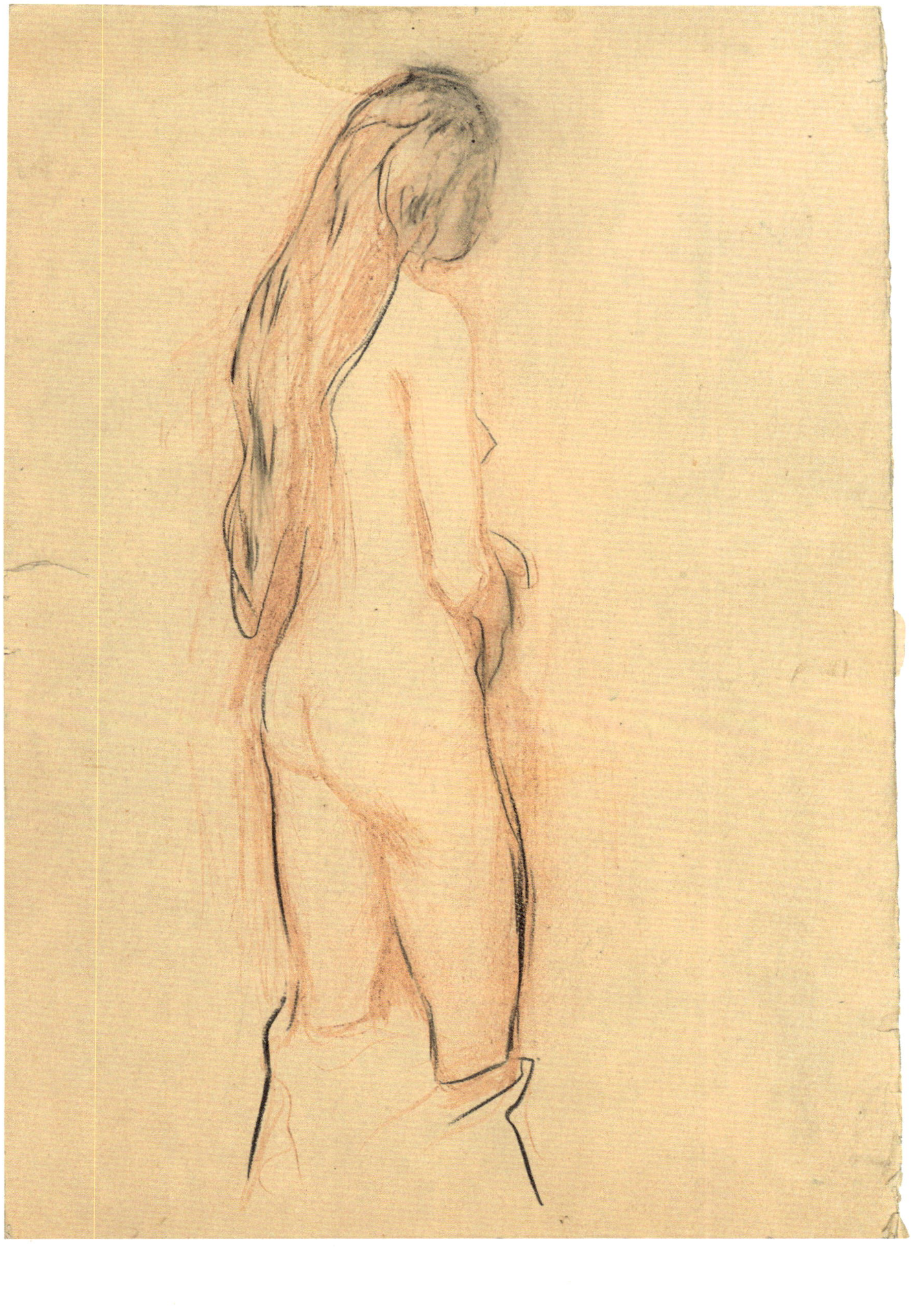

Standing Female Nude with Back Halfway Turned
1896
Crayon
560 × 410 mm

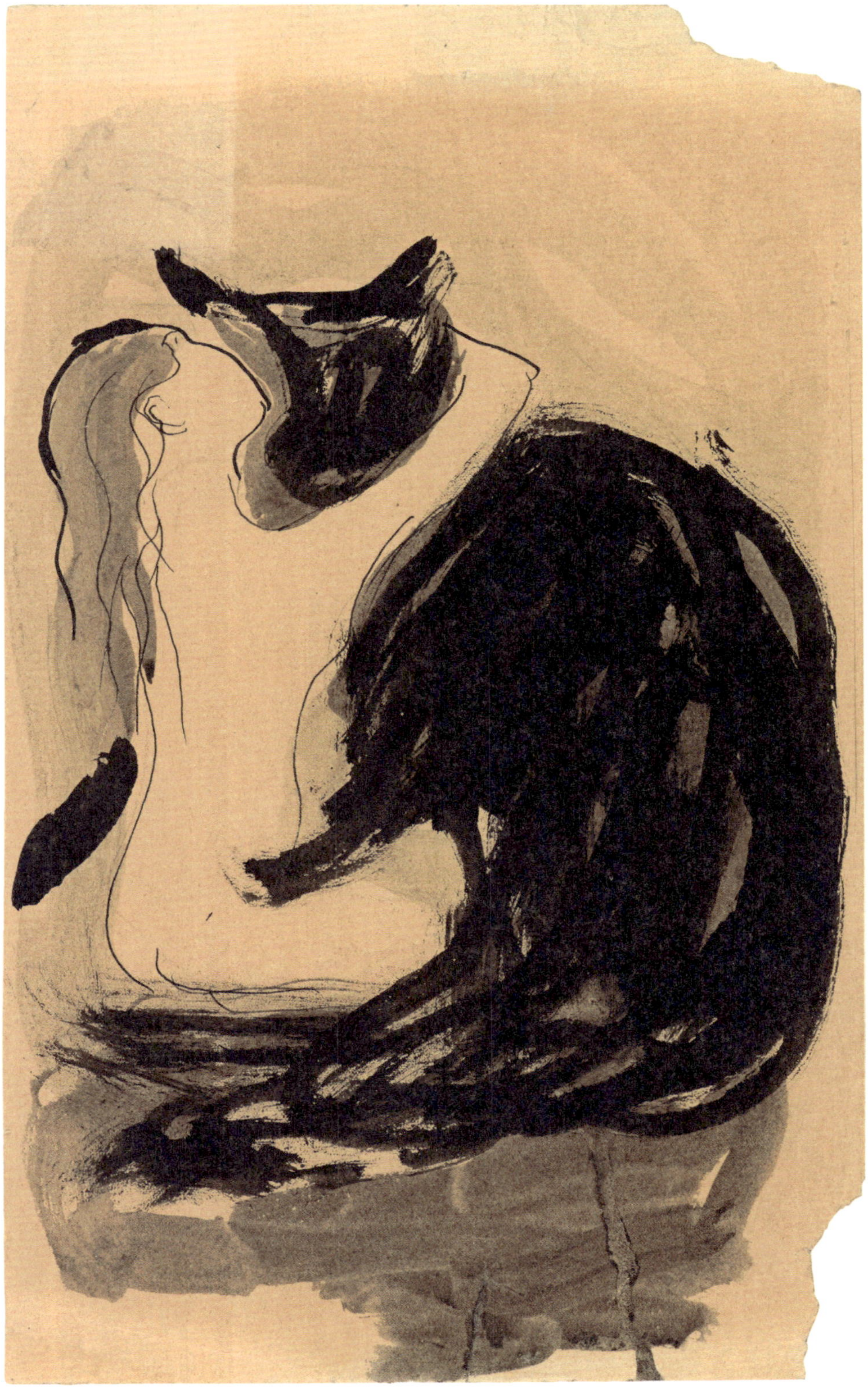

The First Human Beings:
The Woman and the Bear
1895–96
Pen and brush
321 × 202 mm

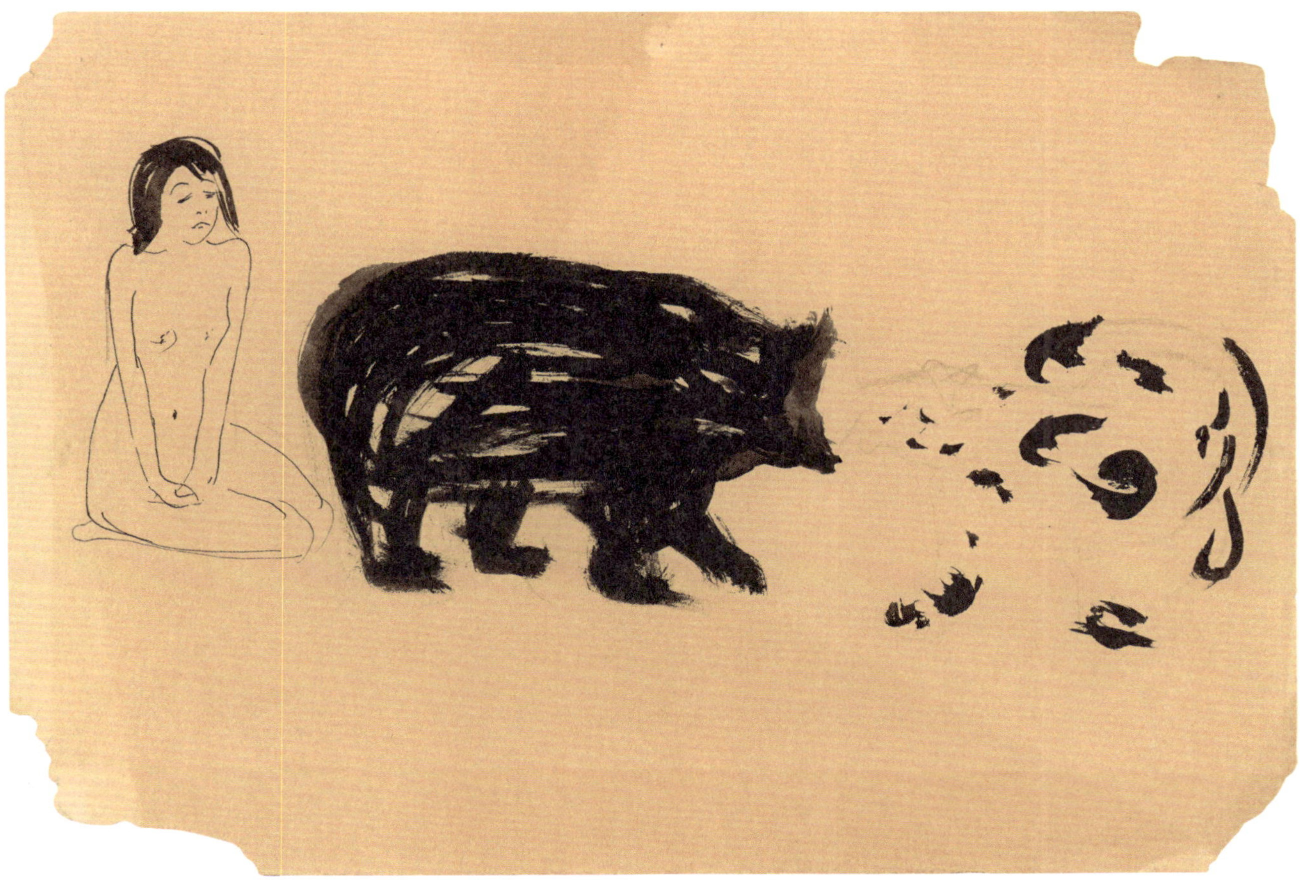

The First Human Beings:
The Woman, the Bear and the Tiger
1895–96
Brush, pen and pencil
322 × 481 mm

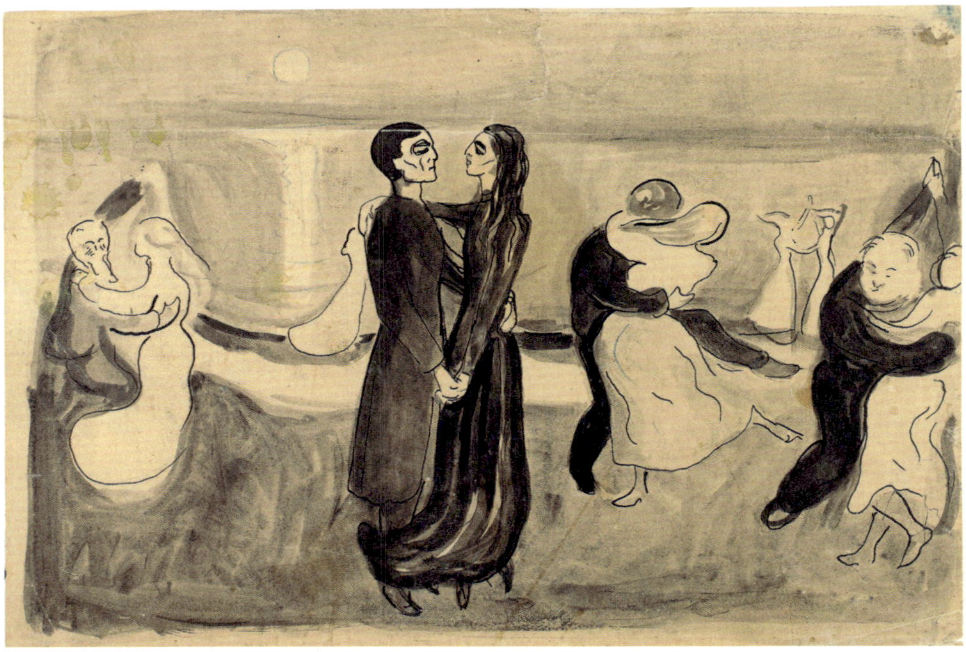

Dance of Life
1898–99
Pen, brush, wash and crayon
323 × 478 mm

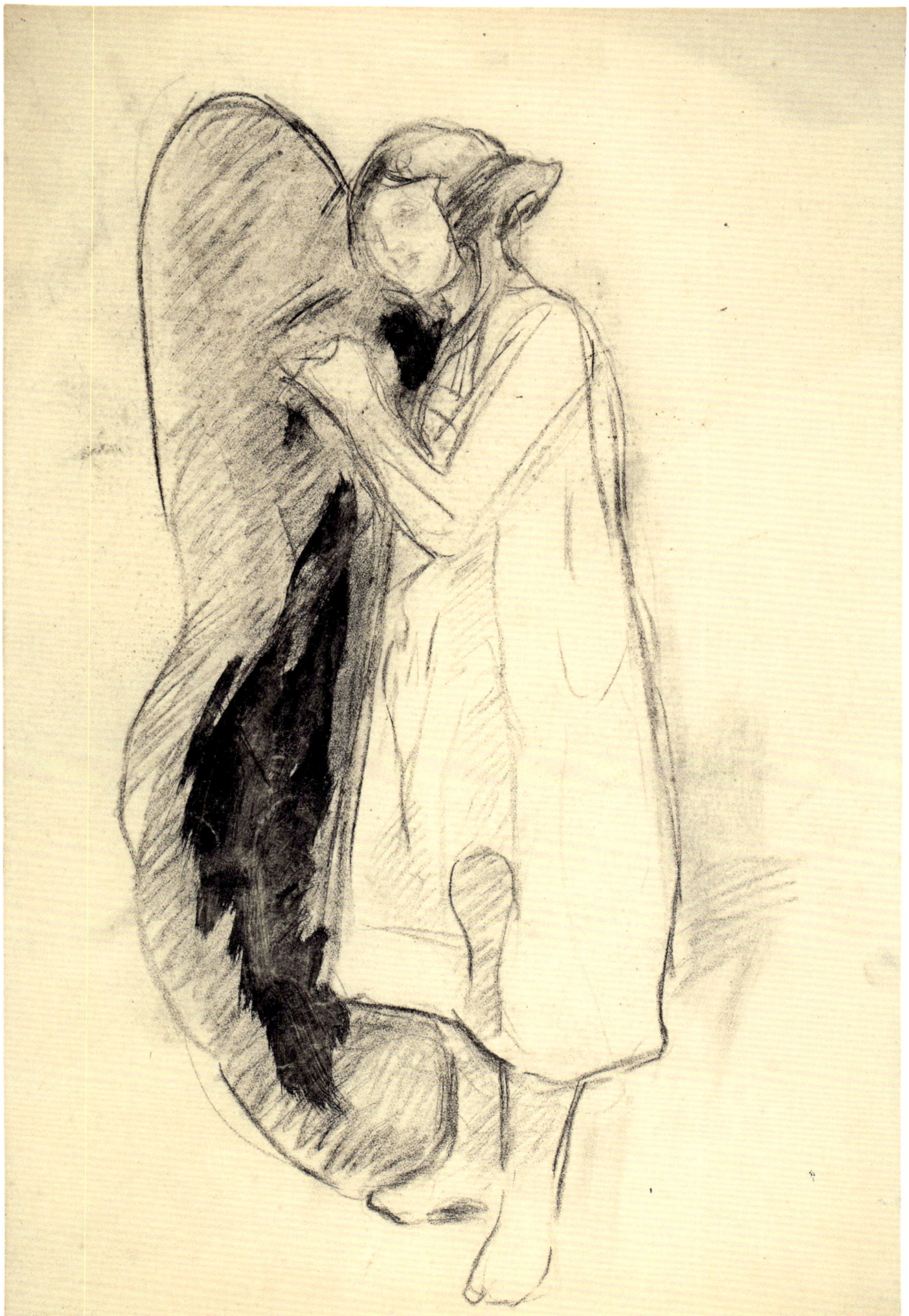

Young Woman Standing
1892–93
Charcoal and brush
630 × 431 mm

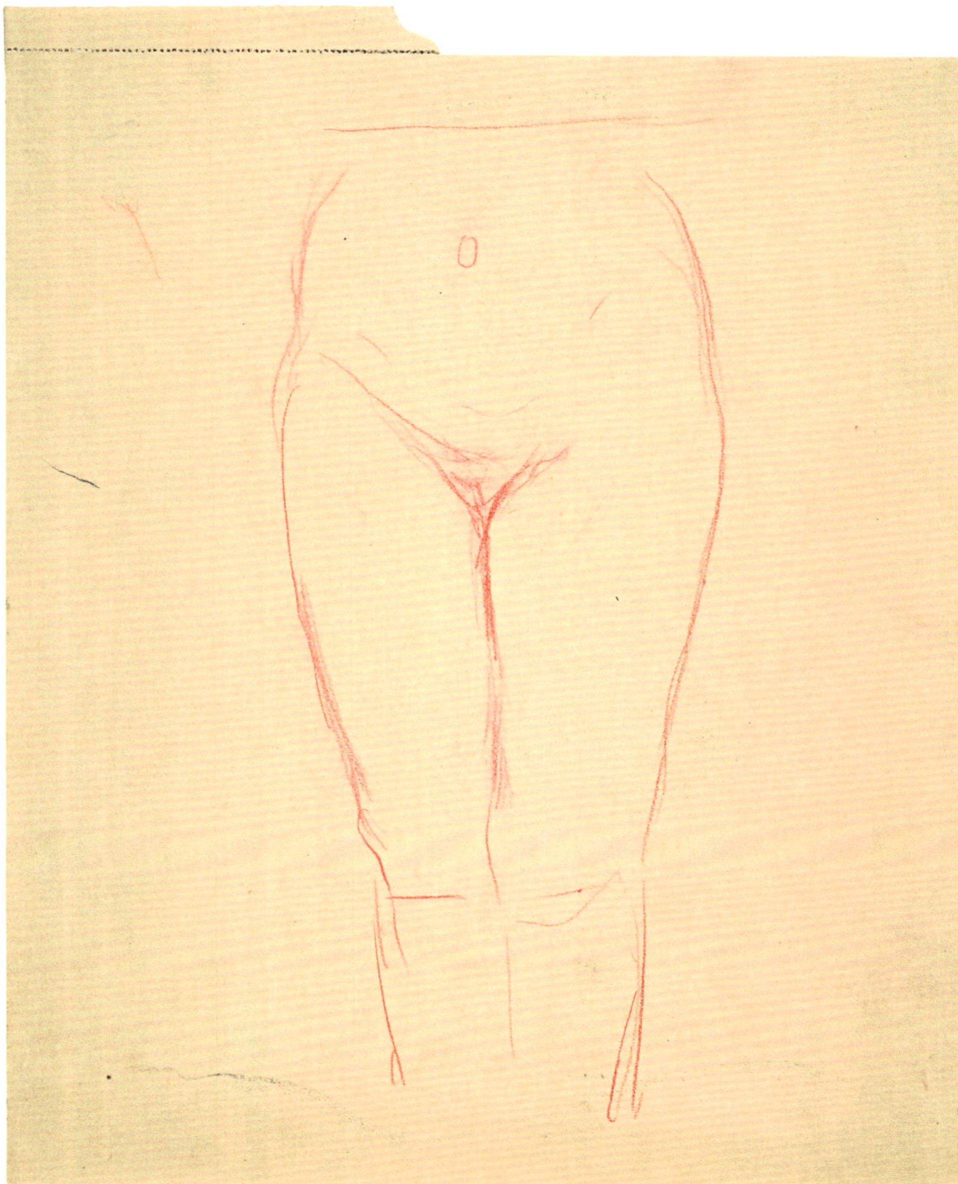

Female Nude from the Waist Down
c. 1895
Crayon
326 × 264 mm

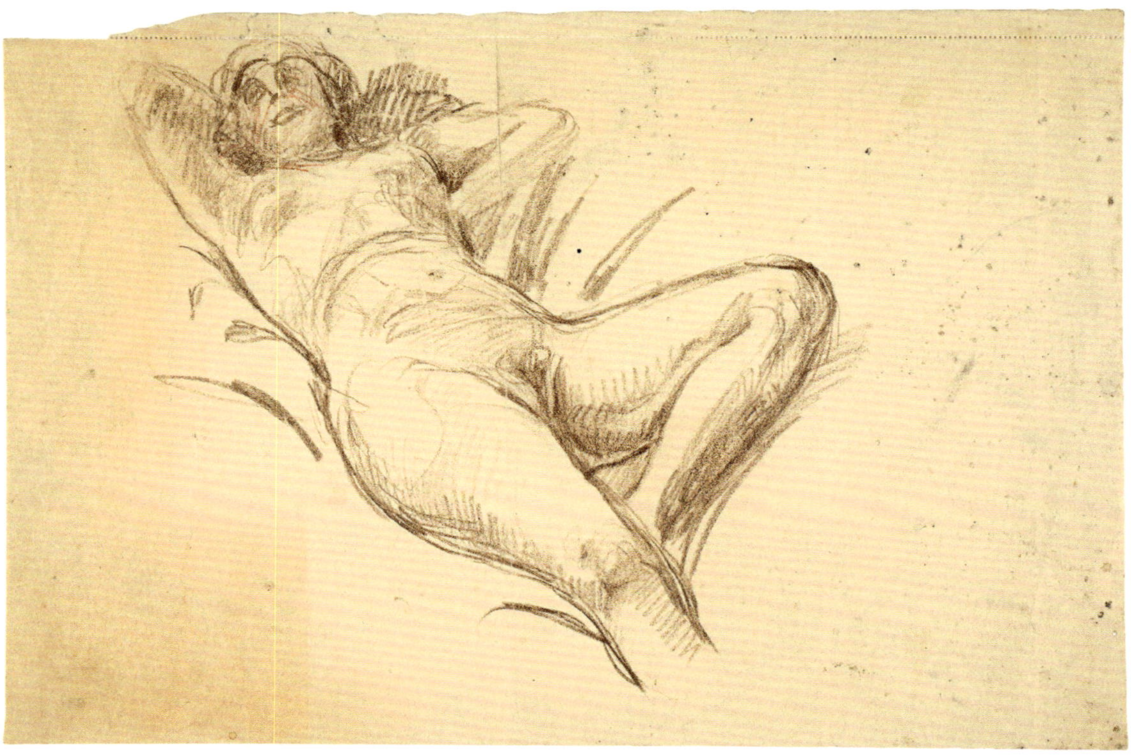

Reclining Female Nude
1911–15
Crayon
270 × 409 mm

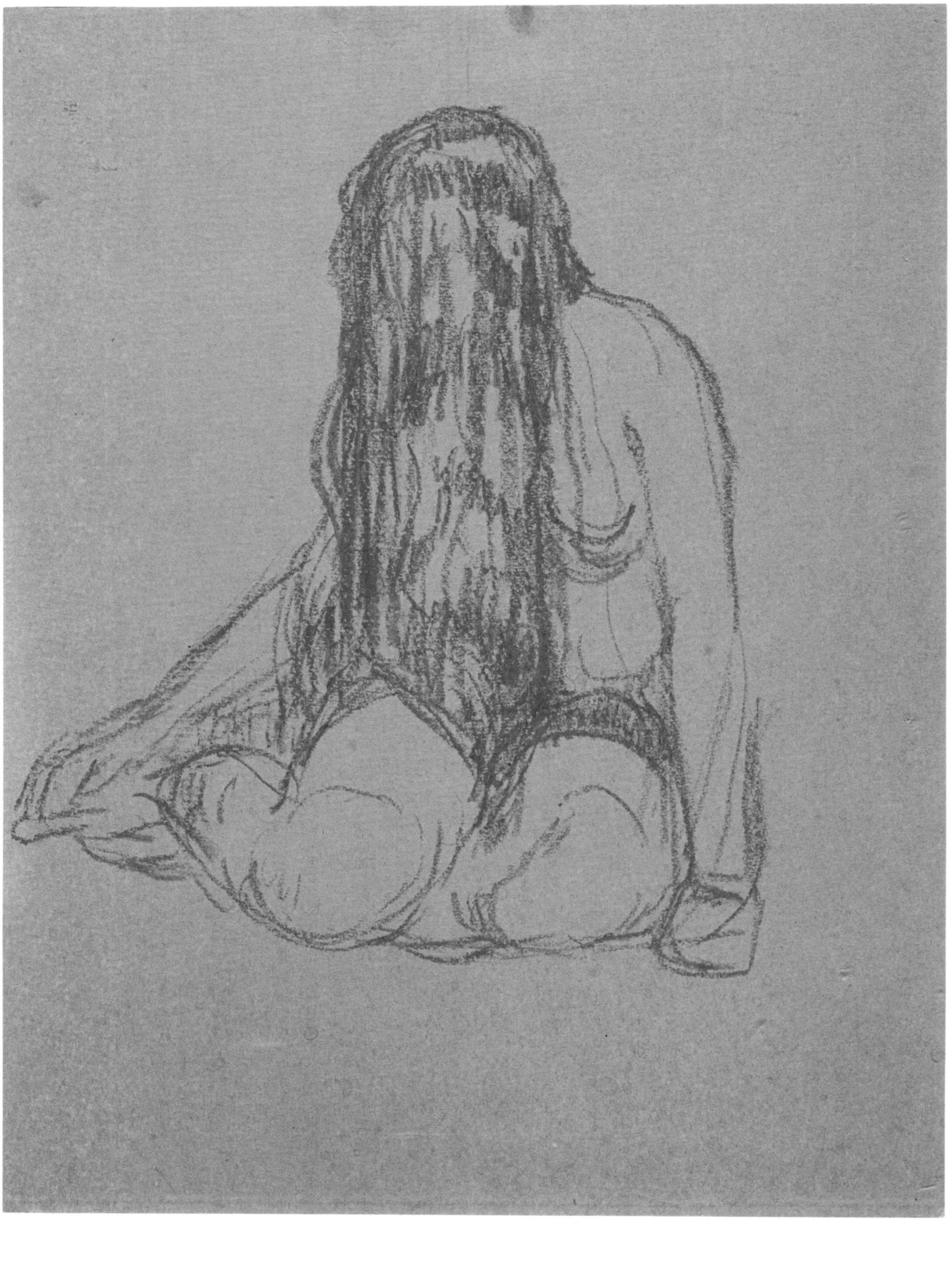

Seated Female Nude with Flowing Hair
1912–14
Crayon
730 × 560 mm

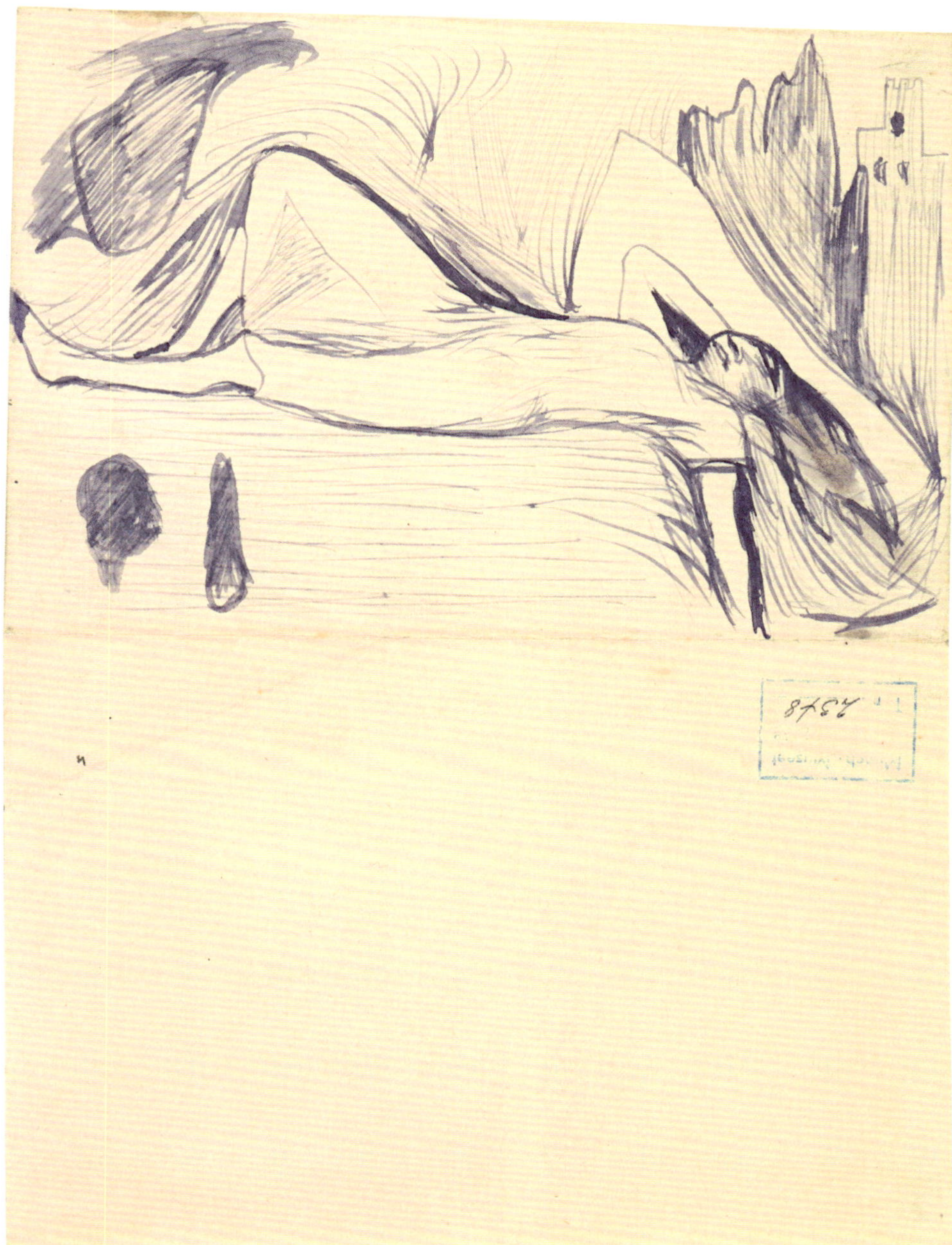

The Day After
1892–94
Pen
229 × 176 mm

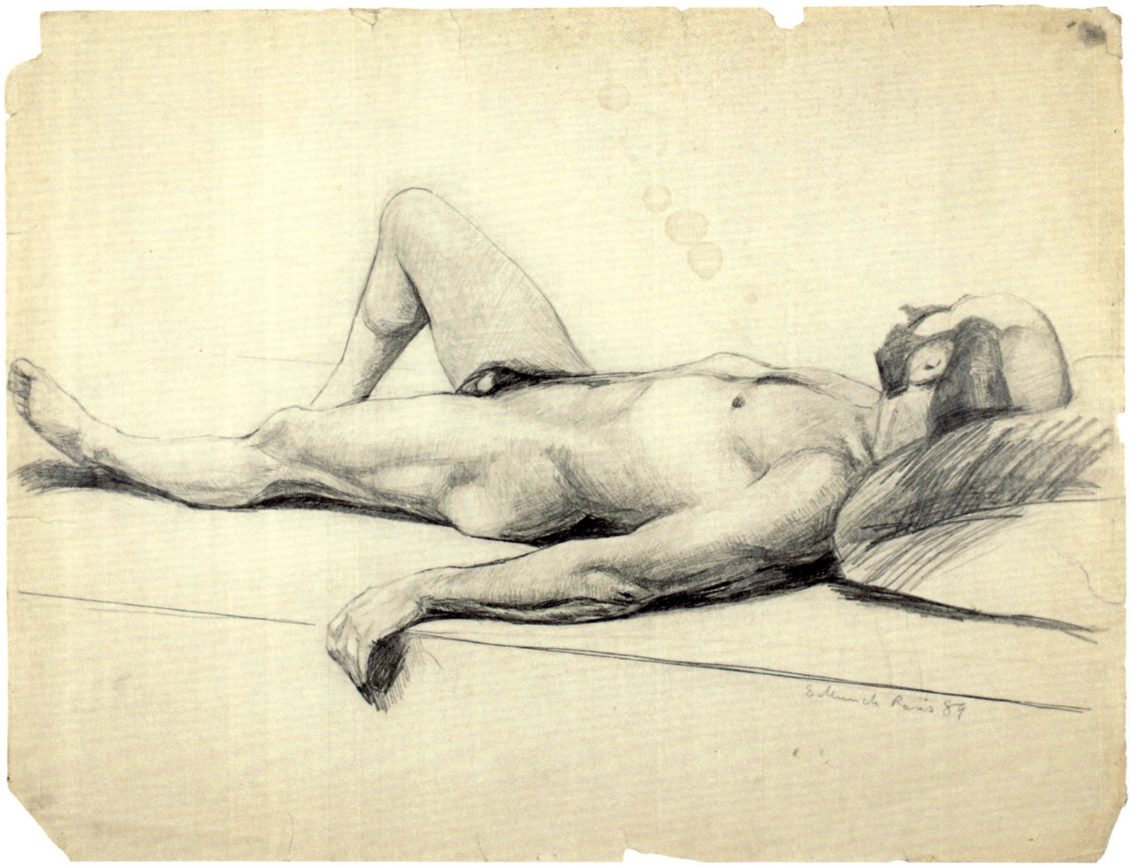

Reclining Male Nude
1889
Pencil
498 × 645 mm

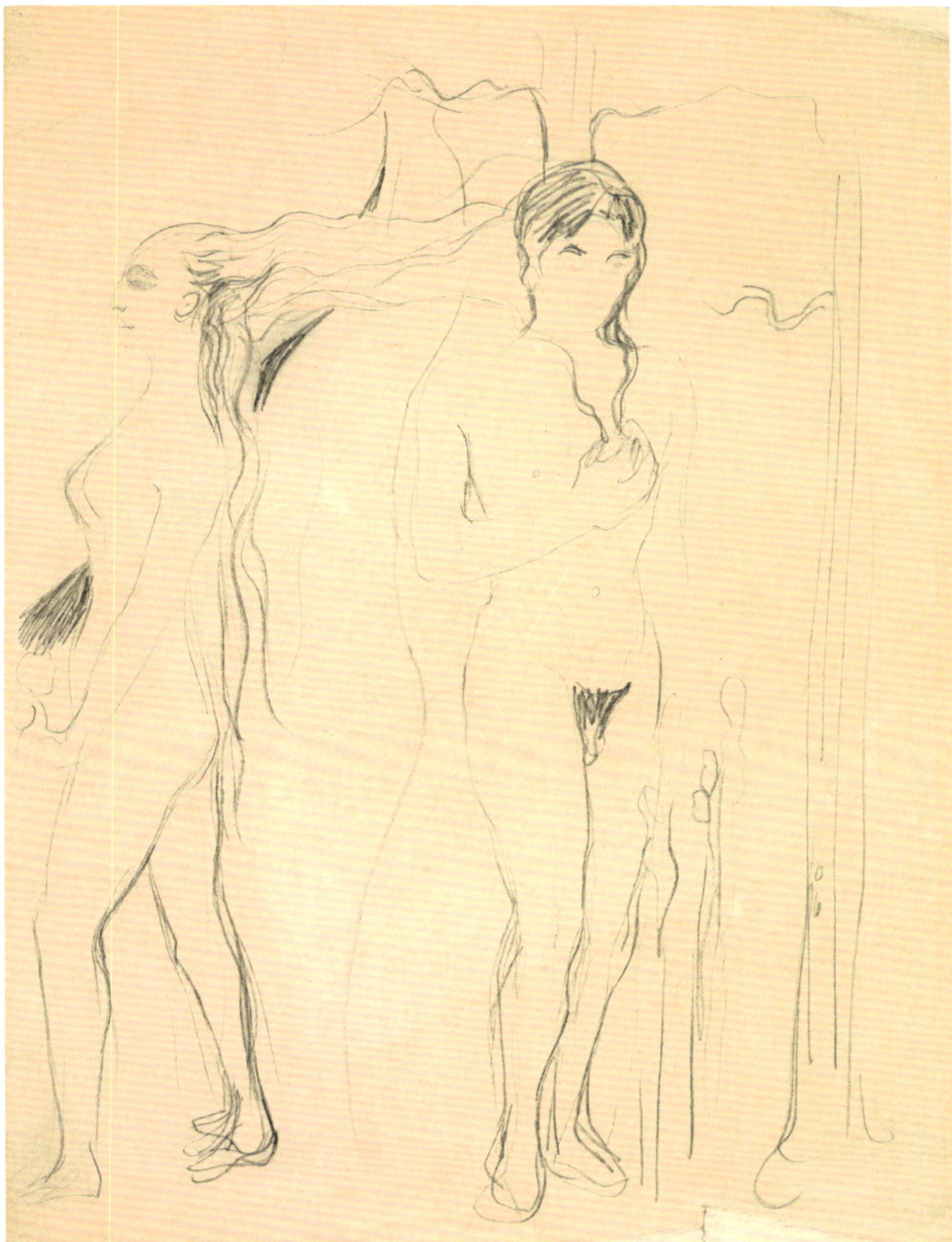

Separation
1893–95
Pencil
483 × 371 mm

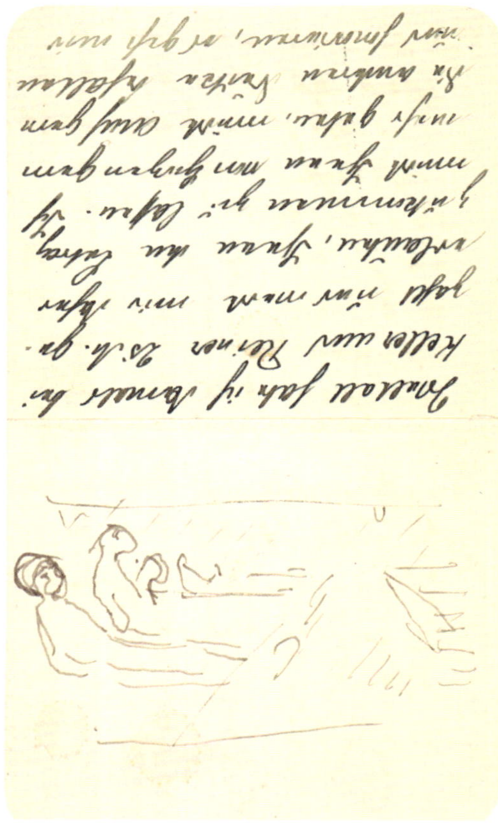

Sketch for *Hospital Ward*
1902
Drawing on a letter from
Eberhard von Bodenhausen
Pen
55 × 100 mm (motif)

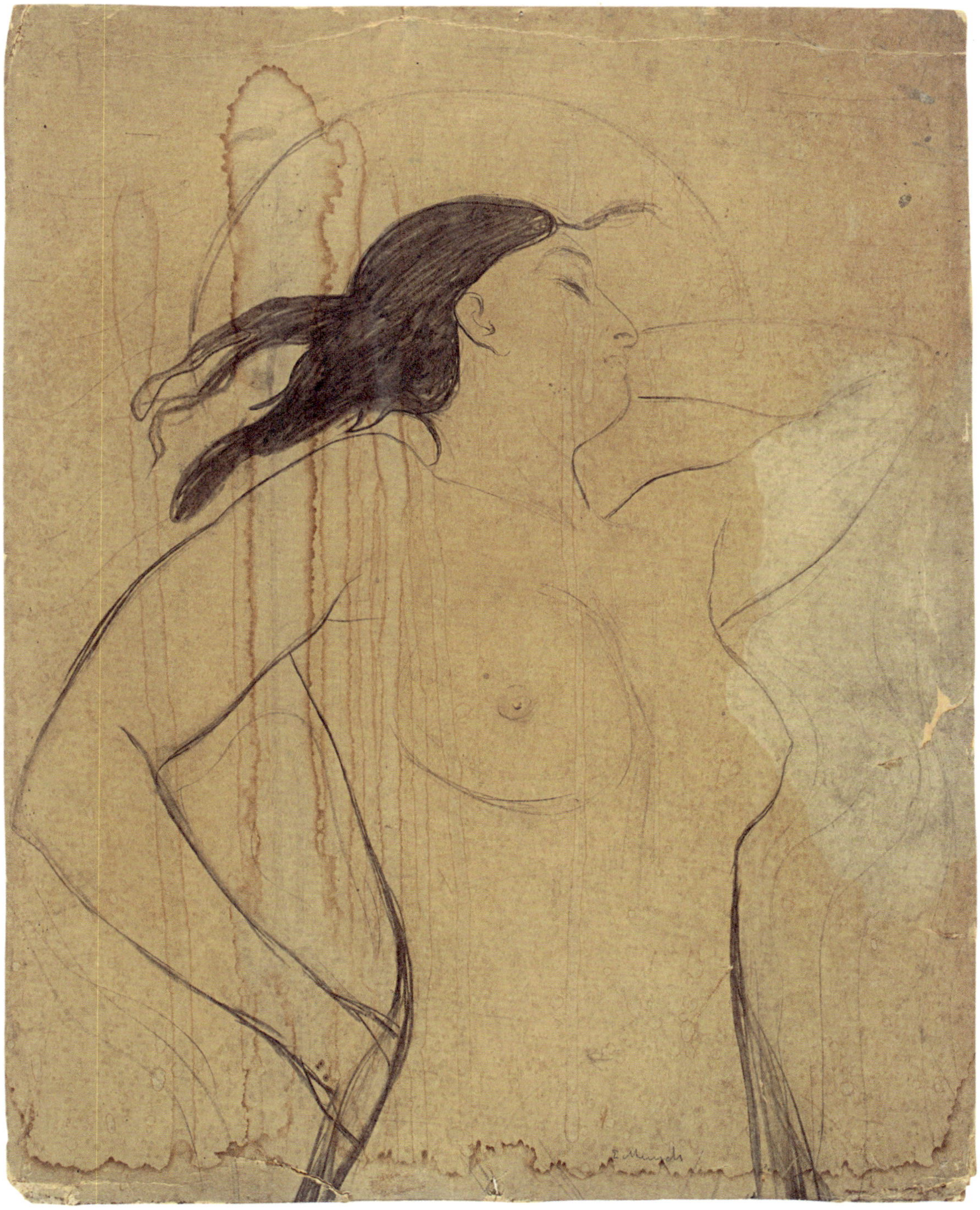

Sketch for Madonna
1893–94
Charcoal
738 × 598 mm

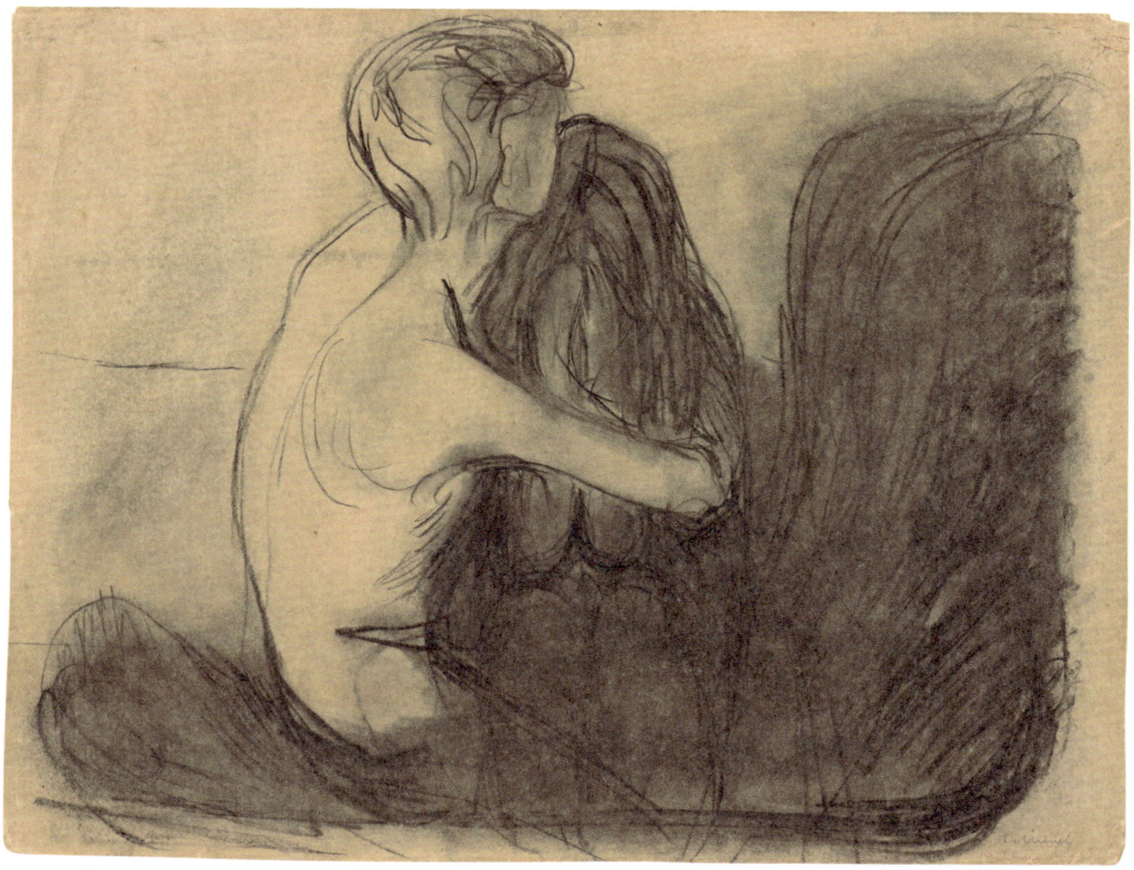

Consolation
1894
Charcoal
478 × 632 mm

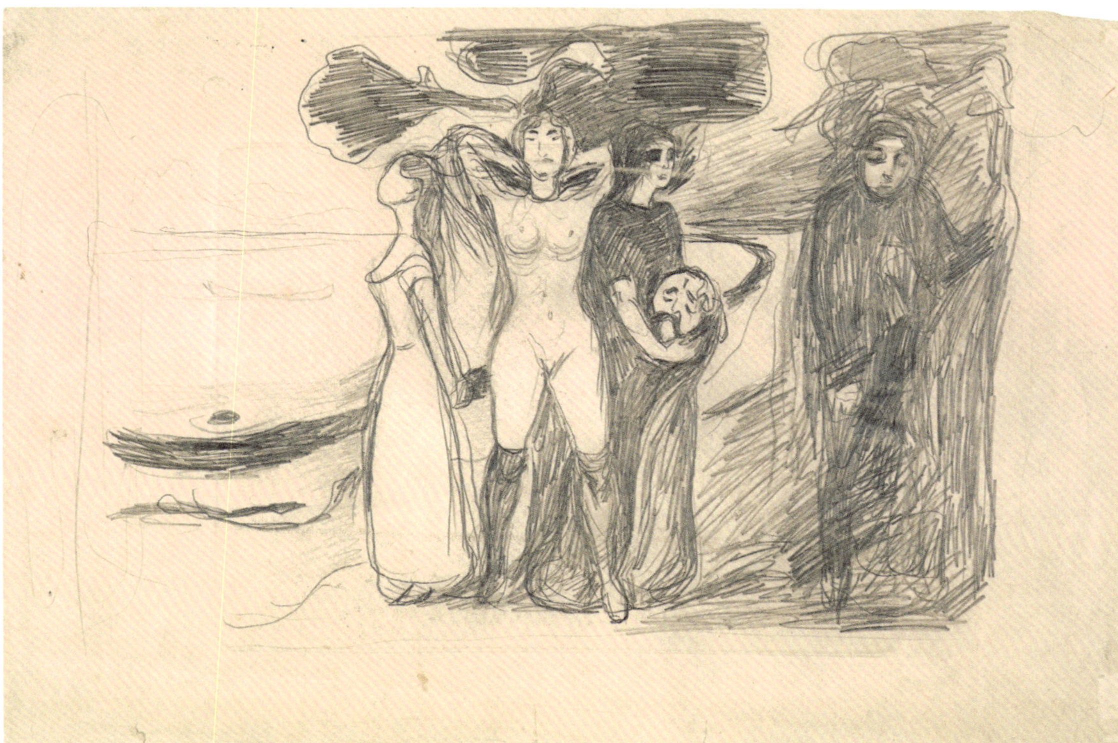

The Woman
1894–95
Pencil
303 × 460 mm

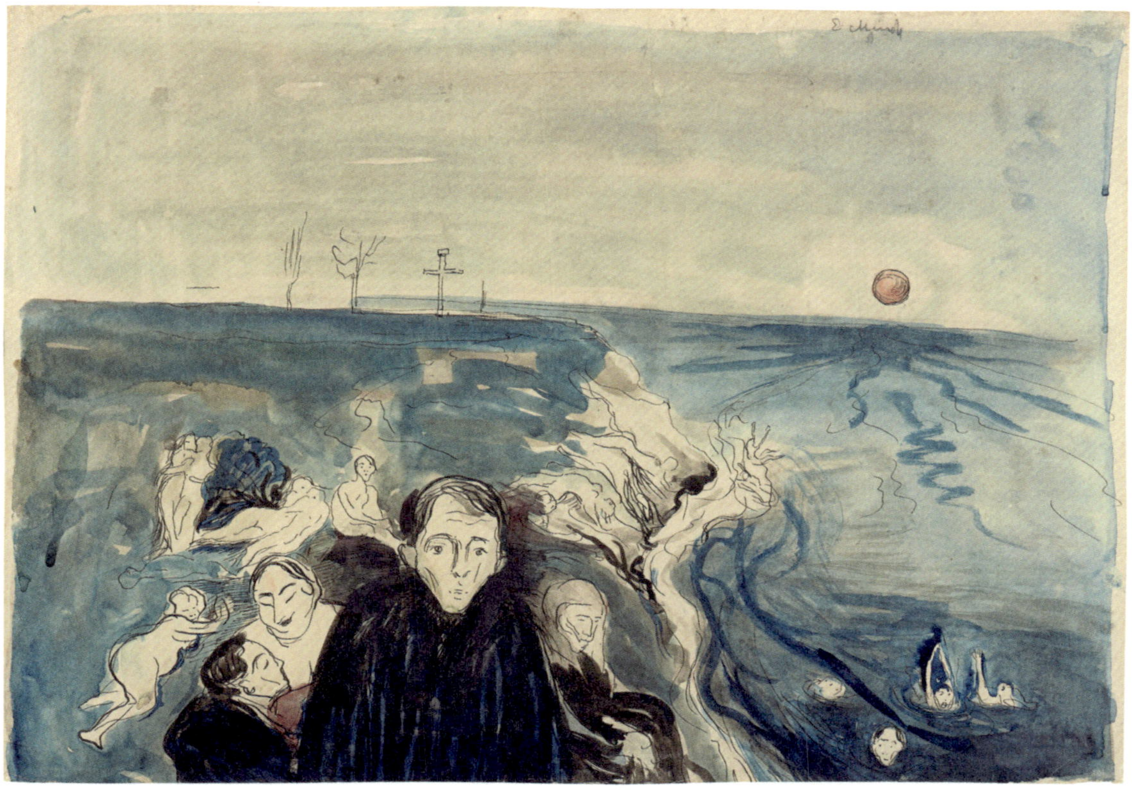

The Empty Cross
1899–1900
Watercolour and pen
433 × 627 mm

I never used a waste paper basket. My Suitcases served the purpose – That is why it is so terribly difficult to separate the wheat from the chaff but also the reason why I preserved so much

Edvard Munch, 1943

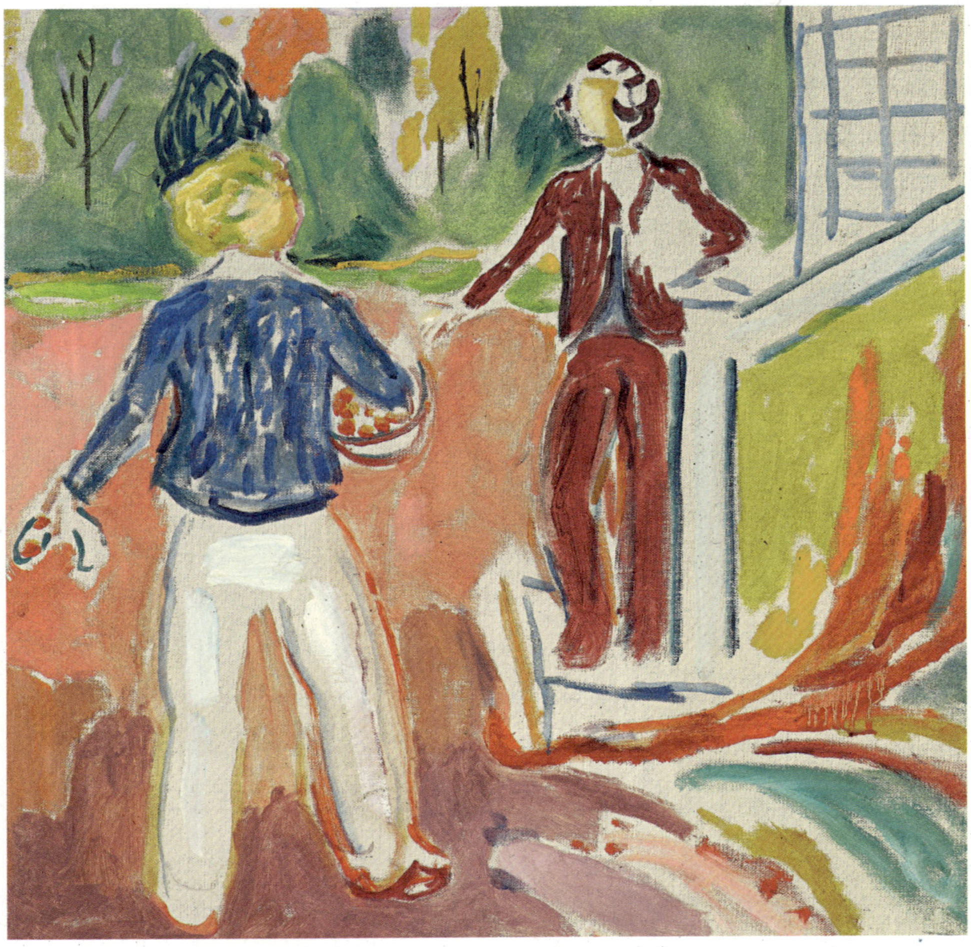

B
Two Women by the Veranda Steps
1942
Oil on canvas
59.5 × 61.5 cm

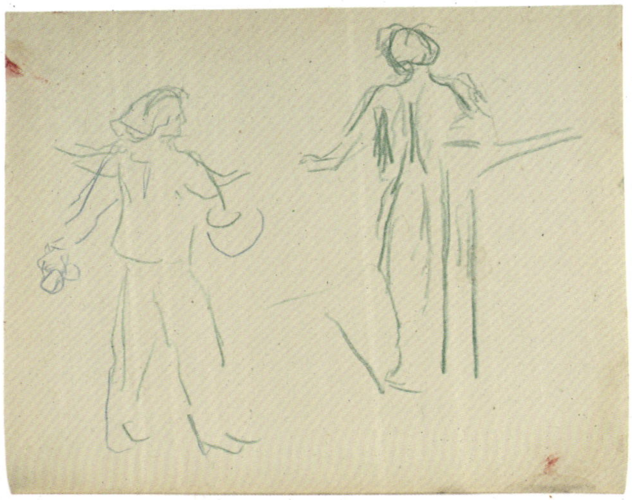

A
Two Women by the Veranda Steps
1942
Crayon on paper
165 × 280 mm

The Work Behind the Catalogue Raisonné of Munch's Drawings

Magne Bruteig

Edvard Munch's production of drawings was enormous, and 7700 of them have survived to this day. One of the explanations can be found in the quote on page 225, taken from a letter Munch wrote to his friend Christian Gierløff in 1943. Today we are grateful that Munch "preserved so much". When we began the work of compiling a catalogue raisonné of his drawings in 2015, we decided that "separating the wheat from the chaff" was something we wished to keep at an absolute minimum. We chose to include everything that could possibly be defined as a drawing – even very simple, unpretentious, unfinished, and yes, artistically rather unsuccessful drawings – because they fill in the picture of how the drawing process progressed for Munch. And there we stood before an overwhelming task with respect to sheer numbers. It soon became clear, as well, that a publication of the complete drawings in a traditional catalogue raisonné on paper would be too voluminous, and that an online catalogue would therefore have to be the main form of publication.

Registration

The first phase of this process consisted of registering all of the material anew. Although the drawings owned by Munchmuseet and from several other collections had already been registered, it was necessary to review every single drawing once more, in order to verify and supplement the existing information. During the course of this review, misleading or inaccurate titles were corrected, dates of origin were assessed and provisionally established, the type of tool used (pen, brush, pencil, crayon, pastel) was noted, signatures and inscriptions were evaluated and the type of paper was examined. In addition, references to comparable works were added, including drawings, prints and paintings, and the type of motif was noted, such as landscape, portrait, nude, interior, etc. This comprehensive and time-consuming registering of the drawings was followed by a phase consisting of quality control, an expansion of related works and a special focus on the dating.

Dating

Dating Munch's paintings and prints can be challenging enough. However, it is possible to turn to the dates noted by Munch himself, even though they are not always one hundred per cent reliable. Many of these works have also been shown in exhibitions, where they are documented in catalogue lists and occasionally with photographs. But the drawings are fundamentally more difficult to date. Only rarely does Munch date them, and although he exhibited drawings relatively often, they are seldom documented. Information in a catalogue that reads, "the exhibition presents a number of drawings as well" is not particularly useful in our context. In addition to purely stylistic evaluations, we have therefore made use of a rather broad system of categories, which together have led to certain, or probable, datings for well over 90% of the drawings. Not always down to a specific year, perhaps, but in most cases at least within a five-year period. Here are some of the most important "pegs" we have used:

For Munch, as for many artists, drawings were often the first step in an artistic process, which might end in a painting or, less often, in a graphic work. Occasionally a final result might also be a fully developed drawing. We have therefore looked for links to such comparable works, in particular where these have a certain or probable dating. The drawing *Two Women by the Veranda Steps* (A, p. 226) is quite certainly a sketch for the painting with the same title (B, p. 226). Since this was conclusively dated at 1942, it is natural to give the same dating to the drawing.

The reason behind the certain dating above is that one of the two women is identified as Dorothy Drewry, who worked as a model for Munch in 1942, and only this year. If we can identify the model or the person from a portrait in a drawing, we can often establish the date of its origin within a specified period, at best to a specific year, as in this case. In other cases, the time frame might be a bit broader: Ingeborg Kaurin was Munch's model from 1911 to 1915. We are quite certain that he did not draw or paint her beyond this period, so the period indicated, 1911–15, can thus be considered as certain, provided we are certain about the identification.

A positive sighting of a location in many cases may also provide a useful narrowing down of the period in which a drawing may have been executed, and at best provide a precise dating. If the motif is from Ekely, we know that 1916 must be the earliest dating; if it is from Jeløya, the time frame can be narrowed down to 1913–15 – the period in which Munch rented Grimsrød manor. Munch visited Åndalsnes only once, in 1925, so *Åndalsnes* and *Nesaksla Mountain* (C) and other drawings from the same place can be safely fixed to this date.

Munch often made his drawings on ordinary paper, which does not provide many clues for dating. But on occasion he used types of paper that were so distinctive that we could obtain an indication of the time frame for the execution of the drawings. Paper containing a watermark is often very useful. The drawing MM.T.02064 (D) has clear similarities with the motif in *The Wedding of the Bohemian* and has traditionally been dated 1925–30, like the painting with the same name (E). However, the paper bears the watermark "Buskerud Bank", which in Munch's archives has only been found in letters from 1937 and 1939. The decision for a late dating is further strengthened by the address "Kirkeveien 106" noted on the reverse side of the drawing, an apartment building in Oslo that was completed in 1936. MM.T.02064 is therefore not a preliminary sketch for the paintings with the title *The Wedding of the Bohemian*, as previously presumed, but a later repetition, and the dating was fixed to 1936–40.

The sketchbooks can provide many different possibilities for determining the date of their origin. Most of them were filled with drawings within a period of one or a few years. A certain or probable dating of one or several drawings can thus lead to a corresponding dating for the remainder of the drawings. However, there are also a good number of sketchbooks that Munch had obviously taken up again and continued to draw in after an interval of many years, so each book must be evaluated meticulously. Some of the sketchbooks may also contain numerous written points of reference, both lengthy notes and text fragments, personal names, place names, the names of hotels, addresses and telephone numbers, etc. The possibilities for researching historical records are many: using a name and address, for instance, we were able to search in digitalised directories for Kristiania/Oslo in order to find out when the person in question lived at the given address.

In addition to these and other "pegs" is of course stylistic analysis. During his youth in particular Munch went through obvious stages of artistic development that are possible to pinpoint with a large degree of precision. He eventually developed a broad repertoire of drawing techniques, which he could alternate between, depending on what he found most appropriate with regard to motif, drawing tools, and the like. This makes it more difficult to say anything certain about the dating based on style.

C
Åndalsnes and Nesaksla Mountain
1925
Crayon on paper
251 × 353 mm

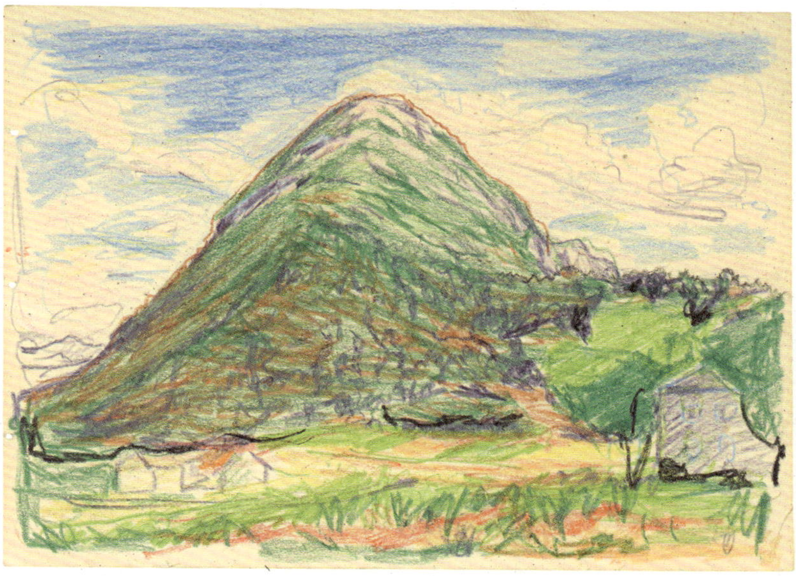

D
Variation on *The Wedding of the Bohemian*
1936–40
Pen on paper
220 × 280 mm

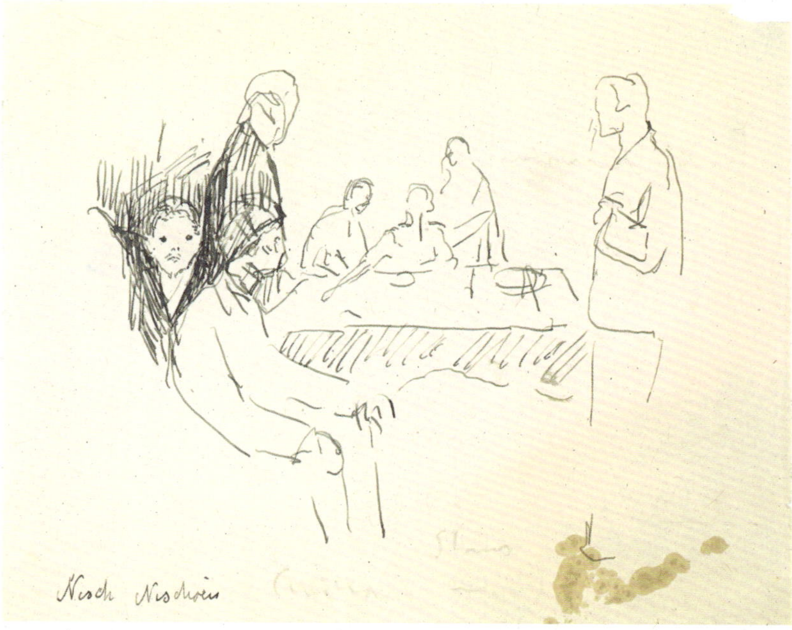

E
The Wedding of the Bohemian
1925–30
Oil on wooden panel
46 × 55 cm

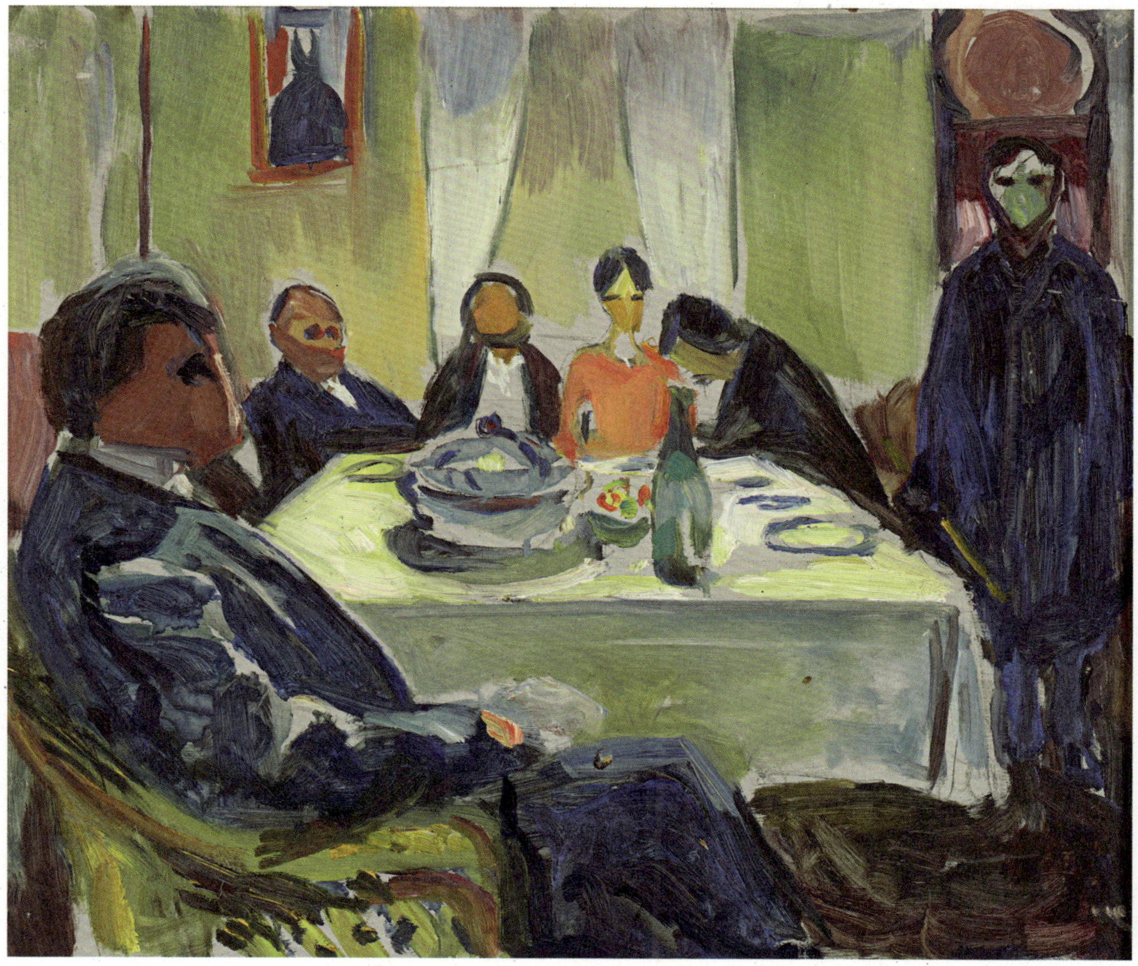

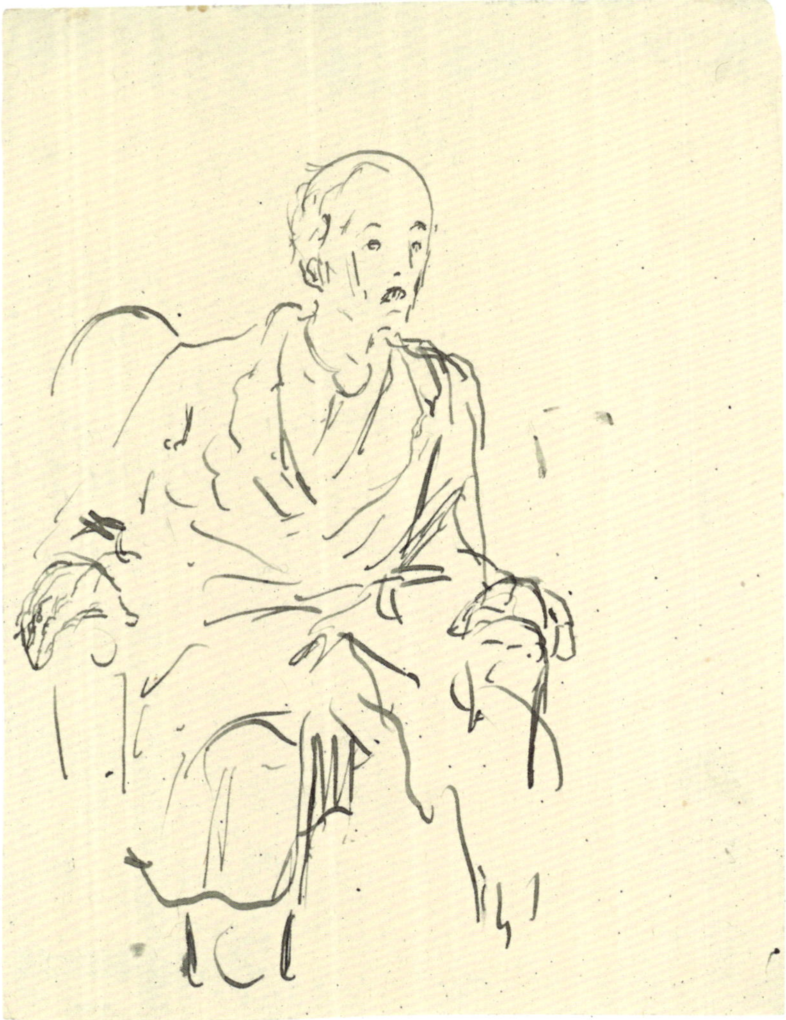

F
Rising from the Chair
1932–34
Pen on paper
226 × 175 mm

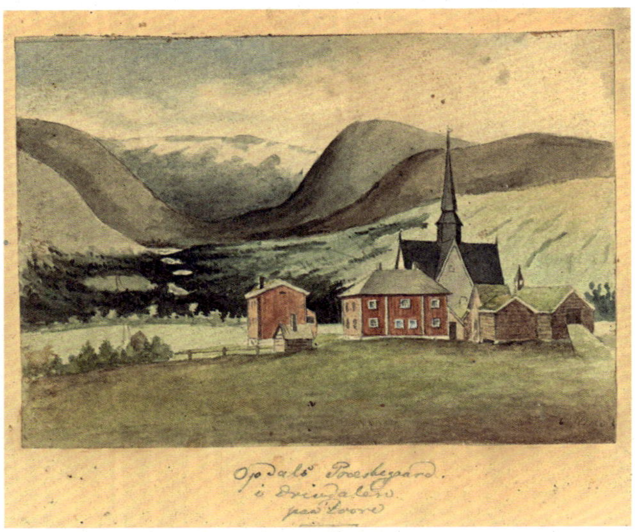

G
Oppdal Vicarage and Church
1879–80
Copy after Edvard Diriks
Watercolour and pencil on paper
111 × 161 mm

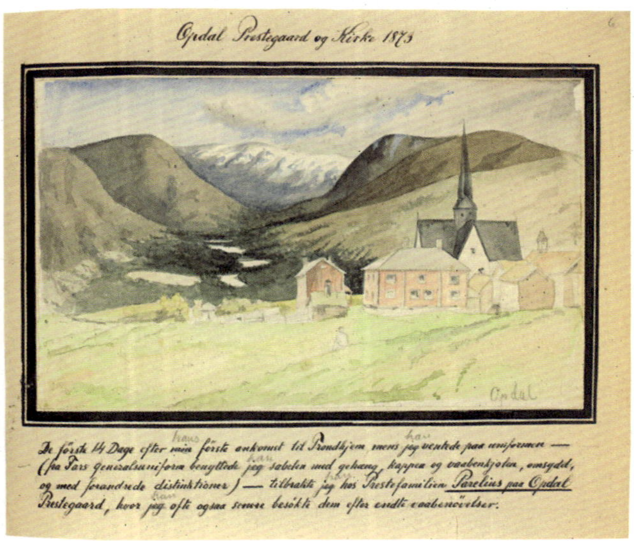

H
Edvard Diriks
Opdal Vicarage and Church
1873
Watercolour and pencil
National Library of Norway, Oslo
Photo: National Library

The drawings from the last decades of Munch's life, on the other hand, have a characteristic shorthand and loose style, in particular the pen drawings, such as *Rising from the Chair* (F).

The work of dating the drawings is not simply a vast canvas to be bleached; it is a canvas that will never be conclusively bleached. New information will most certainly appear, and new evaluations will be made that will change the dating of many of them in the years to come. Nevertheless, we believe that through a systematic and concerted review that focuses not only on individual works but also on Munch's entire production of drawings, we have contributed to significantly elevating the quality of the dating of this extremely voluminous material.

Authenticity

Evaluating authenticity is another important and often time-consuming aspect of working on most catalogues raisonnés. In this case, well over 90% of the drawings are in the museum's collection, with a provenance that can be traced directly back to Edvard Munch. With few exceptions, the drawings in both public and private collections have previously been evaluated and approved by the museum's experts, and the project team has on an independent basis upheld this conclusion.

A collection of drawings in a private collection, all of which stem from one sketchbook that was most likely acquired by Munch in Paris around 1897, has proved to be problematic. The provenance of the sketchbook can with great certainty be traced back to Munch's sister Inger, but there has nevertheless been disagreement among the experts whether it was Edvard Munch or someone else who penned the more than forty drawings in the book. The project team studied the history, the motifs and the design of every single drawing. Following exhaustive discussions the drawings were included in the catalogue.

During the course of our work we received a number of inquiries from the public regarding drawings that may have been made by Munch, and some of these were included, after careful evaluation, in the catalogue. In 2017 we were contacted by a private individual who owned a watercolour of *Oppdal Church* (G). We could immediately see that if it had been done by Munch, it must have been when he was very young. Some of his early watercolours have some of the same precise, detailed and rather meticulous style. This would have been long before he developed a unique artistic idiom, and many others might have painted a watercolour of this kind. The picture was signed "E Munch", but the signature was faint and written in such a way as not to preclude a handwriting that was not Munch's. The question also arose as to why Edvard would make such an ambitious watercolour of a church he had never seen. A web search of Oppdal Historical Society surprisingly revealed a nearly identical watercolour (H). Further research revealed that it was executed by Edvard Diriks in 1873.

Edvard Diriks (1855–1930) was Edvard Munch's cousin. He studied architecture in Karlsruhe and Berlin 1874–75 and received an art education in Berlin and Weimar in 1877–79. Prior to this he was an officer in the army. He painted the watercolour from Oppdal while en route from Kristiania to his military base in Trondheim in 1873. After his studies on the continent he settled in Kristiania in 1879, and it was most likely at that time that Edvard Munch borrowed the watercolour, which he copied. The provenance of the copy could with reasonable certainty be traced back to Munch's aunt Josefine Roll.

This was one of extremely few examples of how Edvard copied works by other artists in his youth. In the museum's holdings we have a copy – a watercolour as well – of a sailboat after an original by another Diriks relative, Carl Fredrik Diriks. With *Oppdal Church* we gained an important confirmation of how Edvard Munch worked diligently towards developing artistically before arriving at his final decision "to become a painter".

Motifs

An online publication provides a whole different possibility for searching than a printed catalogue, and with such a magnitude of material, a well-developed search function provides both an overview and a structure. Here one can of course search by title, inventory number, technique, dating, etc. But in order to take maximum advantage of the search modes, we also invested extensive work in categorising the motifs. Among the 23 main categories, we can mention: "fauna", "flora", "interior", "caricature", "landscape" and "portrait". Most of them also have a number of sub-categories. "Landscape", for instance, has as many as 26, among them: "avenue", "river", "mountain", "waterfall", "coastline" and "forest".

In addition to the motif-based categories, we have chosen to include "place" as a separate category. Among these are eleven countries, with "Norway" having 38 specific locations, all the way down to street addresses (e.g. "Thorvald Meyers gate 48"). In this way you can easily attain results for all the drawings Munch made of motifs from Ekely, for example.

This possibility of making a very specific search among the motifs is useful for those who simply wish to "leaf through" the drawings, while simultaneously being a highly advanced and time-saving tool for students and researchers who wish to immerse themselves in specific themes. To go through thousands of drawings to find the 122 male nude drawings that Munch made would be extremely time-consuming. Now it takes just a few seconds.

The Team

As mentioned, Edvard Munch's drawings encompass a voluminous and multifarious material that is difficult to grasp in its entirety. The catalogue raisonné is the result of three years of intensive work. Thanks to a team that worked with all aspects of the material and contemplated it from various angles, we have been able to discover and develop links between individual works, as well as between various parts of the entirety.

The team consisted of art historians at Munchmuseet; Senior Curator Magne Bruteig, Curator Petra Pettersen, and Researcher Sivert Thue, as well as external Munch experts Gerd Woll and Frank Høifødt, who had previously been employed at the museum. MaryClaire Pappas, a student of art history at the time, was of invaluable help in creating an overview of drawings outside the museum's collection. The museum's digital collection head, Hilde Bøe, was responsible for transferring all the data from the museum's database to the online catalogue. Several other professional groups at the museum have also been involved in the process; paper conservators, librarians, IT staff and art historians. The museum's photographers have done an exceptional job of re-photographing several thousand drawings. Discussions along the way have also helped us to arrive at results that we could hardly have achieved individually. Independent translator Francesca M. Nichols has translated the titles of the drawings and the catalogue texts into English.

Artists' biographies

Marlene Dumas (b. 1953) grew up in South Africa during the apartheid regime and since the mid-1970s has lived in Amsterdam in the Netherlands. The main modes of expression of her oeuvre are drawing and painting, executed in a striking combination of raw spontaneity and great precision. She is especially known for her nudes and portraits that revolve around sexuality, identity and oppression. Many of her pictures are included in comprehensive series, among them "Rejects" (1994–), which consists of portraits she has rejected from other works. Another major series is "Great Men" (2014–), composed of portraits of male homosexual artists, created as a response to Russia's criminalising of LHBT persons. Dumas is also a text artist. Many of her works combine writing and images, and she also has a large production of freestanding poetic texts. In 2018 she made her debut as a curator with the exhibition *Moonrise. Marlene Dumas & Edvard Munch* at Munchmuseet.

Terje Nicolaisen (b. 1964) has since the mid-1990s developed a wide-ranging and unpredictable art production, characterised by a short path from idea to finished work. He is particularly known for his many proposals for art projects that remain unrealised, for uncensored everyday observations, and for his portraits of authors, artists, and acquaintances. In addition to a large number of individual works on paper, Nicolaisen has produced some 450 artist books, and in recent years has also worked with painting on canvas. His productivity is attributable to a ruthless commitment to honesty and a pronounced pride in his occupation. He is a self-assured product of the 1990s' anti-romantic ideals of artistic professionalism, a theme he also frequently addresses in his work. Since 2004, he has been one of the five members of Tegneklubben (Drawing Club), who meet at irregular intervals to cultivate spontaneous expression on paper, always using the A4 format and signing their creations collectively.

Nalini Malani was born in Karachi in 1946, the year before Pakistan was separated from India and the British government relinquished control of the region. Since the 1960s she has combined new and traditional mediums in sweeping visual narratives. In her works she links motifs from Indian and Greek mythology associatively with current political themes, such as Hindu nationalism, the ideology of free trade, and violence against women. A central aspect of Malani's works is the interaction between images and different architectonic spaces. Another aspect is the use of monumental formats together with more intimate modes of expression in the form of notes and sketches. Her multifaceted oeuvre encompasses paintings, installations, books, film, video animation, shadow play, performance, and scenography.

Georg Baselitz (b. 1938) grew up in what, from 1949 to 1990, was called GDR or East Germany. He studied at the art college in East Berlin, but when he was expelled for "socio-political immaturity", he decided to continue his art studies in West Berlin. This was three years before the Berlin Wall was built, which would divide the city in two for the next 28 years. During the 1960s Baselitz worked his way to becoming one of the most prominent young artists in West Germany. With the revival of painting in the 1980s and a newly won international interest in German art, he made a name for himself at the forefront of international contemporary art. Baselitz has always worked in a figurative and expressive idiom, with the human figure as the central focus. Unlike many other German postwar artists, he did not embrace abstract painting, nor did he become infatuated with American Pop art of the 1960s. Instead he insisted upon an idiom with roots in older German art, which many perceived as somewhat backwards and provincial at the time. When, in the late 1960s, Baselitz began to systematically paint his motifs upside down, it implied a form of resetting and liberation of the figure. In doing so, he abolished in his own way the fundamental disparity between abstraction and figuration that defined the art discussions of the time, and which also formed part of the political and ideological schism between Western abstraction and Soviet and Eastern European socialist realism.

Tracey Emin (b. 1963 in England) has been a prominent figure in international contemporary art since the early 1990s. Her art has always been highly autobiographical and personal. She created a great stir with her work *Everyone I Have Ever Slept With* 1963–1995 (1995), a tent onto which she appliquéd the names of everyone she had, in one way or another, shared a bed with. The work was shown in the art collector Charles Saatchi's sensational show *Sensation* in 1997. Another notorious early work is *My Bed* (1998), which was included in the exhibition for the Turner Prize in 1999. It consisted of her unmade bed together with other objects such as bloodstained underwear and used condoms, as they appeared after Emin had spent numerous days in bed during a personal crisis. She has worked in many different mediums, such as drawing, printmaking, photography, textile, neon, painting, and sculpture. During the past 20 years, classical mediums such as painting and bronze sculpture have gained a more prominent place in her oeuvre. A recurring feature of her work has always been an expressive line, brushstroke, or text. This is evident in the flowing handwriting in the neon works and other text-based works, and in the alternately delicate, frenetic, and aggressive lines in paintings and prints. In 2011 Emin was appointed professor of drawing at the Royal Academy of Arts in London.

Contributors

Mieke Bal is an independent cultural theorist, critic, video artist and curator. Her work is based on the cultural analysis of subjects such as gender, migratory culture, psychoanalysis, and critique of capitalism. Bal received her PhD in French and Comparative Literature from Utrecht University in 1977. In 2017 she curated the exhibition *Emma & Edvard. Love in the Time of Loneliness* at Munchmuseet. Her 45 books include a trilogy on political art. As a video artist her latest works include the sixteen-channel video installation *Don Quijote: Sad Countenances* (2019) and the essay film *It's About Time! Reflections on Urgence* (2020). Bal is based in Amsterdam.

Magne Bruteig studied Art History at the University of Oslo, and was employed at Munchmuseet from 1998 until he retired in 2018. He worked in the Department of Prints and Drawings, in his last years on the staff as Senior Curator. Bruteig has written a number of articles about Edvard Munch and is the author of the books *Munch – Drawings* (2004) and *Edvard Munch. Works on Paper* (2013, together with Ute Kuhlemann Falck). From 2013 until 2018 Bruteig headed the museum's catalogue raisonné project of Munch's drawings.

Halvor Haugen is trained as an artist and works as a freelance editor, writer, and translator. Together with Nina M. Schjønsby Halvor runs Tekstbyrået, which in addition to taking on editorial and publishing projects for various art institutions also serves as an independent publishing house. He is the former editor of the art journals Billedkunst and UKS – forum for samtidskunst, and has taught art theory and writing at the Oslo National Academy of the Arts and the Faculty of Fine Art, Music and Design at the University of Bergen.

Jon-Ove Steihaug is Head of the Department of Exhibitions and Collections at MUNCH. He earned his PhD in Art History from the University of Oslo with a dissertation on the Norwegian painter Bendik Riis (2008). He has previously been employed at the Museum of Contemporary Art (now the National Museum), Kunstnernes Hus and the University of Oslo, and has arranged numerous exhibitions as an independent curator. Steihaug has also been an art critic, among other things for the public radio broadcasting corporation NRK P2 during the period 2008–11, and was the initiator and editor of the website kunstkritikk.no from 2003 to 2005.

Illustrated works

Marlene Dumas

14 *Salome can't Decide*, c. 1987
Ink and watercolour on paper
29.5 × 21 cm
Collection of the Artist
Photo: Peter Cox, Eindhoven

17 *Venus with Body of Adonis*, 2015–16
Ink wash and metallic acrylic
on paper
25.5 × 28.5 cm
Glenstone Museum,
Potomac MD, USA
Photo: Peter Cox, Eindhoven

17 *The Dove*, 2015–16
Ink wash and metallic acrylic
on paper
27 × 30.5 cm
Glenstone Museum,
Potomac MD, USA
Photo: Peter Cox, Eindhoven

18 *I Do Not Know / This Man* from the
series "Give Me the Head of John
the Baptist", 1992
Ink, crayon and pencil on paper
35.2 × 26.7 cm
Centro de Arte Visuales Fundación
Helga de Alvear, Cáceres, Spain
Photo: Centro de Arte Visuales

20 *The Dance* from the series "Give Me
the Head of John the Baptist", 1992
Ink, crayon and pencil on paper
35.2 × 26.7 cm
Centro de Arte Visuales Fundación
Helga de Alvear, Cáceres, Spania
Photo: Centro de Arte Visuales

21 *About Heaven*, 2001
Ink and crayon on paper
16 × 22 cm
Collection of the Artist
Photo: Peter Cox, Eindhoven

24 *A (Young) Girl's Problems /
Or Thinking about / Give Me the Head
of John the Baptist* from the series
"Give Me the Head of John the
Baptist", 1992
Ink, crayon and pencil on paper
74.2 × 58.2 cm
Centro de Arte Visuales Fundación
Helga de Alvear, Cáceres, Spania
Photo: Centro de Arte Visuales

Dumas chooses Munch

26 *Stooped Man Looking at Himself
in the Mirror*, 1919
Crayon
128 × 178 mm
MM.T.00218-07-verso

27 Sketch of *Vision* with text, 1892–93
Pen
181 × 230 mm
MM.T.02908

28 *Le Mort Joyeux.*
Illustration for Charles Baudelaire's
Les fleurs du mal, 1896
Pen, wash and pencil
280 × 205 mm
MM.T.00402

29 *The City of Free Love*, 1908–09
Lithograph
310 × 230 mm
MM.G.00330

30 *Standing Man and Dancing Woman*
1908–09
Watercolour
240 × 314 mm
MM.T.00560

31 *Caricature of a Couple*, 1909–11
Pen
339 × 223 mm
MM.T.02734-007

32 *Frame with Caricatured Figures*
1905–06
Pen
280 × 215 mm
MM.T.01370

33 *The City of Free Love: The Lap Piggy*
1908–10
Brush and crayon
480 × 650 mm
MM.T.01335

34 *Caricature: Women, Toad-Piglet
and Dog*, 1908–09
Watercolour
260 × 361 mm
MM.T.01316

35 *Caricature. John the Baptist's Head
on a Platter.* Variation of the
engraving *Ghosts*, 1905
Pen and crayon
214 × 280 mm
RES.B.00468

35 *The City of Free Love: The Dollar
Princess with the Singer's Head
on a Plate*, 1905–06
Pen
215 × 280 mm
MM.T.01292

36 *The Wedding Present*, 1909–11
Pen
339 × 223 mm
MM.T.02734-012

37 *Caricature. Tulla Larsen, Sigurd
Bødtker, Gunnar Heiberg and
Christian Krohg*, 1905–06
Pen
214 × 280 mm
RES.B.00471

38 *The City of Free Love*, 1909–11
Pen
339 × 223 mm
MM.T.02734-011

39 *The Dancer Kicked into the Grave*
1909–10
Pencil, crayon and brush
504 × 632 mm
MM.T.02756-04-verso

40 *Desire*, 1898
Crayon
395 × 355 mm
MM.T.01373-recto

41 *Peer Gynt: Anitra's Dance*, 1916–20
Crayon
208 × 265 mm
MM.T.00198-16

42 *Peer Gynt: Anitra's Dance*, 1916–20
Crayon
208 × 265 mm
MM.T.00198-24

43 *Peer Gynt: Anitra*, 1916
Crayon
411 × 268 mm
MM.T.00200-29-verso

44 *Peer Gynt: Anitra's Dance*, 1920
Pen
206 × 128 mm
MM.T.00202-12

45 *Peer Gynt: Anitra's Dance*, 1935–39
Crayon and pen
267 × 410 mm
MM.T.00206-33-verso

46 *Peer Gynt: Anitra's Dance*, 1916
Crayon
329 × 253 mm
MM.T.01601

47 *Peer Gynt: Anitra's Dance*, 1913
Crayon
411 × 258 mm
MM.T.01608

48 *Peer Gynt: Anitra's Dance*, 1932–34
Brush and pencil
225 × 290 mm
MM.T.01616

49 *Peer Gynt: Anitra's Dance*, 1932–34
Brush
225 × 290 mm
MM.T.01627

50 *Peer Gynt: Anitra's Dance*, 1932–34
Brush
225 × 290 mm
MM.T.01628

51 *Peer Gynt: Peer og Anitra*, 1930–33
Pencil and carbon paper(?)
313 × 233 mm
MM.T.01643

52 *Peer Gynt: Anitra's Dance*, 1916
Crayon
325 × 253 mm
MM.T.01644

53 *Peer Gynt: Peer og Anitra*, 1913
Crayon
355 × 253 mm
MM.T.01645

54 *Peer Gynt: Anitra's Dance*, 1916–17
Pencil
112 × 183 mm
MM.T.02741-03

55 *Peer Gynt: Anitra's Escape*, 1916–17
Pencil
112 × 183 mm
MM.T.02741-04

Terje Nicolaisen

58 *Encounter on the Landing*, 2020
Oil on canvas
80 × 100 cm
Collection of the Artist
Photo: Tor Simen Ulstein

61 *At the Bar*, 2013
Ink and watercolour on paper
390 × 267 mm
Christian Torp Collection

62 *Two Lovers*, 2015
Ink on paper
280 × 210 mm
Collection of the Artist

65 From the Artist Book *Proposals*, 2001
Ink and watercolour on paper
173 × 255 mm
National Museum of Art, Architecture and Design, Oslo
Photo: National Museum / Dag André Ivarsøy

66 *Dag Solstad*, 2017
Ink and watercolour on paper
760 × 560 mm
Collection of the Artist

67 *Allen Ginsberg*, 2007
Ink and watercolour on paper
1100 × 780 mm
Stiftelsen Litteraturhuset i Oslo
Photo: Tor Simen Ulstein

68 *From the Studio*, 2016
Oil on canvas
80 × 100 cm
Kai Johnsen Collection
Photo: Tor Simen Ulstein

Nicolaisen chooses Munch

71 *Unidentified Motif*, 1916
Crayon
355 × 253 mm
MM.T.00181-89-verso

72 *Doodle Drawing*, 1902
Pen
164 × 110 mm
MM.T.00133-18-verso

73 *Sketchy Map of the Oslo Fjord*, 1904
Pen
137 × 80 mm
MM.T.02738-04-recto

74 *Man Bending Over*, 1929–30
Crayon
112 × 144 mm
MM.T.02346

75 *Man Bending Over*, 1929–30
Crayon
144 × 112 mm
MM.T.01803

76 *John Gabriel Borkman: Foldal in the Ditch*, 1928–30
Crayon
205 × 176 mm
MM.T.00243-84

77 *John Gabriel Borkman: Foldal in the Ditch*, 1928–30
Crayon
205 × 176 mm
MM.T.00243-83

78 *John Gabriel Borkman: Foldal in the Ditch*, c. 1925
Charcoal
190 × 253 mm
MM.T.02230

79 *John Gabriel Borkman: Foldal in the Ditch*, 1914–15
Crayon and pencil
252 × 357 mm
MM.T.00165-18

80 *Two Men Fighting*, 1889
Pencil
177 × 134 mm (cropped)
Private Collection

81 *Falling Asleep in the Chair*, 1928–30
Pen
170 × 208 mm
MM.T.00195-068

82 *Falling Asleep in the Chair*, 1928–30
Pencil
208 × 170 mm
MM.T.00195-050

83 *Falling Asleep in the Chair*, 1930–33
Crayon
290 × 223 mm
MM.T.00568

84 *Landscape*, 1932–33
Pen
106 × 179 mm
MM.T.00240-13

85 Original Drawing for *Ragnarok: Two Escapees on the Beach*, 1914
Crayon
199 × 266 mm
MM.T.02044

86 *Explosion*, 1943
Gouache and oil
650 × 510 mm
MM.T.01442

87 *Winter at the Farmhands' Quarters* c. 1930
Watercolour, gouache(?) and crayon
425 × 575 mm
MM.T.01502

88 *Gunnerud's Dog*, 1938–39
Crayon
267 × 410 mm
MM.T.00206-42

89 *Gunnerud's Dog*, 1938–39
Crayon
267 × 410 mm
MM.T.00206-36

90 *A Cod's Head*, 1938–42
Pen
103 × 136 mm
MM.T.00248-36

91 *A Cod's Head*, 1938–42
Pen
103 × 136 mm
MM.T.00248-49-verso

92 *Female Nude on the Bed*, 1919–24
Watercolour
600 × 408 mm
MM.T.01130

93 *Portrait of a Man with Hand in Front of his Face*, 1914–15
Pencil
278 × 175 mm
MM.T.00160-28-verso

94 *Male Head in Front of a Window*
1916
Crayon
277 × 213 mm
MM.T.00197-21

95 *Female Head*, 1923–33
Watercolour
460 × 330 mm
MM.T.00654

96 *Male Portrait*, 1928–30
Crayon
410 × 267 mm
MM.T.00215-43-verso

97 *Male Portrait*, 1936–42
Pen and wash
203 × 130 mm
MM.T.00185-37-verso

98 *Two Nudes. Man and Woman, Half Figure*, 1912–15
Charcoal
269 × 409 mm
MM.T.00459

99 *Handicraft*, 1927
Pen
210 × 268 mm
MM.T.00174-68-verso

Nalini Malani

102 *A Tree in Lohar Chawl*, 1995
Watercolour on papier d'Arches
76,5 × 127 cm
Peabody Essex Museum, Salem MA, USA
Photo: Prakash Rao

105 *Grieved Child* from the series «His Life», 1981
Oil on canvas
122 × 122 cm
Private collection
Photo: Vivan Sundaram

106 *Living in Alicetime: Broken Alice II*
2005
Watercolour, acrylic and enamel on reverse painting on acrylic sheet
152.5 × 122 cm
Private collection
Photo: Girish Patil

108 *Can You Hear Me?*, 2018–20
Animation Chamber, 9 channels, 88 iPad-animations, sound.
Whitechapel Gallery, London
Photo: Luke Walker

109 *Onanism*, 1969
Digitalised 16 mm b/w reverse stock film, no sound, 3:52 min
Museum of Modern Art, New York
Photo: Nalini Malani

111 *Can You Hear Me?*, 8 February 2020
iPad-animations, sound
60 × 13 meters
Taj Mahal Palace and Tower Mumbai
Commission for Goethe Institut / Max Mueller Bhavan Mumbai
Reproduced with permission from Goethe Institut / Max Mueller Bhavan Mumbai
Photo: Ranabir Das

112 *City of Desires*, 1992–2017
Charcoal Wall Drawing / Erasure Performance
Stedelijk Museum, Amsterdam
Photo: Gert Jan van Rooij

Malani chooses Munch

114 *Portrait Sketch*, 1928–29
Pen
158 × 98 mm
MM.T.02811-12

115 *Caricatures and a Drunkard*, 1911–15
Pen and pencil
269 × 408 mm
MM.T.01297

116 *Caricatures*, 1907–08
Pen
280 × 222 mm
MM.T.02638

117 *Figures and Animals. Bødtker, Heiberg and Toad*, 1908–09
Crayon and pastel
337 × 439 mm
MM.T.01324

118 *Caricature: Old Man with Horns*
1899–1900
Pen
110 × 180 mm
MM.T.01305

119 *Two People Eating Bread*, 1874–76
Watercolour and pencil
82 × 57 mm
MM.T.02960-recto

120 *Interior with Girl* and *Bird*, 1874
Watercolour and pen (left motif), watercolour (right motif)
98 × 110 mm (left motif), 19 × 37 mm (right motif)
MM.T.02751-verso

121 *Five Illustrations*, 1874
Watercolour and pencil
122 × 193 mm
MM.T.02751-recto

122 *Construction Work*, 1929
Watercolour and charcoal
300 × 395 mm
MM.T.01831

123 *Bricklayer*, 1929
Crayon on unprimed canvas
85,5 × 78,5 cm
MM.M.00967

124 *War Invalid. The Beggar*, 1916–18
Crayon
266 × 208 mm
MM.T.00179-11

125 *Seated Female Nude*, 1912–17
Watercolour
490 × 614 mm
MM.T.01079-recto

126 *Seated Female Nude with Hands Holding Her Knees*, 1918–22
Watercolour
497 × 637 mm
MM.T.01133

127 *Omega Weeping*
Original drawing for the lithograph *Omega Weeping*, 1908–09
Crayon
312 × 205 mm
MM.T.01382

128 *Caricatured Figures. Peer Gynt(?)*
1932–34
Brush and watercolour
270 × 353 mm
MM.T.01314

129 *Anxiety Motif*, 1928–30
Pen and pencil
170 × 208 mm
MM.T.00195-116

130 *Grenadierstraße in Berlin after the War.* Original drawing for the lithograph *Genthinerstraße in Berlin after the War*, 1920–21
Crayon
270 × 401 mm
MM.T.00441

131 *The Scream*, 1893
Crayon on unprimed canvas
74 × 56 cm
MM.M.00122b

132 *The Veil* and *Sketch for Theatre Programme for Peer Gynt*, 1896
Crayon (left motif), pencil (right motif)
472 × 618 mm
MM.T.00257-recto

133 *The Veil*, 1896
Crayon
448 × 315 mm
MM.T.00258

134 *The Splitting of Faust*, 1932–35
Watercolour, gouache, pencil and crayon
700 × 860 mm
MM.T.02125

135 *Standing Woman.* Study of detail for *The Splitting of Faust*, 1932
Gouache on canvas
90 × 60 cm
MM.M.01125

136 *The Afflicted Eye. Kneeling Female Nude with Eagle*, 1930
Watercolour
500 × 322 mm
MM.T.02151

137 *The Hands*, 1893
Charcoal, gouache and crayon
679 × 452 mm
MM.T.02442

138 *Woman with a Samoyed*, 1929–30
Watercolour
679 × 424 mm
MM.T.00687

139 *Kiss of Death*, 1933
Brush and pencil
219 × 282 mm
MM.T.00366

140 *Autopsy of a Male Body*, 1928–32
Watercolour and charcoal
703 × 865 mm
MM.T.00566

141 *Peer Gynt: Mother Aase's Death*, 1933
Brush and pencil
282 × 220 mm
MM.T.01602

142 Edvard Munch's drawing of a man on skis and a dog, added to postcard of two women on skis; sent to the artist Thorolf Holmboe as a New Year's greeting on 9 January 1912
Private collection

143 Edvard Munch's drawing of hanged men added to postcard of "Oslo by Night. The University"; sent to the artist Thorolf Holmboe as a New Year's greeting on 31 January 1929
National Library of Norway, Oslo
Photo: National Library of Norway, Oslo

Georg Baselitz

146 *Triangle between Arm and Torso*
1975
Gouache and oil on paper
56 × 40.7 cm

148 *Untitled*, 2006
Pen, watercolour and ink on paper
65.4 × 50.5 cm
Photo: Jochen Littkemann

149 *Untitled*, 2015
Pen and ink on paper
mounteed on canvas
331 × 148.5 cm
Photo: Jochen Littkemann

150 *io*, 2018
Pencil and pen on paper
66.4 × 50.4 cm
Photo: Jochen Littkemann

151 *Blue North*, 2009
Pen on paper
67 × 50.8 cm
Photo: Ulrich Ghezzi

152 *Untitled*, 2013
Ink wash and watercolour on paper
66 × 50.4 cm
Photo: Jochen Littkemann

155 *Head (Munch)*, 1960
Pen and ink on paper,
and opaque white on cardboard
15.5 × 10.4 cm
Photo: Lothar Schnepf

Baselitz chooses Munch

158 *Male Head. Self-Portrait(?)*, 1913–15
Crayon
400 × 281 mm
MM.T.00175-68-verso

159 Sketch for *Between the Clock and the Bed*, 1940–43
Charcoal
652 × 498 mm
MM.T.02437

160 *Self-Portrait*, 1919
Crayon
184 × 132 mm
MM.T.00218-09-verso

161 *Self-Portrait with Afflicted Eye*, 1930
Charcoal, oil and crayon(?)
90 × 72 cm
MM.M.00207

162 *Self-Portrait in Profile*, 1918
Pencil
128 × 163 mm
MM.T.00224-22-verso

163 Original drawing for *Self-Portrait with Hat I*, 1927
Crayon
328 × 220 mm
MM.T.00572

164 *Self-Portrait*, c. 1905
Charcoal
564 × 346 mm
MM.T.00576-recto

165 *Self-Portrait*, c. 1925
Charcoal
598 × 462 mm
MM.T.00577

166 *Rising from the Chair*, 1932–34
Pen
292 × 224 mm
MM.T.02000

167 *Rising from the Chair*, 1932–34
Pen
275 × 216 mm
MM.T.02003

168 *Seated Male Nude. Self-Portait*
1933–34
Pen and pencil
216 × 275 mm
MM.T.02005

169 *Self-Portrait, Sitting on the Floor*
1921–35
Watercolour and pencil
700 × 862 mm
MM.T.02462

170 *Self-Portrait, Standing*, c. 1940
Ink
279 × 220 mm
MM.T.02295

171 *Self-Portrait*, c. 1940
Pen
276 × 215 mm
MM.T.02294

172 *Rising from the Chair*, 1932–34
Pen
226 × 175 mm
MM.T.02296

173 *Self-Portrait. Quarter Past Two in the Morning*, 1940–43
Watercolour and gouache
302 × 500 mm
MM.T.02433

174 *Self-Portrait*, 1920–30
Crayon
205 × 176 mm
MM.T.00243-33

175 *Self-Portrait*, c. 1935
Crayon
142 × 115 mm
MM.T.02417

176 *Self-Portrait*, c. 1915
Charcoal
600 × 600 mm
MM.T.02448

177 *Male Head*, 1896
Brush and crayon
445 × 225 mm
MM.T.00408-verso

178 Sketch for *Between the Clock and the Bed*, 1940–43
Pencil
241 × 322 mm
MM.T.02016

179 *Self-Portrait*
c. 1915
Crayon
675 × 483 mm
MM.T.00580

Tracey Emin

182 *The Truth Is I wanted you*, 2019
Acrylic on canvas
182.6 × 214.3 cm

184 *I love you*, 2015
Acrylic on paper
35 × 35 cm

185 *Mother 6*, 2017
India ink hand painting on lithograph
76.5 × 103 cm

186 *Dark Mind*, 2015
Gouache on paper
30.5 × 40.6 cm

187 *Love is coming*, 2015
Gouache on paper
28 × 38 cm

189 *The thought of you, 2112 HK*, 2016
Gouache on paper
40.5 × 50.8 cm

190 *I said I would say goodbye*, 2019
Acrylic on canvas
182.1 × 152.2 cm

192 *The Kiss*, 2020
Acrylic on canvas
20.3 × 25.4 cm

Emin chooses Munch

195 *The First Human Beings: The Woman and the Bear*, 1895–96
Pen, brush, wash, and charcoal
322 × 324 mm
MM.T.00492

196 *Metabolism*, 1896–98
Gouache and pencil
473 × 618 mm
MM.T.02547-a53-verso

197 "Nothing is small nothing is great"
c. 1930
Handwritten text
Crayon
649 × 501 mm
MM.T.02547-a31

198 *The Wave.* "Moonlight glides across your countenance", 1896
Handwritten text
Gouache and pencil
618 × 473 mm
MM.T.02547-a53-recto

199 *Alpha and Omega*, 1908–09
Watercolour, pastel and crayon
640 × 496 mm
MM.T.00334

200 *Landscape*, 1881
Watercolour and pencil
113 × 270 mm
Privat eie

201 *Sketches of People with Animals* and *Couple Kissing*, 1886
Pen and pencil
154 × 87 mm
MM.T.02571-24-recto

202 *Seated Man* and *The Dead Mother*
1890–94
Pencil and pen
350 × 263 mm
MM.T.00291-recto

203 *Crucifix on a Country Road*, 1905
Pen
148 × 229 mm
MM.T.00132-12-recto

204 *Crucifixion*, 1890–1900
Pen
260 × 208 mm
MM.T.02902-recto

205 Sketch for *Metabolism*, 1896
Pen
225 × 445 mm
MM.T.00408-recto

206 *Towards the Forest (The First Human Beings)*, 1896
Watercolour and crayon
302 × 500 mm
MM.T.00356

207 Two Sketches for *Vampire*, 1892–93
Pen
284 × 220 mm
MM.T.00382-recto

208 *Man's Head against Woman's Breast*
1890–92
Pen
384 × 290 mm
MM.T.00388-verso

209 *Standing Female Nude with Back Halfway Turned*, 1896
Crayon
560 × 410 mm
MM.T.01081

210 *The First Human Beings: The Woman and the Bear*, 1895–96
Pen and brush
321 × 202 mm
MM.T.01383

211 *The First Human Beings: The Woman, the Bear and the Tiger*, 1895–96
Brush, pen and pencil
322 × 481 mm
MM.T.01394

212 *Dance of Life*, 1898–99
Pen, brush, wash and crayon
323 × 478 mm
MM.T.02392

213 *Young Woman Standing*, 1892–93
Charcoal and brush
630 × 431 mm
MM.T.00547

214 *Female Nude from the Waist Down*
c. 1895
Crayon
326 × 264 mm
MM.T.00890

215 *Reclining Female Nude*, 1911–15
Crayon
270 × 409 mm
MM.T.00821

216 *Seated Female Nude with Flowing Hair*, 1912–14
Crayon
730 × 560 mm
MM.T.00796

217 *The Day After*, 1892–94
Pen
229 × 176 mm
MM.T.02348

218 *Reclining Male Nude*, 1889
Pencil
498 × 645 mm
MM.T.02429

219 *Separation*, 1893–95
Pencil
483 × 371 mm
MM.T.02402

220 Sketch for *Hospital Ward*, 1902
Drawing on a letter from Eberhard von Bodenhausen
Pen
55 × 100 mm (motif)
MM.T.02819

221 Sketch for *Madonna*, 1893–94
Charcoal
738 × 598 mm
MM.T.02430

222 *Consolation*, 1894
Charcoal
478 × 632 mm
MM.T.02458

223 *The Woman*, 1894–95
Pencil
303 × 460 mm
MM.T.02762

224 *The Empty Cross*, 1899–1900
Watercolour and pen
433 × 627 mm
MM.T.02452-recto

Published by MUNCH

Head of Publications: Josephine Langebrekke, MUNCH
Editor: Halvor Haugen, Tekstbyrået
Curatorial Editor: Jon-Ove Steihaug, MUNCH
Editorial Contributor: Karen Elizabeth Lerheim, MUNCH
Design: Jens Johan Tandberg, MUNCH, and Ian Brown, Feed
Photographic Consultant: Halvor Bjørngård, MUNCH

Cover:
Female Nude on the Bed
1919–24
Watercolour
600 × 408 mm

Typeset in: Magister (Source Type), Antique Legacy (Optimo)
Paper: Munken Print White, Lenza Top Recycling Pro,
UPM Sol Matt
Printing and binding: Conti Tipocolor
Repro: JK Morris

Translations from Norwegian:
Foreword, Introduction, Baselitz interview, Bruteig essay:
Francesca M. Nichols
Nicolaisen interview: Peter Cripps, The Wordwrights

www.munchmuseet.no

ISBN: 978-82-93560-71-5

This book and the digital catalogue raisonné of Edvard Munch's drawings have been made possible through the generous support of the Bergesen Foundation

Bergesen-
stiftelsen